MILES LORD

MILES LORD

The Maverick Judge Who Brought
Corporate America to Justice

ROBERTA WALBURN

University of Minnesota Press
Minneapolis • London

Published by the University of Minnesota Press
111 Third Avenue South, Suite 290
Minneapolis, MN 55401-2520
http://www.upress.umn.edu

Printed in the United States of America on acid-free paper

The University of Minnesota is an equal-opportunity educator and employer.

22 21 20 19 18 17   10 9 8 7 6 5 4 3 2 1

Library of Congress Cataloging-in-Publication Data
Names: Walburn, Roberta, author.
Title: Miles Lord : the maverick judge who brought corporate America to justice /
    Roberta Walburn.
Description: Minneapolis : University of Minnesota Press, 2017. | Includes
    bibliographical references and index. | Identifiers: LCCN 2017011917 (print) |
    ISBN 978-1-5179-0231-5 (hc) | ISBN 978-1-5179-0232-2 (pb)
Subjects: LCSH: Lord, Miles. | Judges—United States—Biography. |
    District courts—United States—Officials and employees—Biography. |
    Judges—Minnesota—Biography.
Classification: LCC KF373.L56 W35 2017 (print) | DDC 347.73/2234 [B] —dc23
LC record available at https://lccn.loc.gov/2017011917

To my mother, Harriet Walburn,
and in memory of my father, Sid, and brother, Glenn

I am only one,
But I still am one.
I cannot do everything,
But I can do something;
And because I cannot do everything
I will not refuse to do the something that I can do.

—*Edward Everett Hale (1822–1909)*

Contents

Prologue

Early one morning, my phone—ringing off the hook—jarred me awake. I picked up; an angry man yelled. This was the spring of 1982, when I was finishing my second year of law school at the University of Minnesota and working part-time as a reporter for the *Minneapolis Star Tribune*. As a reporter, I was no stranger to irate calls.

But not at home.

Not at 5:00 a.m.

Not from a federal judge.

"This is Chief Federal Judge Miles W. Lord!" he thundered.

I had just written an article for the paper about Judge Lord ordering the city of Minneapolis to allow a Gay Pride block party in the heart of downtown. The judge ruled that the city's denial of a permit, typical politics for the time, violated the free speech rights of the Gay Priders. "It is the unpopular cause that needs protections," the judge wrote in his order.

My article quoted the reaction of a city alderman: "The federal courts are in control of the streets," he complained.

Now the judge who wrote the decision was yelling at me as I tried to wake up. "You got the facts wrong! You got the law wrong!" he shouted. "Your career as a journalist is ruined because I am going to make sure no one in town talks to you again!"

I had met Judge Lord a couple of months before, at lunch with a newsroom colleague who had known him for decades. But I really didn't know the judge except by reputation, as with his controversial decisions and larger-than-life personality, he was a journalist's dream (although not on this morning).

The judge continued his tirade until I mustered the wherewithal for a response. "Thank you for calling," I finally said. "Can you tell me exactly what was wrong with the story so we can correct it?"

"Ha! Ha! Ha!" The judge exploded with laughter. "The story is fine," he said. "I just want to know if you want to be my law clerk after you graduate next year."

I froze; my head spun. I had gone back to school after working for a few years as a reporter with the idea of using a law degree to help my journalism, not to become a lawyer. Now, on the phone, I didn't want to make a major decision about my future while half-asleep. But the judge started to yell again, bellowing something about how many people would love to clerk for him.

I said yes.

Later, after I hung up and thought about what happened, I found it hard to believe my good luck.

Most federal judges have a rigorous protocol for selecting law clerks. But Judge Lord charted his own varied course, as he so often did on the bench. Sometimes he hired based on the standard qualifications for the job: grades and the pedigree of the law school. But oftentimes a clerk would be the son or daughter of a longtime friend or someone he'd met, in one capacity or another, around the state. He tended to like Democrats, but party affiliation was not a prerequisite. ("You're a fucking Republican!" he shouted at one applicant, when he saw his résumé. Still, he hired the young man, who, in fact, had bipartisan credentials.) I wasn't sure why I was hired—the judge never even asked for a résumé or transcript—but it was probably because he liked the idea of a clerk with a journalism background, as he loved being in the press.

My clerkship would start some fifteen months down the road in the fall of 1983, after I graduated and took the bar exam. In the meantime, I continued my routine of school by day and reporting on nights and weekends. On slow days, when there was no breaking news—no fires, no murders, no snowstorm-of-the-century stories to report—I pulled old clips about the judge from the newsroom library, filed away in envelopes bulging with newsprint. I also started to hear stories about the judge from, it seemed, just about everyone in town.

"Miles!" people called him—first name only, exclamation point—no further identification needed.

He was a judge who believed that the formal rules of law and inequities in wealth and power, along with the shenanigans and skullduggery of attorneys, stood as obstacles to fairness and justice. He was outrageously colorful and exuberantly outspoken, roiling the powers that be and discombobulating his buttoned-down brethren, but leaving the man on the street cheering. He made no attempt to hide what he was doing behind the closed doors of chambers, as he—in his words, "rootin', tootin', shootin'"— said what he thought. He thought that the deck was stacked in favor of the rich and powerful and set out to balance the scales for "the little guy."

By the time our paths crossed, the judge was in the twilight of his career. But he was still "romping and stomping," as he liked to say.

Indeed, as it turned out, my clerkship would coincide with the judge taking on one of the largest lawsuits in history—the Dalkon Shield intrauterine device (IUD) litigation—involving a product that injured women by the thousands, with many suffering horrific infections that resulted in infertility and sometimes death. The litigation had stymied other judges for years; Judge Lord would preside for only three months. But in that time he would set in motion a sequence of events that resulted in the disintegration of one of the nation's largest companies. In the end, more than two hundred thousand women would receive nearly $3 billion in compensation for their injuries, ranking at the time behind only asbestos in terms of personal injury claims; "one of the most disastrous episodes of American corporate misconduct in this century," wrote the *Washington Post* reporter who covered the debacle.

This book is a firsthand account of my days with Judge Lord, along with a more in-depth narrative of the Dalkon Shield litigation—drawn from thousands of pages of court records, internal company documents, multiple interviews, and Judge Lord's personal files (which I had access to during my research)—to place the judge's exploits in context. It is also the story, in alternating chapters, of what made Miles Lord, the man and the judge, and the wide swath that this hell-bent crusader had cut through history in the decades before my clerkship, both on and off the bench.

■ ■ ■ ■

He was a scrawny brawler from the rough-and-tumble Iron Range of northern Minnesota . . . a hotshot prosecutor of gangsters and racketeers (Jimmy Hoffa chased him through courthouse corridors in one free-for-all) . . . the early friend and confederate of a cadre of coming-of-age, Depression-era young men who, with their social-gospel populism, banded together to forge one of the greatest political dynasties in American history . . . a behind-the-scenes envoy between his lifelong comrades Hubert H. Humphrey (who Miles loved unabashedly as a brother) and Eugene McCarthy (whose stubborn independence, along with Humphrey's White House influence, was instrumental in Miles's appointment to the bench), as they battled each other for the soul of the Democratic Party in the blood-in-the-streets presidential campaign of 1968 . . . and finally, a federal district court judge who fought battles aplenty on behalf of the poor, the disadvantaged, and, as he would say, "the meek," and whose bold rulings—holding big corporations accountable, protecting the environment, standing up for consumers, defending the rights of women, and weighing in on issues ranging from disability rights to education reform to nuclear disarmament—reshaped jurisprudence for decades to come.

In the process, he scorned the very basis of American jurisprudence—the adversary system—with its blind faith in the premise that truth and justice will emerge from opposing attorneys duking it out.

He thrilled to enter the ring himself.

Inevitably, this led to repeated clashes with his superiors on the Eighth Circuit Court of Appeals. To Judge Lord, the Eighth Circuit judges—a bunch of ivory-tower "stuffed shirts," he thought—were all that stood between himself and complete freedom and independence. To the Eighth Circuit, Judge Lord was an uncontrollable free spirit who lived by his own rules.

Before the Dalkon Shield cases, they had come to blows, most notably, over an environmental lawsuit involving the Reserve Mining Company and its massive iron ore processing plant in northern Minnesota, which spewed thousands of tons of waste, laden with asbestos-like fibers, into the pure blue waters of Lake Superior. As the case dragged on—in what became the longest and most sensational trial of the early environmental era—Judge Lord became increasingly exasperated by the intransigence of Reserve Mining and its corporate parents. Ultimately, the judge faced off against the company's top officials in a high-noon courtroom scene—and ordered the plant to shut down.

Then he faced off against the Eighth Circuit.

"Judge Lord," wrote the appeals court when it booted him off the case, "seems to have shed the robe of the judge and to have assumed the mantle of the advocate."

These words would set the stage for all that followed—including, most fatefully, the Dalkon Shield litigation—and demarcate the battle lines over the judge.

He was loved and he was hated, a hero and a villain. He was named the best federal judge in the country—and one of the worst. At times, he left even his most ardent supporters baffled and bewildered. "They broke the mold," said one prosecutor who worked with him, "*before* they made him."

Journalists who covered his career all but ran out of ways to describe him: "an unforgiving, unregenerate, unabashed Prairie Populist of the old school"; "live-wire slayer of corporate behemoths"; "a Mark Twain in judge's robes"; "Trumanesque champion of the underdog"; "folksy"; "feisty"; "impulsive, fun-loving, compassionate, vindictive, opinionated." They described his courtroom in "Oz-like terms": "the land of Miles, where anything can happen and often does" and "where the unexpected is commonplace, the unusual is ordinary."

His enemies were equally expressive: "a disgrace to the bench"; "an out-of-control judicial zealot"; "reckless"; "an embarrassment"; "Miles God."

"A World War II mine loose in the channel," the A. H. Robins Company would call him, after its battle royal with the judge.

It was a collision course—Judge Lord versus A. H. Robins, the manufacturer of the Dalkon Shield—that had been years in the making.

■ ■ ■ ■

At the time of Judge Lord's early morning call to me, the judge had not yet been assigned any Dalkon Shield cases. But A. H. Robins (or its insurer) had already spent millions of dollars defending thousands of claims and was winning the majority of cases that went to trial in other courtrooms.

The A. H. Robins Company, of Richmond, Virginia, was a bastion of the Old South, founded by Albert Hartley Robins at the end of the Civil War in the capital of the old Confederacy. From humble beginnings, the company—still controlled by the Robins family—would grow into a Fortune 500 colossus. In 1970, the company purchased the rights to a new birth-control device and within one year had catapulted the Dalkon Shield to the top of the market: the best-selling IUD in the country and, soon, the world, with millions sold.

But the Dalkon Shield had a deadly flaw. Its threadlike tail string, tied to the bottom of the device, created a pathway for bacteria to ascend into the uterus.

Before long, women by the thousands suffered ravaging infections—pelvic inflammatory disease (or PID)—spreading into the upper reproductive tract: fallopian tubes, ovaries, and surrounding tissues. Women also suffered perforations of the uterus (and migration of the Dalkon Shield into the pelvic cavity); unplanned pregnancies (the Dalkon Shield wasn't as effective as A. H. Robins represented); ectopic pregnancies in the fallopian tubes or ovaries (a life-threatening condition); septic abortions, where the fetus became infected and spontaneously aborted (also life-threatening); and birth defects in children carried to term (including blindness and cerebral palsy).

Often, women were rendered infertile from surgeries or from scars and adhesions that formed like glue around their reproductive organs.

There also were deaths.

The lawsuits had begun in the early 1970s.

A. H. Robins dug in for the long haul, building a litigation juggernaut and waging war in courtrooms across the country: hiring more than one hundred law firms; retaining a platoon of physicians and other experts to rebut the women's claims with scientific (and pseudo-scientific) jargon; attacking women who sued by probing their personal lives—sex partners, sex practices, which way they wiped in the bathroom—with a cross-examination litany that came to be known as the "dirty questions"; concealing damning internal documents, including secret studies of used tail strings; and attempting to buy off experienced plaintiffs' attorneys so they wouldn't pursue future lawsuits, all of which made the litigation expensive and oppressive, if not impossible, for the injured women and their attorneys.

The company was no longer selling the Dalkon Shield; it had been pulled from the market in 1974. But A. H. Robins steadfastly refused to fully warn of the dangers or issue a recall to the legions of women still using the device.

"Robins feels that if they issued a recall, it would kill them in court," said one plaintiffs' attorney.

As a result, the injuries and deaths continued.

By the early 1980s, A. H. Robins had appeared before numerous judges throughout the country. There were scattered indications that some were growing increasingly frustrated by the company's maneuverings. One judge decried the company's know-nothing stance, with "the hard questions posed . . . unanswerable by anyone from Robins." Another sanctioned the company for its "shell game tactics" and failure to comply with orders. Yet another refused to allow the company's Richmond lawyers to appear in his courtroom, citing their actions that "continually thwarted the progress of the litigation."

But no judge had been willing or able to pierce the company's walls of defenses.

Before long, however, Judge Lord would enter the scene. And once more, as in the Reserve Mining case, he would embark on a one-man mission against a mighty corporation, this time the A. H. Robins Company, with the Eighth Circuit Court of Appeals again waiting in the wings.

It would be the judge's final round as a jurist.

■ ■ ■ ■

All roads had led Miles Lord to this last showdown: from his hard-born, hard-fought years on the Range; to his life-shaping fellowship with Hubert Humphrey and disciples who, in their glory years as neophyte midwestern reformers, shared the improbable belief that they could change their state, their nation, and their world; and through his formative years as a judge, when he would come to appreciate that his black-robed status need not cloak his born-and-bred proclivities but could be used as the most potent weapon in his devil-be-damned battle on behalf of the least fortunate.

Indeed, the Dalkon Shield cases would be the natural consequence of his life's journey.

And for me, as a young law clerk with a ringside seat to the action, it would be the beginning of my education into how the legal system *really* works when individual citizens face off in court against a corporation and its multitudes of lawyers.

I would also learn how one judge—one man—can make all of the difference in the world.

In fact, federal judges have uncommon power and independence—appointed for life and unbeholden to any electorate—as guaranteed by Article III of the Constitution.

And all judges, who, of course, are people too, have their own personalities, life experiences, and values, and, as a consequence, their own partialities and ideologies on the bench. There is simply no such thing as a judge without any biases to one degree or another, although many—*not* including Judge Lord—like to profess otherwise. "Judges tend not to be candid about how they decide cases," wrote one highly respected appellate judge. "They want their calling to be a mystery, and one way to make it so is to complexify what they do."

That is not to say that a judge's predisposition is at play in every case. Sometimes, it has no impact at all. But other times it is the most consequential factor, where, for example, the law is multiple shades of gray or provides a judge with considerable discretion.

Judge Lord used his discretion—and then some—to the maximum degree. He figured the world could use one jurist like him as a counterbalance to the overwhelming majority of his colleagues who hewed to the status quo, which, in Judge Lord's mind, was a default to the privileged elite.

Like Judge Lord, I do not pretend I am a blank slate. My point of view has been shaped, of course, by the nearly year and a half I spent clerking for the judge. It has also been influenced by my experiences since that time.

After I left my clerkship, I practiced law for more than twenty-five years, primarily representing plaintiffs in litigation against big corporations. I am not an indiscriminate apologist for the plaintiffs' bar; while many of these lawyers are unparalleled professionals and fierce champions for the rights of their injured clients, others, at the opposite end of the spectrum, have been the bane of my existence. But I do believe, as did Judge Lord, that the U.S. legal system—although it may well be the best in the world—is often askew. Too often the wealth of the litigant and how much it, in the case of a corporation, can spend on lawyers sway the fate of justice. And not only in the past, as with the Dalkon Shield cases. To a large degree, the legal system today—in high-stakes litigation against a high-powered corporation—is little changed from the trench warfare days of Dalkon Shield. Change the name of the case, change the name of the defendant, change the names of the lawyers, and you could easily witness much of the same legal maneuvering in many of today's courtrooms.

There is, however, no Miles Lord.

1

Boyhood on the Range, 1919–1937

Miles Lord never forgot the land from which he came.

The Iron Range sweeps across northeastern Minnesota, with Canada to the north and Lake Superior, the grandest of the Great Lakes, to the east, and traversed in part by the northern reaches of the Mississippi River. It is a land with a history—and a people, raw and tough—shaped by the exploitation of its plentiful natural resources and epic clashes between the haves and have-nots. The Range bred class warfare, radical politics, and an independent people, described as "hard, loud, direct," with "a deep distrust of rich people and outsiders" and who "never forget an enemy."

Miles was a Ranger from head to toe.

■ ■ ■ ■

The land had been settled first by the Dakota tribe of Sioux and later the Ojibwe. European explorers—French voyageurs, followed by the English— arrived in the 1600s and with their fur trade began the first wholesale extraction of native riches. By the time Minnesota became a state in 1858, however, the fur trade was already in decline, with pelt-bearing animals, including the beaver, all but trapped out.

But by then, the rise of the lumber industry, which beckoned Miles's forebears, had begun.

Both sides of his family—Scotch-Irish on his mother's, British on his father's—had been early immigrants to the New World, arriving in pre-Revolutionary War days and settling first along the East Coast. In the latter half of the 1800s, the virgin pine forests of northern Minnesota drew them to a new home. The land they found was rugged and unforgiving: the soil thin and rocky, the growing seasons short, the winters the longest and coldest in the continental United States. But the forests, dense and primeval, were magnificent, with white pines towering two hundred feet into the sky.

Frank Lord—Miles's future father—began work in the lumber camps as a boy, deep in the wilderness. For more than two decades, he felled trees in the winter, and, in the summer, followed the logs downstream to the sawmills of Minneapolis, the young river city, some hundred-plus miles away as the crow flies. In 1899, Frank Lord met Rachel (Welton) Terry. The next year, the couple married at her family's homestead in Pine Knoll, a speck of a township. Frank was a relatively old thirty-three; Rachel, only nineteen.

The babies started coming in 1901, baby after baby after baby, for more than twenty years. All told, Rachel Lord gave birth to twelve children. Three did not live past infancy. Miles Welton Lord was the eighth of nine to survive: six boys and three girls. He was born on November 6, 1919, in the Pine Knoll farmhouse, his grandmother tending as midwife.

By that time, the pine forests were largely decimated. Once again, however, another industry—which would give the region its name—had already ascended.

■ ■ ■ ■

The first deposits of iron ore had been unearthed in northern Minnesota in 1865. That spurred further exploration and, in the end, the discovery of the largest and most accessible deposits of iron ore in the world: three bands of formations—the Vermilion Range, the Mesabi Range, and the Cuyuna Range—collectively, Minnesota's Iron Range. For decades, the entire nation's needs for steel would be met in large part with ore mined on the Range and shipped out of Duluth, the growing commercial center on Lake Superior (and soon to surpass New York City as the leading port in the country).

More than one hundred mines transformed the wilderness. Often, the ore lay so close to the surface that steam shovels simply scooped it out, gutting the land with massive open pits. For veins of deeper ore, underground mines were blasted out of the terrain.

Adjacent to the mines, small towns sprang up, and tens of thousands of immigrants poured in. By 1910, nearly 80 percent of the people on the Range had been born in a foreign country. There were at least thirty-five ethnic groups—Finns, Serbians, Croatians, Poles, Slovenians, Italians,

Germans, Irish, Russians, Bulgarians, and Greeks, among them—and also Swedes and Norwegians, the staid Scandinavians who were the dominant population in the strikingly homogenous rest of the state.

The immigrant miners worked long hours for meager pay. The jobs were often seasonal, with long winter layoffs, and the work grueling and perilous. The mining companies—most prominently, United States Steel, the world's first billion-dollar corporation and a major player on the Range—became the enemy.

The first widespread strike, described as "class warfare," came in 1907; the second, in 1916, spread to as many as twenty thousand miners. Still, the only union willing to join battle in 1916 was the militant Industrial Workers of the World—the IWW, or "Wobblies"—whose avowed goal was to "do away with capitalism." (The IWW's most famous song, "Solidarity Forever," had been written the year before: "Is there aught we hold in common with the greedy parasite, Who would lash us into serfdom and would crush us with his might?") The mining companies fought back, recruiting strike breakers and arming thousands of guards. There were mass arrests and violent clashes with several deaths, and, after about three months, the strike was crushed. Around this time, the IWW was also beaten back in its efforts to unionize the region's loggers, including, perhaps, Frank Lord. The IWW left the Range, defeated, by 1921. But these epochal strikes—and other struggles against powerful, out-of-state corporations—left a lasting impression on the Iron Range for generations to come.

As one Ranger would write decades later: "Our Past is a Big Deal."

■ ■ ■ ■

When Miles was born in 1919, the large family lived in a small two-story house in Pine Knoll that his father built by hand. Heat came from two stoves, light from kerosene lanterns. There was no indoor plumbing; outside there were a water pump and an outhouse.

Frank Lord had stopped working in the Minneapolis sawmills after the first babies were born. He continued to work as a lumberjack, however, until his midfifties, when Miles was two or three years old. Then the Lords moved to a nearby mining town. The family of eleven loaded all of their possessions into one wagon, pulled by two horses. The younger children, including Miles, followed in an uncle's car. Miles napped on the ride. As the car topped a small hill, someone yelled, "Milesy, wake up. There's

Crosby!" Miles opened his eyes and saw his first electric lights, the street-lights of Crosby.

Crosby, population 3,500, was the business center of the Cuyuna Range, the last of the three ranges to be developed. The town was carefully planned, with water mains and sewer lines, a community park and beach, and a public school that was the pride of the town. That, in fact, had become the trend across the Range, as the immigrant communities fought bitter battles to raise municipal taxes on the mining companies in order to build schools and other public improvements that far outshone other Minnesota cities. The schools, the families hoped, would provide the pathway for their children to the American Dream.

The Lord house in Crosby was small. There was running water and electricity; the bathroom, however, was still an outhouse. Rachel Lord's relatives filled the neighborhood, with at least two dozen cousins, along with their assorted dogs, cats, horses, mules, and chickens, within a three-block radius. "We ate wherever we found ourselves and we slept wherever we happened to be when we became sleepy," Miles would recall. Grandma Terry—Rachel Lord's mother—lived in the middle of it all. "She seemed as happy as a sparrow in a manure pile," said Miles.

Miles would remember these early years as idyllic. But the harsh realities of life on the Range would also sear his memory.

Sirens pierced the air.

On February 5, 1924, when Miles was four years old, the worst mining disaster in Minnesota history struck a few miles outside his town.

The Milford Mine was an underground operation. Near the end of the afternoon shift, a rush of water and mud cascaded in from an adjacent lake and bog. Within minutes, the entire mine flooded. Only seven miners made it out; forty-one died.

It took almost two months to recover the first bodies, nine long months for the last. The widows locked arms and walked through the streets awaiting news. Eighty-eight children lost their fathers; Miles would grow up with many of them.

The community banded together. "Relatives and friends cared for and shared with the bereaved, and communities became more and more closely knit as everyone tried to help the less fortunate 'make do,'" wrote a local historian. "'We're all family,' is a familiar saying on the Cuyuna."

Miles would talk about the Milford Mine stories—and lessons—his whole life.

■ ■ ■ ■

Around the time Miles started kindergarten, the Lord family moved one last time, a short distance down the road to Ironton—Crosby's twin city— with a population of about a thousand and a grade school that it boasted was "second to none in the state." For the first time, the Lords had indoor plumbing. But the house was a small one-story. Five boys, Miles included, slept in one cast-iron bunk bed, three boys up and two down.

Most everyone was poor in the little mining town, but Miles remembers being the poorest of all, one-bag-of-candy-from-the-church-for-Christmas poor. There was food on the table, but shoes, coats, and mittens were hard to come by and sometimes shared. "My parents," Miles would say, "had just exactly nothing."

Frank Lord struggled to earn money, picking up odd jobs. He had health problems—an illness or injury or both—never really identified but significant enough to affect his ability to work. Rachel Lord, five foot two and stout, kept the family fed with her garden and her chickens out back. She was warm and humble and, as Miles remembered, full of old Irish stories, songs, and poems, and love and hugs for her children.

"In every conceivable way, the most enduring and effective influence on me was that of my mother," Miles would say. Even as an adult, his eyes would brim with tears when he spoke of her.

Religion of varying sorts came early. In Pine Knoll, the family had worshipped as Methodists. In Crosby, when Pentecostal revivalists took over an abandoned dance hall, Miles went with his mother and later with local schoolteachers; he sat on their laps and begged to go up front and be saved. In Ironton, there was a Presbyterian church one block from his house, where Rachel Lord taught Sunday school, and that became Miles's regular church. The sermons made a deep impression. Miles heard the story of Cain and Abel and envisioned the two brothers on the Range, with Cain pushing Abel into an iron ore pit that Abel could not escape.

The young boy was spellbound.

"I never wanted to repeat Cain's mistake and have God ask me about it," Miles would later say.

By as young as six, Miles had started delivering newspapers door-to-door. He was outgoing—learning to turn on the charm—and customers would "take me in just to hear me talk." He also had his favorite houses, like the Zontellis', where a cute, dark-haired girl, a couple of years younger than Miles, waited in pajamas on her grandmother's porch for delivery of the Sunday comics.

Decades later, Miles would still remember the names of the people who lived in virtually every house in town. He could also determine, with uncanny accuracy, the lineage of the children, even where "a few blood lines may have gotten mixed up," he said. "I was the paper boy who saw a lot on my route."

He became a keen observer of people. "You pay more attention to people when you don't have so many things," he would say.

He saw the bootlegging: "Those kids strutted down the street in nice clothes."

He saw the prostitution: "Maybe mom takes some of the guys upstairs."

He saw the "poor but honest": "They had the roughest times."

He saw the immigrant communities. Many staked out their own sections of town and fought to protect their territories.

He also saw the boundaries between men and women, girls and boys, in a community where roles were clearly defined. "I thought they [girls and women] were little nice things and I loved them," he would say, "but basically, it was a man's world."

■ ■ ■ ■

Black Tuesday, October 29, 1929, struck days before Miles's tenth birthday. The Great Depression hit the Iron Range with brutal force, with unemployment reaching as high as 70 percent.

The Lord family struck bottom and, despite their pride, accepted assistance. One day, Miles rode his old bicycle to the Crosby Armory to pick up surplus commodities. He parked his bike on a curb, where the county relief administrator promptly ran it over with her car. Miles's mother admonished him: "Don't say a word." She was afraid any protestation would jeopardize their aid.

His family, Miles learned, was, unlike many Rangers, timid. Not Miles. Already he had learned to talk his way into or out of just about any proposition or predicament. By the time he was twelve, his mother told him, "Miles, you have a lot of answers for a lot of things. You should become a lawyer." This was not a family where law school, or even college, was considered within the realm of possibilities. Miles had never been in a courtroom, never known a lawyer. He had taken the measure, however, of the lawyers in town. "Everybody was afraid of them," he would say. "It was so bad that some folks with unpaid bills would walk on the other side of the street just to avoid them." But his mother told him he should be a lawyer, and that was it: "I never thought about anything else after that." He vowed, however, not to be a bill collector.

The Depression also brought Miles's introduction to politics.

The first politician to make an impression on him was the charismatic Floyd Bjornstjerne Olson—"The People's Governor"—who led Minnesota's Farmer-Labor Party, perhaps the most militant left-wing party ever to capture statewide office anywhere in the United States.

"I am not a liberal!" Olson proclaimed. "I am a radical!"

Olson had gotten his start prosecuting gangsters and crooked officials as a county attorney in Prohibition-era Minneapolis, renowned for its rampant corruption, and moved on to run for governor, where his fiery campaigns—and rousing and theatrical speeches—electrified the state. He was elected to the statehouse in 1930 and reelected in 1932 and 1934. (Farmer-Laborites and Republicans were the two major parties in Minnesota in this era, with Democrats languishing in distant third; in one race, the Democratic candidate for governor failed to reach even 5 percent of the vote.) The Iron Range was one of Olson's strongest areas of support, as he called for state ownership of the mines, along with the banks, utilities, and railroads. (His party platform declared that "capitalism has failed.")

Olson also courted young Minnesotans, giving interviews to school newspapers and urging students to go into careers in public service, not the business world. He took to the radio with weekly shows, the first politician in the state to do so. Miles listened to that "great voice," as he would describe it, and thought of Olson as "a beloved person."

Olson did have enemies, who accused him of inflaming class hatred and running a corrupt political machine with flagrant patronage abuses. For most Minnesotans, however, Olson soared to iconic status.

The end came abruptly. Olson died of cancer in 1936, at the age of forty-four. An estimated two hundred thousand people, in lines more than a mile long, waited outside the state capitol to file by his coffin.

The Communist Party also surged during the Depression years on the Iron Range, literally in Miles's backyard. In 1932, an avowed Communist was elected mayor of Crosby. This was big news—the first Communist mayor in the United States—and put the little Range town in the national spotlight.

Miles was not a Communist. But, as a schoolboy, he did go to some Communist picnics—"they had pretty good food," he said—where party members sang songs like "We Little Bolshevists."

■ ■ ■ ■

Fighting—a common occurrence in Crosby-Ironton—was how Miles first distinguished himself. He began to fight, first in the streets, then in the ring. In high school, he hitchhiked to the nearby town of Brainerd for a boxing lesson. He and a friend also heard about a military training program for students at Fort Snelling in St. Paul. There would be life in the barracks and military drills but also boxing lessons with a regulation ring, gloves, shoes, headgear, and coaches—"all the things we had seen in the newsreels," said Miles. Off they went. "We would have gladly suffered anything in our rush to get boxing lessons."

Back home, Miles "made it his business to tame bullies." He felt that he owed something to the guy who was being picked on. "I was the little guy," he would say, "and so was everyone in our family." No matter his size, a lean—one might say skinny—five feet nine inches, Miles ventured from the school yard to the alleys to the pool and dance halls. "There were some mean bastards around. They'd intimidate whole towns," Miles said later. "I would go out of my way to aggravate a bully, and I mean a big bully, just for the sake of having him take a swing at me so I could avenge some of the wrongs he had done to others."

Fighting, in fact, was Miles's most notable achievement in high school, followed by his budding as an actor (he scored the lead male role in virtually every school play) and his mastery of the jitterbug. He also participated in more than his share of schoolboy mischiefs, from overturning outhouses to drinking moonshine. In 1937, he graduated from Crosby-Ironton High School, with only a couple of brief mentions in his graduation flyer: one for his letter in dramatics and the other for his "beautiful sense of rhythm" and "fascinating wink."

■ ■ ■ ■

Miles reached young adulthood.

Despite the privations of growing up, he had come to believe that he was a fortunate one, especially by comparison with his older siblings. He saw how his older sisters' clothes didn't measure up, even by Crosby-Ironton standards, and how they had to share a coat and skip school on alternate days in the winter. He saw his older brothers defer high school to help support the family; three eventually went to work in the mines. He believed he was blessed and wondered why, since all of the siblings had the same parents—"We all sprang from the same thighs," he would say—and the same upbringing.

In later years, he would spend no small amount of time analyzing himself. (He loved to do this.) He would attribute his lifelong crusade as his self-professed brothers' and sisters' keeper to his boyhood days and the deep-rooted lessons of the Range, at times sounding more like a preacher than the judge he became. As an adult, as a Lutheran, Miles would harbor plenty of doubts about his faith, even about God and the hereafter. But he continued to embrace—and preach—the moral teachings of the church.

"You know, when they talk about 'are you your brother's keeper,' my answer to that question was yes," he said. "I felt a terrible allegiance to my family and, in a way, later to my extended family and to anybody who was in trouble."

And Miles was always finding people in trouble.

2

The Dalkon Shield Quagmire

As I go through my last semesters of law school, in the 1982–83 school year, I drop by Judge Lord's chambers from time to time to get a preview of what to expect when my clerkship begins.

I'm plenty nervous the first time I stop in, not sure if the judge will even remember me, let alone that he has extended the offer of a clerkship. (His early morning phone call now seems like a dream.) But the judge looks pleased; he loves company. At day's end, I walk with him out of the courthouse. On the way, he stops to banter with a couple of janitors. He seems to know everyone who works in the building: who they are, what they do, the names of their spouses and kids. The janitors tell the judge about rumors that they might be replaced by private contractors; the judge assures them he will find an attorney, with "spunk," he says, to fight back. Then he gets into his car—he's known for driving old beaters; now he's in a Volkswagen diesel Rabbit—and drives off for the day, holding a pocket recorder to his lips and dictating up a storm.

Other days when I visit, the judge kicks back in chambers in storytelling mode, rambling through tales so fast, some current, some decades past, that I can hardly track what he is saying. One minute he is laughing about a recent wedding he officiated, where the guests mistook him for a preacher. Ha-ha-ha! The next minute he is reminiscing about his mother—he's got an old recording in chambers of her singing Irish songs—and, as he listens, he is moved to tears. Next, he is talking old-time politics. One day, he tells a tale that has something to do with Karl Rolvaag (a former Minnesota governor), the judge (before he was appointed to the bench), a trip to the north woods, lots of whiskey, and as a result, the judge says, the appointment of a U.S. senator. I try to follow along but can't put the pieces together and don't have a chance to ask before the judge darts back onto the bench.

The judge also takes me under his tutorial wing on my visits with a font of down-home judicial philosophy. Over and over, like a mantra, he repeats his central refrain. "There is one set of laws for the rich and powerful and another for the poor and oppressed," he'll say. "One for the mighty and one for the meek!"

Meanwhile, back in the newsroom as the year progresses, I start hearing about big-league litigation gearing up in Minnesota involving the Dalkon Shield IUD. From what I know—not much other than the litigation has been going on a long, long time—it seems strange that after so many years, these cases are still going to trial. But I don't pay too much attention to the talk, as these cases are not assigned to Judge Lord.

■ ■ ■ ■

As I later learn, the ongoing litigation had already shed much light—although not the whole story (not all of the bombshells have exploded)—on the history of A. H. Robins and the Dalkon Shield.

The concept of an IUD—embedding a foreign body in the uterus as a method of birth control—dates to ancient times. For centuries, Arabs and Turks inserted small stones into the uteruses of camels to prevent pregnancies on long journeys across the desert. Some women also began to use primitive IUDs, made of glass, gold, or ivory, but infections and uterine perforations discouraged widespread use. As late as 1959, a prominent medical journal "thoroughly condemned" the devices.

But by the 1960s, there was a growing belief that a properly designed IUD could be the solution to fears of a purported population explosion and provide an alternative to birth control pills (approved by the Food and Drug Administration [FDA] in 1960, but with high-estrogen doses, igniting a "pill scare" about blood clots and strokes). The sexual revolution was also in full swing, further stoking the clamor for a new generation of IUDs.

No one was sure how an IUD worked: interfering with the ability of sperm to reach an egg in time for fertilization; promoting a foreign-body inflammatory response that attacked sperm; preventing a fertilized egg from attaching to the uterine wall—a contraceptive preventing fertilization or an abortifacient interrupting the growth of a fertilized egg.

But IUDs were easy to use (insert and leave in place for years) and inexpensive to make (pennies per device). Inventors of all types began experimenting with plastics, inert and moldable into any shape, to design an improved, modern IUD.

The potential for profits was enormous.

One inventor was Dr. Hugh Davis at the Johns Hopkins School of Medicine in Baltimore. By 1967, Dr. Davis had designed an IUD shaped like a policeman's badge (or shield). He teamed with a friend, Irwin Lerner, not a doctor but an electrical engineer. Lateral fins were added to anchor the IUD in place. And for reasons unknown, but perhaps because of the strength needed when pulling on the string to remove the device, a multifilament tail string was selected. (Other IUDs on the market had monofilaments.)

In January 1970, Dr. Davis testified before the U.S. Senate. The pill scare was peaking, and Dr. Davis, the lead witness, fed the flames. He warned of the dangers of oral contraceptives and touted the promise of IUDs.

Dr. Davis was asked if he had a commercial interest in any IUD. He told the Senate no.

Dr. Davis also published an article in a leading medical journal endorsing the Dalkon Shield as "a superior modern contraceptive," with, he wrote, a remarkably low pregnancy rate of 1.1 percent, nearly equal to the pill and better than any other IUD. Again, Dr. Davis did not disclose his conflicts of interest: his role as coinventor of the Dalkon Shield or his financial stake in the device.

Dr. Davis and Lerner, along with two other men, formed a small company. In May 1970, one of them was staffing an exhibit booth for the Dalkon Shield at a medical conference in New Jersey and met a detail man from A. H. Robins. ("Detail men" promote and sell drugs and devices to physicians.) The detail man alerted his headquarters in Richmond to the exciting new product.

A. H. Robins had no experience with contraceptives or medical devices of any kind. It was known instead for its cold treatments and gastrointestinal medications, as well as a line of pet products. Within weeks, however, the company purchased the rights to the Dalkon Shield.

The company, wrote one employee, would "learn on-the-job."

What the company learned, even before purchase of the Dalkon Shield, was that Dr. Davis's claim of a pregnancy rate of 1.1 percent was false. A. H.

Robins also learned—from Lerner, the coinventor—that the tail string wicked, which could allow bodily fluids and bacteria to be drawn up through capillary action. "The string or 'tail' situation needs a careful review," an A. H. Robins executive wrote, "since the present 'tail' is reported (by Mr. Lerner) to have a 'wicking tendency.'"

This memo, titled "Dalkon Shield: Orientation Report," was sent up the chain of command to thirty-nine A. H. Robins executives. First on the list was E. Claiborne (E. C.) Robins Senior, CEO and chairman of the board.

■ ■ ■ ■

One day when I visit chambers, the judge gives me a copy of his best-known speech, which he had delivered a couple of years before to a gathering of prominent religious leaders sponsored by the Minnesota Council of Churches. To me, it reads more like the amalgamation of a preacher's sermon and old-time Wobbly oratory (I studied the IWW in college) than remarks from a federal judge. In this speech, the judge blamed corporations—and their sins, as he said—for many of the wrongs in American society. (He often ponders sins and sinners and, most of all, redemption.) He stated that a corporation—a person in the eyes of the law but certainly not in his—allows executives to sublimate their individual responsibilities to a system demanding "instant profits." He also pronounced his version of the Ten Commandments: "Thou shalt not steal applies to every corporate official who sells shoddy, dangerous, or unusable merchandise in the name of profit. . . . Thou shalt not kill applies to the corporations . . . who are killing through industrial pollution." And while he qualified his remarks by saying they applied only to "people and institutions that are doing wrong," the speech, from a sitting judge, was a shocker nonetheless. "Many people denounce crime in the street," the judge had proclaimed, in a line that I would often hear him repeat, "but few examine crime in the skyscraper."

I'm sure the speech is by now in the files of all defense lawyers with any prospect of ever appearing before him, including, as we would later learn, those representing A. H. Robins.

■ ■ ■ ■

The A. H. Robins Company did not test for wicking—in fact, did no safety testing at all on the Dalkon Shield—before its national market launch.

At the time, there was no FDA requirement to do so, unless the IUD contained a component intended to enhance its contraceptive effectiveness. That would make the product a "drug" instead of a "device," in regulatory parlance, and require years of premarket testing and regulatory approval. The Dalkon Shield did contain copper, added "for the express purpose of improving effectiveness," according to an internal company memo. But A. H. Robins told the FDA that copper was added only to improve the physical or mechanical characteristics (for example, strength and opacity), while failing to disclose its contraceptive effect.

Then the company rushed to market.

National sales of the Dalkon Shield started in January 1971 with an all-out promotional blitz: advertising to doctors (not only ob-gyns, the traditional targets, but also to general practitioners) and directly to women (virtually unheard of at the time for a product sold only through doctors); hiring a public relations firm to plant favorable articles in newspapers and women's magazines (*Ladies' Home Journal, Cosmopolitan, Glamour, Mademoiselle*); pressuring its detail men to increase sales ("No excuses or hedging will be tolerated, or look for another occupation"); and promoting a smaller version of the device for use in women who had never given birth (a huge market, but previously thought unsuitable for IUDs due to the risk of impaired fertility).

Soon A. H. Robins had captured the vast majority—80 percent—of the U.S. market for IUDs and was also distributing the Dalkon Shield in seventy-nine countries around the world.

That was no small feat of salesmanship. The Dalkon Shield was described by one gynecologist as a "gruesome looking little device" and "veritable instrument of torture." Other IUDs on the market folded into a slender linear shape to ease insertion into women through the vagina and cervix and into the uterus. But the Dalkon Shield was broad and shield-shaped, a thumbnail-sized piece of translucent plastic, with four or five spikes angling down on each side. (Less judgmental descriptions included "a law enforcement officer's badge," "a butterfly with sharp ridges," "a fishing lure," and "a skeleton of a fish with a string.") Little thought, it appeared, had been given to the mechanics of pushing or pulling the device through the narrow cervix. For insertion, the device, perched atop a blue plastic stick, was thrust into women, often without anesthetics. Some women passed out from the pain. Removal could be even more excruciating. "The most traumatic manipulation ever perpetrated on womanhood," wrote one doctor.

But that was not the most serious problem with the Dalkon Shield. The most serious—and deadly—problem was its tail string.

A black tail string, a couple of inches long, like a thick thread, was tied to the bottom of the device and hung down into the vagina. The tail string served two purposes: a woman could check periodically to make sure the IUD was still in place, and a doctor could pull on the string to remove the IUD (when, for example, a woman wanted to get pregnant). To the naked eye, the tail string looked like a single strand, a monofilament. In fact, however, it was a multifilament with several hundred tiny strands encased in a nylon sheath. The sheath was supposed to keep the inside of the string dry, but both ends were cut and left open. This was the fatal flaw: a tail string with open ends and interstices between the multiple filaments, providing a channel for the wicking of fluids—laden with bacteria—from the vagina into the uterus. The uterus is normally sterile. But the vagina is a "bacterial garden" bursting with microbes. "Similar to the mouth, similar to the rectum," said one doctor.

■ ■ ■ ■

Sometimes when I stop by, I find the judge continuing to riff on themes from his Council of Churches speech. "I am not anti-corporation," he likes to say, "but I am anti-hoodlum, anti-thug, anti-bank robber, and anti-wrongdoer." And, he adds, in case anyone misses his point, "some of these wolves wear corporate clothing."

■ ■ ■ ■

The Dalkon Shield lawsuits started as a trickle, in 1972.

The earliest cases were for perforation of the uterus. The A. H. Robins defense was to blame doctors for faulty insertion: for ramming the Dalkon Shield, atop its inserter stick, through the uterine wall. There were also suits for pelvic inflammatory disease (although, in the early years, the women, their lawyers, and even their doctors didn't know that the tail string wicked bacteria). Again, A. H. Robins blamed doctors, claiming that they inserted the Dalkon Shield without examining women for preexisting disease and placed the device "in a contaminated field."

A. H. Robins had little experience with litigation at the time—despite its long history, it had rarely been sued—and only a small in-house legal department. In the early years of the lawsuits, Roger Tuttle, a young in-house lawyer—pink-cheeked, bespectacled, and, in the eyes of one colleague (if not more), a bit peculiar—was in charge of the company's defense.

Tuttle turned to the medical department for guidance. They told him the problem was "with the physicians who pushed too hard inserting the IUDs or inserted them when the women were already suffering from infections," Tuttle would recall. "They told me all those liberated women were hot to go and just couldn't wait for the infection to clear up."

Tuttle was a born-again Christian. He walked through the halls of A. H. Robins speaking in biblical terms. "We'll smite the Philistines," he would say.

■ ■ ■ ■

Judge Lord tells me that the legal system can be more effective than government regulation in pressuring manufacturers to either improve defective products or withdraw them from the market. "Only the courts can make it too expensive to kill," he likes to say. "It is the only place that corporations haven't been able to buy into government."

But most judges are too cautious, he says, because they are too concerned about their reputations if they are reversed on appeal. Their main concern is not the U.S. Supreme Court, which grants only about 1 percent of petitions for review, but the federal Circuit Courts of Appeal—like the Eighth Circuit, based in St. Louis and covering seven states—where there is a right of review after a trial court's final judgment and the possibility of review even for certain intermediate (or "interlocutory") decisions made before the end of a case.

Judge Lord doesn't like to be reversed on appeal, either. But he would still rather do what he believes is "exactly the right thing"—whatever the consequences.

■ ■ ■ ■

The first deaths were reported, from septic abortions, in 1973. The next year, A. H. Robins sent out a "Dear Doctor" letter advising physicians to remove the Dalkon Shield upon confirmation of a pregnancy.

The letter did not mention the tail string or wicking or infections in nonpregnant women.

By this point, the FDA, alerted to several septic abortion deaths but still without full knowledge of the dangers of the Dalkon Shield, requested that A. H. Robins halt sales until the agency could study the issue. Tuttle, among others at A. H. Robins, opposed the move. He told A. H. Robins executives:

> If this product is taken off the market it will be a "confession of liability" and Robins would lose many of the pending lawsuits.

Two FDA advisory committees, however, continued the pressure, and some agency staffers urged not only a cessation of sales but also a recall so that women still wearing the Dalkon Shield would have it removed. (Many wore the device for years.) Ultimately, A. H. Robins recognized the inevitable—although the FDA did not have premarket authority, the agency could take action in these circumstances after the device was on the market—and lobbied for the weakest option, a voluntary suspension of sales. In June 1974, the FDA commissioner agreed.

The FDA, however, still planned to hold a hearing in August on the safety of the Dalkon Shield and other IUDs and requested that A. H. Robins turn over relevant documents. One week before the hearing, William L. Zimmer III—at the time, the president (E. C. Robins Senior was chairman and CEO; his son, E. C. Robins Junior, was still being groomed for leadership)—sent a memo to fifteen key executives:

> You are requested to immediately search your pertinent files for any letters, memos or notes on oral or written communications relating in any way to the thread utilized for the tail for the Dalkon Shield and send them to Ken Moore. Of particular interest are any references to "wicking" of the tail.

The documents were collected, as requested. But they were not provided to the FDA when the hearing began.

Or ever.

Indeed, the documents—*of particular interest*—appeared to vanish into a black hole.

■ ■ ■ ■

The judge often tells me how big corporations hide their most sensitive documents from pretrial discovery. "They move the documents around," he likes to say, "like pheasants in a cornfield."

■ ■ ■ ■

Later in 1974, a jury was selected in the first Dalkon Shield case that would go to verdict.

The plaintiff was Connie Deemer. She had become pregnant while wearing the Dalkon Shield, after the device perforated her uterus and migrated into her abdominal cavity. (She carried her baby to term.) The trial, in Wichita, lasted more than two months, with A. H. Robins calling nine expert witnesses: eight doctors and one engineer. The company's defense was to blame Connie's doctor. Connie's doctor, in turn, testified that based on what she had learned about the Dalkon Shield (too late for Connie), she wouldn't put it in a dog.

The jury reached its verdict in February 1975, awarding compensatory damages of $10,000 and punitive damages—awarded only when a defendant's conduct is egregious—of $75,000.

Punitive damages are meant to send a message to corporate wrong-doers to mend their ways. But the A. H. Robins response was to shore up the company's defenses. The top in-house lawyer, William A. Forrest Jr., traveled to Connecticut to meet with the Aetna Casualty and Surety Company, which insured the Dalkon Shield, to discuss the ongoing defense. Aetna executives told Forrest to get rid of Tuttle; "demanded my scalp" for losing the trial, Tuttle said.

Tuttle was relieved of his Dalkon Shield duties and left A. H. Robins the next year.

Aetna took charge and showered money into the litigation. McGuire, Woods & Battle, one of Virginia's largest law firms, was hired to direct the defense, along with, eventually, scores of additional law firms around the country.

The legal strategy was revamped. A. H. Robins would stop blaming doctors and instead stress causation, arguing that other factors—venereal disease, sex practices, personal hygiene, etc., etc., etc.—caused the women's infections, not the Dalkon Shield. Most women with pelvic infections never used the Dalkon Shield or any IUD, the company would argue. A. H.

Robins would also claim that the Dalkon Shield was no worse than other IUDs and therefore was not defective.

In addition, the outside lawyers began to hire experts to conduct studies of the tail strings. With lawyers commissioning these studies, any unfavorable results—for example, bacterial migration along used strings—could be hidden behind claims of attorney-client privilege or the work-product doctrine. (In fact, the law of privilege is not so simple, but this type of tactic was—and is—commonplace.) These secret studies were conducted or funded, at least in part, through Aetna, the insurer.

■ ■ ■ ■

Judge Lord makes no secret of the fact that he hates insurance companies.

On one visit, when I'm sitting in on a trial about insurance coverage, the judge motions me up from my seat at the clerk's table by the side of his bench. While the trial continues—and with the judge still managing to listen to every word of testimony—he tells me a tale about how as a young man he once worked as an insurance adjuster, an ill-fated endeavor that ended after he paid a woman multiple times *more* than her demand of $50 for a broken knee.

Later, he calls me up to the bench again to sum up his view of the insurance industry. "Sons of bitches," he mutters.

■ ■ ■ ■

The number of Dalkon Shield cases continued to grow. By late 1975, there were several hundred, enough so that to handle them efficiently, all of the federal lawsuits were consolidated in multidistrict litigation (MDL) proceedings before a single judge, Frank Theis, in Wichita. In the MDL, Judge Theis would handle pretrial proceedings for issues common to all of the cases, including the production of documents and depositions of company personnel, and then send the cases back to the jurisdictions where they had been filed for case-specific discovery and trial.

Judge Theis was passionate about the rule of law. He grew up in a small southeastern Kansas coal town, became active in the state and national Democratic Party (where he met a young Hubert Humphrey in 1938 and later a young Miles Lord), and was appointed to the bench by President Lyndon B. Johnson in 1967. He entered a series of orders directing A. H.

Robins to produce the company's internal documents, including a 1976 order that covered:

> A copy of *all files, correspondence, memoranda,* promotional material, and all other written or printed matter *which pertains in any way to the Dalkon Shield,* including but not limited to, its *design,* purchase, *testing,* promotion, manufacturing and marketing.

A. H. Robins responded by producing more than two hundred thousand documents (after further agreement about the parameters of the order) and establishing a depository, called the "Source Files," intended to be the comprehensive collection of all relevant Dalkon Shield documents for plaintiffs' attorneys to access.

■ ■ ■ ■

Judge Lord's views about document discovery are well known in the legal community, as I quickly discover. "You never go before Lord in a position where you are opposing discovery," one lawyer will later tell the press. "He'll not only overrule you; he'll think of six other things the plaintiff ought to have."

■ ■ ■ ■

In late 1977, Judge Theis in Kansas began remanding the MDL cases back to their original jurisdictions. (The MDL, however, would continue for years with the constant filing of new cases.) Minnesota, because of early advertising by two young plaintiffs' attorneys, had more cases than any state except California, making Minneapolis, in the words of one national magazine, "a boom town of Dalkon Shield litigation."

Once in Minnesota, A. H. Robins lawyers launched into discovery in each individual case, summoning women who had filed suit for pretrial depositions and the "dirty question" interrogations:

> "At what age did you first have intercourse?"

> "How many different sexual partners have you had?"

> "What was the frequency with which you were engaging in intercourse?"

"Have you ever engaged in oral intercourse with your partner or he performed oral intercourse on you?"

"Have you ever used any marital aids, for instance, vibrators, artificial penises, anything of that nature?"

"Have you ever engaged in anal intercourse?"

"Do you douche? . . . How often?"

"When you went to the bathroom did you wipe from front to back or back to front?"

The A. H. Robins lawyers argued that they needed this information to prove alternative (other than the Dalkon Shield) theories of causation; critics countered that the company's real intent was to make the women think twice about continuing to pursue their claims.

■ ■ ■ ■

By late 1982, Judge Lord is starting to talk a bit about the Dalkon Shield cases when I drop in, as the first trial in Minnesota is now on the horizon. Still, he doesn't seem too focused on the matter since all of the cases in the district are assigned to another judge, Donald Alsop, across the river in St. Paul. Mostly, Judge Lord complains about how the litigation is clogging the district's dockets.

To date, A. H. Robins has won ten of the fifteen cases to go to verdict in other parts of the country. If the company can keep up this winning percentage, it is another way to scare off many women and their attorneys, with the expense and difficulty of these cases. To a large degree, A. H. Robins can control which cases are tried, which is one reason it wins so often. If a strong case is selected for trial, A. H. Robins can simply offer enough money to settle, while it moves on to a weaker case on the docket.

In Minnesota, the A. H. Robins attorneys go down the list of trial-ready cases. They get to one where the company can attempt to introduce arguments about multiple sex partners, abortion, venereal disease, diabetes—

anything to divert the jury's attention from A. H. Robins and the Dalkon Shield.

The case, however, is not without its strong points as well. Few cases are one-sided; virtually every trial has many shades of uncertainties.

The woman is Brenda Strempke, who was born and raised outside of Little Falls, Minnesota, a small town in the center of the state. In 1971, when Brenda was twenty-three, she had a Dalkon Shield inserted. Eight years later, in February 1979, she felt excruciating pain in her abdomen and was rushed to a hospital, going into shock. A surgeon cut open her abdomen from pubic bone to belly button and removed her right ovary, with pus pouring out, and fallopian tube. Several days later, the doctor stood at the foot of Brenda's bed and told her that because of the severity of her infection and the surgery, she would have difficulty getting pregnant.

"The first thing I thought of was no babies, no babies," Brenda would say. "I will never have a baby."

The Strempke trial starts in February 1983.

Judge Alsop allows A. H. Robins wide latitude to delve into Brenda's personal life, over the repeated objections of her attorneys. (Judge Alsop is well respected but also known for his conservative bent. He was nominated to the bench by Richard Nixon in August 1974, on Nixon's last full day as president before resigning in the Watergate scandal.) A. H. Robins lawyers cross-examine Brenda about how many sex partners she had while wearing the Dalkon Shield, even though her husband was her only partner for a year and a half before her pelvic inflammatory disease. They argue that Brenda had herpes (there is a reference in her medical records but no confirming culture); they cross-examine Brenda and her doctors about her diabetes (arguing she increased her risk of infection by not taking proper care of herself); and they raise the issue of Brenda's abortion before she used the Dalkon Shield (an abortion that Brenda's mother first learned about from the press during trial).

The trial drags on, days turning into weeks turning into months.

The A. H. Robins attorneys are masters at delay, battling to keep company documents out of evidence (claiming they lack proper "foundation"); battling to keep out evidence of other lawsuits ("highly inflammatory") and evidence of septic abortions and deaths ("irrelevant and prejudicial"); battling to keep out evidence of A. H. Robins's false claims of a 1.1 percent pregnancy rate ("clearly collateral issues"); battling to keep out evidence of a new study from the Centers for Disease Control (which found that the Dalkon Shield's infection rate was at least five times higher than other IUDs); and battling over virtually every legal issue (endless in a case like this).

Finally, in May, the end of trial is in sight. But as the case comes to a close, Brenda calls her attorneys with startling news. She tested *positive* in a blood test for pregnancy.

For months, Brenda's attorneys have tried her case on the premise that the Dalkon Shield rendered her infertile. One of her experts had testified that the odds of her conceiving were "essentially zero." A pregnancy now would be a miraculously wonderful event for Brenda, but devastating to her lawsuit.

Brenda's attorneys, Dale Larson and Michael Ciresi, are experienced trial lawyers from the Twin Cities, although this is their first Dalkon Shield case. Ciresi knows they must report this news to Judge Alsop, even though he and Larson are not certain that Brenda is pregnant or, even if so, that she could carry to term, given her injuries.

In the courtroom, one of Brenda's doctors comes back to testify that Brenda is most likely pregnant but is at a great risk of an ectopic pregnancy, which will terminate when her fallopian tube, where the fertilized egg would be implanted, ruptures. Brenda also retakes the witness stand. "I want to be happy, but I am just too worried and too concerned," she says.

Then it is time for closing arguments.

Richmond attorney Deborah Russell argues for A. H. Robins. The Dalkon Shield, Russell says, is "safe and effective" and did not cause Brenda's infection. There were "many, many other factors in her life that put her at high risk," Russell asserts, and runs off the list: "Out of control diabetes, failure to follow the advice of her doctors and nurses, multiple sexual partners, sexually-transmitted diseases, and elective abortion." Moreover, she says, "Mrs. Strempke is pregnant."

Ciresi stands up to argue for Brenda. He says how proud he is to represent her. "She had the courage not only here but in her deposition to stand up to this company. She bared her personal life to you and to anyone else who came into this courtroom. How many have that courage?" He attacks A. H. Robins. "Their defense, ladies and gentlemen, reminds me of an octopus. You know an octopus when it is attacked expels a murky liquid to confuse whoever is attacking it and then it tries to swim away and escape while the confusion and deceit exist." He takes aims at the top corporate officers. "Where is E. C. Robins?" he asks. E. C. Robins Senior, he argues, owns half the shares of the company worth hundreds of millions of dollars. "You must reach him and tell him that he can't come up here to Minnesota and blow a whole bunch of smoke at you and bring in experts from all over the world . . . and take on that lady from Little Falls, Minnesota, thinking she is going to buckle under." Ciresi also gives the jury his send-the-message argument. "You can send a message from this courtroom this day: 'We are not going to tolerate that type of activity, it must end, you shall not do it again.'"

The jury begins to deliberate. The verdict must be unanimous, with all eight members of the jury agreeing.

Day one passes. No verdict.

Day two. No verdict.

Day three, a Friday. Brenda telephones her lawyers. She has begun to bleed, consistent with her menstrual period. Larson and Ciresi ask to reopen the testimony. But A. H. Robins lawyers argue it is not unusual for bleeding and spotting in the early stages of a pregnancy. Judge Alsop declines to call back the jury, at least pending further reports from Brenda's doctors. The jury will continue to deliberate, without this news.

The weekend passes with the jury off.

Day four, Monday. At 2:00 p.m., word comes in. The jury has reached its verdict.

There are fourteen questions on a special verdict form. The first question: Was the Dalkon Shield worn by Brenda Strempke defective by reason of design?

"Yes," the jury answered.

The second question: Was the defect a direct cause of the pelvic infection experienced by Brenda Strempke?

"Yes."

And so on down the line, a blowout for the plaintiff: was the Dalkon Shield defective by reason of inadequate warnings? ("yes"); was A. H. Robins negligent? ("yes"); did A. H. Robins negligently fail to warn physicians? ("yes"); and on and on, until the question on the amount of compensatory damages, for which the jury awards $250,000.

And that is not all.

Despite (or maybe because of) A. H. Robins's arguments about multiple sex partners, sexually transmitted disease, abortion, diabetes, etc., etc., the jury also finds that A. H. Robins demonstrated "a willful indifference to the rights or safety of others." That warrants punitive damages, which the jury awards in the amount of an additional $1.5 million.

It is the second-highest Dalkon Shield verdict in the country to date.

But at what cost? The trial lasted more than three months and cost Brenda Strempke and her attorneys (working on a contingent fee) more than $1.5 million in attorneys' time and expenses, almost the amount of the entire verdict. And the case is not over. A. H. Robins lawyers challenge the verdict as "excessive," "shocking," and "unconscionable." There will be months of post-trial proceedings before Judge Alsop and then an inevitable appeal to the Eighth Circuit. The costs will continue to mount. (And Brenda, as it turns out, was not pregnant or, if pregnant, swiftly miscarried.)

A. H. Robins, even when it loses, still manages to make the litigation too expensive for many women and their attorneys to fight to the end.

"Something has got to be done," Judge Alsop tells the lawyers after the Strempke verdict. "We can't do what we just did. The system just won't handle it."

He calls a hearing for all of the hundred-plus Dalkon Shield cases jamming federal court in Minnesota. (There are also hundreds more cases in Minnesota state court.) Judge Alsop has performed yeoman's work in the Strempke trial, but the backlog of cases, and A. H. Robins's tactics, are simply too much for a judge who operates in a business-as-usual manner. So Judge Alsop announces that he will no longer be the sole federal judge handling Dalkon Shield cases in Minnesota. The five other active federal judges in the state, he says, will also start to try cases.

That will include Judge Lord.

Judge Alsop may have been patient—too much so in the eyes of some plaintiffs' lawyers—but he knows what lies ahead.

"I want to see when you get in front of my friend Miles Lord," he has already warned one particularly obstreperous A. H. Robins attorney.

The trials will start in the fall, shortly after my clerkship begins.

■ ■ ■ ■

Finally, I graduate from law school.

The added bonus, as if I need one, is that our commencement speaker is Judge Lord. He tells us that we have the most expensive legal system in the world, yet fail to protect the rights of all of our citizens. He calls on us to make "a renewed commitment for justice for all" and to "rectify the wrongs in your profession and in society." He gives us a little sermon about being "your brothers' and your sisters' keeper." But he also warns that, for many of us, our idealism will be "crushed" in the real world. "The sad reality is that most of you, like most people, will be led around by your wallet," he says.

The judge knows his words are harsh. He does not apologize. "You asked for this," he says. "You invited me."

We line up to march on stage and receive our diplomas. When my turn comes, the judge stops the procession, steps forward, and gives me a big hug.

3

Young Man in the Cities, 1939–1948

His brother gave him twenty dollars and said, "Go sign up." Miles took the cash and registered at Crosby-Ironton Junior College, a small school with only a few dozen students.

Academics was not Miles's top priority. He chaired the social committee and organized a fraternity. In the spring of 1939, he also joined the community theater and landed the starring role (as was his custom) in *Aaron Slick from Punkin Crick,* billed as "a clean rural comedy." The role of Little Sis Riggs, a feisty tomboy, went to Maxine Zontelli, the cute girl who used to wait for paperboy Miles to deliver the Sunday comics.

The romance began.

Miles had seen Maxine in town sporadically over the years. She always caught his eye, but her family had moved around as her father built a series of businesses across the region. Emil Zontelli, a first-generation Italian, started with a wagon and a team of horses to haul logs and deliver coal, then began paving roads. He and his wife—he married a Norwegian girl, Anna—lived in a trailer. The pay wasn't much, but Emil worked hard and fast. He partnered with his younger brother, and later a sister, and branched into rural electrification. Eventually, the Zontellis also acquired several iron ore mines. They were small-time compared to the eastern corporate interests, called "citizen-miners" and well respected by the locals. Still, they were substantial enough to employ as many as three hundred men and successful enough that when the Depression shuttered the First National Bank of Ironton, the Zontellis bought the building to serve as headquarters for their varied business ventures.

The days of trailer living were over. Emil Zontelli and his siblings built adjacent houses on a beautiful lake on the edge of Crosby, geographically close to Miles's home but literally and figuratively on the other side of the railroad tracks.

Rich, poor—no matter.

Miles and Maxine made a striking and fun-loving couple. They shared their love of theater—and dance. Miles grabbed his girl and threw Maxine up over his head, down around his back, and through his legs as they won dance contest after contest, jitterbugging their way across northern and central Minnesota.

Miles also continued fighting. He took on carnival fighters at county fairs—he claimed he once fought "a little guy, a big guy, and a giant," all in one day—and took Maxine out to dinner with his winnings. He also entered the Golden Gloves tournament in 1939. He was nineteen years old and still in junior college, hoping to box his way to amateur fame and then turn pro to pay for law school.

The Golden Gloves were a big deal, broadcast on radio statewide and drawing flocks of spectators to watch the fights live. For the northern Minnesota championship, more than two thousand people filled the Brainerd Armory, with another thousand or more turned away at the door. Former heavyweight champion Jack Dempsey refereed one night and, the local press reported, "took quite a fancy" to Miles, instructing him how to throw hooks, coordinate his feet, block punches. Miles, weighing in at 153 pounds and fighting as a middleweight, won his division and moved on to the northwest championships in Minneapolis. The winners would go to the nationals in Chicago.

Miles won his semifinal bout in three hard rounds. He knew he would have to stop his opponent in the finals—a "tough nut," he thought—early. After the first few exchanges, Miles launched an uppercut and, with the force of the blow, broke his right hand. He threw a few more right punches, each one sending shock waves through his body, and collapsed to the mat. He got up. His opponent knocked him down with what Miles would describe as "a beautiful left hook." Miles's brother, ringside with his sister, told Miles to stay down. Miles got up. He got knocked down. Again and again. After about seven falls in all, Miles finally stayed down and lost on a knockout, as Miles recalled the fight.

But the referee, Johnny DeOtis, remembered it this way: Miles was floored repeatedly—maybe six times—by a stronger and more experienced fighter. "But he got up six times and finished on his feet," DeOtis said. "When he left the ring, he got the greatest applause of the night."

DeOtis made these comments in 1974, during Miles's clash with the Eighth Circuit over the Reserve Mining case. "You think Judge Lord has shown guts on the bench lately," DeOtis said. "But that is no surprise to those who saw him get off the canvas time after time."

Miles, too, saw boxing as symbolic of life at large and would remain as proud of his mettle in the ring as of any of his accomplishments. His dreams of turning pro, however, were over. Miles had to find another way to pay for law school. "I would now have to work for a living," he said, "and work I did."

■ ■ ■ ■

But first—marriage.

Maxine graduated in the spring of 1940 from Crosby-Ironton High School. She was eighteen; Miles, now twenty. Miles had been in school his whole life, and not working too hard at that. (His résumé would claim he graduated from junior college, but Miles would tell an interviewer, decades later, that he was "expelled . . . for a little bit" for defending a friend in trouble—no further explanation—and left a couple of courses short.) He was penniless, and his main credentials, as he saw them, were being "a hell of a dancer and a good bar fighter," not likely to impress the Zontellis.

So Miles and Maxine ran away to marry.

Miles borrowed an old car, and they headed to Mora, seventy miles down the road. Halfway there, the wheel axle broke. Miles paid a few dollars to tow the car and another few to replace the axle, which left him broke. In late August, they tried again. This time Miles borrowed a nice car from a rich kid in town. Miles wed Maxine with her class ring; he had no money for a wedding band.

They returned to town, keeping their secret. Except for one night when they snuck away for a honeymoon in a tiny cabin in nearby Aitkin, Miles and Maxine lived apart. Their plan was to keep their marriage secret while Miles enrolled at the University of Minnesota to finish college and go on to law school.

The Zontellis' plan—not knowing any of the above—was to ship Maxine off to the College of St. Catherine in St. Paul to get her away from Miles.

On the appointed day, Emil and Anna Zontelli loaded Maxine and her suitcases into their car for the drive. Miles saw them off and waved goodbye. A couple of hours later, the Zontellis pulled into the college parking lot.

There stood Miles, waiting to open the car door.

But Miles and Maxine still kept their secret. Maxine started school; Miles rented a small apartment nearby. Soon the nuns at St. Catherine's became suspicious, as Maxine was often gone from her dorm. They alerted the Zontellis, who confronted Maxine when she went home for Thanksgiving.

Maxine cried and blurted out: "I married Miles!"

She was also pregnant.

Miles and Maxine moved back to Crosby-Ironton. Maxine dropped out of college. Miles sold refrigerators and worked as a janitor at the local armory. After a couple of months, the couple returned to the Twin Cities. They lived in a tiny room; soot from nearby trains turned their laundry black. Miles washed barrels at a meat-packing plant in South St. Paul. Maxine cried and cried, she was so lonely.

Anna Zontelli came to visit, took one look at how her daughter was living, and ordered Miles and Maxine back home.

Emil Zontelli had foreclosed on a small restaurant in Crosby. He turned it over to Miles and Maxine, who tried to make a go of it for several months. Miles and Maxine were the cooks, waiters, janitors, everything. But the restaurant soon failed, leaving Miles, who had nothing to begin with, several hundred dollars in debt.

Around the same time, in June 1941, Miles and Maxine lost their first child, Mary, at birth. With Maxine still in the hospital, Miles buried their baby alongside Maxine's Italian grandmother.

The young couple—their baby lost, their restaurant failed—headed back to the Twin Cities.

Miles was still such a rube that he had trouble crossing the busy streets. But with the growing war effort, he landed jobs at ordnance plants in the Twin Cities suburbs, first as an oiler on a power shovel and next as a construction foreman. Miles had virtually no experience—"all I had was bullshit, just to tell you the truth," he would say—but there he was, supervising up to 150 men operating cranes, crawler tractors, diggers.

A baby, Priscilla, was born in June 1942.

Miles took a welding course to learn a skill to support his family while he enrolled at the University of Minnesota. Maxine had come from a high-achieving family. She expected the same from her husband. "We are going to achieve things in life," she told Miles.

He was "bright-eyed and bushy-tailed," as he would recall, in a brand-new suit from Brainerd.

Miles registered at the university, ran down the steps of the administration building—and fell. He busted up his knee (he would bear the scar for decades) and ripped a twelve-inch hole in his new suit pants.

He went to college by day and welded by night, until 2:00 or 3:00 a.m., working alone "in a big, spooky room." To free up time to study, he taught himself to work with both hands and weld double-time. Then he would put his schoolbooks inside a box with a small light and read in a dark corner of the room.

Maxine took a job at Dayton's department store in Minneapolis, in the credit department, to help pay off bills from their defunct restaurant. One day, Miles went to visit her at work. He didn't like what he saw. He was possessive and jealous, a product of his time and place. He didn't want men ogling his wife as she walked down the halls "in her little high heels," as he would say later. He told Maxine, "I'll just work harder." She would never work outside the home again.

■ ■ ■ ■

Despite school, work, and family, Miles began to pay attention to local politics.

He heard about a young politician making a run for mayor of Minneapolis. Hubert Horatio Humphrey—a cherubic-faced, joyful, fast-talking, and impassioned small-town populist—was little known but beginning to transfix students and other young volunteers with his energy and oratory. Miles went to a campaign event at a YMCA on the university campus. Humphrey told the students that, together, they could take over the state and create a better world. Miles thought that was outrageously far-fetched. Still, when Humphrey said, "My young friends, I need your help," Miles felt he was talking directly to him.

"He inspired us and taught us," Miles would say, "and bent us like tender willows in a nursery."

It would be a number of years, however, before the two established their hard-and-fast friendship. For now, Miles became a foot soldier peddling campaign literature in Humphrey's run for mayor of Minneapolis in 1943.

Humphrey lost the election.

Miles left college and, with World War II raging, enlisted in the air force.

He was assigned to an aviation cadet training program in Columbia, Missouri. At twenty-four, he was one of the "old men" in the unit and more cynical about the military and the need to obey any and all commands. Nor was he gung ho about the prospect of going into battle. He shuddered at the thought of "dropping bombs" or "shooting down another young boy."

Other cadets pinned up pictures of Betty Grable. Miles, as he would say, had his own "real live pinup, Maxine . . . the cutest little gal you ever saw." Maxine was back in Crosby, taking care of Priscilla. Miles wrote "scorching love letters." But he didn't hang up her picture. "I was so jealous and covetous of Maxine that I didn't even want those other boys thinking about her," he said.

Soon he was transferred to the Office of the Trial Judge Advocate at an air force base in Tucson. He assisted in military court martials, investigated accidents, and researched legal issues. Maxine and Priscilla joined him in Arizona, living just outside of camp, the young family together and happy.

There they stayed until the war ended.

■ ■ ■ ■

While Miles was in the air force, Hubert Humphrey ran again for mayor. The race was nonpartisan, but Humphrey recognized after his 1943 defeat that he nevertheless needed a vibrant party behind him. He was a Democrat, the lowly also-rans in Minnesota, polling far behind the Republicans and Farmer-Laborites. But the party of Governor Floyd B. Olson had been much weakened since his death, and, in 1944, Humphrey seized the opportunity by leading a merger of the Farmer-Laborites and Democrats to consolidate the liberal vote and form the new Democratic-Farmer-Labor Party, or DFL, as the Democrats would be known in Minnesota—unique among the states—from that day forth.

When Humphrey ran again for mayor in June 1945, backed by a contingent of young men known as "the diaper brigade," he won by the largest majority in city history.

The new mayor, a thirty-four-year-old "boy wonder," pledged to clean up a city known as one of the most corrupt in the country.

Minneapolis had been born a classic river city. Back in the days when Frank Lord spent his summers in the sawmills, the young town was renowned for its whorehouses, opium joints, unlicensed saloons, gambling syndicates, thieves, swindlers, pickpockets, and officials—including the mayor and top police officers—who ran a protection racket for them all. (Lincoln Steffens, the famed muckraker, featured the political corruption of Minneapolis in his 1903 article for *McClure's* magazine, "THE SHAME OF MINNEAPOLIS.") By the 1920s, Prohibition-era Minneapolis and its twin city of St. Paul were a hubbub of bootleggers, racketeers, and gangsters. By the 1930s, the U.S. attorney general had labeled the Twin Cities "the poison spot of the nation."

Mayor Humphrey described the Minneapolis he took over as a "wide-open town," with gambling, prostitution, and liquor rackets still thriving openly. The city's most infamous gangster—Isadore Blumenfeld, a.k.a. Kid Cann—implicated but never convicted in multiple murders (including the machine-gun slaying of a local journalist), was widely known for distributing cash by the envelope to politicians and police. "I have the city council in the palm of my hand," he boasted.

Mayor Humphrey named a tough Irish police officer, FBI trained, as top cop. Together, they cleaned up the police department, closed down illegal establishments, and started grand jury investigations of underworld activities. Mayor Humphrey himself, a tornado of energy, rode with cops on night patrols.

He also embarked on a campaign for social justice in a city marked by rabid racial and religious discrimination—one national magazine called Minneapolis "the capital of anti-Semitism in the United States"—leading the effort for the first effective fair employment ordinance in the nation and spearheading the transformation of the culture in the city and the state.

Mayor Humphrey was "out in front all the time, preaching and exhorting," as his biographer would write. He also began to harbor higher ambitions. "He lit the room up like a hundred watt bulb going on suddenly," said one top adviser, "and the idea of his being president didn't seem at all ludicrous."

■ ■ ■ ■

At the end of the war, Miles and Maxine returned to Minneapolis. In 1946, he reentered the University of Minnesota to complete his undergraduate degree—the only one of his siblings to get that far in school—and go on to law school.

Another child, Miles (Mick) Welton Jr., was born in June 1946.

For Miles, school and work filled the day and night, with school in the morning and then job after job after job: 1:00 p.m. to 5:00 p.m., janitor in apartment buildings; 6:00 p.m. to 10:00 p.m., clerk in the post office; 11:00 p.m. to 7:00 a.m., night watchman. He also worked at various times as a hotel bellhop and a tractor operator. In free moments, he studied in his bathtub, surrounded by pillows.

One day a chauffeured Cadillac pulled up in front of Miles's roach-infested apartment in southeast Minneapolis. Out hopped Mayor Hubert Humphrey. The mayor needed a military veteran to testify at a legislative hearing on rent control.

Just like that, Miles was back in the Humphrey sphere. Their first significant mission was to reshape the DFL, still in its formative years.

■ ■ ■ ■

The merger of the Farmer-Laborites and Democrats had fused the parties in name but left acrimonious divides, with extreme left-wing radicals holding considerable power. To this faction, Hubert Humphrey—a tour-de-force liberal—was a "fascist" and "warmonger." At the 1946 state DFL convention, they spat on Humphrey and jeered so relentlessly that he could not finish his speech.

Humphrey and his band of young devotees began to meet in the mayor's office to plot their move. They organized, in part, under the auspices of the Americans for Democratic Action (ADA), a new national organization that sought to promote a liberal movement independent of the Communists. In Minneapolis, Humphrey's troops included his organizational mastermind, Orville Freeman, a tough ex-Marine, "intense" and "highly competitive," as Humphrey would say, and, unlike the warm and cheerful Hubert, unafraid to make enemies. ("Hubert's strong-arm," one friend called Freeman.) Eugene McCarthy, a young professor at the College of St. Thomas in St. Paul, who had studied to be a Benedictine monk, also joined the ranks. Miles was involved in the effort but still in law school and, he would say, not part of the "brain group . . . because they were older and brighter and more learned in those things." Another college student, among the youngest in the group, was Walter (Fritz) Mondale, studying at Macalester College in St. Paul.

These young liberals branded the left-wing faction as Communists and set out to purge them from the DFL.

It was called an "outright war." In the spring of 1948, the Humphrey-ites fought their way precinct by precinct through the DFL caucuses and eventually on to a final victory at the state convention. "Grubby, head-to-head slugging," Freeman, who led the charge, would call it. With the battle over, Humphrey reported to the ADA leadership in Washington that, in his words, the "commies and other left-wingers" were defeated. Humphrey now controlled the DFL and was endorsed as its candidate for the U.S. Senate. The left-wing faction, defeated, left the DFL to form its own party, which soon collapsed.

In later years, there would be substantial debate over how many of the left-wingers had actually been Communists. Looking back, Miles would feel remorse. "We campaigned as the young idealists, but I don't think we were any more idealistic than the people we purged," he said. "It was a struggle for power and it wasn't fair to the people involved."

But Miles threw himself into the new campaigns.

He went to work on Humphrey's run for the Senate, driving young kids to assigned streets and paying them quarters to hang campaign litera-ture on doorknobs. He worked as well for Gene McCarthy in St. Paul, the little-known professor making his first run for office, for the U.S. House of Representatives.

Miles also graduated from law school in the summer of 1948, wearing the same pants—all patched up—as he had the first day when he fell down the steps of the administration building.

His father had died shortly before Miles received his diploma. But his mother, Rachel Lord, was there to see her dreams fulfilled.

■ ■ ■ ■

In July 1948, Miles was working one of his jobs on a farm on the outskirts of Minneapolis, shoveling in a barn and listening to the radio. Hubert Humphrey's voice came crackling above the din of the Democratic Na-tional Convention in Philadelphia.

Mayor Humphrey had gone to Philadelphia to fight for civil rights. (When asked how he got interested in the issue, Humphrey, from a small prairie town in South Dakota, would say, "I got it when I was born. I guess we just were brought up to believe that people are people.") He was not well known outside of Minnesota but managed an appointment to the platform committee, where he advocated a tough, no-compromise civil rights plank. He was told to give it up, that his proposal would split the party, destroy the presidential chances of Harry Truman (who was in trouble in his race against New York governor Thomas Dewey and desperately needed the Southern vote), and ruin Humphrey's own future.

Humphrey refused to back down. The party hierarchy was enraged. "Who does this pipsqueak think he is?" asked one senior senator.

To no one's surprise, Humphrey's plank lost in committee to a watered-down bill with no teeth. On the night before the convention's last day, Humphrey met with his supporters in a college fraternity house, where they argued until nearly sunrise about whether he should continue to push the issue. Finally, Humphrey made his decision. He went off by himself to scribble a speech in longhand.

Hours later, Humphrey stood on the podium at the Philadelphia Convention Hall. He was pale and thin (he had lost fifteen pounds during the committee battles) and sweat streamed down his face in the ninety-three-degree heat (there was no air conditioning). The delegates milled about, fanning themselves, as Humphrey began. Many had no idea who he was and little interest, initially, in what he had to say. But Humphrey's words poured out. His voice rose to a shout. Before long, delegates began to pay attention:

> Friends, delegates, I do not believe that there can be any compromise of the guarantees of civil rights. . . . There will be no hedging and there will be no watering down.

Cheers began to fill the hall. Humphrey thrust out his chin:

> My friends, to those who say that we are rushing this issue of civil rights, I say to them we are 172 years late. To those who say that this civil rights program is an infringement on states' rights, I say this: The time has arrived in America for the Democratic Party to get out of the shadow of states' rights and walk forthrightly into the bright sunshine of human rights.

More cheers rang out. Humphrey left his text to cry out: "People! Human beings!":

> This is the issue of the twentieth century. . . . We cannot and we must not turn from the path so plainly before us. That path has already led us through many valleys of the shadow of death. . . . For all of us here, for the millions who have sent us, for the whole two billion members of the human family, our land is now, more than ever before, the last best hope on earth. And I know that we can, and I know that we shall begin here the fuller and richer realization of that hope, that promise of a land where all men are truly free and equal, and each man uses his freedom and equality wisely and well.

The speech ended. The Minnesota delegation leaped to their feet. Other delegates followed in wild exuberance, jumping on chairs, raising banners, marching through the hall.

Many called it one of the greatest speeches in American political history. "He was on fire, just like the Bible speaks of Moses," said one delegate. An estimated sixty million Americans had listened on the radio. (Miles was not the only one tuned in.) Hubert Humphrey rocketed to fame.

At the convention, segregationist Governor Strom Thurmond of South Carolina led the Dixiecrats out of the hall. But the speech roused the party. The Democrats adopted Humphrey's minority plank, a landmark victory for civil rights. Truman went on to win an astonishing upset in November (notwithstanding the infamous "DEWEY DEFEATS TRUMAN" headline). In Minnesota, Humphrey, thirty-seven years old, defeated the incumbent Republican senator in a landslide—the first Democrat to win a popular election to the Senate in state history—and hit the cover of *Time* magazine as the "No. 1 prospect for liberalism in this country." Gene McCarthy, thirty-two years old, came from nowhere—borrowing a ramshackle 1937 Chevy from Humphrey for a campaign sound truck—to win a seat in the House, along with three other Minnesota DFLers.

The golden era of the Minnesota DFL had begun. In a few short years, Humphrey and his young followers had taken the Democrats from third-party status to a rising dynasty that would reshape politics for decades to come. They were a remarkable crew with, Miles included, strikingly similar backgrounds. They grew up poor, in small towns, forged by the

Depression and hard work. They came to politics young and hardened early in the fierce battle for control of the DFL. They embraced a commitment, rooted in the social gospel, to the least fortunate: "Those who are in the dawn of life, the children; those who are in twilight of life, the aged; and those who are in the shadows of life, the sick, the needy, and the handicapped," Humphrey would say; "my brothers and my sisters," said Miles. There were future governors and mayors and Minnesota attorneys general among these young men. Three would become among the most liberal senators in the nation. Two would become vice president. Three made serious runs for president. Humphrey almost—*almost*—went all the way.

Sometimes they helped each other to extraordinary heights.

Sometimes their ambitions clashed.

Miles Lord would be both the beneficiary of his friends from this early era and, on other occasions, smack in the middle of the internecine strife of dreams and egos.

4

Courtroom No. 1

The first week of my clerkship, in September 1983, is a nonstop blur.

The judge arrives in chambers early each morning, whistling and sing-ing, clapping his hands and shouting out enthusiastic greetings to spur his staff to action. The schedule, this week alone, is packed with trials, sen-tencings, motion hearings, and settlement conferences, with the judge in perpetual motion. He has attorneys flowing in and out of his courtroom, in and out of his chambers, and in a succession of rapid-fire conference calls. He has jurors in the courtroom, more jurors in holding rooms. One courtroom isn't enough; at one point he commandeers the courtroom of another judge down the hall and dashes back and forth between the two.

As the week ends, we prepare for a trip to Duluth, where the judge oc-casionally holds court. Our small entourage will head up on Monday for a few days. To prepare, we sit in chambers on Friday afternoon while the judge phones lawyer after lawyer with cases on his calendar for the trip, trying to get some to settle. With more than four hundred and fifty cases assigned to him—typical for a federal trial judge (with most cases randomly assigned by the clerk's office)—reducing the backlog is always on his mind. The judge puts the calls on his squawk box, a big, brown contraption with multiple red levers, and starts banging heads, pulling legs, and cracking jokes with the attorneys on the line, anything to persuade them to agree to a deal. One of his favorite ploys is to threaten to try a case *immediately*, even if not trial ready, if the attorneys don't settle *now*. Some attorneys are stunned; they don't know if the judge is kidding or not. (Nor do we.) Sometimes, the judge reverses field and threatens an intractable plaintiff's attorney with a wait of years for a trial date if the attorney doesn't take the settlement offer on the table.

Finally, we're done for the week.

Keith Halleland, one of my co-clerks, stops by my desk. "Wait 'til you see the judge in Duluth," he says. "He really loosens up there."

■ ■ ■ ■

The judge is closing in on sixty-four years old when my clerkship starts. He is fit and spry (no surprise he's been compared to a leprechaun); his face is lean and creased, with a strong, sharp chin and gray, thinning hair combed straight back; his hands are gnarled, with cryptic reminders to himself scribbled in ink on the back. His eyes, behind wire-rimmed glasses, are twinkling one moment, fiercely piercing the next; his face, expressive and mercurial, quickly transforms from delight to incredulity to fist-pounding wrath. (He still revels in the role of leading man, as he did in his youth. "He is a natural actor," wrote one reporter, "and the courtroom is his theater.") Woe to the lawyer or litigant who provokes his ire, when the judge's jaw will set and his eyes turn cold and hard. But he loves to laugh—cackle, whoop, and hoot—especially at his own jokes and stories but also at oth-ers'. He is endlessly amused and fascinated by people from all walks of life.

In his courtroom—Courtroom No. 1 of the federal building in down-town Minneapolis—the judge sits on high in a black leather chair. Nothing escapes his scrutiny. He surveys the courtroom like a hawk looking for its next meal, ready to pounce on a recalcitrant witness or wayward attorney or to take note of anyone who takes a seat among the rows of backbenches. He will chat it up or tell a joke or story to just about any person—an old friend, a reporter, visiting schoolkids—who enters, no matter what is going on in court at the time. Most of the courtroom is standard fare: the gold-tasseled American flag, the Great Seal of the United States, the dark mahogany wood. But the judge has added one unique feature (in addition to himself): hidden speakers from which, with the push of a button, he booms music—Mantovani's orchestral pop is a favorite—so jurors can't hear his private sidebars with lawyers or sometimes just for sheer amuse-ment or shock value. There is also a spittoon behind the bench, for when the judge chews his Copenhagen snuff.

Back in chambers, the judge is more partial to cigars. When he does relax, he props his feet up on his desk, lights up, and puffs away.

The judge's staff is small, and we occupy a warren of modest offices con-nected to the judge's inner chambers.

Suzanne (Suze) Laukka, the judge's senior secretary, doesn't say much, but it's clear to me after a week on the job that she rules the roost. She has been with the judge since 1972, and the judge values her above anyone else on staff, as well he should. (Supreme Court Justice Ruth Bader Ginsburg would later tell an interviewer: "As I tell my clerks, 'if push came to shove, I could do your work—but I can't do without my secretaries.'")

There's also a calendar clerk who schedules the judge's days, dealing with the hyperkinetic judge on the one hand, and lawyers by the dozen on the other; a court reporter who can take down a hurricane-of-words a minute, but also knows, from a nod of the judge's head, when the judge wants his remarks off the record; and three law clerks who pass through for one- or two-year stints.

I'm the newest of three. My co-clerks are Keith Halleland and Jennifer Anderson. Jennifer used to be the judge's calendar clerk, then went back and got her law degree. Keith previously worked for a magistrate—judicial officers appointed by the judges of each district to handle a variety of assignments—and got to know the judge that way. The motions and briefs and assorted papers from the judge's cases stack up in our in-boxes; we sort through the piles, filter out what the judge needs to know, draft orders and opinions on old manual typewriters, and work on jury instructions, all standard clerk duties with any judge. We also have to take care of some administrative work, as Judge Lord, by virtue of seniority, is now the chief judge of the district (a title with more bureaucratic than substantive power).

Some judges keep their law clerks toiling away in a back room, but Judge Lord likes to get us in on the action. He makes sure we're all in court when there will be excitement, calls us into his inner chambers when he moves to that arena (spacious but plain, with a portrait of *The Old Man and the Sea* and a few honorary plaques on the wall), and often uses us as sounding boards. He also likes to take us out to eat and drink. If it's a familiar haunt, he is greeted—Miles!—like an old friend, especially at Murray's, the fabled steakhouse with its old-time waitresses, who fuss and fawn over the judge; if it's a new place, he is sure to be the best of buddies with the waiters and waitresses by the time he leaves.

Apart from his staff—and there are a few others from time to time, including additional secretaries and student interns—I'm surprised at how isolated the judge is. He is on cordial terms with the other federal judges in Minnesota, even friendly with a couple, but being a judge is a lonely calling, so at odds with Judge Lord's exuberant sociability. I also get the feeling that some of the other judges and their clerks want to keep a safe distance from Judge Lord and his staff, almost as if the controversies that so often swirl around Judge Lord are a contagious disease.

■ ■ ■ ■

The steady flow of cases continues when we hit Duluth on Monday. In late afternoon, after we wrap up the first day in court, we head to our hotel bar. We've barely finished a round of drinks when the judge jumps up and announces that we should take a trip—right now—to his hometown, one hundred-plus miles away. He wants to check up on his brother-in-law, who is sick.

Five of us pile into one car, with the judge at the wheel: honking away at other cars . . . at state troopers . . . at cows . . . and in time to radio music.

In Crosby-Ironton, the judge gives us the grand tour, including the house where he grew up (smaller than my one-bedroom apartment). The judge visits his sister and brother-in-law, where he spends the night. The rest of us stay in a small hotel.

The next morning, we stop at a local diner for breakfast, where the judge engages the patrons, to much merriment, in his attempts to identify their genealogy from his paper-route recollection of hometown faces. We are late getting back to Duluth but still able to knock off the day's work and even squeeze in lunch by the harbor on Lake Superior. As we munch our sandwiches, seagulls land around us, screeching to be fed. We toss out morsels; one gull starts snapping food from the others; the judge lures it in with food—then kicks it in the butt.

"I don't like bullies," he says.

■ ■ ■ ■

After Duluth, I settle in to the nonstop pace.

All in all, the judge is a great boss. He is quick to appreciate and trust our work. Typically, he doesn't change much in our draft opinions, except for adding an embellishment or two to juice them up. And even when we (or I) screw up—I make a mess of one set of jury instructions—the judge is understanding and puts the blame on himself.

A number of his former law clerks continue to drop by chambers, long after they've moved on to other jobs. They miss the days of exhilaration—

"like taking a running start and jumping on a roller coaster," as one will describe the experience—and the feeling that their work was actually helping real people. Not every clerk, however, was taken with the judge. Some were offended by his unorthodoxy in both his judicial philosophy and his hijinks (as lowbrow as pulling out a rubber snake to frighten restaurant patrons or shooting a spitball in chambers), which upended their notions of the proper comportment of a federal judge. One former clerk also warns me that the judge is a sexist. In truth, the judge is the first to admit that he has not shaken all of the vestiges of his Iron Range roots. He is an old-fashioned flirt and still struggles with, and is amused by, modern (to him) nomenclature; he knows the term "girl" is verboten except for a youngster, so he invented his own terminology: "woman-person" or some variation on that theme. But in substance, the judge, once he saw the light some years ago, has been a pioneer for women's rights. I've read the newspaper stories about a ground-breaking decision that he issued allowing girls to participate in high school sports; he also stewarded a historic sex-discrimination case against the University of Minnesota. He now has two daughters, both of whom are lawyers (along with one of his two sons). He also encouraged other women to attend law school, including Jennifer, my co-clerk; the judge was thrilled when she told him she was going back to school for a law degree. And for my part, I don't detect one whiff of sexism in how he treats me (and, as a reporter, I've been called a lot worse than a *woman-person*).

In fact, the judge and I hit it off splendidly.

It helps that I'm coming out of a newsroom, a faster-paced environment and way less stuffy than the rarified law-school milieu that most clerks are used to. Also, I can double as the judge's de facto press agent, no small plus with a judge who loves attention. ("Pisses me off," he says, when he's been out of the headlines too long.) I'm also eager to soak up the judge's stories about the past. To the judge, the past is the present is the future. He considers Reserve Mining a present-day topic; although the case is long over, I still find him on the phone with medical experts discussing the latest studies on asbestos. His stories about Minnesota politics are especially engaging to a relative newcomer to the state like me. And his tales about the gangster days amuse and amaze; by the time I arrived in Minnesota from the East Coast in the late 1970s, the state was considered so squeaky clean that my editor bemoaned the dearth of scandalous stories to cover.

I'm also entertained by the judge's antics and join in the spirit of things myself. I buy a bunch of those fake glasses with big noses and mustaches, and we—the judge and staff—put them on in a restaurant one day. "I've brought my family to lunch," the judge tells the waiters. Afterwards, he proudly parades us through the clerk of court's office.

It can be easy for some people to miss, through his hell-raising and tom-foolery, the other side of the judge. The judge himself doesn't think he is all that brainy, at least in the highbrow sense. "If I had your brains and my guts," he tells one magistrate. But he has an agile mind and fearsome instincts. And he views his mission as nothing less than to save the world. "A natural-born rescuer," he calls himself, both on the bench and off. (He's been known to carry a towing strap in his car to aid stranded motorists; to chase down hit-and-run drivers; to use his belt as a tourniquet on an injured motorcyclist.)

I had thought before I started with him that the judge was blithely impervious to the criticisms and condemnations hurled his way as he kicked up his storms of controversies. My vision of him was as a judicial Pig-Pen (from *Peanuts*), oblivious to the cloud of dust in his wake. But up close, I see a different side. The judge bears many scars, most notably from Reserve Mining, as well as from other battles. Indeed, his psyche seems to have been forever marked by what the Eighth Circuit did in Reserve Mining, booting him off the case and thwarting his white-knight mission to save the people along Lake Superior from the plague of asbestos-like fibers in the municipal water supply. Some days, he seems tormented by the injustice of it all and consumed with an Iron Ranger's rage at his enemies, with the Eighth Circuit at the top of his list.

"I don't go bouncing along in blissful ignorance," he will say. "I know what price I pay."

He is tiring of the toll. He is also bored with the more mundane aspects of judging. He talks about retiring next year, when he turns sixty-five.

I think again how lucky I am. Even if there is no blockbuster case like Reserve Mining during my tenure, I will be one of the last young lawyers to clerk for him.

But there may be one last hurrah. I start hearing more and more chatter about it around the courthouse: the Dalkon Shield litigation.

Before long, the cases will be divided up among all of the judges in the district. Judge Lord, even before his cases are officially assigned, tells me to start reading the briefs filed with Judge Alsop to pick up some background.

■ ■ ■ ■

For the time being, however, the Dalkon Shield cases remain before Judge Alsop, and not much has changed.

Despite the Strempke verdict the previous spring, the A. H. Robins lawyers know that the system, which breeds delay, is on their side. One A. H. Robins lawyer makes no secret of the company's game plan. "We have more money than you do," he tells plaintiffs' attorney Dale Larson, as a boast—and a warning—of the gridlock that lies ahead.

Indeed, it is not unusual for big-time litigation to bog down for years or even decades. In many ways, A. H. Robins is following the playbook written by attorneys for the tobacco and asbestos industries, unleashing seemingly limitless resources and taking no prisoners. As one tobacco company attorney would write in an internal document (later leaked):

> The aggressive posture we have taken regarding depositions and discovery in general continues to make these cases extremely burdensome and expensive for plaintiffs' lawyers, particularly sole practitioners. To paraphrase General Patton, the way we won these cases was not by spending all of [R. J.] Reynold's money, but by making that other son of a bitch spend all of his.

Often in this type of litigation, General Patton does not meet his match until the defendant is forced to turn over all of its internal company documents in pretrial discovery. This bares the inside story in the company's own real-time words, especially important when company executives stonewall with "I don't know" and "I don't recall" in their testimony. In reality, however, there are countless ready-made arguments to shield the most damaging documents from ever seeing the light of day: claiming attorney-client and work-product privilege; refusing to comply with document requests that the defense deems improper ("burdensome, vexatious, and harassing," "irrelevant and not reasonably calculated to lead to the discovery of admissible evidence"); hiding a harmful document or two in a warehouse filled with thousands or millions of pages of irrelevant material; playing word games over each phrase of each document request (what does "pertains in any way" mean? what does "relating to" mean?).

In the Dalkon Shield cases, A. H. Robins did produce a number of damaging documents in the multidistrict litigation proceedings. Judge Theis—and the plaintiffs' attorneys in Kansas—were hardworking and professional. (Tuttle called the lead plaintiffs' lawyer, Bradley Post, "a bull-dog.") But given A. H. Robins's modus operandi, the MDL discovery has not been sufficient to force a breakthrough in the litigation.

Plaintiffs' attorneys like Dale Larson and Mike Ciresi in Minnesota believe that the most damning documents are still hidden. But they haven't found a judge who will let them go after them in the face of A. H. Robins's arguments that all of the discovery was completed in the proceedings before Judge Theis.

Larson and Ciresi, however, do manage to convince another federal judge, in Wisconsin, to let them take the deposition of E. C. Robins Junior.

Junior is the fourth generation of his family in company leadership. His father, Senior, is now the semiretired chairman, while Junior is, at forty years old, president and CEO, with the responsibility of running the company day to day.

In his deposition, Junior testifies that, despite the flood of litigation, A. H. Robins continues to prosper. The company's stock price has more than doubled over the past two years. That raised Junior's net worth—mostly from a trust fund with company stock set up by his grandmother—to millions of dollars.

Junior testifies that he has not personally reviewed the safety or efficacy of the Dalkon Shield. He cannot recall any conversation with his father about the Dalkon Shield. He cannot recall any conversation at any board meeting about the Dalkon Shield. There is very little talk about the Dalkon Shield at "my level," he says.

The deposition ends with Larson asking if Junior is aware that the Strempke jury in St. Paul found A. H. Robins "willfully indifferent" to the rights of women.

"Yes," says Junior.

"That didn't cause you to take any further action of any kind, am I correct about that?" asks Larson.

"Correct," responds Junior.

■ ■ ■ ■

Judge Lord, meanwhile, is keeping busy with other cases on his calendar.

There are discovery hearings (attorneys arguing, like little kids, about which documents they have to produce); plaintiffs' attorneys fighting each other over who will represent a quadriplegic (the damages, and therefore the fees, will be huge); and a naturalization ceremony for new citizens, which, with the judge's memories of the immigrant families on the Range, brings him endless joy (after the standard Oath of Allegiance, the judge gives an improvised oath more to his liking about the need to be "our brothers' and sisters' keeper," then he descends from the bench to pose for photographs with the children like the proud granddaddy of each happy family).

There is also a never-ending flow of Social Security disability cases, with hundreds of thousands of people previously found to be suffering from serious medical or mental impairments having had their benefits terminated in a systematic purging of the rolls by President Ronald Reagan's administration. Judge Lord makes no secret how he views these cases. "The poorest and most downtrodden are getting it in the neck," he tells the press. As far as I can tell, he orders the reinstatement of benefits in every case that comes before him. But the procession of claims continues on. "I feel like I'm running around with a bucket trying to catch raindrops," he says to Keith and me.

And there is plenty of action outside of the courtroom. The judge, with a prosecutor's blood still in his veins from his early days, is well known for his frequent clashes with criminal defense attorneys. In one dustup, he gets into a public spat with one of the top criminal defense lawyers in town. A jury had convicted one of this lawyer's clients a few years back; the Eighth Circuit, however, recently reversed because Judge Lord had too actively assisted the prosecution at trial. A judge must "respect the role of counsel in the adversary process," the Eighth Circuit's chief judge wrote, and allow "the chips to fall where they may." Fat chance, I think, when I read the opinion. Indeed, when newly disclosed information about the case now hits the press, Judge Lord takes it upon himself to pile on with derogatory comments. Reporters swarm, headlines blare. The judge is happy as a lark with all the commotion he's causing and sings the refrain from an old song over and over.

"The little man has had a busy day," he belts out with glee.

The judge also revels in the company of old friends.

Gene McCarthy stops by for lunch one day, and the judge invites the staff along. While I was a teenager and too young to vote in 1968, I do remember McCarthy from his fervent opposition to the Vietnam War and his against-all-odds campaign against President Johnson and, ultimately, Hubert Humphrey. Now, there are three hours of the former senator, long white hair flowing, reminiscing with the judge: their political campaigns in the 1950s (appearing on radio and television together, with Miles serving as the attack dog for the entire DFL ticket); the Kennedys (oh, how the senator hates them still!); and McCarthy's visits to the Johnson ranch in Texas (with LBJ bullying his guests into shooting deer).

They also touch on the 1968 presidential race. My memories of that campaign, albeit slight, are of McCarthy as the knight in shining armor and Humphrey as the establishment lackey and apologist for an unpopular war. But I have begun to ponder my view of Humphrey (who died in 1978) given how the judge so obviously loved the man with all his heart. By now, I've heard so many stories about Hubert as the judge's dearest friend. And I wonder as the lunch talk merrily proceeds, didn't McCarthy have a lot to do with Humphrey—or, as the judge sometimes calls him, "the Hubie"— losing in 1968?

But I stay quiet as the judge and McCarthy laugh over shared memories.

The judge is also in constant demand as a speaker and often heeds the call. Soon he is asking me to help draft his speeches.

Suze has just gotten the first permanent computer in the office. She names it Exxie (after Exxon, its manufacturer). Since I can type as fast as most people talk, from my days of reporting on deadline, I sit at Suze's desk while the judge stands over my shoulder, dictating and whooping and hollering as he goes. I type up a storm and offer comments along the way.

One speech is for an event at Hamline University in St. Paul. The judge is blunt, as always, and asks whether people are shocked "to hear that politics, that personal philosophy" influence judges. He draws an analogy to the Ouija board:

> The words of the law—in the Constitution, in the statutes—are subject
> to varying interpretations. The law is not some mystical truth floating in
> the clouds waiting to be discovered by judges. Their philosophy, back-
> grounds, views of current events consciously or subconsciously enter
> into the decision-making process. I think of it somewhat like a Ouija
> board. You will recall that if you know the answer and hold your fingers

on the Ouija board's pointer, it will ultimately—no matter how careful you are—work its way over to that answer. In the same way, judges have a feeling of what is appropriate and just under the circumstances. . . . Having decided what it is that we want to do, it is easy to then back up this predilection with legal jargon and case law, as precedent can be found to back nearly any proposition.

But, he says, a judge's "harmonious relationship" with the appeals court is "often the high price paid for doing what in the individual judge's opinion is right."

■ ■ ■ ■

As we move into the fall of 1983, some of the other federal judges in the district start on their assignments of Dalkon Shield cases. Judge Lord, however, is not in a rush. He wants to gain a better understanding of the litigation and tells me to keep track of what is happening in other courtrooms.

One case is called for trial down the hall from us before Judge Diana Murphy. The plaintiff's attorney is George Gubbins Jr., a sole practitioner without the wherewithal to try the case. (Later, it will be discovered that Gubbins was issuing dozens of insufficient fund checks around this time, and he will be temporarily suspended from the practice of law for various financial improprieties.) A. H. Robins attorneys know that Gubbins can't afford a trial; they tell him, as he later says, that they will "grind me down." The jury returns its verdict during the second week of November. One more win for the defense.

Next door to us, in Judge Harry MacLaughlin's courtroom, the case set for trial involves only minor injuries, and the woman requests a settlement of a modest $12,500. But A. H. Robins is reluctant to do any deal. This is another case that the company can win; the plaintiff and her attorneys are not likely to spend enough to properly try a case where the expenses would far exceed any potential verdict. Judge MacLaughlin, however, pressures A. H. Robins, and on the eve of trial the case settles for $8,000, with the plaintiff's attorneys waiving their fees.

Two other trials in the district—before Judge Robert Renner and, again, Judge Alsop—will result in verdicts against A. H. Robins, but without punitive damages.

Mike Ciresi is also back in trial before Judge Paul Magnuson in St. Paul.

Ciresi's client is Martha Hahn. She was born and raised in a small town in Iowa, went to college in South Dakota, and in 1973 was inserted with a Dalkon Shield. In late 1978, when Martha was twenty-four, married, and living in Reno, a sharp pain ripped through her midsection, "as if someone was stabbing me from the inside with a knife." A doctor diagnosed pelvic inflammatory disease (PID) and pulled out the Dalkon Shield. The pain, as she would describe it, was "like pulling an old razor blade through you." One month later, the pain returned, and her husband rushed her to the emergency room. Her infection was the worst the doctor had ever seen. He feared for her life.

On December 24, Christmas Eve day, Martha's surgeon operated. He removed her entire reproductive system: both ovaries, both fallopian tubes, her cervix and uterus, a total hysterectomy, "a clean-out." When Martha came to, her first awareness was the sound from her heart monitor. She listened to her heart beating. She thought, "I am alive."

At trial, an A. H. Robins attorney tells the jury in opening statements to focus on what caused Martha Hahn's PID. He runs off a list of her "risk factors," including, he says, exposure to gonorrhea. (In fact, Martha had a negative culture for gonorrhea, but her medical records, as is not uncommon, contain an inaccuracy.)

Ciresi believes in Martha and believes in the case against A. H. Robins. But his law firm has hundreds of pending Dalkon Shield cases, and he wonders how many of these trials—months long, with astronomical costs in time and expense—he will face. Any lawyer can lose any case, no matter how strong. And a plaintiffs' lawyer, like Ciresi, needs a unanimous jury to win: the agreement of every single juror, from vastly different walks of life, with vastly different politics and values, a seemingly impossible feat. A. H. Robins, by contrast, needs only one person in order to deadlock—or hang—the jury: for *one* juror to accept *one* of its umpteen arguments, to believe, for example, a cryptic (or erroneous, as in Martha's case) notation buried in hundreds of pages of medical records that the causative culprit is venereal disease, not the Dalkon Shield.

For Ciresi, there is no end in sight.

Then—toward the end of the Hahn trial—a letter arrives.

■ ■ ■ ■

"Dear Ladies and Gentlemen," Judge Lord writes on December 5 to all of the attorneys on the Dalkon Shield cases assigned to him. "It is my present plan to have a Pre-Trial Conference on Friday, December 9, 1983, at 10:00 a.m. in Courtroom No. 1 of the United States Courthouse, Minneapolis, Minnesota."

The judge is now primed for action. He has waited—and watched—as the other judges in the district have taken on their first Dalkon Shield trials. Now he outlines his tentative plan: to try *all* of his Dalkon Shield cases together, one big trial, for twenty-one cases.

The judge tells the attorneys in his letter that he is "interested in hearing your views" on his proposal for a consolidated trial. But he also sets an anticipated trial date: January 3, 1984, less than one month away.

5

Hotshot Prosecutor, 1951–1952

The benefits to Miles from the DFL's smashing victories in 1948 were not immediately apparent.

He set out to practice law from shared space in a cheap office in downtown Minneapolis. The pickings were slim. He handled whatever cases he could get his hands on: workers' compensation, divorce, personal injury, rent control. He also hired out as a public defender for five dollars a case. That didn't pay the bills but did gain him experience and his first exposure to federal court, where he was struck by the high caliber of the men on the bench—all of the federal judges in the district were men—and their power. For the first time since his mother had said, "You should be a lawyer," Miles formed a vision of a path to follow.

More immediately, however, he needed to feed his family. Miles and Maxine now had three children, with James born in November 1948. Miles helped make ends meet by taking care of a pediatrician's farm near suburban Chanhassen. He milked cows, fed pigs, and then drove downtown to his little law office.

In 1950, Miles decided to run for the state legislature. It was a doomed mission, as his district was solidly Republican. But "the howl of the creditors," as he would say, left him few choices. By running for office, Miles would get his name out, make more DFL connections, maybe attract some clients, maybe land a government job.

"Lord for the Legislature," his campaign signs read. "A liberal! For liberals!"

It was not the most compelling message for his conservative district.

Miles didn't much care. "There is not the faintest possibility that I will prevail," he wrote that fall.

While campaigning, Miles heard about an opening for a prosecutor in the office of the U.S. attorney for Minnesota. (U.S. attorneys are appointed by the president as the top federal prosecutors for a state or district; each U.S. attorney then hires his own assistants.) Miles applied in October 1950. He told the U.S. attorney that he was willing to immediately withdraw from the state ballot, or if he were not offered the assistant's job until after the election and if "by some strange quirk I should be elected," he would then resign from the legislature. Miles coveted the federal appointment; it was prestigious, and as he would later say, "it sounded like groceries."

The assistant's position was not filled right away, and Miles went on to lose the election.

Hubert Humphrey, however, took note of Miles's effort and congratulated him on his "splendid race." "This was a tough year for the liberals," Humphrey wrote, in a letter to Miles typed on U.S. Senate stationery. "Thank goodness we had men like yourself who were willing to carry the liberal fight." On the bottom of the page, in handwriting, Humphrey added, "Thanks Miles for everything. You've been a real fighter."

Miles seized on the opportunity to speak with Humphrey about the position in the U.S. attorney's office. As he hoped, he had also gained the recognition of other well-placed DFLers during his run for the legislature. In January 1951, he started his new job.

■ ■ ■ ■

It did not take long for Miles to hit the headlines as an energetic—and publicity-seeking—prosecutor.

Not long after his appointment, an inmate escaped from the St. Cloud Reformatory and called Miles, whose name was known from his days as a public defender. The escapee told Miles horror stories about the reformatory, including the use of narcotics by inmates and brutality by prison officials. Miles called state officials (at the Minnesota Bureau of Criminal Apprehension), federal officials (at the FBI), and a local TV station—not necessarily in that order. A sensational investigation ensued, involving allegations of widespread barbiturate trafficking and other lawlessness by officials and even, Miles charged, possible murder by guards at the state-run prison.

Miles testified before a state grand jury, highly unusual for a federal prosecutor. He also corresponded with Senator Humphrey to urge that "our Minnesota penal institutions be brought out of the dark ages." "Although I am a federal employee," Miles wrote, "I continue to feel strongly, as I am sure you do, about a situation which so vitally affects the welfare of our own state."

Indeed, this should have been a state, not federal issue, and presumably outside of Miles's jurisdiction as a federal prosecutor.

But there was wrongdoing.

There were headlines.

There was Miles.

And soon, he began to make an even bigger name for himself as a prosecutor.

Minneapolis was still fertile ground for an ambitious crime buster.

Hubert Humphrey, as it happened, had gotten rid of many—but not all—of the racketeers while he was mayor. In fact, although Mayor Humphrey was widely credited for cleaning up the city, not all agreed he was so pure. Some even claimed that Mayor Humphrey's crackdown had in fact helped Kid Cann—the "most notorious citizen" in Minneapolis—by forcing his gangland rivals into exile and closing down street gambling, but allowing Kid Cann's sports-betting business to thrive as the "nerve center" for high-stakes gambling nationwide. In the early 1950s, Kid Cann still ruled the streets of Minneapolis.

Another longtime gangster, Tommy Banks, also flourished. Banks had been a bootlegger in the 1920s and 1930s, frequently arrested but convicted only twice: once for involvement in an alcohol ring whose bookkeeper, a reputed snitch, was machine-gunned down. (Banks was fined $2,000.) Now Banks was believed to be in a gambling syndicate and the owner, through various fronts, of multiple nightclubs and bars. But his slot machines had been one of the casualties in Humphrey's reign as mayor. Indeed, Banks was known as a political enemy of Humphrey.

Miles went after Tommy Banks.

The investigation of Banks had begun when Humphrey, as mayor, called in the FBI and the Internal Revenue Service to investigate whether Banks had paid taxes on his ill-gotten gains, and it was just beginning to bear fruit when Miles started in the U.S. attorney's office. Miles lobbied for and got the assignment, even though he had never before prosecuted a significant case. In early 1952, a federal grand jury, led by Miles, indicted Banks for defrauding the government out of thousands of dollars in taxes. The crux of the charges was that Banks spent more than he declared as income, making this one of the first "net worth income tax cases" in the country.

The case was front-page news, day after day.

But Miles was scared.

He was scared for the safety of his family. (Miles and Maxine now had four children, with Virginia, who would be their last child, born in December 1950.) One night, their oldest daughter, Priscilla, picked up the phone to hear a voice say, "Is your Dad there? You tell him if he knows what is good for him and his family he'll lay off of Tommy Banks."

Miles was also scared because this was his first big case and his first, of many to come, centered around complicated financial transactions. As trial approached, he worked further and further into the nights to piece together the paper trail. Two federal revenue agents assisted him and took turns taking naps, so one would be awake at all times.

The trial took place in May 1952. When Miles stood to speak, his voice came out high and squeaky. Forty-seven witnesses testified over six days. The jury deliberated for one hour and fifty minutes.

And Miles had his first significant conviction.

After that, Miles was an unrelenting prosecutor and on his way to becoming a regular presence in the headlines. He also looked the part, like a young G-man, with an intense gaze and heavy black-framed glasses set atop his sharp, hard-cut features.

Along the way, Miles got a visit from someone in Senator Humphrey's circle. The visitor said the senator was hearing some grumbling that Miles was too aggressive in prosecuting certain underworld figures.

Miles went to Senator Humphrey to clear the air. The senator stood by Miles.

They had known each other for years. But this would mark the beginning of their lifelong bond of brotherhood.

■ ■ ■ ■

Miles and Hubert had much in common.

Hubert described himself as "a poor boy from a small country town." He was born in a bedroom above his father's drugstore in Wallace, South

Dakota; raised by a deeply religious mother, who wanted her son to be a minister, and a politically active father, who read him bedtime stories about great figures from American history; saw his family lose their home during the Depression, his father crying as he sold the house to pay debts; and, after dropping out of school for a few years to help in the drugstore, worked his way through college by cleaning toilets, caretaking apartments, and selling ten-cent sandwiches made by his wife to fellow students.

From their hardscrabble years, the two men—Hubert and Miles— emerged much alike.

They believed that every hurdle could be overcome, that no problem was unsolvable, and that each person—each *human being*—could make a difference. They had faith in, and a bottomless love for, the human spirit. They embraced a social philosophy that, as Miles described, was imbued with the moral teachings—"blessed are the meek"—of the Sermon on the Mount.

It is, indeed, striking how many traits inscribed by Humphrey's biographer would equally define Miles as his career progressed: "fiery prairie progressiv[e]"; "free spirit"; "impulsive"; "irrepressible"; "ambitious, shrewd"; "strong flair for publicity"; "bursting with affirmation of life"; and "filled with faith in the brotherhood of man."

Of course, they had their differences as well. Indeed, to some, Hubert and Miles were the odd couple, with Miles along for the ride to amuse the usually (but not always) more serious Hubert.

Especially in their early years, Miles marveled at the fact that Hubert would embrace him as a friend. Hubert had been the hallowed leader— and Miles, eight years his junior, a low-ranking devotee—when they had first met in the 1940s, and had risen to national stature by the time he and Miles conjoined. "I felt very humble and proud that he would adopt me as a friend," Miles would say. "If he hadn't been for picking up stray cats and dogs, he never would have put up with me." From the start (and until the end) Miles worshiped Hubert. "Hubert Humphrey stood head and shoulders above any man I ever met," he would say. "Being with Hubert Humphrey was just like riding on a magic carpet as we used to imagine it in grade school."

Their wives—Maxine and Muriel—also bonded, and the two families, each with four children around the same ages, celebrated holidays, marked family events (birthdays, graduations, weddings), and spent untold hours and days together. Hubert also came to rely on Miles as a surrogate family counselor; when a Humphrey son would face troubles back in Minnesota, Hubert, in D.C., had a standard refrain for his child: "Go talk to Miles about that." Miles even gave the Humphrey children a pony. ("I have never seen Bobby and Douglas so happy as when you brought out that pony," Hubert wrote to Miles. "We will take good care of him.") Miles and Hubert also fished together and hunted together, sometimes with a son or two in tow, although Miles was much more the outdoorsman.

"Hubert's concept of an outdoor experience is to walk around on somebody's back lawn," said Miles.

They often traveled to the Lord family cabin on a small island in Leech Lake, in north-central Minnesota, which had once belonged to Maxine's father. The cabin was one room, more of a hunting shack, with spiderwebs covering the outside walls, insects and rodents with run of the place, and no indoor plumbing or electricity. Hubert, known for his fastidiousness, would do his best to tidy the place: carrying in pails of water from the lake—boiling, washing, scrubbing, sweeping—while Miles and the boys went out to catch walleye and pickerel. Hubert also once tried to rid the island's outhouse of its resident garter snakes by grabbing a rifle and firing away, turning the two-seater, Miles would say, into "a fifty-eight holer."

Miles, in fact, was forever laughing at his fussbudgety friend. He perfected a drawn-out routine describing how the Hubie cleaned up after shaving: Hubert cleaned the razor, cleaned the shaving cream can, cleaned the mirror, cleaned the faucet, cleaned the drain, cleaned the sink, folded the towel, and, as he was about to leave the bathroom, exclaimed, "My, this doorknob is sticky!" and grabbed the towel again to finish the job.

The good-natured Hubert was an easy mark for Miles, who would never outgrow his love of a good prank. One time, when Miles and Hubert were on a fishing trip up north, both unshaven and slovenly (especially by Hubert's standards), they came upon a broken-down bus filled with tourists from California. Miles jumped aboard to greet the captive audience. He told the out-of-staters there was a local fellow who looked a lot like Senator Hubert Humphrey and even believed that he was. "A harmless nut," said Miles. Soon after, Hubert boarded the bus, announced that he was Senator Humphrey, and was greeted by roars of laughter. It didn't take him long to figure out what was going on. "Miles, God damn you, what have you done?" Hubert shouted. Then Hubert had a good laugh, too.

(Some of Miles's best capers took place at a hunting lodge in southern Georgia, owned by a Minnesota businessman who often invited down his favorite politicos, including Hubert, Miles, and their pals. There, they would hunt, talk politics into the night, and, especially Miles, plot elaborate practical jokes on each other. On one trip, Walter Mondale joined them and was promptly hoaxed with a fake murder scene; he awoke from a nap, and, as he descended from his second-floor room, there was his businessman-host splayed out across the staircase and bleeding from the throat, all quite convincing—even the ketchup.)

But there was also a serious side to the relationship between Miles and Hubert that many did not perceive, especially since Miles would be shunted into the background, not a natural state for him, at some of the senator's more dignified gatherings.

In private, however, the two talked politics and philosophy, for hour after hour.

Miles listened—and learned—when Hubert taught him that educating the public about the issues of the day was one of the most important duties of public officials in a democracy and that, with public opinion on their side, their goals could be within reach. "The power," as Miles would later repeat, "lies with the people."

Hubert also tried to teach Miles about the more pragmatic side of politics and counseled Miles to make peace with some of the power brokers from the corporate world, including the big pharmaceutical and steel companies. "Miles," said Hubert, "if you ever want to be kept in style, you either go with a pharmaceutical company or Big Steel."

That was one bit of advice that Miles failed to heed (and he would often laugh about the irony in later years: Dalkon Shield and Reserve Mining, ha-ha-ha). Indeed, Miles, the Ranger, would rarely try to make peace with his enemies. He remained untamed, true to his north-woods roots, and, Hubert thought, courted too much controversy.

"Too much static, Miles," Hubert would say. "Too much static."

As the years went by and even as their friendship deepened, this difference would grow more pronounced. While Hubert continued his bold leadership on many progressive issues—including, most notably, civil rights—he also perfected the art of compromise. "I would rather get something than nothing," he would say. Hubert's admirers would attribute his legislative accomplishments—ultimately, he would be heralded as one of the greatest legislators in the history of the Senate—to this trait; "the art of the possible," it was called.

But Miles would see the price—eventually, in 1968, the ultimate one—that Hubert's accommodations would extract.

At times, Miles would come to think that Hubert wasn't tough enough. Hubert was too nice, even sweet. "He was a terrific fighter but no killer," wrote his biographer. "Men were not afraid of him."

The same would not be said of Miles as he ascended to power.

6

Meeting the Enemy

The judge is revved up—darting around chambers, clapping his hands—as he prepares to enter the courtroom on the morning of December 9, 1983, for his first hearing on the Dalkon Shield litigation.

But first he has another, short matter to address: a plea bargain by a big defense contractor for overbilling the government on a missile system. This hearing should be perfunctory, as the deal has been agreed to by both the company, Sperry Corporation, and federal prosecutors. But the judge is angry. He thinks Sperry is getting off easy because of its status as a billion-dollar contractor. He is also perturbed because no one—no person—is being held accountable. To Judge Lord, living breathing persons, with souls and consciences, must be held accountable. Otherwise, he tells the lawyers before him, personal responsibility "disappears in the deep, dark recesses of corporate power."

He launches into his familiar themes, one justice for the rich, and one for the poor; one for the mighty, and one for the meek; and adds a new line, one for the defense contractor, and one for the road contractor.

As the judge speaks, attorneys for the Dalkon Shield cases begin to filter into the courtroom. The judge and I watch—the judge from the bench, me from the clerk's side table—and exchange glances as more and more lawyers take seats on the backbenches. I try to figure out who all these suits are. We have been expecting a brigade of defense attorneys. But as the judge continues his tirade against corporate America in the Sperry case, I'm thinking that they look like mostly plaintiffs' lawyers.

They are smiling.

■ ■ ■ ■

The Sperry hearing ends. The judge tentatively accepts the plea deal. "I don't know if I have any authority to reject this," he says, but "I have the capacity to resent it."

Now he turns to the Dalkon Shield lawyers.

Despite his excitement this morning, the judge is not sure where he is heading with these cases. His predilections naturally lead him to side with the victims, and he is acutely aware of the punitive damages verdict, the red flag for corporate misconduct, in the Strempke trial across the river in St. Paul. But his main goal is to break the litigation logjam. If this means getting A. H. Robins to quickly settle without any fireworks, not only in Minnesota but also around the country, that would be fine by him.

In the meantime, he has a big-time case on his hands, and he loves the excitement—and attention—that will bring.

The first matter of business is who is who. The judge wants to know who everyone is in the courtroom—sometimes attorneys try to hide in the back rows—and whom they represent. He has an insatiable curiosity about people (stemming, he says, from his old paper-route days), and he also wants to know whom he can hold accountable once things heat up. He asks the attorneys representing A. H. Robins to stand. Only two local attorneys—Jack Fribley and Mary Trippler from Faegre & Benson, a large Minneapolis law firm—rise.

The big guns from Richmond that we have heard about aren't here, not yet.

The judge asks the plaintiffs' attorneys to stand; forty-some rise, a few with clients by their side.

He asks if the plaintiffs have selected lead counsel to represent the group. Dale Larson says that will be himself and Mike Ciresi. Ciresi is still in trial in the Martha Hahn case in St. Paul, but the attorneys have been given a day off for this hearing.

"Well, come up here," the judge says. "And defense counsel, come up here, too."

The attorneys take their places at the two counsel tables in front of the bench, with Larson and Ciresi claiming the table near the jury box, where they will want to be, closest to the jurors, once trial starts.

Larson and Ciresi are with Robins, Zelle, Larson & Kaplan (RZLK), a law firm based in Minneapolis and founded by Solly Robins (no relation to the A. H. Robins family of Richmond) in the Depression days of 1938. Robins grew up in St. Paul, the son of Jewish immigrants. He couldn't get a job with any of the major firms after graduating from law school due to the Twin Cities' infamous anti-Semitism (in pre–Mayor Humphrey days). So Robins set up his own firm with a law school classmate. He took on all kinds of clients but made his name in personal injury and products liability cases. His partner was a business lawyer, and the combination of the two—representing both plaintiffs and businesses—was unusual, especially as the firm grew. By 1983, the firm has about one hundred attorneys. That makes it one of the largest law firms in the Twin Cities, and it has largely outgrown its Jewish roots. But with its unique history and continued representation of not only corporations, as with most big law firms, but also plaintiffs, the firm is still considered an outcast, often called a sweatshop, by the blue bloods of the legal establishment, the firms that wouldn't let a young Solly Robins in their doors.

In 1983, Robins still has an active practice but no longer leads the firm's blockbuster cases. The baton has been passed to Dale Larson, in his forties, and Mike Ciresi, age thirty-seven.

Larson is now a name partner. Most of his work is on behalf of corporations and insurance companies—not injured plaintiffs—and he looks the part, with dark, well-coiffed hair, elegant three-piece suits, a deep and measured voice. He is an exceptional trial lawyer. He is smooth. He is feared. "I don't know which hand he has got in my pocket," an A. H. Robins lawyer grumbles at one point.

Mike Ciresi, a passionate Sicilian, is a study in contrasts. His most distinguishing feature—he is average height and build, with dirty-blond hair—is his round face, which, unlike the studied deadpan of the lawyers around him, brims with expression. Ciresi's mother died of breast cancer when he was young. His father was a first-generation Italian who spoke broken English, quit school after the seventh grade to sell fruit and vegetables from a cart in St. Paul, and later opened a liquor store. When Ciresi graduated from law school and landed a job at RZLK, his father was bursting with pride but also astonished at the starting salary, a flush $11,000. ("Stupid sons of bitches," the father said of the firm.) Ciresi went to work at Solly Robins's side and by 1983 is also a first-class trial lawyer, with a courtroom style that reflects his personality. "How many women have to lose their reproductive organs before A. H. Robins will take action?" is one of his choice lines of cross-examination. "One hundred? One thousand?" He also loves to get under the skin of opposing counsel. In the Strempke trial, Ciresi sat just a few feet away from A. H. Robins attorney Deborah Russell; he would swivel toward her in his chair at counsel table and whisper: "How can you represent these people with what they do to women?" (Ciresi rarely saw her in the litigation after that trial.)

In this first hearing before Judge Lord, Larson carries most of the arguments for the plaintiffs. Ciresi sits at counsel table, beaming his smile and looking like there is no place else on earth he would rather be.

Jack Fribley, representing A. H. Robins at this hearing, is a young partner at the old-line Minneapolis law firm of Faegre & Benson, which dates back to 1886. Fribley is in his early thirties but looks younger, with a mop of curly brown hair. His roots are all Iowa: he grew up in Ames; had a distinguished law school career at the University of Iowa, including serving on the law review; and clerked for a federal judge in the state. Then he headed for what he called the "big city," Minneapolis, and the Faegre firm. Fribley has an open, nice-guy demeanor. And Judge Lord has nothing against big-firm defense lawyers from Minnesota. He even has a son-in-law whose St. Paul law firm, Oppenheimer Wolff, has been retained by A. H. Robins. (That firm made its first appearance in the litigation when Judge Alsop was preparing to divvy up the cases; it was agreed, however, that its lawyers would not appear before Judge Lord.) The judge is generally comfortable with the names and faces he recognizes, as opposed to out-of-town defense lawyers—classic corporate outsiders to his Ranger sensibilities—who do flybys in his courtroom. He knows Fribley and his background. "You're a fine, honorable guy," the judge will tell him. But Fribley, as we quickly confirm, doesn't call the shots in the Dalkon Shield litigation. The orders come from Richmond.

Mary Trippler, who is with Fribley at this hearing, is a young associate at Faegre & Benson. We will see little of her—and no more women lawyers in Minnesota for A. H. Robins—after the Richmond team arrives.

Once in place at counsel table, Fribley wastes no time in objecting to the judge's plan for a consolidated trial. He says there is too much work to do on the individual cases—including obtaining volumes of medical records and taking depositions of the women and their doctors—to be ready for trial by January 3. Fribley does have a point: only one of the twenty-one consolidated cases has been certified "trial ready," with all of the case-specific pretrial work completed. The judge, however, has heard this argument—too much work, too little time—from countless other corporate defendants and is not impressed. He knows there is an army of defense attorneys, even if not in court today.

Fribley also tells the judge that "consolidation at this time is not an efficient solution to the court's backlog." He says a trial of twenty-one cases, all together, would be "too confusing and potentially prejudicial." Besides, Fribley says, A. H. Robins is working diligently to settle cases through a process set up by Judge Alsop.

"We share this court's desire to reduce that backlog," Fribley says.

The judge listens politely. "I called you here to hear from you," he says. "My conclusions were *tentative*."

The lawyers understand the code. The judge wants to leave himself flexibility in order to stave off a final decision that A. H. Robins can immediately appeal to the Eighth Circuit. In legal-speak, this is "protecting the record." (Judge Lord, as with most judges, is quite adept at protecting the record when he wants to; unlike other judges, however, he is quick to transmute into his more famed persona as his ire rises.) In most cases, there is only one appeal, at the end of a case. But where a litigant has the time and the money—as does A. H. Robins—interlocutory review may be possible at any time, within the discretion of the appeals court; the more tentative the order, however, the less the chance of immediate appellate review.

So the judge proceeds to set forth his "tentative" plan for a consolidated trial.

"As I understand it," the judge says, "the question is, 'Did the A. H. Robins Company produce and market a device which, when used in a manner in which it would ordinarily be anticipated to have been used, create an unreasonable danger to the user?'" That is a generic liability question, says the judge, "it goes right across the board." It makes no sense to him to try the same issue—with the same witnesses, the same exhibits, the same attorneys—twenty-one times over. But A. H. Robins lawyers don't see it that way. The trial threatens their strategy of litigation by attrition. It also undermines their dirty-question approach, as it is hard to blame a single individual for one thing (multiple sex partners) or another (venereal disease) when twenty-one women face the jury and the only thing they have in common is the Dalkon Shield.

The judge also lets the plaintiffs' attorneys have a piece of his mind. He tells them that to move the cases along, they will have to streamline their evidence and claims. The judge thinks that the lawyers, from both sides, overcomplicate the issues. To the judge it's pretty simple. "If they tell you that there is a string hanging down there and sucked up germs, and that once the germs get there they cause an infection, then is it important that you know all about everything else?" he says to the lawyers. The trial of the generic case, he says, should only take about two weeks, not months as in previous trials.

He also tells a well-worn tale from his past about how he learned to handle huge litigation. He once presided over a group of antitrust cases, called "the biggest lawsuit in America," involving price-fixing for broad-based antibiotics. The defendant pharmaceutical companies demanded that millions of purchasers—each one allegedly overcharged—be compelled to testify. The judge asked the companies how long that would take.

"They said, 'eight thousand years,'" he recounts.

The judge brings the message home to Dalkon Shield. "If this goes on over and over across this country, do you realize what will happen?" he asks.

He answers his own question.

"Actually, it has been observed, the ladies will be dead and gone before their cases get litigated."

For the rest of the hearing, the judge flies through A. H. Robins defenses in quick succession.

First, he brings up the issue of the A. H. Robins dirty questions, "alibi evidence," he calls it. "I don't mean that in derogation," he says, "but that's really what it is, it's 'Something else did it.'"

He doesn't wait for Larson and Ciresi, or any other plaintiffs' lawyer, to raise the issue, as would most judges. He dives in on his own.

"The depositions are not going to go into all of the things that they have gone into, from what I have read in the papers, about the ladies' past sex lives fifteen years ago," the judge says. "That kind of thing we are not going to talk about in this case. . . . We are just not going to do that here."

Questions about abortions, says the judge, are out. "Not to be referred to, not to be inquired into."

The judge turns to Larson and Ciresi. "What else?" he asks. "What is the other stuff that embarrasses these women into not filing their claims?" Larson stands. "Oh, they ask them, you know, which way they wiped, how many sexual partners they have ever had, when they've had sex—"

The judge cuts him off. "None of their business," he rules.

Next issue up: the admissibility of A. H. Robins documents.

The A. H. Robins attorneys have argued, in case after case, that many of the company's documents are not admissible into evidence because they are not business records (and are instead hearsay), even though authored by A. H. Robins personnel and produced in the MDL directly from the company's own files. Again, Judge Lord raises this issue before Larson and Ciresi do. Judge Alsop had told him that A. H. Robins took up an extraordinary amount of time arguing over documents in the Strempke trial.

"We are not going to have a lot of arguments on exhibits," Judge Lord says. "Any exhibit that got by Judge Alsop will be received without any argument."

Later, the judge goes further with his ruling, shortcutting the myriad and often intricate rules of evidence. "If they pulled the documents out of the company files, foundation is laid," he says, simple as can be.

Larson raises another issue: compelling the live testimony of A. H. Robins executives at trial. Judge Lord feigns surprise that there would be any resistance to this. "Oh, I think they would do that, wouldn't they?" he says.

Of course not.

Everyone in the courtroom knows that corporations almost never want their executives to testify, not in pretrial depositions and certainly not live at trial. They "mummy up and play dumb," as the judge likes to say. The more senior the executive, the more vehemently his attorneys typically resist. Among other things, defense lawyers will want to argue that if there was any improper conduct (which they deny), it was perpetrated by some wayward employee at the bottom of the organization chart. This is a critical issue, as a key factor in assessing punitive damages is whether top management is implicated in the wrongdoing.

There are some plaintiffs' attorneys who, uncertain of their skills or too lackadaisical, don't care if they can get top executives to testify or don't even want them.

But not Larson and Ciresi. "Live meat," Ciresi often says, with relish.

Larson tells Judge Lord which executives the plaintiffs want for trial, starting at the top with E. C. Robins Senior.

"You can have them here live," says the judge. "That will be an order."

Fribley begins to argue that at least some of the executives, who live and work in Richmond, are outside the subpoena power of a judge in Minnesota.

The judge cuts him off. "You don't want to stand on that, do you?" the judge asks.

"As a legal position, yes sir," says Fribley.

"You stand on it as a legal position, and as a practical position you better have the people here," says the judge.

Finally, as the hearing wraps up, the judge says—one more time, for emphasis—that his rulings today are only *preliminary* and *interlocutory*. He speaks to the lawyers in the courtroom. But his words are meant primarily for the lawyers in Richmond, who will soon be reading the transcript.

The judge knows that his orders today—preliminary or not—have gone a long way toward dismantling A. H. Robins's traditional defenses. In one sense, what he has done should not be seen as radical at all. He has scheduled a trial for related cases, eliminated extraneous lawyer-made defenses, and ordered the testimony of top executives to test both sides on the merits of their claims. But in the legal world, where the search for the truth is often trumped by process and procedure—ritualistic steps performed in slow motion—the judge's actions are a lightning bolt. His rapid-fire rulings on this single day would typically take, before other judges, months or more of briefing, arguments, and written orders. The message is clear. This judge is more than ready to slice through the flotsam and jetsam of ten-plus years of lawyers' games. And while the consolidated trial is for only twenty-one cases out of thousands nationwide, one enormous verdict, as the attorneys well know, can change the course of the entire litigation.

■ ■ ■ ■

After the hearing, Mike Ciresi drives back to St. Paul for the closing arguments in Martha Hahn's trial. The old rules—not Judge Lord rules—are still in force here.

Charles Osthimer III, an attorney from San Francisco arguing for A. H.

Robins, blames Martha's PID on multiple factors other than the IUD, including, he says, her exposure to gonorrhea. (Never mind her negative culture.)

Ciresi argues for Martha Hahn. He denounces the Dalkon Shield as "a time bomb ticking away" in the uterine cavities of women. He says A. H. Robins treated women as guinea pigs, inserting an untested product into their wombs. He blasts the dirty-question litany: "When they sold this product, did they tell people not to have sex?" he asks. "Did they sell it to nuns?" He tells the jury, as if they didn't already know, that he has not been able to hide his feelings about A. H. Robins. "I detest them," he says.

It is a basic rule that an attorney is not supposed to express his personal opinions to a jury. Ciresi knows that; he can't help himself.

A. H. Robins moves—unsuccessfully—for a mistrial.

The jury doesn't need long to deliberate. It returns the next day with its verdict: compensatory damages of $200,000 and punitive damages of $550,000, a substantial, but not crushing, result. A. H. Robins can keep going at this pace for years, if not decades, to come.

Except that the sands have already begun to shift.

■ ■ ■ ■

A few days after this first pretrial hearing, Judge Lord issues a written order to memorialize and refine his rulings from the bench. The consolidated trial will be held in in three phases. The first phase will address issues common to all of the cases: Whether the Dalkon Shield was defective and A. H. Robins negligent in its design, manufacture, warning, or marketing; whether the Dalkon Shield has been a cause of septic abortions, ectopic pregnancies, unwanted pregnancies, perforations, pelvic inflammatory disease, infertility, deformed children, and deaths; and whether A. H. Robins acted in willful disregard of the health and safety of women. The second phase will address individual issues—causation and damages—for each of the women, and the third phase, the amount, if any, of punitive damages.

The judge's pretrial order also addresses other matters from the first hearing. On the issue of A. H. Robins's dirty questions, his order bans questioning women on "which way they wipe"; "use of marital aids"; "methods of intercourse"; "the number or identity of sexual partners"; "elective abortions"; or "any other intimate details that are designed to intimidate or embarrass the claimants." The order leaves an opening if A. H. Robins can produce evidence "that such personal practices caused or contributed to a plaintiff's injuries." In other words, A. H. Robins lawyers can ask these questions only if they first demonstrate that the inquiries are relevant to an individual woman's case.

Also, on the issue of witnesses for trial—Ciresi's "live meat"—the order requires the appearance of E. C. Robins Senior and Junior, plus three additional A. H. Robins executives "and such others as may become necessary."

I help put this order together; a large part of my job is to tie up loose ends after each hearing. After setting out the above provisos, I also make sure to include the magic words: "This is an *interlocutory* order and is *subject to amendment* if it becomes apparent that it is working an undue hardship on any party."

If there's one thing I've learned by now, it's to try to protect the judge's record for whatever challenge might come in the Eighth Circuit.

Meanwhile, as they have from the start, lawyers on both sides of the case continue to file lengthy memoranda, with mountains of attachments, on every issue imaginable. (Why these are called "briefs" is to me just one of the mysteries of the legal profession.) On other cases, the judge typically doesn't read lawyers' briefs; he gave that up long ago. With his years on the bench—and his dismissive view of legal precedent, which in any event many lawyers twist beyond recognition—he usually relies on his clerks to filter through what he needs to know. But on Dalkon Shield, he gobbles up the filings as soon as they come in.

One A. H. Robins brief, forty-nine pages long, plus attachments, asks the judge to rescind his pretrial order. The A. H. Robins lawyers throw in every argument they can think of (sometimes, it seems, they must get paid by the word), going paragraph by paragraph through the order and arguing, among other things, that the judge's rulings will "make it impossible for Robins to receive a fair trial"; that the time allowed for pretrial preparation is "wholly inadequate and deprives Robins of due process of law"; that the prohibition on asking women personal questions (absent a showing of relevance, which A. H. Robins argues it can't make without asking the questions in the first place) deprives the company "of the ability to obtain evidence critical to its defense"; and that the A. H. Robins executives ordered to appear at trial are not "within the subpoena power of the court."

A young associate from Fribley's firm in Minneapolis signs the brief, but in chambers we're all pretty sure it was drafted by the Richmond lawyers, whose names don't appear on the filing.

■ ■ ■ ■

"Do you have some friends to introduce?"

The judge starts the next hearing, on December 20, with this question to Fribley. There are some new faces on the backbenches, and the judge presumes they are from Richmond. He wants them identified on the record and admitted to practice in Minnesota as out-of-state lawyers (known as *pro hac vice* admission).

Fribley stands and introduces Alexander Slaughter and William Cogar, both from Richmond (but from two different law firms: McGuire, Woods & Battle, and Mays, Valentine, Davenport & Moore, respectively). Slaughter and Cogar stand, not enthusiastically. Cogar doesn't say a word during the hearing. Slaughter—who, as it turns out, is the top outside lawyer for A. H. Robins—raises only one issue: the judge's order that A. H. Robins executives testify at trial. The fact that Slaughter speaks to this issue telegraphs its significance to the company. But Slaughter does not want to defy the judge in his first appearance, so—in a low-key manner, in polite Southern cadence—he says that A. H. Robins hasn't yet decided what position it will take in response to the order to appear. The judge also feels no need to force the issue yet and sets it for "a little hearing" after the first of the year.

Much of this hearing focuses on plans for the consolidated trial.

The judge tells the attorneys that "we're in the middle of a mess." He repeats his story from the antibiotics litigation—*eight thousand years to try the case*—for the benefit of the lawyers from Richmond. "And if we judges and lawyers can't work this out," says the judge, "then—like Pogo says— 'We have met the enemy, and he is us.'"

But the judge also says that he is impressed enough with A. H. Robins's arguments about time pressures—the lawyers estimate they will need seventy-two depositions of the women and their doctors—that he will push back the start of trial to January 15.

Fribley, however, continues to complain. The judge isn't moved. He rifles through a mound of pleadings on his bench looking for the "wonderful brief," he says with a smile, that A. H. Robins filed—the forty-nine pager—most of which the judge considers a waste of time and effort. He tells Fribley that with the A. H. Robins lawyers toiling away on briefs like that, "I can understand why you didn't have time to take any depositions."

The plaintiffs have a much smaller legal team than A. H. Robins, and as much work to do, but we never hear a peep of complaint from them. Larson and Ciresi can't wait to get to trial. We can see it in their faces as they sit at counsel table, especially Ciresi, who is looking ever more cheerful as the hearing proceeds.

The judge gives Fribley a bit of advice. "Just pretend that you are on the plaintiffs' side and that you want to hurry these cases through and you will see how quickly the clouds roll away," he says.

He also tries to convince the A. H. Robins lawyers that the consolidated trial might not be a bad thing for the company. (Another judge in Oregon has also consolidated cases, although that judge left A. H. Robins defenses, including the dirty questions, largely intact and dismissed the plaintiffs' claim for punitive damages.) Maybe there will be a smaller punitive damages award, the judge says, if assessed on a consolidated basis instead of over and over in individual cases. Maybe Aetna, the insurer, can "assess their losses and get the thing over with," he says. The judge is sincere. He doesn't understand why A. H. Robins wouldn't want to put the litigation—the expense, distraction, and bad publicity—behind it and move on.

The judge still isn't personally invested in these cases. He just wants to move the litigation to resolution and protect the women still wearing the Dalkon Shield.

The judge raises A. H. Robins's refusal to recall the Dalkon Shield at this hearing as well.

"I read in the plaintiffs' brief that A. H. Robins had never even up to now got hold of the women and told them to take those things out," the judge says. "Is that true?"

Fribley complains that the plaintiffs want A. H. Robins "to contact every customer who ever had a Shield inserted."

"Do you have a computer?" the judge asks. "Within three days, with the technology we have now available, we could notify every woman in the country."

Still, the judge lets the issue of a recall drop. For now.

Instead, he attempts to move the cases along in a more peaceable manner. "I urge you to get on with your settlement talks," he says. He turns
to the plaintiffs' attorneys. The judge knows what many are thinking.
"And I don't want you plaintiffs to get so encouraged—now that you have
Judge Lord here, thinking I am going to run roughshod over these defendants—so that you raise your prices too high," he says. "So I want you to
be realistic, take fair settlements and go home."

"I would not be disappointed if on the fifteenth of January there was
nothing for me to try," the judge says. "I have plenty of other work to do."

■ ■ ■ ■

We do have plenty of other work in the month of December on a host
of matters, some ongoing (we continue to pound out decisions in Social
Security disability cases) and some new (including a suit brought by environmental groups to stop the trapping of wolves under the Endangered
Species Act).

There's also more of the extracurricular—and headline-grabbing—
action that the judge seems to find on a regular basis. One day, a small
group of women shows up to protest the country's nuclear arms policy.
They spill blood over an assortment of items on the floor of the courthouse lobby—baby bottles, a christening gown, booties—then await arrest. The judge goes down to check out the scene and brings me along. He
chats awhile with the women. Then he calls in the federal marshals, not
to arrest the activists but to protect them from being harassed by another
judge or the U.S. attorney. By this point in his life, the judge is a full-blown
pacifist. "We have three rooms dedicated to recruiting their sons," he tells
the press, "and they're welcome to the use of this lobby for their protest."
No arrests on this day, he says.

■ ■ ■ ■

We greet the new year with a Dalkon Shield hearing on January 5, 1984,
and the first thing on the judge's mind, as everyone should know by now,
is who's who among the lawyers. "When do I get to meet the lawyer who is
actually going to try this case?" he asks. We have seen a number of lawyers
for A. H. Robins—including Alexander Slaughter, who directs the show—
but not the lawyer with the performance skills, and often the biggest ego,

who will try the case. On the plaintiffs' side, Larson and Ciresi are a one-stop shop; they do it all, backed by a small team. But A. H. Robins, it seems, has a squad of lawyers for every aspect of the litigation.

Fribley says he will be one of the trial lawyers, but the lead will be another new face, Chuck Socha from the Tilly & Graves firm in Denver. Socha, it turns out, is in the courtroom today. He stands and greets the judge.

"This is a pleasure to be here," Socha says.

The judge smiles. He decides that a bit of ribbing is in order.

"Are you the man who litigated with the great George Gubbins?" the judge asks. He can't forget the only trial that A. H. Robins won in Minnesota, against sole practitioner Gubbins, and it bothers him to no end. Judge Lord would never let anything like that—*chips falling where they may*—happen in his courtroom.

"No, I don't believe so, Your Honor," says Socha, looking puzzled.

In large part, this first hearing of the year focuses on compelling the live testimony of A. H. Robins executives.

In truth, a judge's authority to order out-of-state executives to appear at trial is not crystal clear, even in federal court. So the judge tries to use his powers of persuasion. "Don't these people want to tell their story?" he asks.

The judge's entreaties gets nowhere. In fact, Slaughter raises an additional obstacle to the testimony of E. C. Robins Senior and another top executive, both of whom, he says, have heart problems that would make travel "medically unwise."

The judge cuts off Slaughter midsentence.

"Would you mind bringing in his medical records," the judge says of Senior, "so I can have an independent doctor make an evaluation of them, please?" He says he doesn't want to order anyone to appear if they are truly sick. "But I don't want anybody to say they are sicker than they are, either," he says.

By now, Larson and Ciresi are worried about getting the testimony live at trial. So they want to take depositions, videotaped in Richmond, of the executives before trial starts, just in case. There is no question—at least no legitimate question—that a federal judge has the discretion to order the executives to appear for depositions in their hometown. Still, Fribley objects. He complains again about all of the work A. H. Robins has to do before trial. He also argues that the depositions are unnecessary because the executives were previously deposed, primarily in the MDL proceedings.

This argument has convinced other judges around the country. But not Judge Lord. He does agree, however, to push back the trial date again, this time to late January.

■ ■ ■ ■

In the meantime, the judge will be heading soon to a judicial conference, with a vacation tacked on. Before he leaves, we need to wrap up a few matters.

He issues his opinion in the wolf trapping case; by now, as the press writes, it is "a nationwide cause celebre for wolf lovers." Keith writes the opinion, and the judge, as is his practice, changes little in the draft. He does add, however, a bit of flourish: "Each person who would slay the wolf must stay his hand."

The judge also holds hearings to catch up on his more routine cases and is in no frame of mind to put up with the ever-tedious lawyer bickering. On one case, with a small amount of money at stake, the judge warns the lawyers that they better settle or they'll be cooling their heels indefinitely before he gives them a trial date. On another case, with complicated securities and tax issues, the attorneys are making life difficult for the judge (and me, as I'm assigned to the matter). The judge had asked both sides to have their experts resolve an accounting issue, but their submissions only made matters more confusing. Now the judge tells me to take the witness stand to explain exactly what we need from the expert accountants. He warns the lawyers to cooperate or he will find them "in contempt of *clerk*." He makes it clear he is not jesting.

In fact, the drivel of lawyers—day in and day out—is sapping our spirits. But the judge soon lifts us out of our funk with a small act of kindheartedness. One of the janitors in the building comes to ask the judge for help. He says that his new government supervisor is switching his shift, which will force him to give up his second job. The judge picks up his phone, calls the supervisor, and tells him to work things out. It's not an order, but everyone in the courthouse—"the federal family"—knows that you proceed at your own peril if you ignore a request like this from Judge Lord.

We're all feeling good and smiling now.

The judge and I sit in chambers and enjoy the moment. He pulls out a bottle of whiskey and pours two glasses. (His chambers are always well stocked.) There is one last matter to tend to—a Dalkon Shield order to sign—before the judge leaves town. We review the order one more time. The introductory paragraph lays out the groundwork: A. H. Robins, the order says, has "continued to question this court's authority" to compel the appearance of the company executives at trial. So the judge formally orders—"IT IS HEREBY ORDERED"—that videotape depositions of five executives, including E. C. Robins Senior, take place in Richmond, starting on January 16. There is nothing preliminary—nothing interlocutory—about this order; there can be no more delay if the plaintiffs are to get this testimony before trial starts. And in any event, an order like this to take depositions is not the type of issue for which the Eighth Circuit would likely grant discretionary review.

The judge signs the order, tells me to keep him posted on any Dalkon Shield developments, and leaves for Arizona. The depositions will start while he is gone.

7

Political Wunderkind, 1954–1960

Miles's days in the U.S. attorney's office were coming to an end. In the late summer of 1952, when he saw the imminence of Dwight Eisenhower's election and, with a Republican in the White House, a new U.S. attorney in Minnesota who would select his own assistants, Miles resigned his post and returned to private practice.

By now, he had gained some measure of renown and quite a bit of experience. He had turned himself into an ace trial attorney, with a combination of fierce preparation (all-nighters, seriatim), street-fighter combativeness (go for the jugular), knack for sizing up witnesses (a master at reading people), and leading-man theatrics (jurors loved him). Now he had far more success in attracting cases than in his old milk-the-cows, feed-the-pigs, five-dollars-a-case days.

Still, he viewed private practice as a way station. He began to look, "with covetous eyes," he said, at the position of the Minnesota attorney general, the chief state (not federal) law officer, an elected position. In 1954, he won the DFL endorsement for the post and hit the campaign trail with a fury.

Much was at stake in the 1954 Minnesota elections. The emergent DFL had a watershed year in 1948, but its notable victories were for federal offices: Hubert Humphrey for the U.S. Senate, Gene McCarthy and other DFLers for the U.S. House of Representatives. The elections of 1950 and 1952 did not do much to boost the DFL candidates to state offices; indeed, Republicans had held the top office for more than fifteen years, since the last of the Farmer-Labor governors. Orville Freeman—the hard-nosed ex-Marine and organization man for Humphrey—had run for attorney general, then governor, in 1950 and 1952, respectively, and lost both times, badly in his run for governor. Even one of Freeman's closest associates acknowledged that Freeman was not a natural on the campaign trail and hoped that he would continue as Humphrey's drill sergeant.

In 1954, Freeman ran again for governor. Humphrey and McCarthy both ran for reelection. (Humphrey was in his first reelection bid for the Senate, McCarthy in his third for the House of Representatives.) And Miles Lord, for the first time, joined the statewide ticket, running for attorney general.

At times, the entire slate of candidates campaigned together, Senator Humphrey, Representative McCarthy, Freeman, Miles Lord, and the rest of the DFLers.

Often, however, Miles was out front, leading what one reporter would call a "free-swinging" brawl of a campaign.

He loved the fight. He loved meeting people. He crisscrossed the state nonstop: cities, farms (mooing into a bullhorn as he drove past grazing cows), and, of course, the Iron Range. He was described as "quick on his feet, hard-nosed, charming"—the traits that also marked him as a trial lawyer—but also "just a trifle unpredictable."

He ignored the Republican candidate for attorney general—"why donate to my opponent any free publicity," he would say—and assailed the administration of Republican Governor C. Elmer Anderson. He denounced the Republicans for turning state government "into a breeding ground for influence peddling and corruption." He charged them with what he would call "hanky-panky" for purchasing an office building owned by prominent supporters at an inflated price. ("Pretty profitable work—if you can get it!") He drubbed the administration for placing delinquent girls, as young as ten, in a reformatory with "hardened, habitual offenders." ("How much humanity would be needed to see to it that a little girl who steals from the local dime store is separated from degenerate women who work at the world's oldest profession?") He challenged Governor Anderson to a debate, and when the governor didn't show—Miles, after all, wasn't his opponent—debated an empty chair on TV. He brandished more theatrics with the television appearance of his entire family, including "my dear old mother" and his young son Jim, who on cue stole the show by asking for a nickel as a reward for sitting quietly through the program.

Miles reminded voters that he was a law-and-order man. But he also showed his compassionate side, telling how he forgave "small, oppressed" debtors when he was an assistant U.S. attorney. (He recounted the tale of a man living in a chicken coop who owed the feds a few hundred dollars. "Well, I have prosecuted many criminals," he told a TV audience, "but when people have a story like that to tell me I don't feel very much like 'Mr. District Attorney.'") He hit a theme that would define him—as a prosecutor, as a judge—for decades to come, assuring voters that he would protect "people who need help," while doing all he could to hold accountable "wealthy, powerful, special interest groups."

Republicans called it "an earthquake."

Humphrey and McCarthy won big.

Freeman—unsuccessful in two previous tries for a state post—was elected governor, at the age of thirty-six.

Karl Rolvaag, another young veteran of the Humphrey brigade, was elected lieutenant governor.

Indeed, DFL candidates won every statewide office except one.

At the new governor's inaugural ball, the receiving line filled the capitol rotunda and flowed down the stairs and into the basement, as Governor Freeman and his wife greeted well-wishers. A newspaper photographer captured a shot of the feet of the waiting masses. He also snapped a picture of an older woman, clad in a dark dress and dark hat, a bouquet on her chest, standing with dignitaries.

Rachel Lord had come to celebrate the election of her son as the attorney general of Minnesota. Miles Lord, thirty-five years old, was the new "wunderkind in state politics."

He was also far and away the most controversial figure in state government.

He was lauded as "a brilliant and resourceful chap," "charming and personable," with "uncanny political instincts" and "a genuine compassion for the underdog." He was lambasted as a man who "forgot to think before he spoke," whose actions were "intemperate" and "not in keeping with the decorum one usually associates with the attorney generalship," and who had "a positive genius for riling the public."

He was on the go, day and night, night and day, no matter too trifling (on the scene to direct a "two-bit raid" of a gambling house, where unfazed patrons continued to drink whiskey and dance all the while), no matter too big or too difficult (continuing his pursuit of mobsters), whether popular (extending state aid to GIs and senior citizens) or unpopular (ruling that pregnant girls—"rotten, pregnant apples," he would call them, mimicking their detractors—could not be expelled from school), often accompanied by a bit of theatrics and a blast of shameless publicity as he alerted the press—and cameramen—to catch him in action, any time, any place. "MILES LORD LIKES DRAMATICS," a newspaper headline declared.

He viewed himself as the attorney not only for the state and its agencies but also for all of its people and insisted that the lawyers working under him help anyone and everyone with their pleas for assistance. (His staff chipped in to buy a portrait of a white knight to hang in his office.) He drafted hundreds of attorney general opinions, paving the way for Minnesota to lead the nation in the adoption of prepaid health care plans (the early HMOs), extending workers' compensation benefits, opposing antiunion right-to-work laws, and stopping armed guards from crossing picket lines.

He did not fear to tread where no man—or legal precedent—could be found. When he faced the issue of supplemental unemployment compensation for iron ore miners, "I didn't worry about the legal niceties of it," he would say. Instead, he thought back to the long winter layoffs at the mines on the Iron Range. "All they had to do was tell me that this would give the men more money in the winter time and bang, let's legal[ize] it," he said.

Some praised his opinions. "He has compiled an impressive record on his opinions and is rarely overruled by the Supreme Court," one newspaper wrote. Others disagreed. Indeed, he was lampooned at the local Newspaper Guild's annual dinner in 1956, with a spoof sung to the tune of the "Battle Hymn of the Republic":

Mine eyes have seen the folly of a ruling by Miles Lord;
He is short on legal knowledge that a law school would afford;
He hacks the law to pieces but it's speedily restored;
He's always overruled.

Miles attended that dinner, as he rarely missed a chance to mingle with the press. He also rarely missed a chance to take center stage, and he leaped on up to join in song:

Oh, Miles then got elected as the state's top legal gun;
No sooner in the office than his mouth began to run;
If Freeman doesn't shut him up the DFL is done;
He's always overruled.

■ ■ ■ ■

Miles also continued to personally prosecute cases as attorney general—he wasn't one to sit behind a desk for long—and in 1956 lost his first trial as a prosecutor.

It came in the prosecution of an official from the International Brotherhood of Teamsters, Gerald P. Connelly, who was indicted for ordering the dynamite bombings of two rival union officials (the home of one in St. Paul and the car of another in Minneapolis). Connelly was in Florida at the time of the bombings but allegedly gave the orders. After ten-plus days of trial for the St. Paul bombing, however, the presiding judge struck much of the testimony as hearsay and directed an acquittal.

Notably, the verdict was directed by a judge, not delivered by jurors, whom Miles generally swayed. And Connelly was convicted of the other bombing—the car in Minneapolis—with Miles aiding county prosecutors who tried that case.

Still, the St. Paul trial was a stinging defeat and the only such loss in Miles's career, out of one hundred or so cases tried.

Miles refused to let it go. He was now on the trail of the Teamsters. There were allegations that prior to the dynamiting, Connelly had been encouraged to "get rough" with rivals by Jimmy Hoffa, who was rising to the top of the union's national leadership. There were also rumors that another man closely affiliated with Hoffa—Twin Cities businessman Benjamin Dranow—was with Connelly in Florida at the time Connelly gave the orders.

Miles began to focus on Dranow as a way to get to Hoffa, but soon Dranow absconded. With his Range roots, however, Miles would not let this (or any) enemy slip from mind, no matter how long the wait to settle the score.

■ ■ ■ ■

Miles also got his start tangling with appellate judges—most notably the chief justice of the Minnesota Supreme Court—during his attorney general years. His biggest imbroglio came in a fight over the time of day.

In the late 1950s, the state erupted in a roiling dispute over whether to adopt daylight saving time (DST). Nearly all states east of Minnesota were already on DST—or "fast time," as it was known—and most Minnesotans favored the switch. But farmers and drive-in theater owners, who feared that longer daylight hours would be the "death knell" of their business, put together a powerful lobby in opposition.

It was the most hotly disputed issue at the state capitol, setting off what was called "one of the greatest legislative battles in Minnesota history." The legislature—courting compromise but spewing confusion—passed several bills. One allowed some cities and counties, generally the most populous, to establish DST on their own, regardless of what happened in the rest of the state. Another bill, little noticed and ambiguous, may (or may not) have revoked that authority.

Three urban counties—Hennepin (including the City of Minneapolis), Ramsey (including the capital of St. Paul), and Anoka—passed resolutions to switch to DST on Sunday, April 26, 1959, at 2:00 a.m.

With just hours to go, on the morning of Saturday, April 25, an attorney for the theater owners filed an emergency petition in the Minnesota Supreme Court. The court, normally closed on Saturdays, just happened to be open. Indeed, Chief Justice Roger Dell—a Republican stalwart, who himself owned a movie theater, albeit indoors, in outstate Minnesota—was there to sign a writ to block the move to fast time. The three counties received no advance notice and no hearing, even as extensive plans had been made to switch to DST, with many clocks already set forward when the weekend began.

The writ, said one newspaper editorial, "dropped with bombshell suddenness."

Chaos ensued. Miles jumped in.

He met with Governor Freeman and told him that in his opinion the writ merely restrained the counties from taking any further action but did not rescind their prior adoption of fast time. (This was in truth a questionable view; in any event, however, it would have been virtually impossible for the counties to comply with the last-minute order.) Miles then went on radio and TV to advise the public to, in effect, ignore the court's mandate.

No one knew what time it was, where.

At the state capitol, Governor Freeman's office was on DST, the legislature and Minnesota Supreme Court on standard. Most, but not all, railroads were on standard time; airlines on DST. Bus lines, schools, and businesses were all over the clock.

Chief Justice Dell held firm. "We do not intend to permit mass hysteria to influence us in rendering our opinion," he told the press.

After almost two weeks of chaos, Miles appeared before the seven justices in a hearing described as "a three-and-a-half hour slugfest." Chief Justice Dell repeatedly "hammered" Miles, the press wrote, and several other justices were openly hostile. Miles "gave as good as he took," it was reported. But he also paced nervously.

"Am I on trial here, Your Honor?" Miles asked.

In effect, he was.

After the hearing, the court ordered Miles to appear again to answer questions about his "professional conduct" for advising the public and the counties to disobey its writ. Many thought he would be held in contempt or even disbarred.

Governor Freeman upped the ante by directing that Miles, his attorney general, decline to comply with the court's directive to appear, which Miles was inclined to do in any event. The fast-time issue was now a full-blown, separation-of-powers constitutional crisis, with Freeman calling the Minnesota Supreme Court's summons "a serious infringement of the independence of the executive branch of government."

When the court convened again, the courtroom overflowed with spectators and the press. Chief Justice Dell pounded the bench. "We do not intend to permit the governor or the attorney general to step in and run the judicial branch of government," he said. But Miles was not there to hear him; he stayed in his office, directly below the courtroom in the capitol building.

The court issued its order the next day. Miles was hit with a "severe censure," unprecedented in the history of the state. The justices berated Miles for "improper and unethical acts" and acting in "defiance of our order." They were particularly incensed with Miles's statements to the media, saying that he had "intended to deliberately mislead the public."

Ultimately, the issue that got it all started was resolved when Governor Freeman and the legislature ordered fast time for the entire state. But the Minnesota Supreme Court's censure would dog Miles for years.

And Miles was soon back on the hot seat, along with the governor.

■ ■ ■ ■

This time the issue was a violent labor strike at a plant in southern Minnesota.

In October 1959, thousands of union workers walked off their jobs at Wilson and Company in Albert Lea, one of the nation's largest meat-packers. Tensions—and violence—built. There were brawls and rock throwing along the picket line, with reports of knifes, blackjacks, and guns and threats to life and limb as replacement workers were brought in. Tires were slashed, windows shattered. Night riders roamed the countryside.

Finally, in a midnight order on December 11, Governor Freeman declared martial law. That morning, he sent National Guardsmen—two hundred strong, bayonets drawn—to Albert Lea and, perhaps even more controversially, ordered the plant to suspend operations.

Wilson and Company challenged the governor's actions in federal court. A standing-room only crowd—including Miles's wife, Maxine, and Freeman's wife, Jane—packed in. In private discussions, Miles had argued that a military solution was not warranted. But in court, Miles backed the governor. Governor Freeman, however, also wanted Miles to openly threaten to disobey the federal court should it rule against them. Miles refused to do so, not on the heels of the DST fiasco, especially when his advice this time (against sending in the National Guard) had been rebuffed.

On December 22, the federal court struck down the declaration of martial law and harshly criticized the governor:

> A free people do not surrender to mob rule by the expediency of martial law until all means available . . . have proved futile.

The court ordered the state to reopen the plant. The National Guard could assist local authorities, but under civil, not military, authority.

The strike settled two months later, in February 1960. But the rift between the governor and the attorney general—and their two mighty egos—would only deepen.

■ ■ ■ ■

Miles Lord and Orville Freeman had been allies dating back to the early days of the DFL. Their political orientation—progressive Democrat—was certainly aligned. They were close in age, Freeman only a year and a half older.

But there was no mistaking one for the other.

Freeman was a square-jawed Scandinavian, called ornery by some and, by Miles, pompous. A clash was all but inevitable: the obstinate ex-Marine versus the free-spirited Ranger, neither one known, as one journalist noted, "for timidity."

Their big falling-out was over an opening on the Minnesota Supreme Court.

Miles had secured a promise, he believed, that Governor Freeman would appoint him to fill the next opening for a justice. True, this would be a state court appellate judgeship, not the federal trial bench where he longed to be. (Among other things, state judges in Minnesota, while usually appointed by the governor in the first instance, have to run for reelection. Also, on an appellate bench, Miles would have no power to act on his own; he would have to persuade fellow justices to adopt his views.) Still, it was a distinguished position and would afford Miles an opportunity to put controversy behind him.

In February 1960, a justice died. Miles reminded Governor Freeman of his promise. It was not clear, however, that the governor believed he had ever made that commitment. Undaunted, Miles floated his own trial balloon, and the press was soon abuzz with the likelihood of his appointment. Governor Freeman, undeterred, appointed his former law partner. The governor also told Miles that he would not make a good judge. (Miles's critics in the press agreed. "What a travesty on justice that would have been," wrote the *Minneapolis Tribune*.)

Publicly, the governor and Miles pronounced all was well. Privately, however, Miles was bitter. He believed that the events of the Albert Lea strike—when "I hadn't been quite faithful"—had led to the governor's snub.

■ ■ ■ ■

By this time, Miles—and Maxine especially—were both fed up with politics.

Miles had won reelection as attorney general twice. The 1956 race was a squeaker, with Miles eking out victory only due to lopsided margins from the heavily DFL regions of northeastern Minnesota, including the Iron Range. (On election day, his mother, Rachel Lord, hovered over the returns at the DFL headquarters in Minneapolis; she died the following year at age seventy-six.) Miles's political popularity rebounded, however, and within two years he was one of the most popular Democrats in the state and among the top choices to run for the U.S. Senate. Miles took a pass on Washington but went on to handily win his third term as attorney general in 1958. (McCarthy ran for that Senate seat and won, leaving the House to join Hubert Humphrey in the Senate.)

But the political wars—Republicans often focused their fire on the on-the-loose attorney general—had taken their toll. Miles also loathed what he called "the rotten business" of politics: fund-raising from people looking for favors.

Maxine, for her part, was no fan of politics or politicians. Among other things, she thought that politics bred infidelity. She had spent years watching "who comes out of which hotel room," said Miles. (But not Hubert, he was quick to add.)

Miles and Maxine beheld each other jealously.

Miles hadn't wanted Maxine in the workplace or her picture pinned up in an air force barracks; Maxine didn't want Miles to be a politician.

"Maxine didn't want me in those politics," said Miles. "Oh, it's a terrible place to be."

Then the 1960 presidential campaign got under way.

Hubert Humphrey was making his first serious run for the Democratic nomination. The old posse rallied round. Freeman and McCarthy cochaired the Humphrey for President committee. Rolvaag directed the day-to-day operations.

Despite his disenchantment with politics, Miles succumbed to Hubert's entreaties and crossed the border into Wisconsin—the most important early primary—as an advance man. He found the Humphrey operation in shambles, "an amateurish band of Minnesota volunteers," wrote one journalist. There was little organization. There was no money. "I had kids writing bad checks all over that state," Miles said. And they faced an opponent, John F. Kennedy, with seemingly unlimited funds, a topflight organization, and, with the help of his brothers (particularly Bobby), a no-holds-barred campaign style.

On April 5, Kennedy swamped Humphrey.

Miles returned to Minnesota, more disillusioned than ever with politics. (He had been harshly critical of Bobby Kennedy, in particular, in Wisconsin.) When Hubert called to ask for help in West Virginia, the next major primary, Miles did the unthinkable.

He said no to Hubert.
Three times Hubert asked.
Three times Miles said no.

■ ■ ■ ■

Maxine insisted that he delay no longer.

In late April 1960, with Maxine by his side to keep him from changing his mind, Miles went to see Governor Freeman to hand in his letter of resignation. Freeman asked Miles to stay through the November election. The governor wanted Miles on the DFL ticket, as Freeman faced a tough reelection battle. (Miles was much more of a natural on the campaign trail than Freeman.) But Miles resigned effective the following week, catching nearly everyone by surprise.

The postmortems on Miles's years as attorney general ran the spectrum.

"An impartial judgment will show that he has served in that office ably and well," wrote the *Shakopee Argus Tribune*.

"Few tears will be shed," countered the *Minneapolis Tribune*.

And from the *Albert Lea Tribune*: "It is a pleasant prospect for those of us who enjoy serenity."

To take his place as attorney general, Miles recommended a young member of his staff: Walter Mondale. There was no disagreement here with Governor Freeman. Mondale was a charter member of the DFL family and another Humphrey acolyte, one of the youngest to join battle in the late 1940s and cut from the same small-town, grew-up-without-a-dime mold. (His father was a farmer and prairie preacher in southern Minnesota who lost everything when farm prices collapsed in the 1920s; his mother ran Sunday school at the local church.) Mondale had gone on to gain experience as a DFL operative and managed Freeman's 1958 reelection campaign. But he was still little known to the public, and, when he took Miles's place as the state's top legal officer, thirty-two years old, less than five years out of law school, and so shy—the quintessential Scandinavian succeeding the quintessential Iron Ranger—that he entered the office in his early days through a private door to avoid small talk with his staff, in contrast to Miles, who greeted any person (or creature) with gusto. Still, Miles thought that Mondale was exceptionally bright and able. Before he departed, Miles bestowed upon his successor two gifts. One was a list of enemies—lawyers who had signed a newspaper ad supporting Miles's opponent in the last election—which Miles kept within easy reach in his desk. The other was the file on an unfinished investigation of a charitable foundation. "Take a look at this," said Miles. "This is going to be big." Indeed, the investigation—that Miles began, that Walter Mondale would continue—uncovered a blockbuster scandal at the Sister Kenny Foundation, which ran a famed treatment center in the Twin Cities for children with polio. The Sister Kenny headlines—including allegations of kickbacks to the foundation's top executives—would propel Mondale's victory that fall, in his first electoral run, to his first full term as attorney general.

■ ■ ■ ■

Miles returned, for the time being, to private practice.

By now, Miles and Maxine and their four children were living on Christmas Lake, a small lake in the western Minneapolis suburbs. Work still kept Miles on the go much of the time. (His youngest child, Virginia, missed her dad so much that one night when home with a babysitter, she started to cry when Miles appeared on the TV news. "Why are you crying?" asked the sitter. "I want him to be home," she said.) But when Miles was home, there was not one minute to waste. Early in the mornings, usually by six, he would walk through the house, banging pots and pans to wake up his children lest too much of the day go to waste. He taught them about justice and fairness. "I heard about the 'little guy' a thousand times," Virginia would remember. "It came from his soul," said Priscilla, "deep, deep, deep." The idyllic lake setting also offered Miles a chance to relax and engage his children in a fashion of his own. He showed his kids how to catch minnows and swallow them live. He had them eat sandwiches of poison ivy, which, he claimed, built up their immunity to the plant. He took them out on the lake in a boat; he would don a skin diver's outfit, plunge underwater to locate fish, then climb back aboard to cast his rod. He amused them with his tinkering: fixing old machines, welding, woodcutting, and weekend mechanics of all sorts. He kept a menagerie of animals, including several horses (which he sometimes paraded through the house to startle visitors) and, at various times, one or more goats, chickens, rabbits, dogs, Siamese cats, birds (sparrows and an owl), and even alligators (in the basement).

In later years, Miles also befriended a group of baby geese living in their yard; he fed them, talked to them, led them on walks, and, as the goslings grew, tossed them into the air and flapped his arms to teach them to fly.

"They think I am their mother!" he proudly proclaimed.

■ ■ ■ ■

Meanwhile, in the 1960 presidential primaries, Hubert Humphrey's presidential hopes had been dashed in West Virginia. The Kennedy machine broke him with mudslinging accusations—reportedly fueled by Bobby— that, in contrast to John F. Kennedy's heroics in the South Pacific, Humphrey had dodged the draft in World War II. (In fact, Humphrey tried to enlist but couldn't pass the physical.)

It was one of the few times that Miles would see his friend, normally so ebullient, deeply upset and sad.

Orville Freeman, however, wasted little time lamenting the bruising defeat of his mentor. With Humphrey out of the presidential race, Freeman's own ambitions rose to the fore, and he set his sights on the vice presidency. Humphrey was also considered to be in play for the second spot on the ticket, but he initially declined to endorse JFK's nomination for president, even knowing this would end his vice presidential chances. (Humphrey harbored doubts about JFK's commitment to the liberal cause.) At the outset of the Democratic National Convention in Los Angeles, Humphrey— along with Gene McCarthy—supported Adlai Stevenson. (McCarthy gave a passionate nominating speech for Stevenson, which helped elevate the junior senator from Minnesota to national prominence.) Miles attended the convention, with Maxine, and accused Freeman of not displaying appropriate loyalty to Humphrey by moving too quickly to embrace JFK. Freeman, in turn, was furious that Humphrey had not been sufficiently helpful in his own vice presidential quest. "They love each other," Miles would say of Humphrey and Freeman, "but they love to beat each other, too. Like brothers and sisters." Ultimately, Freeman placed JFK's name in nomination but lost his bid for vice president to Lyndon Johnson. In November, Freeman also lost his race for reelection as governor, with Miles sitting out the campaign.

By now, however, even with the disappointments and turmoil of 1960, these young men who had banded together in the formative years of the DFL had landed on the center stage of American politics, with one national magazine naming Humphrey ("the elder statesman," who turned forty-nine that year), McCarthy, Freeman, Rolvaag—and Miles Lord—as "the most impressive group" of Democrats "in any of the fifty states."

The year, however, had opened fissures.

Indeed, Miles would nurture some of these blood feuds—with Freeman, among others—with fellow DFLers for decades to come (while, at the same time, cultivating a fair number of friends and allies who were solid Republicans).

But he had emerged in ever stronger stead with both of the senators from Minnesota, Humphrey and McCarthy.

And he would need these friends.

Miles may have left electoral politics in 1960, but he knew he would not remain content for long in the private practice of law. More than ever, he was thinking of a federal judgeship, where he could rise above politics—that *terrible place to be*—and act boldly without having to answer to anyone. But Miles had left a long trail of controversy in his wake as attorney general, the Minnesota Supreme Court DST censure included, and seemed a most unlikely prospect for the prestige of a lifetime appointment to the federal bench.

Home-state senators, however, as Miles well knew, held great sway in the nomination process. While many judges after their appointment prefer to believe otherwise—and merit surely has much to do with selection—it was still in large part a patronage position.

As one federal judge would say, "My merit was that I worked for a United States Senator."

8

Lawyers Objecting,
Witnesses Stonewalling

Doctor, assume that there were one hundred women who had suffered loss of reproductive organs as a result of the Dalkon Shield. Would that have been clinically significant to you?

Would it be significant to you if three hundred of those women suffered loss of reproduction organs and were never able to bear children?

Would it be significant to you if a thousand of those women suffered loss of reproductive organs and were unable to bear children?

You simply don't know, doctor, how many women it would take to lose their reproductive organs as a result of the Dalkon Shield before you would consider it clinically significant. . . . Is that correct, doctor?

Mike Ciresi is in the A. H. Robins offices in Richmond, starting the Judge Lord–ordered depositions. The witness is Dr. Ellen Preston, an in-house physician at A. H. Robins and product monitor for the Dalkon Shield, who received all of the communications—reports, complaints, questions—about the Dalkon Shield from doctors and women, as well as from the company's detail men in the field.

Chuck Socha, defending this deposition, raises a slew of objections: "improper hypothetical," "assumes facts not in evidence," "irrelevant," "abusive," "harassing," "argumentative." Ciresi plows ahead. Dr. Preston answers, "I don't know," again and again, the best she can muster. She sits in the witness seat—her eyes puffy and short hair turning gray—and answers in a soft voice with little emotion, except an occasional hint of disgust at the whole affair.

Ciresi hones in on the words "clinically significant."

By this point in the litigation, it is difficult for A. H. Robins to deny that the tail string wicks, so its lawyers—and witnesses, presumably well sandpapered, which is routine in big litigation—say that even if there is wicking (which they sometimes still deny), that has no *clinical significance,* meaning, as Dr. Preston testifies, that "it would not cause any problem" in women.

For several days, Ciresi continues to pound away on Dr. Preston, while his partner, Dale Larson, thumps on another A. H. Robins official. But the process is tedious. Many answers from the witnesses are nonresponsive or *I don't know/I don't recall.* There are also countless "speaking" objections from the A. H. Robins lawyers—interruptions, sometimes long-winded, to slow the pace and throw off the momentum of the cross-examination— and endless squabbling over everything from the definition of mundane words to where the video cameras should be aimed.

But the cracks are growing. Judge Lord, by allowing these depositions, has provided the opportunity for Ciresi and Larson to push the door open, inch by inch.

■ ■ ■ ■

Larson and Ciresi are bringing a new focus to the litigation.

For years, the plaintiffs' lawyers in the MDL had focused on defects in the *product.* Larson and Ciresi turn their attention to A. H. Robins's *conduct.*

If the company's conduct demonstrates a willful disregard for the rights or safety of women, a jury will get angry. An angry jury awards punitive damages.

Punitive damages are a game changer, the holy grail of litigation (and despite popular misconception, extremely uncommon). The whole premise of punitive damages is to punish and deter and make it too costly for a company to continue business as usual, especially since these awards are often not covered by insurance.

There have been a few punitive damages verdicts against A. H. Robins— Larson and Ciresi have two themselves—but the size and number have not been sufficient to break the litigation open.

So Larson and Ciresi begin to focus on what they call the Watergate questions: What did the A. H. Robins executives know? When did they know it? And what did they do about it? As with Watergate—which started as a two-bit burglary and ended with the downfall of a president—it is often the case with corporate misconduct that the cover-up is worse than the initial malfeasance. If senior company officials—the corporate counterparts to the president and all his men—have knowledge of a dangerous product and fail to fix it or warn about it or issue a recall, and instead cover up, the case becomes tailor-made for punitive damages.

Day by day, Larson and Ciresi press on.

■ ■ ■ ■

Not all plaintiffs' lawyers are alike—far from it—as A. H. Robins knows all too well. Years before Larson and Ciresi got involved, two other plaintiffs' lawyers, young and without much experience—the yin to the yang of Larson and Ciresi—had represented a large number of the women with Dalkon Shield claims in Minnesota. Robert Appert and Gerald Pyle, partners not long out of law school, began advertising for Dalkon Shield cases in 1977. Earlier that year, the U.S. Supreme Court had struck down a ban on attorney advertising as a violation of the First Amendment. Many attorneys, however, still viewed such marketing as too controversial or distasteful. But Appert and Pyle seized the opening with aggressive advertising for Dalkon Shield cases and signed up women by the hundreds. They did little work for their clients, seldom even filing suit. Instead, the lawyers quickly—and cheaply—settled claims with A. H. Robins's insurer. (Appert had befriended one of the adjusters at Aetna.) The women got little, the average settlement in 1978 was only $10,000, while Appert and Pyle, with their large volume of cases, made several million. Their offices, said a former employee, "reeked of wealth," decorated with antiques and Oriental carpets.

Before long, A. H. Robins officials began to look into why Aetna was settling so many claims in Minnesota. Eventually, the company accused Appert and Pyle of an improper relationship with the Aetna adjuster, as well as other improprieties. In the fall of 1980, A. H. Robins filed a motion with Judge Alsop to disqualify the two lawyers. The next year, under fire, Appert and Pyle withdrew from the litigation (denying any wrongdoing and claiming they had been "harassed" by A. H. Robins lawyers). The Minnesota Supreme Court would later temporarily suspend them from the practice of law.

But the hundreds of women whom Appert and Pyle represented would need new lawyers. Most signed on with Larson and Ciresi and their firm. A. H. Robins, for all of its efforts, bounced two young lawyer-fleas, only to end up with two professionals at the top of their game.

■ ■ ■ ■

A. H. Robins knew that Larson and Ciresi would be trouble. By August 1983—even before Judge Lord took on his Dalkon Shield assignment—the company tried to resolve all of their cases in a global settlement. But Larson and Ciresi were demanding too much money for their clients, substantially more than other plaintiffs' lawyers. And on the other side of the table, A. H. Robins was demanding, Larson would say, that he and Ciresi agree to not accept any future Dalkon Shield cases. This was a condition that plaintiffs' attorneys accused A. H. Robins of attempting to impose on others as well; if the company was going to settle, especially at a high price, it wanted to get rid of attorneys like Larson and Ciresi once and for all. Larson, however, rejected the ultimatum, accusing A. H. Robins of violating the lawyers' Code of Professional Responsibility, which prohibited a lawyer from entering into any settlement agreement "that restricts his right to practice law."

After Judge Lord entered the scene, A. H. Robins redoubled its efforts to settle with Larson and Ciresi, as well as other attorneys with cases in the judge's block. One by one, some—but not all—of the cases start to drop away.

Settlement, of course, is one possible route to escape from Judge Lord's courtroom. The other, if settlement fails or is too expensive, would be a run at the Eighth Circuit.

Larson and Ciresi want to get as much discovery as they can before the door slams shut.

Together, the two lawyers entrench in Richmond, simultaneously questioning witnesses in separate conference rooms at the A. H. Robins headquarters. A court reporter takes down every word, with a video technician also recording the testimony to play to future juries. (Larson and Ciresi often preface their questions with, "Is it your testimony here today before the ladies and gentlemen of the jury. . . ." With a jury nowhere in sight, some witnesses seem a bit perplexed.) On breaks, Larson and Ciresi meet in stairwells for privacy and whisper about the latest testimony of their respective witnesses.

At night, they go back to the Commonwealth Park Hotel, across from the state capitol, where they feel all eyes upon them, the Yankee lawyers who have come to attack one of the largest employers and most esteemed families in Richmond. (One morning, however, as Ciresi eats breakfast alone in the hotel restaurant, his waitress asks if he is the lawyer suing A. H. Robins. "Yes, I am, ma'am," says Ciresi. "Kill them," says the waitress.)

Larson and Ciresi are making progress. But the objections, the obfuscations, the *I-don't-recalls* stymie their efforts. Each witness's testimony drags on, day after day.

■ ■ ■ ■

Mr. Attorney, I fail to recognize any connection whatsoever between the issues at hand and the line of questioning.

I am not going to sit here and undergo a lot of meaningless and repetitious and pointless questioning.

I instruct myself not to answer.

Ciresi is deposing Dr. Frederick Clark Jr., the former medical director at A. H. Robins (now retired).

Dr. Clark has had two heart attacks. He appears, however, to be strong and is certainly combative. There are two attorneys in the room for A. H. Robins, one from Cedar Rapids, Iowa, and Jack Fribley from Minnesota. There's also an additional attorney from Richmond to represent Dr. Clark personally. "Primarily to assure that Dr. Clark isn't harassed or in any way put upon," says the lawyer.

Dr. Clark, however, hardly seems like he needs any lawyer, let alone three. He repeatedly objects to questions (the proper purview of attorneys, not the witness). He quibbles over the meaning of words like an old pro ("I don't understand the words in your question"; "I'm not sure what you mean by 'responsible'"). When he does deem to answer a question, he gives long, rambling, and largely nonresponsive monologues.

Dr. Clark was one of the senior A. H. Robins officials involved in the purchase of the Dalkon Shield in June 1970. That month, he had visited Dr. Davis, the coinventor, in Baltimore and then authored a memo that reported the actual pregnancy rate was significantly higher than Davis's claim of 1.1 percent. There should be no disputing these facts, as they are confirmed in A. H. Robins's own documents, including Dr. Clark's trip report, which was produced years ago to plaintiffs' attorneys.

But that doesn't deter Dr. Clark in this deposition, as he starts out by denying that he was involved in the acquisition of any product for A. H. Robins during that period of time.

Ciresi presses the issue; he knows this isn't true. Dr. Clark hedges and asks for clarification of what "any involvement" means. For example, says Dr. Clark, if a secretary sharpened a pencil for someone looking up a phone number for a company, that "could be said to have some involvement in the acquisition." Dr. Clark says that would be "silly," but asks what exactly does Ciresi have in mind.

Dr. Clark's personal attorney enters the fray. He asks Ciresi to define "involvement" or drop the inquiry.

Dr. Clark laughs. "I second the motion," he says.

Ciresi defines the term as gathering information to pass on to any individual who will make a judgment about acquiring a product. Dr. Clark says that definition is too open-ended. By the time Dr. Clark and Ciresi agree on a definition, Dr. Clark needs the original question repeated. Ciresi complies: "In June of 1970, did you have any involvement with the purchase of any product for the A. H. Robins Company?"

Before Dr. Clark can answer, however, his attorney asks Ciresi—again—to define "involvement."

Ciresi reminds everyone that he just did.

Reversing course, Dr. Clark's attorney now says it would be better to ask a fact question instead of trying to define "involvement."

Another attorney seconds—or thirds—the motion.

Ciresi repeatedly threatens to call Judge Lord, who has made it clear that he is just a phone call away if there are any problems in the depositions. That has no effect, however, on Dr. Clark and the attorneys. Indeed, Dr. Clark's personal attorney says that in his view Judge Lord has no jurisdiction over the deposition, since it is taking place in Richmond, not Minnesota.

For the time being, Ciresi refrains from dialing the judge. He knows the judge is out of town for two weeks, and doesn't want to impose.

■ ■ ■ ■

The judge would have loved to take the call.

Even while he is away, he can't get the Dalkon Shield off his mind. He has time to reflect back on the initial pretrial hearings and is increasingly troubled by what transpired: A. H. Robins's resistance to the consolidated trial and to its officials testifying (*don't they want to tell their story?*); the dirty questions (*which way they wipe?!*); the appearance of out-of-town lawyers (*why are they hiding on the backbenches?*); and the refusal to recall the Dalkon Shield (*what could explain that with the product already off the market?*). He also continues to read—like a fiend—briefs and other materials that are coming in and asks to have these all sent to him via Federal Express. He calls me incessantly to talk about the case and to ask how the depositions are going in Richmond. I try to check in with the lawyers, but when I pass on the little bits and pieces I pick up, it only agitates him more.

When he returns to chambers—he is the first one in on Monday morning, January 23—he is in whirlwind mode. He zooms through mounds of paper on his desk, on all sorts of cases, before I get in. When I do arrive, it's clear to me that he has rocketed into a different orbit.

That same morning, in Richmond, Larson starts the deposition of E. C. Robins Senior.

Senior's grandfather, Albert Hartley Robins, founded the A. H. Robins Apothecary in 1866; Albert's son, Claiborne Robins, began working in the business but died in 1912 at age thirty-nine, leaving his wife, Martha, and two-year-old son (later known as Senior). Martha Robins ran the small establishment while her son grew up; Senior helped out by waiting on customers and delivering prescriptions. He went on to graduate from the University of Richmond and earn a degree in pharmacy from the Medical College of Virginia. That was in 1933, when the business had annual sales of less than $5,000 and only two employees. Then Senior took charge—single-minded and working nonstop—and the business took off. Before long, the A. H. Robins Company mushroomed into a multimillion dollar enterprise, with an aggressive sales force and expansion into international markets. In 1963, Senior took the company public; the Robins family, however, retained a controlling share of the stock. By the end of that decade, Senior was one of the wealthiest men in the country—and beloved in Richmond for his philanthropy. In 1969, he gave $50 million to the University of Richmond, the largest gift by any individual to any university at that time. (The majority of the donation was in A. H. Robins stock.) He also showered other colleges and charitable organizations with contributions and earned a spot on the list of the top five "Most Generous Americans."

At the time of his deposition, Senior is seventy-three and has had two heart attacks. But he still serves as chairman of the board, presides over board meetings, and comes into the office every morning for about three hours of work (and a daily massage).

Larson starts the deposition with a short lecture:

Mr. Robins, my name is Dale Larson and I am a Minnesota lawyer and I represent women who have been diseased wearing the Dalkon Shield, and they have suffered the loss of organs, they have suffered an inability to bear children, many are nulliparous women, that is women who had never had an opportunity to bear children. Today I am going to be asking you some questions bearing upon the Dalkon Shield on their behalf.

Senior sits a few feet from Larson. He hunches forward, his hands folded on the table before him. He stares at Larson. Then he responds, in a soft voice.

"Those things," Senior says, "have not been proven."

As the deposition proceeds over the next two days, Larson asks over and over whether the A. H. Robins Company will warn women of the dangers of the Dalkon Shield:

As a matter of fact Mr. Robins, as chairman of the board of the A. H. Robins Company, is it your testimony here today before the ladies and gentlemen of the jury, that the company has absolutely no intent whatsoever to warn Dalkon Shield wearers that they have a higher risk of pelvic inflammatory disease with the Dalkon Shield than with other IUDs?

Am I correct, Mr. Robins, that as you sit here before the ladies and gentlemen of the jury, there is no current intention of the A. H. Robins Company to ever warn physicians or women users about the fact that the tail string on the device has a wicking tendency?

You don't have any intent to warn about it as we sit here today in front of the ladies and gentlemen of the jury, correct?

Over and over, Senior's lawyer, Charles Osthimer III, objects:

Objection, argumentative, irrelevant, assumes facts not in evidence.

I will object on the grounds that it is argumentative, it is a question which basically cannot be answered, a when-did-you-stop-beating-your-wife-type question, it is irrelevant, it is vague and ambiguous, and it assumes facts not in evidence; namely, that the facts assumed in the question have ever been proven to a medical certainty.

Objection, vague and ambiguous, compound, argumentative, assumes facts not in evidence; namely, that in the use situation, the Dalkon Shield tail string has never been proven to have a, quote, "wicking tendency," unquote.

Over and over, Senior waits for his lawyer to finish the cascade of ob-jections and then defends his company:

We have always acted responsibly and with integrity.

Well, of course, the question starts off with a false assumption.

I don't see how we can warn about something we don't believe is there.

It has never been proven to my knowledge that the Dalkon Shield causes wicking in humans.

Over and over, Larson moves to strike Senior's answers and asks the court reporter to read back the questions verbatim:

Move to strike as nonresponsive. Would you read the question back, Mr. Reporter?

Let's try again, read the question back, please.

It is enough to wear down anyone, and Senior does not look well. Still, he stands fast on his defense of the Dalkon Shield and, when pressed, his fallback of *I-don't-know* and *I-don't-recall* answers. Among other things, he testifies that he doesn't know the tail string is a multifilament:

I don't even know what you mean by a multifilament.

I don't recall it being discussed.

I would know nothing about that.

He also testifies that he cannot recall any specific discussion with his son—the president and CEO—about the Dalkon Shield. Nor can he recall much of anything about discussions relating to the Dalkon Shield at board of directors meetings. In fact, the only board discussion he testifies about in detail involved Brenda Strempke's case, where "the lady claimed that she was made sterile by the Dalkon Shield," but, Senior recounts, "lo and behold she got pregnant during trial." The board, Senior testifies, thought that was "very remarkable" and "rather humorous."

Senior testifies, however, that he has no idea how much the Strempke jury awarded. "You say a million how much?" he asks, when Larson states the amount.

"A million seven hundred fifty thousand," Larson replies.

Senior gives Larson a serious look. "A miscarriage of justice," he says.

There are a few more questions—including about Senior's personal wealth (how much money he received when the company went public and his current stock holdings), which Senior refuses to answer—and the deposition nears the end of one of the sessions. Larson turns to Osthimer and asks the company to produce copies of the board minutes so that Larson can attempt to refresh Senior's memory on any discussions about the Dalkon Shield when the deposition resumes.

Osthimer refuses.

Larson wraps up. "We need to call the judge, in any event," he says.

The call comes into chambers while the judge is still in rocket-man mode. Larson describes the scene in Richmond as a classic deposition food fight, with too many interruptions by lawyers and too few responsive answers by the witnesses.

The judge is in a no-messing-around frame of mind.

There will be no more objections in the depositions, the judge says, except for attorney-client privilege, in which event the attorneys should immediately call him for a ruling. Senior must answer the questions about his personal finances. (It turns out, he is worth some $70 to $75 million.) The judge also says he will hire an independent doctor to evaluate Senior's health and ability to travel. (He tells me to track down a cardiologist in Richmond.)

He also orders A. H. Robins to produce the minutes from board meetings to refresh Senior's recollection. If the company claims that any entries are privileged or irrelevant, the judge will review them *in camera* (in chambers) to determine whether the objections are valid.

The judge gives A. H. Robins two days—the blink of an eye in lawyer time—to turn over the minutes. The typical procedure, set out in the Federal Rules of Civil Procedure, is that a party requesting documents serves a written document request; the opposing party has thirty days to respond by either producing the documents or raising objections; if the party objects, the requesting party files a motion with the court; the opposing party files a responsive brief; there may be oral argument before a judge or magistrate; and, finally, an order. If a magistrate issues the order (most federal judges use magistrates to rule on discovery disputes in the first instance), the losing party may file for review by a judge, in which case the process starts all over again before the judge.

But we are on Judge Lord time. An oral request by Larson. An immediate order to produce.

■ ■ ■ ■

On Wednesday, January 25, Judge Lord time speeds up.

Trial is only one week away (pushed back again, to February 1, to accommodate the discovery). Carpenters are in the courtroom—pound! pound! pound!—building extra jury boxes for all of the jurors needed for the consolidated trial. The judge would hammer the nails himself—he loves to work with his hands—except he has plenty else to keep him busy.

We start the day with a hearing on various Dalkon Shield motions and a discussion of the logistics for trial.

Then the hearing shifts to the issue of the depositions in Richmond, where Larson and Ciresi are ensconced. One of their partners who is appearing today, Roger Brosnahan, wants to fill in the judge on continuing problems in Richmond, "all the interjections and instructions and speeches," he says. Slaughter, in turn, complains about Larson and Ciresi taking "long and trying and emotionally-charged depositions," the "Robins Zelle technique," Slaughter says.

By now, I have found a well-qualified cardiologist in Richmond, who

studied at the trusted Mayo Clinic in Rochester, Minnesota. He has reviewed Senior's medical records and confirms that Senior cannot travel
to Minnesota.

The judge has another idea.

"What about having the judge go down and preside over the depositions?" he asks. "We could maybe give some safeguards to everybody there."

He tells the attorneys to report back later in the day with an update.
Then, he says, he will decide whether to "just get on an airplane tonight"—
maybe with a law clerk in tow—"and hitchhike around."

In the middle of this, the judge motions me up to the bench and whis-
pers that he really doesn't plan on going to Richmond; he is just proposing
the idea in an attempt to get the attorneys from both sides to be more co-
operative. (Judges rarely take the time to preside over depositions, let alone
travel halfway across the country to do so.) That, however, is before we proceed to the next act of the day, reviewing the A. H. Robins board minutes.

In chambers, we gather around the conference table, the judge, Keith
(my co-clerk), and I, along with Slaughter and Brosnahan and a couple
more attorneys. Slaughter has shipped a box of the board minutes from
Richmond. Brosnahan—even though sitting right there—is supposed to
be kept in the dark about the contents of the documents while the judge
considers A. H. Robins's claims of privilege and relevancy. At first, the
judge reads silently. Then he starts to point me and Keith to certain sections. Soon he starts to read aloud, giving Brosnahan a bit of a sneak, but
oblique, preview.

The fact is, the judge can't contain himself. He is seeing entries that he
believes show Junior—in contrast with his deposition testimony last fall
that he didn't know much about the Dalkon Shield—was in fact extremely
knowledgeable about the affairs of the corporation, at least on other issues, and he wonders about the implications of this new information. We
also see references to periodic status reports on the Dalkon Shield litigation that Roger Tuttle—the former in-house lawyer who directed the defense in the early years—provided to the board of directors. These reports,
which have not been disclosed in discovery, should bear on the top officers'
notice of problems with the Dalkon Shield.

What did they know? When did they know it? What did they do about it?

■ ■ ■ ■

Meanwhile, the depositions of Senior and Dr. Clark have been continuing throughout the day in Richmond, with Senior looking weak and subdued as Larson parades a series of internal A. H. Robins memos before him.

Dr. Clark, for his part, is as prickly as ever in his jousting with Ciresi. He threatens to walk out of the deposition. ("We won't take a whole lot of this today, I can tell you.") He talks back when Ciresi moves to strike non-responsive answers. ("I figured you would.") He says the issue of wicking is "a pure unadulterated red herring." He responds to Ciresi's *how-many-women* questions by saying that the questions are "entrapment of some kind." "Baloney," he says, when Ciresi tries to tell him otherwise.

Midafternoon, the judge calls the lawyers in Richmond for a progress report, with Slaughter and Brosnahan again sitting around the conference table in chambers. Larson and Ciresi pile on their complaints. The judge asks, again, how about if he goes to Richmond to help out.

He is fired up from the board minutes and eager to get his hands on the Tuttle reports. Now he is serious about the trip.

No one objects.

The judge asks if both sides will pick up the travel costs for his law clerks, so Keith and I can go, too.

No problem, the lawyers say.

And just like that, the judge, Keith, and I, after quick stops at our homes to pack our bags, are on our way to the airport that afternoon.

9

Persecutor of Organized Crime, 1961–1965

With the change in administrations in Washington after the 1960 election—Kennedy replacing Eisenhower—came new opportunities for Democratic loyalists. Almost immediately, Miles and Hubert began planning for Miles's rebound into public life.

Hubert suggested to Miles an appointment as the U.S. attorney for Minnesota. Miles resisted. Although the U.S. attorney—the top federal prosecutor for the state—was a prime post and Miles had a wonderful time as an assistant in that office, nothing in Miles's mind could measure up to being a federal judge. There was also the matter of timing: a judgeship was expected to open up within months and, with only four federal judges in Minnesota (more seats would be added in the 1980s), it could be years of waiting for another vacancy, and even then no guarantee for Miles.

Hubert, however, persisted in pushing the U.S. attorney position, recognizing that it would be no small feat to elevate his lightning-rod friend—*too much static, Miles*—to a prestigious federal judgeship. He counseled Miles that a stint as U.S. attorney would be a way to clear his name from past embroilments—including his censure in the daylight saving time fiasco, which still had people talking—and to neutralize his enemies, including some within the DFL itself.

The U.S. attorney post, said Hubert, could be "a stepping stone" to a judgeship.

Miles listened to Hubert. In fact, he was rather easily persuaded.

Then came the hard part. Hubert and Gene McCarthy would have to convince the new president to appoint Miles. Scrutiny of U.S. attorney candidates, while less penetrating than for judges, was still acute. And while presidents typically deferred to the home-state senators, Hubert, Gene, and Miles himself—who had run smack into the Kennedy machine while stumping for Hubert in the Wisconsin primary—had been adversaries and rivals of the Kennedys: not only the president but also his brother Bobby, who now served as U.S. attorney general and would surely weigh in on the appointment, as all U.S. attorneys reported to him.

But Hubert and Gene had also been growing their influence in Washington.

■ ■ ■ ■

In the Senate, Hubert was thriving.

At first, he'd had a rough reception in Washington. After sweeping into office in the exhilarating aftermath of his 1948 civil rights speech, he had become too famous, too fast; he was too outspoken, too long-winded, and too fast-talking ("Hubert has been clocked at 275 words a minute with gusts up to 340," Senator Barry Goldwater would say); too brash, too strident, too self-righteous; too buoyant and too optimistic (a "by-gosh-and-by-golly spirit," as later described). Other senators—especially, but not only, the Southerners—were quick to cut him down. They shunned him; they were openly hostile. "Can you imagine the people of Minnesota sending that damn fool down here to represent them?" one Southern senator said, loud enough for Hubert to hear as he walked by.

These were his "dark days," Hubert would say, "the most miserable period of my life."

Slowly, the ice began to break. Texas Senator Lyndon B. Johnson began to introduce him around—LBJ saw Hubert as a useful ally for his own ambitions—and as others got to know the senator from Minnesota, it was virtually impossible not to like him, so decent and kind. At the same time, Hubert blossomed into a powerful force in the Senate, with eloquent and impassioned speeches—historian Robert Caro would call him "one of the mightiest orators of his generation"—and a nonstop work ethic. He was still a bleeding-heart liberal. But he was learning the art of compromise. ("FIREBRAND SENATOR COOLS DOWN," one national magazine would write.) And Hubert moved on quickly from the bitterness of the 1960 campaign to energetically assist the new president on the legislative front. The *Washington Post* called him "the idea factory for many of the Kennedy administration bills." (The Peace Corps, in fact, was a Humphrey idea.) Indeed, by the time of the Kennedy administration, Hubert Humphrey was rising, according to one biographer, to "the epicenter of Senate power."

When Gene McCarthy had joined Hubert in the Senate in 1958, it had given Minnesota the distinction of being represented by two of the most liberal senators in the nation.

As with so many who had begun their political careers by rallying round Hubert in the early DFL years, Gene was a small-town (Watkins, in central Minnesota) child of the Depression. His father was a livestock buyer, Irish and domineering; his mother, quiet and religious. Gene grew up an altar boy and devout Catholic, distinguished himself as a brilliant student (and talented baseball player), and spent years studying at nearby schools run by the Benedictine monks of Saint John's Abbey. He entered the monastery himself but gave up plans for the priesthood after nine months. However, he remained deeply religious; in Washington, he went to mass every day and filled the bookshelves in his office with the works of Aquinas, Augustine, and Thomas More. He became known for his immense intellect and, when he turned it on, his wit and Irish charm. He was also quite handsome. ("Too handsome to be true," his wife-to-be Abigail thought when she first met him.) He also established both his courage and liberal bona fides early, when he became the first congressman to publicly debate the red-baiting demagogue from Wisconsin, Senator Joseph McCarthy (no relation), on national television.

Although Hubert and Gene were bound by their shared history and ideology, their political styles were worlds apart.

The effervescent Hubert—"the Happy Warrior"—rejoiced in the company of people and worked tirelessly to form coalitions and pass legislation. Gene was a loner. He had the soul of a philosopher and poet and, although he could be intensely ambitious, was soon to exhibit ambivalence, and even disdain, for Washington and many of its inhabitants. Already, he was wearying of politicians, in particular the Kennedys. He had served with JFK in the House and Senate and was unimpressed, and he was offended by the cutthroat tactics of the Kennedy campaign in the 1960 presidential primaries. He seemed to harbor that anger longer than Hubert, the target of the attacks.

But Gene was a senator of stature and, with his headstrong personality, a force to reckon with.

Gene also held Miles in special stead. Indeed Miles was on "a very small list of people who were liked by McCarthy," Walter Mondale would say. The two men—Miles and Gene—had the utmost respect for each other, as they saw in one another an uncommon streak of independence and a resolve to follow their own path, even (or especially) down a lonely road.

■ ■ ■ ■

Hubert and Gene went forward and recommended to the White House that Miles be appointed the U.S. attorney for Minnesota.

But Miles had created enemies even within the state DFL, and he was certain that Orville Freeman—now serving in the Kennedy cabinet as secretary of agriculture (where his signature achievements would include initiating the federal food stamp and school breakfast programs for the poor)—was among those opposing his nomination. Publicly, Freeman was tight-lipped, but the press was quick to note his past row with Miles over the Minnesota Supreme Court appointment.

Miles's name was also met "with a marked lack of enthusiasm" at the top levels of the Justice Department, the press reported. Bobby Kennedy took one last stab at changing the minds of the two Minnesota senators and paid a last-ditch personal visit to their offices at the Capitol.

Hubert and Gene refused to budge.

Days later, the appointment was made official. Hubert tore out the announcement from the Congressional Record and sent it to Miles, "so that you may be absolutely assured that your nomination was confirmed," he wrote in an accompanying note. "Congratulations!" Hubert added.

At the White House, however, officials made it clear to the press that the appointment was made with reluctance. If things went bad, as some in the Justice Department feared, they wanted to be able to deflect the blame.

Things went well, very well.

Miles took office in April 1961, at age forty-one. There would be some controversy—Miles was Miles, after all—but he was also a hard-nosed and hard-working prosecutor. He was soon in the newspapers, day after day, not for getting into trouble but for the bread-and-butter work of an industrious crime fighter: prosecutions for counterfeiting, tax evasion, mail fraud, narcotics, extortion, gambling, price-fixing, bank robberies, forgery, embezzlement, and "white slavery." He was not content to play the role of a behind-the-desk bureaucrat; the courtroom was still his stage, and, as he had in the past, Miles continued to try many of these cases himself.

He also continued to reach out to the less fortunate. "UNCLE SAM SHOWS HE HAS KIND HEART," read one headline, when Miles initiated a policy of "compassion and fair play" for small-time debtors. Thousands of Minnesotans, many elderly and infirm, owed the U.S. government amounts as little as $50 for debts dating back to the 1940s, for GI and farm loans, among other things. The Justice Department had been threatening to sue these hardship cases, until Miles came along. He called the situation "pathetic" and either wiped the debts off the books or made arrangements, if possible, for affordable monthly payments.

But first, Miles made sure to get approval for his debt forgiveness program from his boss, U.S. Attorney General Robert F. Kennedy.

Bobby Kennedy was keeping a tight rein on all his U.S. attorneys. On some matters, Miles reported to Washington on almost a daily basis. The close contact, however, brought mutual admiration and respect. Soon Bobby Kennedy and Miles Lord were working side by side on the biggest racketeering cases of the day.

Miles found Kennedy, six years his younger, to be charismatic but also blunt and no-nonsense.

Kennedy proclaimed Miles to be one of the best federal prosecutors in the country. "If Lord isn't the best district attorney in the country, he's next best," he told a reporter.

■ ■ ■ ■

Their main target was Jimmy Hoffa.

Hoffa was now president of the Teamsters, and, although suspected of connections to organized crime, he had eluded the grasp of law enforcement authorities for years. That included Bobby Kennedy, who had begun his pursuit of corrupt unions—in particular, the Teamsters and Jimmy Hoffa—in the mid-1950s as chief counsel to a Select Committee of the Senate. He continued his quest after he was sworn in as attorney general and enlisted Miles in his efforts.

Kennedy told Miles to focus on Benjamin Dranow, the Twin Cities businessman whom Miles had run across in the early 1950s during the

Teamsters car-bombing case. Miles had continued to investigate Dranow on and off for years for his rumored role as a bag man for Hoffa. Now there was a renewed effort, with Miles eager to impress his new boss. With Miles's assistance, federal prosecutors quickly convicted Dranow of financial crimes relating to the bankruptcy of a Twin Cities department store. (Dranow had taken over the store with a rumored loan from the Teamsters and absconded with its assets.) Then Miles tried and convicted Dranow on additional charges of income tax evasion.

"BOB KENNEDY TELLS LORD 'WELL DONE,'" one headline read.

These convictions were unrelated to Hoffa, but Miles hoped Dranow would turn state's evidence in exchange for a deal. Instead, Dranow, out on bail, absconded as he had before.

Miles was beside himself with his prize catch on the lam.

The phone rang in his office. "I know where Dranow is," said an unidentified man. "He's camped out at a northern lake called Lake de Mille Lacs. I can't tell you more than that because I want to survive. I have to look out for myself." Then the man hung up.

Turns out that was Hubert, pranking Miles.

Miles got down to business. He convened a grand jury and hauled in a score of Dranow's relatives, friends, and associates for questioning on the whereabouts of the fugitive. (Dranow's girlfriend was among those summoned and was photographed leaving the courthouse, "clad in mink.") The FBI led a nationwide manhunt, with "WANTED" posters plastered across the country. Eventually, Dranow was tracked down at a posh home in Miami, with an ocean-going yacht moored alongside the estate. Apparently, he was planning to flee to the Bahamas.

Now Miles had Dranow where he wanted, in the federal prison at Sandstone, some ninety miles north of Minneapolis.

Dranow, however, was not about to rat out Hoffa.

Miles upped the pressure, hounding Dranow and piling on more charges, including indictments for bail jumping and another for mail fraud. "I am being persecuted, not prosecuted, by Lord," Dranow complained at a hearing on the new charges. At another hearing, he shook his finger at Miles. "He laughs at my misery," Dranow lamented. "He snickers at me."

Still, Dranow refused to squeal.

Miles came up with a different plan.

He knew another inmate at Sandstone, Fred Ossanna, a onetime prominent Minneapolis attorney. Ossanna was in prison for his role in the demise of the Twin Cities streetcar system, among the finest in the nation until Ossanna led a group of racketeers—including Kid Cann—to take over the Twin Cities Rapid Transit Company. Cann, Ossanna, and several others went on trial in 1960 for dismantling the system and selling off its assets at below-market prices in return for payoffs. All were convicted—except Cann, who kept his storied acquittal streak intact. (This was before Miles's appointment as U.S. attorney; he was not involved in the case.)

Miles offered Ossanna a deal: he would help Ossanna shorten his prison sentence if "you get me the goods on this guy Dranow," Miles told him. "Get him to tell you all about Hoffa."

Ossanna agreed. He started a course in business law for prisoners and recruited Dranow to help teach. As they planned their lectures, Dranow would brag about his work for Hoffa. Every couple of weeks or so, Ossanna reported back to Miles. ("I suppose it would be illegal now," Miles would say years later; at the time, however, he had no qualms.) Miles shared the information with Bobby Kennedy, who collated it with information from his own investigators. Piece by piece, the case came together.

In June 1963, Bobby Kennedy indicted Hoffa and seven others—including Dranow—for siphoning off funds from the Teamsters pension fund. The trial began in April 1964 in Chicago. (Earlier that year, Kennedy had secured his first conviction of Hoffa in Tennessee, for attempted jury tampering.)

Miles was not trying the case, but he stayed in the loop. In mid-July, as the trial neared its end, Dranow was scheduled to take the witness stand. Miles went to Chicago for the testimony. By this point, Dranow was a broken man, the once dapper sophisticate now described as "rumpled and dispirited."

The morning of his testimony, Dranow saw Miles in the courthouse.

That's all it took.

The scene was bedlam: Dranow ran after Miles, shouting obscenities; Hoffa followed, screaming at Miles as well; Dranow, who had a heart condition, collapsed but was still pronounced fit to testify by a doctor. The press had a field day: "HOFFA TRIAL FIGURE TESTIFIES, BUT THE ACTION'S OUTSIDE"; "ENRAGED AT PRESENCE OF MILES LORD, DRANOW COLLAPSES AT HOFFA TRIAL"; "HOFFA ASSAILS U.S. ATTORNEY AS AGITATOR," the headlines read.

Soon there was more pandemonium. On a break in the trial, Miles stood in a courthouse hallway talking with Carmine Bellino, Kennedy's top investigator. The sight of Miles and Bellino together was too much for Hoffa, especially in his riled-up state.

Hoffa approached and spit in Bellino's face. The spray hit Miles.

Miles's first instinct was to floor Hoffa. The feared labor boss was only five foot five inches tall, an easy mark, Miles figured, as he had routinely punched out much bigger men. (Others would have handicapped that fight differently, with a nod to Hoffa's fearsome reputation.) "So here I am looking at Jimmy Hoffa, public enemy number one, who just spit in my face," Miles would later recount. "I thought, should I deck that little bastard now?"

There was only one thing that stopped him. Miles still wanted to be a federal judge.

"So I wiped the spit off my face and walked away."

Hoffa soon got his due in the courtroom; by the end of the month, July 1964, he and Dranow were convicted. Bobby Kennedy hailed the conviction in the national press. Those headlines, Miles was sure, would help down the line.

■ ■ ■ ■

Miles's other big splash as U.S. attorney came in another case that he pursued, on and off for years: fraud involving the Sister Kenny Foundation. This was the investigation he had started toward the end of his tenure as Minnesota attorney general in 1960. Walter Mondale, when he succeeded Miles, then secured the indictment and conviction of the foundation's executive director, Marvin Kline, for grand larceny.

But as soon as Miles was back in an office with the power to prosecute— in federal court now, as the U.S. attorney—he picked up the trail.

To most, Kline had been no small catch. He was a prominent Minneapolitan—he had been Hubert Humphrey's predecessor as mayor in the 1940s—and headed the Sister Kenny Foundation.

But to Miles, Kline was a "minnow." Miles wanted the "big fish."

He had his eyes on Abraham Koolish, the owner of a cluster of Chicago firms that solicited funds for well-known charities, including Father Flanagan's Boys Town and the Disabled American Veterans.

Miles thought Koolish ran the biggest charity racket in the country. And he was seething that Koolish preyed on the Sister Kenny Foundation, a world-renowned Twin Cities institution, and on children—"the sweetest and brightest," Miles said—crippled with polio.

The foundation was named for Sister Elizabeth Kenny, an Australian bush nurse who had come to Minneapolis, destitute, in the 1940s to promote a radical new treatment for polio. She was not a nun; "Sister" was an honorific Australian military title for nurses. She did not even have formal training as a nurse. But she revolutionized treatment for the dreaded illness that, prior to development of an effective vaccine, was paralyzing children by the tens of thousands. The accepted practice had been to immobilize limbs with splints or braces and, for more serious cases, to encase the young bodies in iron lungs. Sister Kenny, however, used massage and exercise. Soon patients were traveling to Minnesota from across the world for treatment. By 1951, Sister Kenny—white-haired and with a flair for hats and corsages—topped a Gallup poll as the most admired woman on earth.

Sister Kenny died in 1952, but the Sister Kenny Foundation lived on as a multimillion dollar operation. The funding came in part through the Koolish operation, which was hired to conduct nationwide mail solicitations. Miles thought too much of the money ended up in Koolish's own pocket and the pockets of certain foundation executives. He indicted Koolish and seven others for conspiracy to commit mail fraud. The allegations included supersized profits (only 40 percent of the solicited funds reached the foundation), bribes and surreptitious payments to foundation executives, and falsified financial statements.

Trial started in March 1963 and lasted ten weeks, with media coverage—press, TV, and radio—nearly every day. It was described as a "mammoth production," with eighty-five witnesses and the longest transcript in the history of the district. It was also bitterly contested, with repeated clashes between Miles and a preeminent lawyer from Chicago, Albert Jenner, who represented Koolish. Jenner was well respected and well connected in legal and political circles, and his law firm, Jenner & Block, was one of the most elite in the nation. He didn't much take to Miles's courtroom style and accused Miles of inflaming the jury, a charge that found some concurrence with the Eighth Circuit, which noted his "overzealousness." Still, the verdict—as usual, the jury sided with Miles and convicted the defendants—was affirmed on appeal.

■ ■ ■ ■

Miles still had his eyes on a judgeship.

Hubert still had his eyes on the presidency.

The next year, 1964, would bring a presidential election. For now, the presidency itself was out of the question for Hubert. With the assassination of JFK in November 1963, Lyndon B. Johnson had assumed the presidency and a lock on the Democratic nomination for his first elected term.

But the vice presidency was wide-open.

Early on, a dozen or so names were floated, including several from Miles's orbit: Hubert Humphrey, Gene McCarthy, Orville Freeman, and Bobby Kennedy, a bitter enemy of LBJ but extremely popular among the party faithful.

Miles was much attuned to the unfolding scenario. He was a politico at heart; these were his friends (Hubert and Gene, longtime; Bobby, newfound; and Orville, former); and politics—and politicians—held the key to any future judgeship.

By August 1964, on the eve of the Democratic National Convention in Atlantic City, it was widely believed that the choice had been narrowed to two names: Hubert Humphrey and Gene McCarthy. In Washington, they were called "the Minnesota Twins."

Publicly, Hubert and Gene stayed on good terms. But Miles knew tensions were rising and headed to Atlantic City to try to keep the peace. His emotions were in overdrive: excitement that one of his friends could be vice president but also fear of the potential fallout from their head-to-head competition.

Hubert was the popular choice by far of most Democrats. The exception was in the South, where Hubert's leadership on civil rights could not be forgiven. Indeed, the ink was barely dry on the landmark Civil Rights Act, signed into law in July after an epic battle, with Senator Humphrey at the helm of the campaign to break the historic filibuster.

LBJ led on both Hubert and Gene. A number of observers, including Miles, believed that LBJ was only playing the two. Others thought that LBJ wanted to keep his options open, at least in public, to generate interest in the upcoming convention, which otherwise lacked for suspense.

As late as Sunday, August 23, 1964, the day before the convention opened, LBJ was still boosting both men. That day, Hubert and Gene appeared back-to-back on NBC's *Meet the Press,* with the moderator opening the program by saying that one of them by most accounts would be LBJ's running mate. ("Senator, it strikes some of us that you have an embarrassment of riches in Minnesota," one of the panelists said to Gene. "How do you account for this? What is there about Minnesota?") Afterwards, LBJ telephoned the studio to congratulate both men on their performances and give them—both of them—"an A-plus." (Lady Bird Johnson, however, who was said to be quite taken with Gene's intelligence and charm, pulled no punches. "You're my candidate," she told him.)

But increasingly the signals pointed to Hubert. On the second day of the convention, Hubert got the word he craved. An LBJ intimate told Hubert that he would be the vice presidential nominee. His selection, however, was to be kept secret until the nominating ceremony the next day.

By this time, the convention buzz had Hubert as the pick. Miles also came to believe that the decision had been made, perhaps even before Hubert knew for sure. (Later, Miles would give conflicting accounts of whether Hubert told him or whether he deduced that on his own.) It is likely that Gene had also come to the same conclusion, in his head if not his heart. But Miles didn't want to take any chances. He worried that the longer the charade played out, the more the relationship between Gene and Hubert would be strained.

Miles decided to have a heart-to-heart with Gene. There was no privacy in the convention hotel—crawling with delegates and press—so they went for a car ride.

"I don't think you're going to be appointed," Miles said.

"Do you have any inside information?" Gene asked.

"No," said Miles. "Hubert hasn't given me any." But, Miles added, "I don't think you're going to get it, and if I were you, I wouldn't let Lyndon Johnson drag me down to the finish line and then reject me."

Gene turned quiet.

Late that night, Gene drafted a telegram to LBJ, which he sent the next morning and released to the press. "It is my opinion the qualifications that you have listed . . . as most desirable in the man who would be vice president with you," he wrote, "would be met most admirably by Senator Humphrey."

Still, LBJ was not done exploiting Gene. The president leaned on Gene to give the nominating speech for Hubert, his rival only hours before. Gene did so, but he would not forget—nor forgive—this debasing.

■ ■ ■ ■

November 1964 brought a landslide victory for the Johnson-Humphrey ticket. (One of the campaign's most notable moments was LBJ's "Daisy" ad: a young girl counting as she pulled petals off a daisy; as she neared ten, her voice morphed into a man counting down a nuclear launch, hyping the fear of Barry Goldwater as a reckless extremist who would doom the nation to nuclear war.)

Back in Minnesota, Hubert's ascent to the vice presidency set off a scramble to fill his seat in the Senate, to serve alongside Gene. Miles had much at stake, as a new face in the Senate would impact his prospects for a judgeship. In addition, Miles was considered in contention for the Senate seat himself. He was also a fishing buddy of the man who would make the appointment, Karl Rolvaag, now governor of Minnesota.

Rolvaag had come up through the ranks, serving in the DFL trenches, then as Orville Freeman's lieutenant governor, and, after Freeman's defeat in 1960, running for governor himself.

Rolvaag asked Miles if he was interested in the Senate appointment.

Although Miles had his eyes on a judgeship, the possibility of serving in the Senate intrigued him. He floated the idea by Maxine, on the offhand possibility that her views of politicians had changed.

"If you go to Washington," Maxine said, "you go alone."

Rolvaag was getting plenty of input—and pressure—for the appointment. At times like this, he liked to do his thinking in the great outdoors. (Rolvaag was much more on par with Miles as an outdoorsman than Hubert, and Miles had had some fun with this in a letter shortly before the election. Miles and Maxine had met up with some of the Humphrey children in New York, where they luxuriated in a large suite at the Waldorf Astoria before two chauffeured Cadillacs whisked them off to a Broadway play. "I asked Maxine who she liked better, Rolvaag or Humphrey," Miles wrote to Rolvaag. "I was not able to interpret her reply. I wonder if you can. She said, 'This beats canoeing.'") Over the years, Miles and Rolvaag had often taken to the woods together: to fish (netting whitefish on cold fall days, icicles on their hands), to canoe, to sit around campfires and discuss life and politics in a setting where, Miles believed, Rolvaag could channel the karma of his Norwegian ancestors. Now, Rolvaag and Miles journeyed up north and camped in a spot frequented by the French voyageurs of old. Well-stocked with whiskey, they pondered the Senate seat.

There were a number of considerations. But Miles made one thing clear. "Appoint somebody who will support me for a federal judgeship," he told his friend.

The picture of the smiling men told the story.

There were Governor Karl Rolvaag and U.S. Attorney Miles Lord, side by side. On their left was a third man. *His* smile beamed the broadest, as he held up the front page of the morning newspaper.

"MONDALE IS SENATE CHOICE," read the headline atop page one.

Walter Mondale—protégé of Hubert Humphrey, onetime assistant and then successor to Miles Lord as Minnesota attorney general—had been appointed, at thirty-six years of age, the new junior senator from Minnesota.

■ ■ ■ ■

It was coming up on four years since Miles had taken Hubert's advice and accepted the post of U.S. attorney. He had come to love the work and would even sometimes say in later years that it was the best job he ever had.

But he still longed for a federal judgeship.

More than ever, he hoped that a judicial vacancy would materialize—and soon—as the stage could not be more favorably set: Gene McCarthy and Walter Mondale serving as his home-state senators; the Democrats with a massive majority in the Senate (a filibuster-proof, two-to-one margin); and Democrats—including Hubert as vice president—in the White House.

If Miles stood a chance, the time was now.

10

Judge Lord Goes to Richmond

We are on the same plane out of Minneapolis as A. H. Robins attorney Alexander Slaughter. In fact, his law firm took care of our travel arrangements: a flight from Minneapolis to Washington, D.C., then a commuter plane to Richmond. We're all in first class, a novel experience for me. I never knew how much free booze there was up here.

The judge and I, sitting next to each other, drink whiskey and brainstorm our way to D.C.

He is especially intrigued by the notion of the Tuttle reports to the board of directors. By now, Roger Tuttle is teaching at the law school at Oral Roberts University in Tulsa, Oklahoma. (The university was founded by and named after the famed Pentecostal faith healer; the goals at the law school are to train students to "integrate their Christian faith into their chosen profession" and to "restore law to its historic roots in the Bible.") The judge, who loves to ponder what makes people tick, has a good time mulling this over: Roger Tuttle, corporate-lawyer-turned-evangelical-teacher-preacher, a tantalizing bit of information. Tuttle also recently wrote an article in the *Oklahoma Bar Journal* titled, "The Dalkon Shield Disaster Ten Years Later—A Historical Perspective." In some parts of this article, Tuttle touts the company line—he calls the tail string a monofilament and never mentions wicking—and is careful to rely on facts in the public record and not privileged. But some of the information he cites—including Dr. Clark's trip report on the pregnancy rates—while now public, is highly damaging to A. H. Robins. And Tuttle's conclusion certainly sounds more like a Christian preparing to confess his sins (right up the judge's alley) than a corporate apologist. Tuttle writes that A. H. Robins had "no trained personnel" when it went to market with the Dalkon Shield;

relied on statistics "from an admittedly biased source"; and overpromoted the device without "sufficient clinical testing." The lesson for corporations, Tuttle concludes, is "to place less emphasis on the profit motive."

What secrets, the judge wonders, is Tuttle still hiding in the dark and deep?

As the judge and I continue to talk, he worries that Slaughter, sitting a few feet away on the plane, may be listening in. The judge passes a note to Keith, who is across the aisle and closer to Slaughter, asking if he can hear our conversation.

"The little corn has big ears," the judge scribbles.

By the time we land in Washington, the judge, after sitting still in an airline seat for a couple of hours, is full of pep and decides to ditch his escort for a few hours of frolicking in the capital. Initially, we walk behind Slaughter as he begins to lead us to our connecting flight. Then we come to a crossroad in the corridor. Whoosh! The judge veers a sharp left, with Keith and me in tow. Slaughter continues straight ahead, no more the wiser.

We hop into a taxi for a nighttime tour of the monuments. Then the judge takes us to visit the Capitol Hill office of a Minnesota congressman, open late because it's the night of Reagan's State of the Union address. Afterwards, we call one of my former colleagues from the newspaper, who is now stationed in Washington, to meet us at a bar for drinks.

Now it is past midnight. It's too late to find a flight to Richmond or even rent a car, so we find a cabbie who is willing—after some cheerful coaxing by the judge, who never lets on that he is a federal judge—to drive us to our final destination, about a two-hour trip.

We arrive at the hotel around 3:30 a.m., place wake-up calls for 7:30 a.m., and begin to walk off to our rooms. As I put the key in my door, the judge continues down the hall toward his room. Suddenly, he stops and wheels around.

He asks me for one more deposition transcript to read before he goes to sleep.

■ ■ ■ ■

"We're like a bunch of skunks at the church picnic!" the judge shouts, clapping his hands.

Thursday morning, January 26, our party of three walks into the headquarters of the A. H. Robins Company. What in the world was Slaughter thinking, I wonder, when he agreed to this? It would be unusual for any judge, regardless of ideology, to enter a defendant's premises to conduct discovery. Yet here is a judge who has made no secret of his provocative views—*many people denounce crime in the streets, but few examine crime in the skyscraper*—on the prowl in the corridors of one of the nation's largest corporations.

The first business of the morning is getting our hands on the Tuttle reports. Slaughter and his crew take us to a conference room in the legal department, where Keith and I will review the reports and dictate summaries. The judge tells us to include only basic factual information that is not privileged—the dates of the board meetings, who was in attendance, the number and types of claims and injuries reported to the directors—to produce to Larson and Ciresi. That information may sound basic, but claims from thousands of injured women are compelling evidence of notice to top management. "And I think the plaintiffs are entitled to do that in their punitive damages suit," the judge says, later in the day. Any privileged information—for example, discussions about legal advice or strategy—will not be turned over to the plaintiffs, he says.

Keith and I read and dictate on and off throughout the day, but we also drop in on the depositions taking place in a conference room off the main lobby.

Senior arrives for his deposition in the late morning. He is pale and frail. His doctors say the stress of the continuing deposition is taking a toll. Presumably, it doesn't help that the conference room is small and poorly ventilated, and, with all of the lighting and electronic equipment, the temperature hits eighty degrees or more.

Judge Lord—in a business suit, not his black robe—starts off by asking whether any of the lawyers object to his presiding at a deposition in Richmond. This situation is so out of the norm that no one, the judge included, is quite sure whether he has the authority to proceed outside of his home jurisdiction without consent of the parties. No one had objected before we left Minnesota. But now the judge is here in the flesh, sitting only a few feet from the venerable chairman of the board. Slaughter murmurs a nonanswer to the judge's question. The judge presses. "I want to know now before I utter the first word and make the first ruling," he says. Finally, Slaughter says that the company consents.

The judge quickly takes control. The tedious pace—this is the fourth session of Senior's deposition—perturbs him. There's plenty of blame to go around. The judge thinks that Larson's questions are too long-winded and ponderous ("Now, come on, move on with your questions."); that the objections from Osthimer are too frequent and frivolous ("Are you making a speech or an argument when you make that objection?"); that Osthimer, who is sitting shoulder-to-shoulder with Senior, is signaling Senior by nudging his elbow ("Move your feet over, too," the judge directs, "I don't like what is going on."); that Senior's incantations of *I don't know* and *I am not aware* are hard to fathom (it is surprising, says the judge, that Senior "has never, during any of this hullabaloo, ever looked at the wicking documents"); and that Senior's answers are too evasive ("I direct you to make a more responsive answer, sir. We can't wait all day.").

In short order, the judge gets things moving. He is quick and crisp: asking simple questions himself, swiftly overruling objections, and ordering that nonresponsive answers be stricken.

The deposition ends for the day around 2:00 p.m. Senior says he is weary and would like to skip the session tomorrow, Friday, and resume on Monday. But the judge says his testimony needs to wrap up quickly as the start of the trial is fast approaching, only six days away, on Wednesday, February 1. He also says that things will move quicker if he is still in town to push the pace.

Finally, Senior agrees. "I would like to take a shot at it tomorrow," he says.

Meanwhile, the tensions have been rising as Keith and I continue to review the Tuttle reports.

At breaks in Senior's deposition, the judge has been scampering through the halls—with frantic A. H. Robins personnel rushing to keep an eye on him—to check on Keith and me. At one point, the judge also holds a mini-hearing, where Slaughter and one of his colleagues argue that all of the information in the reports—even the rudimentary summaries that Keith and I are preparing—is privileged. The judge cuts them off. "I don't want an argument on the law," he says. "That's a sacred privilege, the attorney-client privilege, and we are not breaching it here."

Later, when the judge is out of the room, there's another clash over the reports. The company lawyers demand that Keith and I turn over handwritten notes that we've made while dictating the summaries. They also try to take back some of the reports we had been working with. At this point, the judge pops in and sees me surrounded by attorneys demanding the documents. He tells me I look like an elk surrounded by wolves and gets a kick out of how I hold my ground.

We're starting to think that the document issues—not the depositions— are what's making the A. H. Robins lawyers increasingly jumpy as the day wears on.

In fact, the deposition of Dr. Clark, which begins midafternoon, opens with a veritable lovefest among the attorneys.

"I will welcome the judge here to try to expedite matters," Dr. Clark's personal attorney says. He says he likes the judge's questions—short and focused on specific facts—better than the Larson and Ciresi *when-did-you-stop-beating-your-wife* approach. Another A. H. Robins attorney agrees that the judge's handling of Senior's deposition earlier in the day was "very beneficial."

But Dr. Clark still tries to answer questions with long, nonresponsive monologues. He is still a stickler over the meaning of words. He argues with Ciresi. He argues with the judge. He goes round after round with both of them on whether A. H. Robins told doctors that the Dalkon Shield was "safe." A few minutes later, he talks over the judge as the judge tries to rule on whether an answer is responsive.

The judge attempts to assert control. "Somebody must be in charge of a deposition of this kind," the judge says.

"I agree," says Dr. Clark, nodding his head up and down.

"I am," the judge reminds him.

Dr. Clark's deposition recesses around 6:00 p.m. The judge is still going strong. Slaughter and his crew are tired and testy. They ask me if the judge always works this late. I just smile. They have no idea.

The judge decides to keep going and holds a short hearing in one of the conference rooms. For the first time, Slaughter contests the judge's authority to order any document discovery while he is outside of his home jurisdiction. By now, the fight is over not only the Tuttle reports but also additional documents that Larson is demanding on an insurance dispute between A. H. Robins and Aetna. It turns out that Aetna was contesting its coverage of A. H. Robins (or reserving its rights to do so) for the Dalkon Shield—and Larson wants to know why. He suspects that documents chronicling this conflict may disclose A. H. Robins's dirty laundry, as well as Aetna's behind-the-scenes role in the litigation. (In fact, Aetna will later be named as a direct defendant in some of the lawsuits—a rare event for an insurer—with allegations that it conspired in the destruction of documents, commissioned and concealed studies on the safety of the device, and participated in the decision to refuse to recall the Dalkon Shield.)

The judge, however, says he will hold off ordering the production of any documents until he is back in Minnesota next week. He won't even turn over to Larson and Ciresi the litigation summaries that Keith and I have dictated. He momentarily forgets Tuttle's name.

"What was his name again?" the judge asks.

"Tuttle," says Larson.

The judge smiles as he remembers. "The 'Jesus Freak,'" he says.

Finally, the judge is done with the lawyers for the day. He wants to "gather my troops," he says, so the three of us—the judge, Keith, and I—head back to the hotel restaurant for dinner and to take stock. The judge says he is feeling claustrophobic at A. H. Robins, cooped up in a small, overheated conference room for the depositions, then followed wherever he goes— making quite a scene in the normally staid offices—throughout the building. But soon the judge starts to hoot. In truth, he's been as happy as a pig in shit.

"This is as much fun as you can have with your clothes on!" he shouts.

■ ■ ■ ■

We turn in early. And rise early Friday morning, day two in Richmond.

The judge calls my hotel room. He has been thinking all night and is in high gear. He wants me to call the lawyers to convene a hearing right now.

It is 5:00 a.m.

"Maybe we should wait a couple of hours," I venture.

"But let's you and Keith and I meet downstairs right away," he says.

The judge tells us that he has decided to shake things up, change directions, zig and zag, and keep the lawyers off balance. He has called one of the local federal judges, Robert Merhige Jr., and arranged for the use of a courtroom so he can move the depositions out of the A. H. Robins headquarters.

At 7:30 a.m., I call the attorneys and tell them to meet us at the Richmond courthouse in two hours, with all the equipment and technicians they need for the depositions.

Our threesome takes a cab to the courthouse. The cabbie is fat, with greasy, unkempt shocks of hair and teeth, the few that are left, at all angles. The judge—again, never hinting he is a federal judge—starts chatting away with him, plotting some kind of crazy escapade to make a fast buck. "He's a bird," the cabbie says to me, in his thick Southern accent, as we pull up to our stop.

The federal courthouse in Richmond is within sight of the state capitol grounds. It is not lost on us that this served as the seat of the Confederacy during the Civil War. Majestic statutes of war heroes still keep watch over a main boulevard. Now we are the invading Northerners.

We enter Judge Merhige's courtroom, old and stately. Judge Merhige, another LBJ appointee to the bench, is renowned for his courageous decisions ordering the desegregation of the Richmond public schools in the 1970s. For a time, he was the most hated man in town: protesters spit in his face, his dog was shot, his guesthouse burned down, and after multiple threats to his life, he was guarded round the clock by federal marshals. But Judge Merhige is also no stranger to the power elites in Richmond society, including E. C. Robins Senior, one of his closest neighbors, whose estate is just a few houses away.

Judge Lord welcomes the attorneys.

"Thank you for coming," he says. "Yesterday's experience with the congestion, the confusion, and the climate at the Robins company tempted me to suggest to you that this quiet, serene atmosphere of the federal district courtroom might be a much more appropriate place in which to take the depositions." The judge says there was "almost a carnival atmosphere" at the company, a "congested maelstrom." That, says the judge, "was not good for either Mr. Robins"—he worries that Senior, "that poor old man," will have a heart attack—"or for the decorum of the deposition."

"So let's talk about moving the depositions here," the judge says. "Does anybody have an objection to that?"

"Yes, Your Honor," says Slaughter.

Yesterday, everyone seemed fairly pleased with the judge presiding over the depositions. Today, there is a new attitude. Slaughter won't even agree, as other A. H. Robins lawyers did yesterday, that the judge's presence at the depositions has been helpful. Slaughter also says that holding the depositions in the courtroom—as opposed to the familiar surroundings of the A. H. Robins offices—would be more stressful for Senior.

"And with all deference to the court," says Slaughter, "it seems that there is an element here of either stampeding or harassment to wear Mr. Robins down for a purpose that I don't really understand."

The judge lashes back. "Don't just say that unless you have something to back it up," he says. "That is a pretty serious allegation."

Slaughter retreats. "I don't have anything to back it up," he admits.

The judge advances. "Maybe you would like to withdraw it then; is that right?" he says.

"Yes, Your Honor," says Slaughter.

The judge isn't satisfied. "Have you seen any evidence at all that I had any hostility to Mr. Robins?" he asks.

"No, sir," says Slaughter.

But Slaughter sticks to his position that it would be too stressful for Senior in the courtroom. He says that an A. H. Robins doctor is on his way to the courthouse with the latest information on Senior's health.

Slaughter also lays out his objections to any further document discovery. He complains that "this is probably the most discovered case in history," yet the judge is continuing to order the production of more documents. He complains that the judge is making spontaneous orders—"more or less rambling through the documents, ordering orally here and there that we produce things"—and bypassing the normal rules of court. "Rough justice procedures," he calls it.

"We are moving so fast," Slaughter starts to say, "and with these—"

The judge interrupts.

"Nobody would accuse anyone up to this point of having expedited anything," the judge says. "It's time somebody moved, including A. H. Robins Company and its lawyers." The judge refers to the documents he has seen. "I have read in your own documents that the deal is that you keep talking instead of litigating," he says.

"No," protests Slaughter.

"Your documents show that," counters the judge.

Finally, Senior's doctor arrives. "I really feel that Mr. Robins is at the end of his rope," he says. "I'm very much concerned that he could have a myocardial infarction at any time." He agrees that Senior could be deposed for another hour today, but only at the A. H. Robins offices, not the courthouse.

The judge does not want to second-guess the doctor. "Very well," he says. "We will go back to Robins, and we will start in twenty minutes."

The judge's courthouse plan has come to naught. Except that his plan to shake things up—and get everyone on the run—is working just fine.

The entourage of lawyers and technicians and assorted others reassembles at the A. H. Robins offices. Senior's deposition resumes, and Larson asks a series of questions about the tail string. Senior responds by saying that wicking—or "so-called" wicking, as he puts it—has never been "absolutely proven."

"Could I ask you a question?" the judge says to Senior. "How much proof would it take?"

"Well, you have to be positive," Senior says, "because there is so much conflicting testimony on the part of physicians. Some say one thing and some say exactly the opposite."

Senior doesn't say that the doctors who dispute the dangers of the Dalkon Shield are largely in the employ of the A. H. Robins Company, one way or another. But Senior's answer is fine—in fact, a perfect setup—for the judge's purposes. "Do you think it is appropriate to take the physician who is least concerned and follow his advice," the judge asks, "or in a life-threatening situation of this kind to take the physicians, if they are substantial physicians, who are very concerned to follow their advice and warn?" While Senior tries to answer, the judge tips back in his chair. A smile creeps over his face; he prepares to pounce. He recounts the testimony of Senior's doctor from the hearing this morning. "Dr. Wilkins said your health may be in jeopardy. I have invoked every kind of protection for your health," the judge says. Now he closes the loop. "Should someone have done that for the women who were wearing this device?" he asks.

"Well—" says Senior, before Osthimer, his lawyer, interrupts.

The judge backs off. He's made his point.

■ ■ ■ ■

Later that afternoon, Dr. Clark is back. The nonresponsiveness—by both Dr. Clark and Senior—has been so persistent that the judge tells Larson and Ciresi that instead of waiting for each long-winded soliloquy of an answer to conclude and *then* moving to strike the answer and *then* going back to square one and asking the question all over again (the normal deposition procedure), the questioning attorney should simply raise his hand the moment an answer starts to drift into nonresponsive territory. That will be the signal to the witness to stop talking. But Dr. Clark is still finding it difficult to comport with the program.

Ciresi asks Dr. Clark whether some of the doctors at a 1974 septic abortion conference, sponsored by the company, were part of an A. H. Robins advisory panel. This is merely introductory to a line of questions that Ciresi has in mind; the answer should be a simple yes.

Dr. Clark, however, starts to stray. "I might add . . . ," he says.

Ciresi raises his hand.

Dr. Clark shakes his head in disgust.

"Move to strike," says Ciresi.

"Baloney," says Dr. Clark.

The judge is amazed. Dr. Clark, he says, seems to be in charge. Dr. Clark answers only the questions he wants to. Dr. Clark calls the recesses. "The judge will be the referee here," the judge reminds the witness. "Proceed."

As I watch this scene, I hear muttering behind me. It is Dr. Clark's wife, who has come to observe.

The temperature is rising, literally and figuratively.

"I don't know why you want to come back to a hot, humid place like this, and take a deposition where each one in the room is perspiring," the judge says at one point. "I don't understand. It's crowded, it is hot."

Ciresi chimes in. He asks Dr. Clark if he is warm.

"Perturbed and warm, yes," says Dr. Clark, in another *I-might-add* answer.

Toward the end of the session, Ciresi turns to the issue of A. H. Robins's refusal to recall the Dalkon Shield. He directs Dr. Clark to the internal memo from 1974, now before him in a black binder of exhibits, that expresses the opinion of Roger Tuttle:

> *If this product is taken off the market it will be a "confession of liability" and Robins would lose many of the pending law suits.*

It is getting late now, and the judge has been going all out for two days. But this document, which he hadn't focused on before, brings him to full attention: the A. H. Robins Company—counseled by its Jesus-freak attorney—discussing putting its self-interest in winning lawsuits ahead of the health of the women.

"Do you have any recollection of discussing with your fellow doctors in this company how many women out there might have this device in situ and suffer disease, loss of reproductive organs, or death over the ensuing years if the device was not recalled?" Ciresi asks. "Was that subject ever brought up?"

"Not in those terms that I recall," says the ever-precise Dr. Clark.

"Was it brought up in any reasonable facsimile of those terms?" Ciresi asks.

"Yes," says Dr. Clark.

"And did any doctor suggest to the responsible officials of the Robins company that they hire an outside consultant to go out and collect the medical records to render opinions . . . as to whether the device was causing infection, death, loss of reproductive organs?" asks Ciresi, his voice rising.

"Not to my knowledge," says Dr. Clark.

A few more minutes, and the judge concludes the deposition. He has heard enough for the day.

■ ■ ■ ■

In fact, the judge has heard and read more than enough in these two days: the nonresponsive answers ("I am trying to figure out why it is he can't answer these questions," the judge said after one futile go-round); the selective memories (Senior heard that "frequent sex partners" and gonorrhea could cause PID but couldn't recall, when the judge asked, if "the same people who told you about all the other causes [told] you anything about the tail string causing disease"); Senior not knowing that PID can be deadly ("I have never thought of it as life threatening") or even whether it can cause infertility ("I am not absolutely sure of that"); and the whole Dr. Clark experience, which galls the judge to no end.

At Friday's end, we rush to the airport to catch a plane to Minnesota. Before leaving the A. H. Robins offices, I hear that the company attorneys are searching for an associate to take our flight to keep an eye on us, especially since Larson and Ciresi will be on the same plane. But we board free and clear of any company personnel. Larson worries, however, about the appearance of being seen with us—and potential allegations of an improper, *ex parte* (or one-sided) conversation with the judge—despite the fact that we flew with Slaughter on the trip down (well, at least part of the way).

Everyone is getting paranoid. Especially the judge.

11

The People's Judge, 1966

The stars were still aligned in Washington when, at the end of 1965, a judicial seat opened with the retirement of one of the federal judges on the bench in Minnesota.

For the most part, Hubert's hope that Miles would use the U.S. attorney position to build a solid record on the road to a judgeship was turning out as planned. An editorial in the *St. Paul Pioneer Press* noted that Miles's "former flamboyancy has not been evident" and that "since becoming U.S. district attorney Lord has settled down into a more dignified role."

Dignified . . . Miles Lord.

In the same sentence.

Miles, however, was not a shoo-in for the judicial appointment. Eight or nine serious candidates lined up, including a number with strong DFL ties. Orville Freeman was still in the cabinet, now serving President Johnson and, Miles believed, opposing his nomination. (The *Minneapolis Tribune* noted the "coolness" between the two men that "lingers today.") The daylight saving time censure was a taint that Miles could not shake. And Miles, as the U.S. attorney, was now embroiled in a contentious fraud case against the state's insurance commissioner, a fellow DFLer, who was attacking back with allegations that Miles was pursuing the matter for the sole purpose of advancing his own aspirations.

With a judgeship—*his* judgeship—on the line, Miles was not about to leave anything to fate. He kept in close touch with Hubert, now the vice president. At least one of Hubert's senior staff members believed that Miles lacked judicial temperament—"a wild ass," the staffer thought—and might embarrass the administration. But Hubert stood fast. "Miles understands justice," Hubert told his staffer, "and that's good enough for me." Hubert went to work on his connections in the LBJ administration. He reached out to both the new U.S. attorney general ("You are okay," Hubert wrote to Miles, after that conversation) and the number two man in the Justice Department ("Ramsey Clark tells me things are in good order," Hubert wrote). Hubert also made sure to keep Walter Mondale on board. Miles worried that the junior senator faced pressure to appoint someone else and that Mondale, not wanting to choose between that person and Miles, was pushing a diplomatic solution. "Fritz is trying to work out an arrangement where there can be two or three judgeships announced at once," Hubert wrote to Miles. "I have asked Fritz, however, not to wait for this, but to move on your appointment now."

Miles also kept in touch with the senior senator from Minnesota. But that was hardly necessary.

"McCarthy was steadfast," Miles would say. "Nobody could dissuade Gene."

Indeed, while the popular view was that Miles would owe his judgeship to Hubert, and there was much truth to that, there was more to the story. Gene, Miles would say, was "the primary consistent and dependable source" of support. "A true friend," said Miles.

Gene felt the same devotion toward Miles. After his chastening in 1964 as a contender for the vice presidency, Gene's view of politics had further dimmed. He was not much impressed with the character of many, indeed most, of the men he encountered. But he saw in Miles a man who could be trusted completely and without question. "Miles is the kind of guy . . . that if you were in any kind of trouble, you'd be glad to see him coming," Gene would say, and a man who would "break trail" and "take some chances."

Gene didn't see many men like that in politics.

On February 10, 1966, Gene McCarthy retrieved the official envelope from President Johnson, addressed "From The President of the United States" to "The President of the Senate of the United States." Gene sent it to Miles with a handwritten message:

To Miles—

This is the envelope in which the President's nomination of you as a federal judge was sent to the Senate—

Congratulations—Gene McCarthy

The next step, a hearing before the Senate Judiciary Committee, would take place in the spring. Miles could hardly stand the anticipation and feared that, with his dream so near, something would go awry. The closer he got, the more trouble stirred up. The American Bar Association (ABA) committee that rated judicial candidates was now chaired by Albert Jenner, the Chicago lawyer with whom he had clashed during the Sister Kenny trial. The state insurance commissioner, under indictment, sent a letter to the Senate Judiciary Committee calling Miles unfit for the bench. ("I will be the last innocent person Mr. Lord sends to prison in furtherance of his ambition," he told the press.) Minnesota Republicans also wrote to the Judiciary Committee, attacking Miles for his "obvious lack of judicial temperament . . . not the calm, cool and thoughtful type which is considered necessary for a judge." To show that this was not a partisan attack, the Republicans named nine other DFL lawyers and state court judges and asked: "Would not any one of these . . . have been a better choice?"

Miles did have the benefit of a Democratic-controlled Senate, but the chair of the Judiciary Committee, Senator James O. Eastland, was hardly partial to Miles or his liberal champions. Senator Eastland, Democrat from Mississippi, was a staunch conservative and red-hot segregationist. (He had been one of the Southern leaders who tried to kill the civil rights bill.) He was often at odds with his own party—suffice it to say, he was not on the best of terms with Hubert Humphrey—and ruled the Judiciary Committee with what was described as "an iron hand." As the allegations mounted against Miles, not only in number but also in gravity, Senator Eastland sent an investigator to Minnesota.

Three times, Senator Eastland ordered that the committee hearing be postponed to give the investigation more time.

But the Senate investigator—and the FBI, which put as many as fifteen agents on its own probe—advised Eastland and his committee that none of the charges against Miles had any basis in fact and that some were "ridiculous." Many of the accusations had come from defendants in the insurance scandal, which the investigators chalked up to grievances from "natural enemies" of Miles, their prosecutor. By contrast, the leading judges and lawyers in town—many of them Republicans—praised Miles as "a very able lawyer" and "a man of impeccable honesty." And the ABA gave Miles a "qualified" rating, not its highest ranking but far from its "not qualified" kiss of death. (Albert Jenner had recused himself from the ABA's deliberations given his history with Miles in the Sister Kenny case, but then personally endorsed his onetime adversary.)

Senator Eastland set a new hearing date for April 20. As the day approached, Miles flew to Washington to call on key senators. He walked from office to office on Capitol Hill, accompanied by his daughter Priscilla, now in her twenties, who held his hand to calm his nerves.

The hearing itself was over fast.

Only two witnesses appeared: Gene McCarthy and Walter Mondale, the senior and junior senators from Minnesota, who both spoke in brief but glowing terms. (Mondale would later credit Miles—with his "Wild West approach," as Mondale called it—for accomplishing more big things on the bench than any other district court judge. "Miles is one of the most remarkable human beings I've ever worked with," Mondale would say. "He was a different kind of public servant because he listened to his own drummer.")

Senator Eastland asked the audience-at-large whether anyone wished to testify against the nomination.

Silence.

Senator Eastland asked again.

Again, silence.

There was no opposition. The whole hearing lasted eleven minutes. The committee adjourned to a closed-door session and voted out its approval.

The nomination went before the full Senate the next week. There was no debate or discussion. There was no roll call. By unanimous voice vote, a new federal judge was confirmed.

Hubert Humphrey beamed with pride. He will be "the people's judge," the vice president told the press.

■ ■ ■ ■

U.S. District Court Judge Miles W. Lord was only forty-six years old, but the wait had seemed interminable. He had dreamed of this day since barely out of law school. Now, with a lifetime appointment, a salary of $30,000 a year (no fortune but a sufficient—and dependable—sum, especially for a Ranger), and the power and independence bestowed by Article III of the Constitution, it felt, he would say, "almost like going to heaven."

He could not contain his joy and emotion at his swearing-in ceremony on May 2, 1966. Miles stood in front of a courtroom in Minneapolis and took in the crowd of more than two hundred people. He turned to his extended family, gathered in the front rows, and hailed them in his own inimitable fashion as "my *own*-laws and my *in*-laws and one *out*-law."

Dignitaries, friends, and family cracked with laughter.

(Later, on a visit to chambers, one relative put his feet up on the desk and exclaimed: "Jesus Christ, Miles! You sure done good!)

But there was solemnity as well. The chief judge of the district, Edward J. Devitt, distinguished, highly respected, and well taken to the pageantry of the occasion—known as "the judge from central casting"—presided over the affair. He read President Johnson's official instrument of appointment: "Know Ye; that reposing special trust and confidence in the Wisdom, Uprightness, and Learning of Miles W. Lord of Minnesota, I have nominated, and, by and with the advice and consent of the Senate, do appoint him United States District Judge for the District of Minnesota." Then Judge Devitt administered the oath of office, with Miles repeating the words:

> I, Miles Lord, do solemnly swear that I will administer justice . . . and do equal right to the poor and to the rich, and that I will faithfully and impartially discharge and perform all of the duties incumbent upon me as a United States District Judge . . . agreeably to the Constitution and laws of the United States.

This was the standard oath—*do equal right to the poor and to the rich*—but Miles paid special heed.

Chief Judge Devitt also spoke, with tears in his eyes, of the "awesome responsibility" and "absolute independence" of a federal judge. "We are practically immune from discipline, or censor, or supervision," he said.

Miles paid heed to those words as well.

Maxine, wearing pearls, stood beside Miles. She could not be more proud. She was also, no doubt, relieved. Against all odds—and against her family—she had believed in him from the start, from his early jitterbugging, carnival fighting, run-away-to-elope days. Now she helped Miles into his black robe, with an assist from the U.S. marshal, an old friend.

Miles kissed Maxine. And blew another kiss—at the marshal.

More laughter.

Then it was Miles's turn to speak.

His remarks were short and gracious. He paid tribute to the dignitaries in attendance. He imparted a line of stock wisdom, sounding and looking,

in his new black robe, as dignified as any judge. "The job must seek you,"
he said. "The man can't seek the job."

"Except," he added, "that I have wanted it for twenty-two years."

More laughter.

He grew serious as his emotions welled up.

"And so, folks, my heart is full today. I am happy. I am where I wanted
to be. I think that this is the best job in the world."

■ ■ ■ ■

A few weeks later, the new judge addressed the Minnesota Bar Association
for the first time. He tried to quiet fears—"don't let me frighten you," he
said—but his viewpoint was clear. He spoke of defendants "who find it
much to their economic benefit to delay"; he forewarned that he was "a
firm believer in complete pretrial disclosure"; and he laid down his guiding
commandment "to see that justice is done":

> The federal judge is more than a mere referee. In those instances where
> the litigation takes a direction that makes it apparent that a miscarriage
> of justice will occur, it is his responsibility to take control to insure a
> result which is within proper legal bounds.

Still, the judge wasn't sure in his early days on the bench how far he
could or should take his own words. He was concerned about his reputation and worried that the senior judges on the bench, including Judge
Devitt, for whom Miles had much respect, might think he was not up to
the job. He instructed his first law clerk to meticulously research Eighth
Circuit precedent to make sure that his decisions were properly aligned.
He also harbored the "rather naïve notion," as he would later say, that
judges were "stamped out as though in a production line, each being a
clone to the other black gingerbread men whose only duty was to follow
the law as it existed and not make new law."

But it did not take him long to more fully appreciate that the law was
not black and white and that a judge—not a gingerbread man but *one*
judge—could change the world.

Indeed, once appointed and confirmed, federal judges have an unprecedented degree of power and independence. They never face election—
unlike presidents or congressmen or even most state court judges—and

are the only U.S. officials with lifetime tenure, subject only to the rarely used power of impeachment. In debates over ratification of the Constitution, anti-Federalists warned this would render judges "independent of heaven itself."

But that was the point.

With colonial judges having been subservient to the Crown of England—"He [King George III]," reads the Declaration of Independence, "has made Judges dependent on his Will alone"—our founding fathers created in Article III of the Constitution a federal judiciary that would be insulated from both political and popular pressures.

All three tiers of the federal court system—the Supreme Court, courts of appeal, and district courts (also known as trial courts, where Judge Lord presided)—have extraordinary power. Indeed, district courts, while the lowest tier, handle by far the most cases. And many of their decisions, including intermediary rulings made along the way to a final judgment, are never reviewed on appeal, or if they are, under a lenient abuse-of-discretion standard, which affords great leeway to the trial judge.

Judge Lord, in fact, would often say that being a trial court judge was one of the most powerful positions in the country. He did harbor thoughts of an appointment to the U.S. Supreme Court—if, as he hoped, Humphrey reached the presidency—but even he must have realized that was a pipe dream. At one point, he had the opportunity for an appointment to the Eighth Circuit, when Gene McCarthy asked if he would be interested in an opening. But he passed. He thought that an appellate judgeship would be boring. He would not be able to preside over trials with the action and drama—witnesses, cross-examination, human emotion—he so loved, but would instead sit in secluded chambers surrounded by hefty law books and boring briefs and then listen to oral arguments addressing the finer points of the law. "Dullsville," he said. "I wasn't interested in dying so young."

In addition, as an appellate judge, he would have had to serve alongside colleagues—federal appeals courts typically sit in panels of three—and count votes and compromise, as do legislators, before taking any action.

But a trial judge sits—and acts—alone on the bench.

That would suit Judge Lord just fine. He believed in the power of one.

And with the protections of the Constitution, he said, he would have "the freedom to do what I had the courage to do."

12

On the Trail of Secret Documents

In the days following our trip to Richmond, the judge is on the go, morning, noon, and night. A "stampede pace," the A. H. Robins lawyers complain. The focus turns to discovery: identifying the documents, documents, and more documents that must be produced. To keep the pressure on—nothing like a looming trial for that—the judge also picks a jury on the Wednesday after our return. His plan is to select jurors but then send them home for a few weeks before trial starts to allow time for the discovery to continue.

The judge loves jurors. It's his chance to commune with the people, all too rare in his black-robed world. When February 1 comes, he can barely contain his enthusiasm. He pops into the staging room where the prospective panel members are assembled. Typically, they are nervous; the judge likes to loosen them up. Today he starts by telling the group to bellow out GOOD MORNING, JUDGE LORD! when he comes on the bench in a few minutes.

In the courtroom, we carry in folding chairs to accommodate the crowd. Then the jury pool of one hundred or so squeezes in.

"Good morning, ladies and gentleman," the judge says.

"GOOD MORNING, JUDGE LORD!" they shout back, laughing.

Chuck Socha, the lead trial lawyer for A. H. Robins, looks shaken. Clearly, the jurors are well on their way to bonding with the judge, not a good sign for Socha or his client. (It is not uncommon for jurors, consciously or subconsciously, to mime even the most subtle of clues about how a judge views a case.) The judge sees the look on Socha's face and tries to allay his fears by recounting, with much cheer, how he scripted the jurors' salutation.

That is small comfort, especially as the judge turns to the jurors with his old-fashioned charm. He calls himself an "old goat" and the jurors "fellow judges." He pays special attention to the farmers in the group, chitchatting about whether they will be able to miss chores this spring if chosen for the jury. He encourages all of them to think about whether they will be able to sit for a long trial. ("Are you through thinking?" he asks. "I heard things rattling out there.") He talks about Reserve Mining and how he got knocked off the case, "but not by a tree." (The jurors laugh; everyone, it seems, knows about the Eighth Circuit removing him from that case.) He tells them there is nothing wrong with a smile in the courtroom—"that's allowed anytime"—and even a joke or two to relieve the anxiety. That doesn't detract from the seriousness of the business at hand, he says, comparing the court proceedings to funerals on the Italian side of his wife's family where they break out wine and liven things up, but "it doesn't make us any less reverent or any less serious about the occasion."

By the time the judge gets down to the business of the day—questioning the prospective jurors—the group is ready to discuss their families, their politics, their religion, their use of contraceptives, their involvement in any prior lawsuits. The judge reads off a list of questions submitted by the lawyers. One by one the jurors respond, candidly and to the point:

"I have used an intrauterine device and also a diaphragm. I have had no abortions. I have had no miscarriages. I have an undergraduate degree in biology and chemistry. . . . I'm a Democrat. I do not listen to the Moral Majority."

"I was raised Catholic. But I'm not a real good one any more."

"I have used birth control, the pill, and foam. . . . I have had two miscarriages."

"I'm a Baptist and I'm Republican."

"I was raised Lutheran, and I was bit by a dog and sued because the owner didn't even say so much that he was real sorry or anything."

"Premarital sex—I guess between consulting adults it's their business."

"I do not agree with the church's opinions on birth control. At the same time I feel that we should do what we can to save the lives of the unborn or the elderly."

"I'm Catholic. And my wife uses the birth control pill, and I vote for the best person."

"I am 100 percent against abortion, but I am also 100 percent for anybody that limits their family."

"I have four young children . . . and I don't have too much time for politics, and I do use oral contraceptives."

"After fifteen years of marriage and arguing with my husband who's a Catholic and with the priest, I finally gave in and let him baptize my youngest and myself. So I have joined the church."

The judge doesn't probe too deeply and keeps a light touch. One juror tells the judge that he has fifteen children. "If you used anything, it failed," says the judge, much amused. "We're going to mark him as an exhibit." Another juror says she wishes "they would have come out with a good male contraceptive." A few jurors later, a man says he had a vasectomy. The judge looks back at the wishful woman. "There is your man!" he shouts.

The jurors come from the Twin Cities and a radius of 120 or so miles: cities, suburbs, farms. There's a meat cutter, a janitor, a secretary, a nurse, two mail carriers ("mail-person?" the judge asks one; "mail-miss," she says), a lunchroom supervisor, a forklift driver, a homemaker, a science teacher, a welder, an electrical engineer, a machinist, a sales associate, a road constructor, and farmers—a true cross section of citizens and a living testament to our founders' belief, embodied in the Constitution, in the power of the people to render judgment on even the most profound issues of the day.

There is only one person in the group who gives the judge pause.

"I was in the insurance business for twenty some years," says one prospective juror. "I was a general agent. . . . I worked with claims people."

"I think I'm going to have to let you go," the judge says.

Socha jumps to his feet. At the bench, out of hearing of the jurors, he lodges his objection. The judge tells Socha to put his reasons in writing.

"You don't want it now?" says Socha. "No," says the judge brusquely. After Richmond, his patience is in short supply with A. H. Robins. Still, I wonder about this decision. Even with my limited experience, I'm pretty sure that simply working as an insurance agent is not sufficient reason for a juror to be summarily dismissed. At a minimum, the judge should inquire further, for example, asking the juror if this would affect his view of the case. But, in any event, the man is excused.

The judge handles all of the questioning. Then the attorneys exercise their peremptory challenges—seven strikes per side, without stating any reason—and just like that, in less than one day, a jury of thirty-one is selected for the consolidated trial. The judge proudly points the jurors to the ongoing construction in the courtroom; one newspaper says that the jury box, when finished, may be the largest in the federal court system. He tells the jurors that they will need to be fair and impartial and to stay away from any media reports on the case. (Socha is already complaining about "massive publicity.") The judge says he has great respect for the media, but, he adds, "with all due deference to the newspaper people, sometimes I wonder if we are in the same courtroom." The reporters on the backbenches smile.

In late afternoon, the jurors are sworn in, and the judge tells them to report back on February 21.

That date will begin to slide back, however, as the discovery picks up.

■ ■ ■ ■

Indeed, Larson and Ciresi have begun an all-out push for sweeping new document discovery. This is delaying the trial, they know. But it could also blow the litigation wide-open. And they may never get another chance like this. Judge Lord, as most lawyers know, will not let anything, and certainly not by-the-book rules of civil procedure, stand in the way of full disclosure.

To the judge, discovery under the formal rules is like playing "pin the tail on the donkey." The rules of the game are that the plaintiff's attorney must specify with sufficient particularity which documents he wants produced—before, however, ever having seen them. An additional obstacle is that the process relies on defense attorneys to produce their own clients' documents, or, as the judge likes to say, to "double-cross" their clients by revealing their "most horrible secrets." And to further impede disclosure, the law provides convenient "sanctuaries," as the judge says, for defense attorneys to hide smoking-gun documents under claims of attorney-client or work-product privilege. (These two privileges are similar but distinct. Attorney-client privilege applies to communications between a client and his attorney; the work-product doctrine applies to documents prepared in anticipation of litigation.) These sanctuaries, says the judge, create "an almost impregnable fortress into which documents may be figuratively carried."

He calls the whole process "a charade."

Every day during this first week of February—even on the day the jury is selected—there are continuing arguments about how to define the categories of documents that A. H. Robins must produce, a surprisingly (to me) difficult task. The judge makes it clear that he is not going to stick to the rules: no need for formal document requests, no thirty-day wait for A. H. Robins to respond, no briefing schedules. Instead, he summons the attorneys, sometimes multiple times each day, to listen to the arguments of both sides and probe for information.

Larson and Ciresi want documents that show the top A. H. Robins officers had notice of the defects years ago. They want the Aetna insurance documents. They want—maybe most of all—the secret studies of used tail strings, which they believe will eviscerate A. H. Robins arguments about wicking.

As the pressure mounts on the documents, A. H. Robins continues to try to settle all of the remaining consolidated cases to escape from the judge's grasp. By now, only five plaintiffs remain, and A. H. Robins is offering unprecedented sums of money as the price of flight from Courtroom No. 1.

■ ■ ■ ■

The A. H. Robins lawyers also attack with three motions of their own: one in opposition to producing the board of directors minutes (which they argue are privileged or irrelevant); another to prohibit disclosure of the summaries of the Tuttle reports that Keith and I dictated in Richmond (which they say are "explicitly prejudicial"); and a third catchall motion objecting to "proceedings by way of discovery not conducted in conformance with law."

The judge reads the A. H. Robins submissions—and explodes.

The briefs include an account of the proceedings so far, including the trip to Richmond. The judge blasts the A. H. Robins version of events as "mishmash," "incoherent," and "about as far from here to the moon as to what actually happened." It is clear to him that the briefs are written not for his benefit—he lived the experience—but to concoct a record for the Eighth Circuit.

"I don't want any more garbage like that," the judge says angrily.

He demands to know who is responsible for the briefs. Slaughter isn't sure; maybe, he says, one of his partners in Richmond.

"Now isn't that something," the judge says. "I'm reading a brief here which will be filed in the Court of Appeals which I think is an abomination and even the lead counsel for the company doesn't know who wrote that. . . . [I]t's somebody back in a cubicle back in Richmond."

"I cannot," the judge says, "preside over an enigma wrapped in a fog surrounded by a mystery."

The judge is also set on edge by the new faces he is seeing in court. He complains about the "hit-and-run treatment": lawyers appearing one day sounding sincere but then disappearing, leaving the judge to discover, after they are gone, that the arguments were made of "whole cloth."

"At least I know who Larson and Ciresi are," says the judge, "but I don't know who I'm talking to from Robins half the time."

So the judge says he wants the out-of-town lawyers to take "a little oath" that they will abide by the rules of the District of Minnesota and consent to the jurisdiction of the Minnesota Board of Professional Responsibility, which has the authority to discipline attorneys. In truth, this is not too different from the standard oath that any attorney must take for *pro hac vice* admission to appear in another state. The judge wants to make sure, however, that there will be no question that the lawyers can be held accountable for their actions in Minnesota.

But his request sets off a firestorm.

The company brings in a well-respected Minneapolis lawyer—James Fitzmaurice, one of Fribley's senior partners at Faegre & Benson—to argue against this "loyalty oath," as the A. H. Robins lawyers call it. This is the first time we have seen Fitzmaurice in the Dalkon Shield litigation, but I know him well. He was my own lawyer a few years ago; the newspaper hired him when a small-town sheriff in central Minnesota sued me for libel. (I had reported on various charges of misconduct; Fitzmaurice got the case thrown out.) The judge has also known Fitzmaurice for years, has tremendous respect for him, and even recently appointed him to head a prestigious committee of lawyers and federal judges.

But Fitzmaurice is all-in on this issue.

At the hearing on February 2, Fitzmaurice says that he counseled the out-of-town attorneys not to sign the oath, calling them "an elite group." Slaughter, he says, "has probably appeared in more federal courts than anybody in this room." The same, he says, applies to Duncan Getchell, one of Slaughter's partners, who popped up this week. Socha has "a renowned reputation as an able trial lawyer," says Fitzmaurice. Cogar, he says, is member of American College of Trial Lawyers, "an elite body of competent and able trial lawyers who have stood themselves well over the years before all of the courts of this country."

"None of these lawyers in my opinion needs guidance nor direction nor a reminder as to what is ethical conduct," Fitzmaurice says.

The judge reverts to common sense. "What's the harm of it?" he asks. "What is the harm of saying, 'We'll do those wonderful things' that you have just pledged that they will do?"

The judge and Fitzmaurice face off.

"The lawyers respectfully decline," Fitzmaurice says.

"Very well," says the judge. "Mr. Socha is excused. Mr. Slaughter is excused. You folks may go back to Virginia now." He turns to A. H. Robins local counsel. "We'll proceed with Mr. Fribley."

Fribley begs off. "The client has informed me that I have no authority to proceed alone at this time," he says.

Fitzmaurice asks for a stay to pursue any remedies A. H. Robins might have in the Eighth Circuit. Finally, the judge backs off. He says he will give the lawyers until Monday morning to redraft an agreeable oath.

But the judge is deeply troubled. He doesn't understand why the A. H. Robins lawyers are so "spooky" about the oath. He worries that the hometown lawyers will be swept up in the deeds of no-name out-of-towners, especially if the locals are half-in, half-out of the case—used by the national counsel only when expedient, as they are using Fitzmaurice and his reputation today. "In all due respect, I love you," the judge says to Fitzmaurice. "You have either got to get into this case or get out of it." The judge, alluding to the defense tactics, also tries to warn Fitzmaurice that he may be in the dark about the company's "scorched earth" policies.

"James," says the judge, "you haven't seen any of the confidential documents, apparently."

We also turn back to arguments over the documents at this hearing.

Larson presses for the tail-string studies. Slaughter resists, citing Judge Alsop's previous orders denying virtually identical requests. Judge Lord says that he has read his fellow judge's orders. "And I don't intend to follow that." He directs that absent some good explanation, the testing documents be produced, "every one of them and all of them in their entirety."

Larson also moves on the Aetna documents. He is well versed in how the insurance industry operates, having represented major insurers for much of his career. Here, Larson smells blood. "We may even find, and I don't know, we obviously haven't seen it," he says, "that Aetna and A. H. Robins jointly for economic reasons decided not to warn or not to recall because it was the wisest economic course for them." The judge listens intently. He, too, is experienced in the ways of insurance companies. But he says he will defer ruling on the issue until early next week.

Larson also presses another discovery issue at this hearing. The plaintiffs want to take the deposition of William Forrest Jr., the general counsel. This is the top in-house lawyer at A. H. Robins, who would typically be immune from most discovery, protected by privilege. That, however, gives the judge no pause. He orders the deposition for next Thursday, one week from today, in Minneapolis.

Larson also asks for an order directing Forrest to bring all of his documents relating to the Dalkon Shield.

A request for any—let alone all—of a general counsel's files is extraordinary. "You're talking about getting this court looking at documents that are as intimate as the place where they put the Dalkon Shield," the judge says to Larson. He says that he will probably appoint a special master—a private attorney, or sometimes a retired judge—to look at the documents and make initial determinations of privilege, in the first instance.

The judge has made no secret over the years that he believes special masters—too rarely used—are the key to solving the conflict-of-interest dilemma of partisan attorneys. A special master, with no allegiance to a client, is able to clean out a corporation's files, as the judge says later, right down "to the bare walls."

■ ■ ■ ■

As I watch the judge this week, it's clear that day by day he is becoming more and more consumed with these cases. The rush of events—the wild trip to Richmond, the document games, the loyalty oath, briefs written by unnamed attorneys ("some mischievous gnome," he says later), and his courtroom overrun with unfamiliar attorneys ("jumping up and down," he will say, "like pistons")—is pushing him to the brink. On top of this, he is deeply offended that a company would treat women this way. It has been the women in his life—his mother, who raised him; his sisters, who cherished and protected him; and his wife, Maxine—who have nurtured him his whole life. He also has two daughters, both the same age as many of the plaintiffs in the Dalkon Shield cases. "Maybe women had too much to do with my life," the judge will say by way of explaining his increasing wrath.

If A. H. Robins had done this to men—"chopped off their balls," the judge tells me—the company would have been dismantled by now.

■ ■ ■ ■

Friday comes, February 3, the last day of a busy week.

Before court starts this morning, Fitzmaurice meets with the judge in chambers to say he is withdrawing from the consolidated cases. Then he leaves, never again to be seen in our courtroom.

In court, there is a new request by A. H. Robins to ask the dirty questions in the ongoing depositions of the plaintiffs. The company has filed a document—titled "Statement Respecting Causation"—that purports to set forth the specific showing that the judge has demanded before inquiring about a woman's sexual history. The submission is only a half-dozen pages but packs a wallop, detailing the alleged medical problems of the few remaining plaintiffs: gonorrhea, trichomonas, and venereal warts; cervicitis, vaginitis, cystitis, cysts on the cervix and vagina, and a bladder infection from which E. coli and enterococcus were cultured; cervicitis and a long-standing history of menstrual problems; congenital cysts, monilial infections, and erosion on the buttocks folds and labia major; trichomonas, cervical polyps, and cervical erosion; and recurrent cystitis, chronic cervicitis, and vaginitis.

The judge is taken aback and doesn't know quite what to make of it all. He is hardly a prude, but is certainly not used to thinking about women-persons in this way. "If this is the way the average American woman is . . . , I wouldn't want to live with one of them," he says, when he first addresses the submission. "I'm not sure we'd want them in the courtroom if they're that bad, it might not be safe for the rest of us." He asks Larson if all of the RZLK firm's cases are that bad.

Larson assures the judge that the same allegations, "made out of 'whole cloth,'" could apply to "just about every woman who walks the streets of Minnesota."

"But they don't all have a couple doses of clap," says the judge.

"Neither do the plaintiffs, Your Honor," says Larson.

The hearing on Friday focuses on two women, both RZLK clients. Howard Bergman, another attorney at Fribley's firm, starts out strong in discussing the first:

> We actually have a doctor who believes that infection was caused by a sexually transmissible disease. And you had mentioned that was the criteria you were looking for before we could ask about the woman's social history, in particular the number of sexual partners other than the husband.

Bergman explains that the disease at issue is chlamydia, but that most doctors don't test for this because it is "a hard bug to culture." Nevertheless, an A. H. Robins expert will testify that the woman's "symptoms are consistent with a chlamydia infection," he says.

"Did the doctor culture it?" the judge asks point-blank.

"No," Bergman says. "The only way we can find out whether there is a possibility of this woman contracting chlamydia is to find out about her social history."

"No way," the judge rules. "Forget it."

Bergman moves on to the second woman. He says she had no symptoms while wearing the Dalkon Shield and that a dye test performed after the IUD was removed showed her tubes were still open. In other words, there was no sign of infection after her Dalkon Shield use.

Martha (Marti) Wivell takes the podium to respond to Bergman's allegations. She is a senior associate working with Larson and Ciresi and is immersed in the case, especially the medical issues. She is also one of the few women I see during my clerkship, in any case, to address the court. I sit forward in my seat and thoroughly enjoy the opportunity to watch a woman-person in action, especially as she takes Bergman apart:

Mr. Bergman has represented to the court that this woman's tubes were patent; that means they were open, in 1976. What he did not tell the court was that medical records . . . show that she had problems with the fimbriated ends of her tubes, consistent with hydrosalpinx, which is an indication of an infection, at the time that Mr. Bergman says her tubes were patent.

Bergman remains undeterred. "We want to know about the social history of this woman," he tells the judge.

"And suppose that she had a milkman once a week together with a little love," says the judge, thinking back to the days of his newspaper route in Crosby-Ironton. "What would you argue about it?"

"If she had a milkman who is coming by," Bergman says, "it would indicate that there was an increased risk of her getting a PID."

"Forget it," the judge rules.

It turns out that these two women are the only RZLK clients in the judge's block of cases who have not yet settled their lawsuits. (The other women with remaining cases are represented by other law firms.) To me that explains, at least in part, A. H. Robins's focus on their medical histories. If the company can settle these two cases, the company will be rid of Larson and Ciresi, at least before Judge Lord.

Slaughter stands up and asks whether the judge would "indulge us in settlement conferences."

"Are you ready to talk settlement at the time?" the judge asks Roger Brosnahan (Larson's and Ciresi's partner).

"I don't think today is an appropriate day," Brosnahan responds.

RZLK's last two clients are holding out as long as possible, knowing there is more at stake than their own personal claims. As long as they hang on, Larson and Ciresi can continue to pursue the discovery, which will help all of the women who have been injured, all across the country.

■ ■ ■ ■

The next week, on Monday morning, February 6, the judge picks back up with the loyalty oath. By now, however, the issue is anticlimactic. The judge has decided that he has more important battles—he doesn't want to divert his attention from the documents—and agrees to a watered-down order drafted by A. H. Robins. Essentially, all the order says is that designated partners from each law firm will be accountable for all work by their firms and that all pleadings will identify the partners involved in the preparation. That's it. (Not a word about consenting to the jurisdiction of the Minnesota disciplinary board.) The attorneys and the judge are even laughing about the whole affair: a loyalty oath, ha-ha.

For the moment, the judge also seems to be getting along fine with A. H. Robins's top outside lawyer. Slaughter—with thick salt-and-pepper hair, big glasses, and a comfortable Southern accent—has an unassuming presence and circumspect demeanor, the perfect approach to the judge in a case like this. He tries his best not to antagonize the judge: "no, oh no, no, no, no, no, no," he stutters when judge accuses him of wasting time; "no, no, no, no, I know," he says when the judge reproaches him about the documents; "yes, no—no, yes—it's no, yes, excuse me, I didn't mean to not stand, no, yes," he says when the judge asks him about another issue. Fitzmaurice, before his hasty exit, had told the judge that Slaughter is "a great guy" and a "wonderful person." The judge has also seen more and more of Slaughter and is warming to him as a person. No one should be fooled into thinking, however, that the judge has forgotten that Slaughter, in large part, is running the litigation for A. H. Robins.

Indeed, the judge turns steely as the A. H. Robins attorneys grow increasingly resistant to the notion of any additional discovery. "We basically are reopening the MDL in the District of Minnesota when it has been assigned to Judge Theis in the District of Kansas," Slaughter complains.

Judge Lord had already dispatched with this argument. Now he also tells Slaughter, "I just talked to Judge Theis." On the phone, Judge Theis—a buddy from the judge's old DFL days—told Judge Lord that nothing in his MDL orders precludes the production of additional documents, as long as there is good cause to do so.

"So there is no problem there," Judge Lord says.

The judge is also ready to address the appointment of a special master. He now has not one but two masters in mind, and not only for the general counsel's documents but also for all of the document discovery. The two lawyers—both with tried-and-true pedigrees—are sitting in the back of the courtroom: Peter Thompson, a former law clerk and now law professor, and Thomas Bartsh, the son of a longtime friend. (Thompson clerked for the judge during both the Reserve Mining and antibiotics cases; Bartsh worked as a special master on antibiotics.)

Nothing personal, the judge tells the A. H. Robins lawyers, but "discovery is a terrible test of any lawyer's loyalty."

But Slaughter fights back. "I want the record to be clear that we object to this procedure, Your Honor, of sending down basically agents of the court to conduct the discovery," he says.

"That's the order," says the judge.

He says he will send the masters to Richmond tonight or tomorrow— "have gavel and travel"—to supervise the process of identifying and numbering the documents. The masters will also separate out the documents on which A. H. Robins asserts privilege for later review, first by themselves and then by the judge, to rule on the validity of the claims.

Slaughter asks for an opportunity to make a more formal argument tomorrow. "You may," says the judge, "but the masters will be on their way down there."

The next morning, Tuesday, February 7, Slaughter calls on one of his partners, Duncan Getchell, to make the last-ditch arguments against discovery. Getchell starts off by calling the proposed discovery "a direct assault" on privilege.

"You may manufacture that ground, but it is not so intended," the judge says. "So we will have no further arguments about the attorney-client privilege. You may forget it. Next?"

Getchell argues that the proposed discovery is unduly burdensome, calling for a "huge mass" of material without the requisite specificity.

"Excuse me, please," says the judge. "I will hear this no more." The specificity arguments—the defining and redefining the categories of documents—have been argued over and over in the previous days. "Move on," the judge says.

Getchell says his last argument "goes directly to the heart of our objections": that the prior MDL proceedings preclude any further discovery. This is the umpteenth time that A. H. Robins has made this argument, and it doesn't fare any better now.

The judge enters a formal order appointing the two special masters.

He also says he will issue another order tomorrow morning to delineate the document categories as they have been defined in arguments over the past week and a half. He says the order will include a memorandum that will detail the history of recent events—to counter, in effect, the "garbage" brief that A. H. Robins submitted—and that it will be ready at 9:30 a.m.

That is news to me, the drafter-to-be of the memorandum.

I rush home after the hearing and start typing away on my own computer. (I can't commandeer Exxie today.) Around 6:30 p.m., the judge and Keith show up at my apartment. They bring a pizza, and I open a bottle of cheap wine. The judge starts to dictate; I type his cavalcade of words. By the time he's done, the draft is twice as long—and twice as scorching—as my original. After a couple of hours, he tells me to tone the final version back down and leaves me alone to finish up.

I spend a couple of hours editing the narrative to about eight pages. Then I attach three pages that describe the documents that A. H. Robins must produce—ten categories, labeled paragraphs A–J, including tests or studies of "the safety and characteristics of the Dalkon Shield," and a large sweep of Aetna documents. The order says the documents must be produced to the masters as soon as possible, "the exact date of production being dependent upon the report of the two masters."

By 6:00 a.m., I am in the office at Suze's desk, transferring the draft into Exxie and inserting the final touches. I make sure to protect the record on privilege issues, the most likely target of any A. H. Robins appeal:

> The defendant objects to this discovery as a "direct assault" on the attorney-client and work-product privileges. This argument is, at best, premature. The court is scrupulously protecting these privileges at this stage of the proceedings. The sole endeavor at present is to identify and accumulate the specified documents and segregate them into privileged and nonprivileged categories.

The judge makes some minor edits, and at around 9:30 a.m., we head to the courtroom. He asks the whole staff to come in. "Let the phones ring!" he says.

In court, I hand out copies of the order to the attorneys at both counsel tables.

"Any stay is denied," the judge says.

The special masters are ready to begin work in Richmond. Slaughter has no choice. He rises from his seat.

"I have said there will be no further argument on this," the judge says.

"The court is requesting me to sit down?" asks Slaughter.

"Yes, if you please," says the judge.

There is a brief discussion about the trial, lest anyone forget that a jury still awaits.

Slaughter tries one more run at a stay.

"I will not hear further argument," says the judge. "That's all, period."

He leaves the bench.

The rest of the day, Wednesday, February 8, the judge roams the courthouse handing out copies of his order to anyone he can corral, including fellow judges.

He is excited that his order will result in the production of documents, as he later says, "from here to hell." And he's also got the deposition of William Forrest, the general counsel, to look forward to tomorrow morning.

Things are starting to move.

By first thing the next morning, however, when the doors open to the clerk's office for the Eighth Circuit, A. H. Robins is ready to file its papers to try to stop Judge Lord in his tracks.

13

Presidential Politics, 1968

Miles was barely a year and a half into his judgeship and busy with the routine fare of federal court. But now—in 1968—his focus would be consumed by the turmoil of a presidential campaign, with Hubert Humphrey and Gene McCarthy, despite their shared roots in progressive Minnesota politics, fighting an impassioned battle—"stained with blood," as a leading historian would write—for the nomination of their party.

Miles could not help but place himself in the middle of this story line, not as the leading man (too much to hope for in every instance in real life), but in a substantial character role for a drama playing out on the national stage. He refused to accept that the schism tearing his friends and country apart might be irreconcilable and went back and forth between Hubert and Gene and their campaigns—calling himself the "unofficial envoy"—trying to ease frictions, trying to mute personal attacks, trying to find common ground.

He knew that the canons of judicial ethics prohibited judges from engaging in partisan politics. But he was prepared, he would say, to sacrifice his judgeship for his most improbable scheme: Hubert Humphrey, his most beloved friend, for president, with Gene McCarthy as his running mate.

■ ■ ■ ■

Hubert Humphrey had gone into the vice presidency believing that would be his best route to the presidency. He did not heed his advisors who warned that LBJ, controlling and often cruel, would "cut his balls off." True to form, LBJ as president dominated, subjugated, and humiliated Hubert. "Took him captive," wrote Hubert's biographer, "he was Johnson's prisoner."

On no issue was this more evident than the war in Vietnam.

Early on, within the confines of the White House, Hubert expressed doubts about the growing American entanglement in the war. But LBJ demanded unquestioning allegiance, and Hubert fell in line, even as more and more young men were drafted and shipped into jungle warfare. The country divided, dove against hawk, much of the split generational, young against old. LBJ, entrenched and embattled, summoned his vice president to duty, and Hubert now obliged. His critics, including longtime liberal supporters, branded Hubert a sellout. But those who knew Hubert best— Miles included—attributed his actions to his respect for the presidency, his rationalization that the spread of Communism had to be stopped in Southeast Asia (the "domino theory"), and his unfailing optimism that led him to believe that the United States was on the path to victory. "He was eternally optimistic about getting out of it," Miles would say. "He went along with Johnson because it was his duty, but he could always rationalize that one more step of escalation would lead him into [peace] negotiations."

Meanwhile, antiwar activists had been searching for a Democrat to challenge LBJ for the presidential nomination. This was seen as political suicide: taking on the powerful—and vengeful—incumbent president of their own party. The potential candidates, leading Senate doves, one after another, said no: Bobby Kennedy, now senator from New York, no; Senator George McGovern of South Dakota, no; Senator Frank Church of Idaho, no.

Gene McCarthy stepped into the void.

In November 1967, he declared that he would run in several primaries. Few believed this was a serious campaign for president. In the eyes of many, he was a "candidate-martyr" on a quixotic mission to rally the antiwar movement. Some thought his candidacy was driven by revenge for the way LBJ exploited him during the 1964 vice presidential selection process. But there was no doubt about the fierce authenticity of Gene's opposition to the war. He believed that the war was wrong on military grounds, wrong on economic grounds, wrong on diplomatic grounds. "And in my judgment," he said, "it has long since passed the point in which it can be morally justified."

In January, he took to the snows of New Hampshire, backed by young peace activists, mostly college students, who cut their long hair and went "Clean for Gene."

■ ■ ■ ■

Miles, perhaps surprisingly, had little sympathy for the antiwar movement.

He had never been much of a military enthusiast (although he had not yet evolved into his later-stage, full-bore pacifism), and his instincts would seem to side him with the young protesters standing up for their convictions against the establishment. But whether or not swayed by Hubert's predicament, Miles fought his own predispositions and trivialized the antiwar protesters as "teeny-boppers" and "hippies." And when the first draft resisters came before him in court, he dealt with them harshly.

In one case, in the early months of 1968, two prominent Twin Cities protesters who had refused to report for induction appeared before him. The judge was unforgiving. He scolded the men and said he hoped they would "get a taste of prison" so that "they might more seriously consider the course they are taking." In the end, however, the defendants were able to post bail. And the judge, perhaps because he was hopelessly conflicted (even if he couldn't admit it to himself), would not decide another Selective Service case until after the election.

Miles saved his harshest remarks about the war for Gene. He told Gene that he was a traitor to his country and that the way to end the war was to end the dissent at home. "What you're saying is un-American," Miles said. "You're costing American lives."

Miles spoke these words in private discussions with Gene—then reported on them to Hubert.

Indeed, Miles met with both Gene and Hubert throughout the year and regularly passed on information about his conversations to each of them. Both Gene and Hubert knew—and took advantage of the fact—that Miles was acting as a conduit.

One conversation with Gene, in early 1968, lasted hour after hour. "He is very pessimistic about our prospects of winning in Vietnam," Miles wrote to Hubert afterwards. (Miles often reported to Hubert in a memo or a letter.) In Miles's view, Gene was also dejected about his own campaign, which was being written off by the establishment and the press. More importantly, Gene did not enjoy the glad-handing, baby-kissing, fire-up-the-crowd spectacle of a typical campaign. Gene was an intellectual, low-key and restrained on the campaign trail. He felt his staff—"amateurs" and "strangers," Miles wrote in this memo—was pushing him to campaign in ways that were at odds with his sensibilities.

All in all, Miles saw his friend as "very downcast and tense."

"He is a lonesome, pathetic figure," Miles wrote to Hubert. "For goodness sake, counsel everyone not to attack him."

■ ■ ■ ■

Events took a dramatic turn in the war at the end of January 1968 when North Vietnamese and Vietcong forces launched the Tet offensive with a series of daring attacks. It was now clear that the enemy was stronger than portrayed by the administration and that the war's end—"the light at the end of the tunnel"—was nowhere in sight.

Even Hubert, in private, turned pessimistic. He wrote to Miles in early February, on stationery that said simply: "The Vice President."

Dear Miles:

It was good to talk to you on the phone. If I sounded a bit snappy and irritated, it wasn't because of you. It was only because of some of those news stories that I thought were so unfair. . . .

Do keep your contacts. You are mighty helpful to me in doing this. And do keep in touch with Gene. I am very sorry that Gene went off on this political expedition, but I bear him no ill will and do hope that out of all of this we can preserve a friendship that we have had for many years.

These are troublesome times for all of us. It is mighty difficult to maintain even the image of happiness, much less the substance of it. But I see no easy way out of our present troubles. We simply have to do the best we can and hope and pray that the resources of this great country will be sufficient for the tasks both at home and abroad. . . .

You are a dear friend, and you know how much I cherish that friendship. Never hesitate to speak freely to me, and please share your thoughts. I need a friend who is willing to tell me what he thinks, what he hears, even if it is distasteful to my ears.

Best wishes.
Sincerely, H.H.

The letter jolted Miles.
Hubert—his joyful and optimistic friend—was rarely down and seldom complained, Miles would say, even about his treatment as vice president, "no matter how mean Lyndon was."

■ ■ ■ ■

The antiwar sentiment surged as the primary season approached.

In Minnesota, McCarthy supporters engaged in furious clashes with LBJ forces in precinct caucuses—infighting reminiscent of the 1948 battle for control of the DFL—and stunned political insiders with the strength of their numbers and organization. Miles had rounded up some law clerks to attend the caucuses in support of the Johnson-Humphrey ticket, only to be overwhelmed by the opposition.

In New Hampshire, young people flooded the state.

Still, there were shock waves on the night of March 12, the first primary, when McCarthy captured 42.4 percent of the Democratic vote in New Hampshire. He didn't win—LBJ pulled in 49.5 percent—but given expectations that the president would score a landslide, it was deemed a stunning victory for McCarthy. "A triumph of heroic magnitude," wrote *Newsweek*.

Gene McCarthy was now a serious contender for the presidency.

Four days after New Hampshire, Bobby Kennedy entered the race.

Miles liked Bobby—he would never forget their days of tracking down Jimmy Hoffa—but Bobby certainly wasn't in the same stratum for him as Hubert or Gene. In fact, Miles saw Bobby's candidacy as an opportunity to unite his two friends against a common adversary. There was plenty of animosity to go around in this field of Democrats. LBJ and Gene each had long-standing hatred for Bobby Kennedy; Kennedy, in turn, despised both of them, too. Gene was also angry that Kennedy used him as a stalking horse in New Hampshire and only entered the campaign, splitting the antiwar forces, after the first primary demonstrated the president's vulnerability. And LBJ feared Kennedy—his electric charisma, hard-core organization, and deep pockets—more than anyone.

Hubert called on Miles for help.

They spoke when Hubert paid a visit to Minnesota, soon after Bobby Kennedy's announcement, as Miles drove with Hubert back to the airport. Miles said that, unfortunately, he would be out of pocket for a while. But after Miles got home, he reconsidered his plans. "Dear Hubert," wrote Miles, on March 21:

> At the time I spoke to you on the way to the airport I had not fully considered the implications of the matter of our trip to Europe. Maxine and

I have planned for several years to go this spring. She has been swiping money out of my pockets and tucking it under the mattress for four years. . . . But we have canceled our plans.

We are not going to go around feeling like martyrs either. It is a small sacrifice. Neither of our sons is in the Service as yet. You and the President have bestowed upon me the finest position in America. Maxine and I have been privileged over the years to know you and Muriel and your family as our close and lovely personal friends. . . . Maxine and I voted unanimously to stay home and sweat out these primaries with you and the President.

We are proud to do it.

On the same day as this letter, Miles also wrote Hubert a note about his most recent conversation with Gene, which included a discussion about the next primary, on April 2, in Wisconsin. This would be another head-to-head battle against the president. (Kennedy's campaign was just getting off the ground.) Gene, gathering momentum from New Hampshire, told Miles that he expected to win the state.

"I am therefore pessimistic about what can be done to prevent it," Miles wrote.

Days before the Wisconsin primary, Lyndon Johnson planned a nationwide address on Vietnam. That morning, he paid an unusual visit to Hubert's apartment in southwest Washington. (At the time, there was no official vice presidential residence.) LBJ showed Hubert two drafts of his speech and said he hadn't decided which ending to use. That evening, March 31, 1968, LBJ faced the live cameras and delivered his stunning announcement:

I shall not seek and I will not accept the nomination of my party for another term as your President.

Initially, Hubert was undecided about entering the race, thinking Bobby Kennedy might be invincible. But two days later, when Gene won in Wisconsin, Hubert began to believe that Gene could weaken Kennedy in the upcoming primaries and clear a path for Hubert himself. Before Hubert could announce, however, the country was rocked by the assassination of

Martin Luther King Jr., slain by a sniper's bullet on April 4 as he stood on a hotel balcony in Memphis. City after city exploded in rioting. In Washington, fires and looting reached within two blocks of the White House. Politics was on hold.

Finally, on April 27, Hubert Humphrey officially declared his candidacy for president of the United States. "Here we are, the way politics ought to be in America," he said at his announcement, "the politics of happiness, the politics of purpose, the politics of joy."

This was classic Hubert, the Happy Warrior. And in the spring of 1968, tone-deaf.

Miles agonized for his friend.

■ ■ ■ ■

Before the month of April was out, Miles broached with Gene the subject that had been keeping him awake at night: the vice presidency.

Miles researched whether there was any constitutional prohibition to a president and vice president coming from the same state. He concluded there was not (and that, in fact, William Henry Harrison and John Tyler, who ran together in 1840 and won, were both born in Virginia).

He met with Gene, and, as Miles recounted in a note to Hubert, "I suggested that he might want to run as second man on your ticket." Miles recorded Gene's response as ambivalent: "'Well, something like that might be worked out later.'" That was more than enough to keep hope alive for Miles.

In this same meeting, Miles scolded Gene for his attacks on the president, which Miles called "unpatriotic, unfair, unwise" and "a dastardly deed." It was not right, Miles said, to have Gene and Bobby Kennedy "criticizing the president's every move" in Vietnam. Instead, Miles said, Gene should declare a moratorium on attacks and give the president "a free hand to settle this mess." Miles recognized, however, this would cause Gene problems with "his 'teeny-boppers.'"

Miles also told Gene in this meeting that it was up to Gene "to take care of Bobby," as it would be not be wise for Hubert, as vice president, to go into attack mode. But Miles suggested in his note to Hubert that "Gene will accept the benefit of any research concerning Bobby's history."

That wasn't the only help that was discussed.

The Humphrey camp believed it was crucial that McCarthy receive sufficient funds to take on Kennedy, and there is little doubt that money did pass hands. (McCarthy's campaign manager confirmed, after the fact, that they "definitely received money" from Humphrey's campaign or its supporters.)

One potential big-time funder who was discussed in this meeting between Miles and Gene was Hubert's longtime money man, Dwayne Andreas. Hubert had met Andreas in 1948, when Hubert was first running for the Senate. They became close friends, and, over the years, Andreas, a wealthy businessman, regularly contributed large sums not only to Hubert's campaigns but also to other candidates at Hubert's request. By 1968, Andreas was rising to the top of the Archer Daniels Midland Company, a global agribusiness giant, and on his way to establishing a reputation as one of the most prolific campaign contributors of his time. "Tithing," he called it, as he showered his largess on both Democrats and Republicans alike.

Miles, of course, hated fund-raising—that was one of the main reasons he had walked away from elected office himself—and as a federal judge should have steered far, far away from that *rotten business*.

But Miles wrote to Hubert that he had discussed the prospect of funding for Gene, from Andreas. For now, Gene demurred. "He has suggested that Dwayne's offered help should be held in reserve for a later time," Miles wrote after this meeting with Gene.

Miles's note to Hubert also contained a cryptic reference, apparently to other money for which Miles himself was the conduit. "Gene said what I was doing for him was peanuts (and it really was)," Miles wrote.

■ ■ ■ ■

By now, Miles was traveling with both Hubert and Gene so frequently that the cities and states were a blur. "I'd hop off Humphrey's plane and get on with McCarthy and ride, and then at night I'd get them on the phone to confer," Miles would say. Despite his status as a federal judge, he did little to conceal his political activities. "I never trumpeted my political activity but I didn't hide it either," he said. Sometimes, but not always, Miles flew under an assumed name. But this was only a cursory (and inconsistent) effort to camouflage his involvement, as he was a well-known figure to most politicos and the traveling press. Sometimes, but not always, Miles also attempted to hide his identity on his notes to Hubert by omitting his name. "From a friend in the boondocks," he signed one note; "This message will self-destruct in 10 seconds," he signed off on another. But again, his identity would be clear from even a quick read, and Miles also wrote formal letters to Hubert on his official stationery: "Chambers of Miles W. Lord." (Hubert likewise wrote to Miles on his vice presidential stationery and sent them to the judge's chambers.) Miles also telephoned Hubert on his White House line. And he was well known to Hubert's staff. He called Hubert's aides with advice, and he (or his secretary) dictated memos to Hubert's secretary over the phone when time was of the essence.

His efforts were endless. On one occasion, he started the day breakfasting with Hubert at the Waldorf Astoria in New York City, then jumped on a plane to D.C. to lunch with Gene, then flew back to New York to meet Hubert for dinner.

No doubt, Miles could be exasperating with his know-no-bounds intensity. But both candidates continued to turn to Miles. And Walter Mondale, cochair of Hubert's campaign, was glad that Miles had taken on the role of a go-between. "Someone needed to talk to McCarthy, and Miles was the best," Mondale said later.

■ ■ ■ ■

Miles was also unceasing in his attempts to get Hubert and Gene together, and the two candidates did talk and meet with each other during the campaign.

Their relationship was long and complex.

Over the years, they had done much to support each other and were aligned as committed liberals on most issues in the Senate. But the war in Vietnam was a titanic dividing line. And they were simply two very different personalities.

Hubert was enthusiastic and optimistic, warm and compassionate, described as an "honest, happy, wonderful fellow" and "a very human and emotional man." Miles thought of Hubert as loving and sentimental and a man who never expressed "rancor or ill will."

Gene, by contrast, was introspective, cerebral, and aloof, described as "a scholar, meditant and poet, an inner-oriented person who remains an enigma to those who love him most." Miles thought of Gene as "a loner" and "an aesthetic, quiet, distant person."

Gene also had a dark side.

Hubert knew that Gene frequently ridiculed him. Gene mocked

Hubert's "subservience to Johnson," one biographer wrote, "and even his intellect."

Hubert shrugged it off. "He does that to most people," he said of Gene. Hubert also recognized their differences, "in style, temperament, and interests," he said, and that they even liked "different kinds of people."

Except for Miles.

The two campaigns were also poles apart: the old politics versus the new.

Hubert had entered the race so late that he was bypassing the primaries and amassing a substantial lead by focusing on the large number of states where party kingpins—the Democratic machine—still controlled the delegates. He was beholden to an unpopular incumbent, hopelessly out of touch with the mood of the times, and, with his balding hair, protruding forehead, and, in his words, "my wattles," looked the part of an old-time pol. (He turned age fifty-seven during the campaign.) Everywhere he traveled, antiwar demonstrators hounded him. "He would speak and they would howl," said one of his top aides.

Gene, by contrast, was receiving enthusiastic welcomes (although his stump style often left audiences nonplussed). The national press was glowing, even swooning, glorifying him as valiant, erudite, sophisticated. He was tall and handsome at age fifty-two, with thick, swept-back silver hair, an intellectual—and a poet!—who refused to spout political pabulum. (*Time* magazine ran a gushing article, "A POET'S VOICE STIRS THE LAND," enthusing over the possibility of "a poet-President" and sparing McCarthy no praise: citing his "richness of mind," "nobility of his ideas," and "true dignity.")

But Gene was increasingly disaffected on the campaign trail. Now he no longer held the moral high ground by himself but was locked in a series of bitter—and personal—primary battles against Bobby Kennedy.

■ ■ ■ ■

Kennedy won their first head-to-head confrontation, in the Indiana primary—Miles stayed with Gene that night, watching the results—and then again in Nebraska. Oregon, set for May 28, loomed large.

Shortly before that primary, Miles met up with Hubert. "Tell Gene to get up there to Oregon to campaign hard in that primary," Hubert told Miles. "Our public opinion polls show that he can win up there."

Miles passed on the word. Gene invited Miles to join him in Oregon. One day, Miles was walking down a sidewalk in Portland with Gene's wife, Abigail. There was no telling who was most surprised, Miles, Abigail—or Bobby Kennedy—when they ran into each other on the street.

"Miles, what are you doing here?" Kennedy asked.

"I'm trying to get Hubert Humphrey elected," Miles responded.

Kennedy surveyed the scene—a federal judge from Minnesota, walking down the street in Oregon with the wife of one presidential candidate, professing his allegiance to another candidate, both of whom were campaigning against Kennedy, and, according to Miles, threw up his hands in bewilderment.

McCarthy won the Oregon primary, handing Kennedy the first electoral defeat for any member of the Kennedy clan.

The next showdown would be the crucial California primary on June 4.

Kennedy won California.

"My thanks to all of you," he declared to cheering supporters at the Ambassador Hotel. "And now it's on to Chicago, and let's win there!"

And then, the unthinkable. Shortly after midnight on June 5, after leaving the ballroom and exiting through the hotel kitchen, Kennedy was shot in the head. He died the next day, at age forty-two.

Hubert was "deeply and emotionally shocked," even "unhinged," by the assassination, according to accounts.

Gene seemed worse. He had had enough.

Gene met with Hubert in Washington. He was, according to a Humphrey aide, "trying to find a reason to drop out." But Gene wanted Hubert to make concessions on Vietnam, while Hubert felt locked in by LBJ, whose power he still feared.

Gene stayed in the race. He was attracting large crowds and polling well. But he no longer seemed to have much interest in campaigning. Increasingly, the word used to describe his behavior was "enigmatic."

"Erratic" was also used.

■ ■ ■ ■

In early July, Gene spent several days at Saint John's University, his alma mater, in the central Minnesota countryside. He fraternized with the Benedictine monks with whom he had once studied. He walked the woods. He read his poetry at a nearby coffeehouse.

When he returned from Collegeville to the Twin Cities, he met again with Miles.

Miles was losing patience.

The Democratic National Convention in Chicago was little more than a month and a half away, with no sign of conciliation between his two friends. Miles, however, was not about to give up hope. When he met with Gene post-Collegeville, he continued to push his plan for Gene to be Hubert's running mate.

Some of the people closest to Gene—including a psychiatrist friend who often traveled with him—had urged Miles "to abandon my 'mad scheme' to have Gene become vice president," Miles wrote to Hubert, after this latest meeting. But, Miles added, Gene himself had not made that request.

In fact, Miles wrote Hubert in this note that he was "personally convinced that Gene sees no hope of winning the presidency but is going to come into the Convention so strong that you will have to take him as vice president." Miles added that Gene would most likely "outline the conditions" under which he would accept the vice presidential nomination, including Hubert's break from LBJ on Vietnam.

There was also talk in this meeting of "help"—apparently money—for Gene's campaign. "I gave Gene a small amount of help today and told him more would be forthcoming," Miles wrote. Miles provided no details in his note on the nature of this effort. But it was enough to make Miles nervous—"I was always deathly afraid of it," he said later—and he let Hubert know that these matters were better left to Dwayne Andreas. "I would much rather have Duane [*sic*] do the job which I am about to undertake along the lines I mentioned to you the other night," Miles wrote Hubert in this same note. "Let's hope I don't end up in the Humphrey garbage can." (Miles had cause to worry, and not only about judicial ethics; after the campaign, Andreas would be indicted, but acquitted, for making illegal corporate contributions.)

Miles ended this note to Hubert with another plea to stop any attacks on Gene. Gene had complained that Hubert's staff—not Hubert himself—was disparaging him ("as a poor administrator, lazy, et al.," Miles wrote). "It is rather difficult for me to suggest that you make concessions to a man who is making noises like he would like to destroy you," Miles wrote, "but if you feel like sending a memo to your 'workers' suggesting that they keep the campaign on the issues and making no personal references to McCarthy and get that memo to McCarthy either through me or others, it might be helpful."

"BUT IT MAKES ME SICK!" Miles added. He signed off: "Best wishes . . . Bleeding Heart."

■ ■ ■ ■

As August opened, Richard Nixon won the nomination of his party at the Republican National Convention and picked Spiro Agnew as his running mate.

The Democratic National Convention was set for the end of the month. Hubert Humphrey appeared to have an insurmountable lead in delegates but still struggled to break free from the shadow—and taint—of LBJ and chart his own course on Vietnam. Some advisors begged Humphrey to resign as vice president and assert his independence.

Meanwhile, Miles's vision of a Humphrey-McCarthy ticket was not dead. Or private. In fact, Humphrey said during the summer, in public, that it was "not an impossibility" that he would choose McCarthy as his running mate.

Miles talked to Gene again about the vice presidency in a long phone call in early August.

Gene was coy. He wanted to know precisely what Miles was telling Hubert about their discussions. "You didn't say I *said* I wanted the second spot, you merely said that *you thought* I wanted the second spot," Gene said to Miles, as Miles recounted in a note to Hubert. Miles agreed that's what he told Hubert, "only my own conclusion." Miles tried to entice Gene by telling him that Hubert was talking about "how much fun it would be to run" with his fellow Minnesotan. Gene was conciliatory but opaque. "Well, Miles, I am not sure that I want to be vice president," Gene said. But Gene said he would do "whatever I could do to be of most help to the ticket." Then again, Gene added, "it might be that I could do the ticket more good by not being on it."

Miles—believing what he wanted to believe—saw only one way to interpret the conversation. "His strategy is to keep all of the pressure on you that he can so that you will have to take him on the ticket," he wrote to Hubert.

He also tried to persuade Hubert that even though Gene "has shifted ground many times," Gene could be trusted, as demonstrated by their last few months of conversations. "Gene has never broken a confidence as between the three of us," Miles wrote.

Hubert and Gene met face-to-face one week before the convention, in Hubert's apartment in Washington.

Hubert told Gene that he could not part ways with the president on Vietnam but would be glad to accept a dovish plank if adopted by the delegates in Chicago.

Gene recognized that Hubert would in all likelihood win the nomination. He said that he would not pledge his support to Hubert at the convention—he wouldn't be able to control his supporters if he abandoned them so early—but would do so by mid-September.

And the running mate issue was finally put to rest.

Later, after the campaign was over, Gene would say that he'd never had any interest in the vice presidency in 1968. (He had said the same in 1964, although indications at the time were to the contrary.) Whatever the case now—and Gene may have been deeply ambivalent—time was running out. Gene told Hubert at their meeting that he would not accept the nomination for vice president. Hubert agreed there would be no more talk of that.

But Miles's role as emissary was far from done.

14

Sweeping Corporate Headquarters

The first thing Thursday morning—soon after A. H. Robins files in the Eighth Circuit on February 9, 1984—a clerk from the appeals court calls Judge Lord to request that he voluntarily halt all proceedings until the Eighth Circuit has a chance to rule. The judge agrees; the appeals court could easily issue a stay with the stroke of a pen if he refused to cooperate. We phone the special masters and tell them to stand down. In Minneapolis, where the deposition of William Forrest, the general counsel, is set to begin, I tell the attorneys and video techs in the adjacent courtroom to unplug.

After the rush of activity in the last couple of weeks, we have nothing to do but cool our heels.

In chambers, the judge and I take a closer look at the papers A. H. Robins filed with the appeals court: a motion for a stay and a petition for a writ of mandamus (a request for an appellate court to issue a directive to a lower court). A. H. Robins complains that it is being denied "due process of law," "a fair trial," and "an impartial tribunal"; that the judge is acting as "a partisan advocate" with "an unprecedented degree of hostility and bias"; and that the judge's discovery order of the previous day "completely emasculates the duly promulgated Federal Rules of Civil Procedure." A. H. Robins also cites the Eighth Circuit's decision removing the judge from the Reserve Mining case, a reminder—as if one is needed—of Judge Lord's past transgressions.

In short, there is plenty of rhetoric and rancor.

But, in substance, A. H. Robins's petition seems weak. The focus is the discovery: the production of documents and the Forrest deposition. (The company says it will also seek to disqualify the judge at a later date; typically, a motion for disqualification must be filed first with the trial court—

here, Judge Lord—and A. H. Robins hasn't done that yet.) Discovery, however, is generally within the discretion of the trial court. Recognizing this, no doubt, A. H. Robins tries to amp up its petition by highlighting the privilege issues, where a trial judge has less latitude. But as of yet Judge Lord has not ruled on whether any specific documents are, or are not, privileged. And not a single question, objectionable or not, has been asked in the Forrest deposition. To the judge, there doesn't seem to be anything set in stone for the Eighth Circuit to review.

The judge is agitated—just the thought of the Eighth Circuit is enough to provoke him—but he also can't help but chuckle. He thinks that A. H. Robins panicked—it was, after all, his far-reaching order for the production of documents, signed only yesterday, that precipitated this morning-after run to the appeals court—and pulled the trigger too soon.

Then again, the judge has lived through enough battles with the Eighth Circuit to know that, at least when he's involved, anything can happen.

This time, however, he doesn't have to wait long.

At day's end, about 5:00 p.m., the Eighth Circuit issues an order, signed by Chief Judge Donald Lay. It is an interim ruling that addresses only A. H. Robins's request for an immediate stay, which he denies. Judge Lay says that Judge Lord's discovery order is "couched in protective terms," with "no specified documents . . . nor specified questions to which objection has been made." He also says that the probability of A. H. Robins ultimately prevailing on its petition is "slight." But he sets an expedited hearing for the merits of the appeal: February 16, one week away.

We call it a day, with the Forrest deposition now set to begin tomorrow morning.

Soon after I get home, however, the judge calls. He is still worried that the Eighth Circuit might pull the rug out from under him at any moment and halt the ongoing discovery. There will be a panel of three to consider A. H. Robins's appellate petition; who knows, the judge tells me, which of his longtime antagonists will be sitting in judgment of him once again.

So the judge says that he is going to appoint a U.S. magistrate, Patrick J. McNulty, to supervise the discovery in his stead until the Eighth Circuit rules. The judge hopes that this will insure the discovery can continue without any interruption no matter what the Eighth Circuit does, even if his own involvement is sacrificed in the interim. This will also take the judge out of the line of fire—unable to create any new controversies—in the days leading up to the Eighth Circuit hearing.

The judge has already called Magistrate McNulty, who works out of Duluth, and asked him to drive to Minneapolis. He tells me that we need to have a written order formally appointing Magistrate McNulty ready to file as soon as the clerk's office opens tomorrow morning.

He says he'll be my wakeup call at 4:00 a.m.

The judge calls me as planned. We meet in chambers, with the early morning sky pitch black. The judge walks to a window and looks out at the office of the Faegre law firm just a few blocks away. He draws the curtains so the A. H. Robins lawyers—if they are up at this hour—can't see him at work. I get on the computer. The judge stands behind me and dictates:

> As the arguments against production of the documents exhaust themselves, the tribunal itself becomes the target. This court has tasted of this cup before; it has had its fill.

He doesn't have to explain the reference. Virtually every lawyer who ever heard of Judge Lord knows what happened in Reserve Mining.

When we're finished, Suze puts the order in final form. The judge signs on the last page and certifies the time in handwriting: "Time 7:31 AM." Keith walks down to the clerk's office to file it.

A few minutes later, Magistrate McNulty arrives. We all go to breakfast at the Sheraton Hotel next door. Shortly before 9:00 a.m. we return to chambers, where the judge and the magistrate don their robes.

The judge does not need to make an appearance in court today. Most judges would simply have their clerks place copies of the order at the counsel tables for the attorneys to read when they arrive. But this judge likes drama.

The lawyers, including Ciresi and Socha, are assembled in the courtroom for the start of the Forrest deposition. The judge enters from a door behind the bench, with Magistrate McNulty on his heels. Without a word, the judge and the magistrate seat themselves on two black leather chairs, side by side. Judge Lord, stern-faced, reads his order. Then he walks off, leaving Magistrate McNulty alone behind the bench.

"You may proceed," Magistrate McNulty says to Ciresi.

■ ■ ■ ■

Ciresi steps to the podium and starts in without missing a beat.

He runs through a series of questions to get a better sense of how the A. H. Robins law department files are organized, which might help the special masters as they begin their work in Richmond. ("If I were a young lawyer in your office, Mr. Forrest, and you wanted me to go retrieve these documents for you, what would you tell me? Where would I go?") He gets the name of Forrest's paralegal, Patricia Lashley, who, it turns out, knows more about the documents than anyone else at the company. (Ciresi requests her deposition.) He probes Forrest about the secret tail-string studies; Forrest confirms that outside consultants were retained by Slaughter's law firm, not A. H. Robins itself. Ciresi also returns to some favorite themes. ("How many cases of disease caused by a string had to occur before you felt it was significant? . . . If it caused disease in one woman?")

Forrest is polite and well spoken, with a soft Southern accent. He wears a dark suit and striped tie, his hair neatly combed. He looks like a grown-up Boy Scout. His nickname is "Skip."

Ciresi tries to shake him up.

It turns out, Forrest's own wife had used the Dalkon Shield. (E. C. Robins Senior volunteered that nugget during his deposition.) This is not something that Ciresi can let pass. Forrest, the top in-house lawyer for A. H. Robins, remains stoic as Ciresi bears down.

"Did she have any problems with the Dalkon Shield, sir?"

"Not that I know of, sir."

"You don't know of any infections or anything she had with the Dalkon Shield?"

"No. I didn't inquire into—this is a matter I thought between my wife and her gynecologist. . . . It was something we didn't discuss."

Ciresi senses there is more to the story.

"Did your wife ever have any operations to her reproductive organs after the use of the Dalkon Shield?"

"She eventually had a hysterectomy, yes."

There it is. Ciresi presses on.

"At or near the time the Dalkon Shield was removed, sir?"

"Sometime afterwards."

"Shortly after?"

"I don't recall."

Will jurors believe that? Ciresi wonders.

"Did her doctor advise her that her hysterectomy was in any way related to the Dalkon Shield?"

"Not that I know of, no, sir."

"Did you ever ask her that?"

"I don't recall."

Forrest maintains his composure, but his lips start to purse.

"Was your wife diagnosed as having pelvic inflammatory disease?"

"I don't know, Mr. Ciresi."

"And are you telling the ladies and gentlemen of the jury, Mr. Forrest,
that you and your wife have never had any discussion about whether or
not the Dalkon Shield played any part in her hysterectomy?"

"I had no reason to believe that it did."

Ciresi leans forward, grabs the podium, and presses on.

I am sitting in on the deposition this day. In fact, I am now assigned to
work under the direction of Magistrate McNulty, who requested that
Judge Lord loan me over since McNulty has no background in these cases.

This is Magistrate McNulty's shot at the big leagues—Judge Lord's call
was his ticket to the show—and he is determined to make the most of it.
He is in his sixties, a big man with a jowly face and a mane of receding
white hair. As a federal magistrate, his typical fare is handling miscellaneous pretrial motions for judges. Literally overnight, he has been plucked
out of his relative obscurity to preside over one of the biggest and most
contentious cases in the nation.

Magistrate McNulty knows that even though Judge Lord has stepped
aside, these are in the end Judge Lord's cases. I have noticed in other cases
that it is not uncommon for a magistrate to adopt the worldview of the
presiding judge. After all, a party who loses an issue before a magistrate can
seek review by that judge; the magistrate knows the best way to be affirmed
is to issue an order with which the presiding judge will agree. Magistrate
McNulty is not known as a champion of women. (In coming years, he will
get in hot water for his rulings in a sexual harassment suit brought by
women who worked at an Iron Range mine; among other things, McNulty
allowed the mining company to probe intimate details of the women's personal lives, including inquiries that could have come right out of the A. H.
Robins playbook: sexual relationships, abortions, rape, domestic abuse.)
But here, McNulty knows enough to follow Judge Lord's lead.

In the deposition, McNulty reclines in his chair, head tilted back, as he listens to the testimony. Socha objects, objects, objects. McNulty overrules him again and again, allowing Ciresi to roam free with personal questions about Forrest's wife.

"Was she having problems of a gynecological nature at the time the Dalkon Shield was removed?" Ciresi asks Forrest, when the deposition picks back up the following week.

Socha tries an objection. "I fail to see the relevance," he says, "of this subject matter which is highly personal."

"This entire lawsuit is highly personal, counsel," Magistrate McNulty says, as he orders Forrest to answer.

Ciresi asks Forrest whether he knows what his wife's gynecologist told her when the Dalkon Shield was inserted:

"Do you know whether she was asked *which way she wipes?*"

"Did you ask her whether her gynecologist inquired as to *how many sex partners* she had?"

"Did you ask her whether or not the gynecologist inquired into the *frequency of sex* that she had?"

"Did you ask her whether her gynecologist inquired whether or not she engaged in *anal or oral sex* at the time the Dalkon Shield was inserted?"

Forrest keeps his steady cool. He says those questions were between his wife and her doctor. When Ciresi draws the inevitable analogy to the questions that A. H. Robins asks women who bring claims against the company, Forrest stands behind his employer. "I think they are appropriate questions to be asked," he says. "And my wife might fairly be asked those questions I think in terms of litigation."

Later, Ciresi gets more personal. He asks Forrest a series of questions involving a hypothetical surgery on Forrest himself—on his scrotum. In Ciresi's imaginary scenario, the doctor tells Forrest that he has a choice of sutures. One is a monofilament and the other, like the Dalkon Shield, is an open-ended multifilament. The doctor tells Forrest that the multifilament suture wicks and might cause disease, in which case Forrest might lose his reproductive organs.

"And you've got your choice," Ciresi says, "between this multifilament one that can wick bacteria up the interior and may result in the loss of your penis or scrotum, and the . . . monofilament."

Socha objects to the hypothetical as argumentative and "totally irrelevant." As Socha argues his point, Ciresi turns around at the podium and looks back at his legal assistant, Ann Barcelow, who is taking notes at the counsel table. Ciresi and Barcelow have been friends since high school; Barcelow recently started to work at the law firm. Ciresi gives her a quick glance and a sly smile, then turns around as Magistrate McNulty overrules Socha's objection.

"Obviously, I am interested in a suture which does not entail my getting a disease or getting injured by it, yes, sir," says Forrest.

Ciresi returns to a familiar refrain but with a gender twist this time. "And it wouldn't make any difference to you if it caused disease in one man who lost his penis or a hundred or a thousand, would it, sir?"

Forrest pauses. "In terms of one person, I am not sure," he says. But as for himself, "I would be interested in it as an individual, yes, sir," he says.

"Sure," says Ciresi, "I am sure you would, sir."

■ ■ ■ ■

As the Forrest deposition proceeds, the special masters are on the ground in Richmond, rotating in and out of town.

Even with special masters, however, most of the work will still be done by A. H. Robins attorneys; the best the masters can do is to try to police the process. The company lawyers must locate potentially responsive documents in the various A. H. Robins departments; affix labels to the file drawers and boxes where these documents have been kept; review the documents for responsiveness and privilege; and log each document and number every page, with the first two digits of the number identifying the department or area within the company where the document was found, and the third digit identifying the box or file drawer. (The location where a document is found—which department, whose files—is often critical in piecing together the puzzle of who knew what and when.)

Throughout the process, A. H. Robins lawyers raise a stream of objections. They need to foot-drag, it seems, until they can get their hoped-for relief in the Eighth Circuit, even if their prospects have been dimmed by Judge Lay's denial of a stay. This leads to multiple calls to Magistrate McNulty, who is quick to lose his patience. And he is growing more suspicious about the document games.

In the Forrest deposition, for example, Ciresi asks about the August 1974 memo sent by then-president Zimmer asking key personnel to search for any letters, memos, or notes—*of particular interest are any references to "wicking"*—relating to the Dalkon Shield tail string. Forrest confirms that these documents were never provided to the FDA. "Not to my knowledge, no, sir," he says. He also testifies that he doesn't know what happened to the documents. "I don't recall putting that question to Mr. Zimmer."

Magistrate McNulty is anxious for the masters to find these wicking documents. With all eyes on him, he doesn't want to muff his opportunity.

McNulty also has Judge Lord huffing and puffing over his shoulder. The judge has stepped aside, but he hasn't tuned out—his bystander status only frustrates him more—and he hasn't avoided contact with Magistrate McNulty. (McNulty is sharing the judge's chambers while he is in Minneapolis.) The judge is fretful that the special masters—new to the case—will be hoodwinked in Richmond. He thinks I can help get to the bottom of things, given my growing knowledge of the case. (He starts telling people that if he were breeding bloodhounds, he would want some of my strain in there.) Magistrate McNulty, whether taking a hint or of his own accord, decides spur of the moment to dispatch me to Richmond.

"Pack your bags," he tells me, during a break in the Forrest deposition on Monday, February 13.

By day's end, I'm heading—unannounced to the lawyers—to Richmond. Magistrate McNulty has not given me any directives except to report what is going on and to make sure we search the desks and credenzas in the A. H. Robins law department. This type of assignment is not typical for a law clerk, to say the least. But while I'm new to the law, I've had a few years of experience as a reporter. The newsroom veterans taught me two basic lessons that apply anywhere: show no fear and stay close to the action. I've also learned how to dig out facts. (I'm not sure, however, that I even know what a credenza is; in the newsroom, all we had were cheap desks lined up row after row.)

First thing the next morning, I need to locate the action. Special Master Thompson won't be arriving until later in the day. So I track down Fribley in his hotel room.

"Where are you?" Fribley asks, when he answers the phone.

"In Richmond."

Long pause.

It's clear to me that Fribley needs instructions from the Virginia lawyers.

He says he'll get back to me and calls later to say that there will be a meeting at McGuire Woods, Slaughter's law firm in downtown Richmond, when Special Master Thompson arrives.

The main subject of the meeting, it turns out, is me. A pack of A. H. Robins lawyers, sitting around a conference table, demand that I leave town.

I gaze from lawyer to lawyer—all men, all white; I feel as if I have wandered into a frat house. I wonder how anyone could make the arguments that they (or their fellow A. H. Robins lawyers) pitch to judges and juries across the country. Some of them—especially the Minnesota lawyers— seem uncomfortable with the positions they must take on behalf of A. H. Robins, at least some of the time. (Throughout the proceedings, Judge Lord repeatedly goes out of his way to exonerate the Minnesota lawyers. "They have acted honorably with the evidence that was available to them," he will say.) In addition, the more senior lawyers—Slaughter and Cogar—seem to have the weight of the world on their shoulders and a fear of the consequences of their actions. But these workhorses, gathered around the table today, seem eager to strut their stuff. I'm not used to being in a roomful of suits like this. (The newsroom was not a men's-only club. And even among the men at the paper, few wore suits; we called one who did, "The Undertaker.") But I am not about to let these guys around the table spook me.

Special Master Thompson, however, says I should leave for the day because the argument about my presence is keeping them from addressing the document production. We call Minneapolis, and, to my surprise, McNulty agrees with Thompson.

That night, Magistrate McNulty, Special Master Thompson, and I speak again. Magistrate McNulty now confirms that he wants me involved. We have another conference call the next morning. McNulty tells the A. H. Robins lawyers that I am to participate fully in the production effort. The A. H. Robins lawyers are not happy, but that afternoon they take me and Special Master Thompson on a tour of the legal, medical, and insurance departments so we can see how the documents are kept in the ordinary course of business.

The next morning, Thursday, February 16, we gather again in the conference room at McGuire Woods and call Magistrate McNulty.

The A. H. Robins lawyers blow up.

For years, these lawyers have been making unilateral decisions about which documents to produce, per the standard practice in discovery. Now they face scrutiny and second-guessing, not only by special masters but also by a law clerk, whose only legal experience has been a few months by the side of a judge whom they consider hostile and biased.

The call starts with Gilbert (Bud) Schill Jr., one of Slaughter's partners, complaining that he doesn't want the special masters or me in the room when they review documents to determine if they are relevant. "There's no possible useful purpose, sir, by having people stare at you while you're trying to think," he says.

Magistrate McNulty says there shouldn't be that much to think about unless the lawyers are trying to come up with "narrow interpretations" of Judge Lord's order and reasons not to produce certain documents. In fact, he says, the order is expansive; "if there's a letter in there that says Dalkon Shield in any context, it's a document that must be produced," he says.

Schill begs to differ. "If it were that simple, we could have orangutans do it," he says.

But what really sets Schill off is Magistrate McNulty's directive that the special masters and I also spot-check documents that the A. H. Robins lawyers decide are not responsive. Schill focuses his attack on me. He says that the nonresponsive documents may contain information that is highly sensitive and unrelated to the Dalkon Shield litigation. He demands—if I am going to spot-check the documents—that I agree to "never accept a position with any law firm in the United States of America that has any cases against the A. H. Robins Company."

Yikes.

I am still not sure that I want to practice law when my clerkship ends. Plan A had been to return to journalism. But I have begun to rethink my future, as I watch the Dalkon Shield cases unfold. At this point, I certainly don't want to shut the door to every single law firm that is suing A. H. Robins, which, given the magnitude of the Dalkon Shield litigation, includes many of the best plaintiffs' firms in the country. I know that I wouldn't be able to work on Dalkon Shield cases, but it's common for law firms to set up ethical walls to shield former law clerks from involvement in any cases that were before their judges.

I stare at the phone and wait for Magistrate McNulty's response.

Yesterday, he wussed out and let the A. H. Robins lawyers kick me out of their office. Now his voice comes over the phone strong.

"That, to my mind, is a little bit ridiculous," he says to Schill. "I certainly am not going to force her to sign any kind of a relinquishment of employment rights on the basis of the fact that she's worked for the court."

Schill doesn't back down. "I want to make it clear if Ms. Walburn does wind up in one of these law firms, we will take appropriate action." He says he also objects, although less so, to the special masters spot-checking the documents.

I wait for Magistrate McNulty to stamp down on Schill again. But now he waivers. "That is fair enough," he says.

I wish the judge were here to protect my back. But any sign of weakness from me would send a bad signal. And, in fact, I am excited. The more the A. H. Robins lawyers carry on, the more certain I am that we are closing in on a buried trove of documents. I'm also kind of proud that the lawyers are incensed about my presence, as if I know enough about what I'm doing to pose a risk of uncovering their secrets. (In all probability, however, their attitude toward me is simply derivative of their view of Judge Lord.)

Schill calls the whole process "bizarre, illegal, and wrong in the extreme." But Magistrate McNulty makes it clear that the work will go forward, with me (whatever that might mean for my future employment) and the special masters. The talk turns to how to proceed for the rest of the day. Special Master Thompson says he is returning to Minneapolis. That leaves me by myself for a couple of days.

"Sounds to me like we have a new master," Schill complains.

■ ■ ■ ■

"We're now in the law department of Robins preparing to identify with labels the units that may contain responsive documents. By units is meant such things as file cabinet drawers, boxes, and receptacles where the documents are generally maintained."

Raymond Scannell, yet another of the Richmond lawyers, announces our arrival that afternoon to collect documents at the company offices. A. H. Robins has arranged for a court reporter to accompany our procession (we're also escorted by a couple of "young ladies," the only identification Scannell provides); as we walk, Scannell provides a running commentary, speaking in hushed tones as if he is an announcer at a golf tournament. "We expect to record on the record virtually everything you do," Schill had said before we began. "We're going to get all that down, because it is illegal."

"We're now in Ms. Lashley's office," Scannell says, as we move into the office of Forrest's paralegal. The young ladies gather loose files from the floor and windowsills and place them in boxes affixed with green fluorescent labels. The first digit of the labels is numbered "1" to identify the law department as the source, followed by "2," the number assigned to Lashley's documents. The young ladies also put green labels on Lashley's credenza—there it is!—and desk.

■ ■ ■ ■

Around the same time as we are marching through the law department, a three-judge panel of the Eighth Circuit, sitting in St. Paul where Judge Lay is based, is holding its hearing on A. H. Robins's appeal.

Robert Payne, another Richmond lawyer, starts things off with a stream-of-consciousness tirade against any and all things Miles Lord: the consolidated trial ("we are not ready to go to trial right now"); the loyalty oath ("we spent two days arguing that"); the prohibition on dirty questions ("that discovery has been fundamentally cut off on these cases"); and even the long-ago advertising for Dalkon Shield cases by the two plaintiffs' lawyers who are no longer involved in the litigation ("one of the reasons Minnesota has so many cases is because of advertising . . . and it isn't our fault that they are all here"). Payne also delivers a defense of the Dalkon Shield, telling the appellate judges that A. H. Robins has won over half of the cases that have been tried to verdict and that there is "a large body of opinion" that the Dalkon Shield is not defective.

The three judges—Chief Judge Lay (appointed by LBJ and known as an intellectual and "unapologetic liberal"); Judge Pasco Bowman (on the bench only one year, appointed by President Reagan); and Judge Gerald Heaney from Duluth (another LBJ appointee and DFL stalwart from the early days, but with whom Judge Lord has clashed in intraparty feuds)— hardly seem to know what to make of it all.

"It's a very confusing thing, you've convinced us of that," one of the judges says.

Payne also complains about how Judge Lord is attempting to reduce the backlog of Dalkon Shield cases. (That's a bad thing? I wonder when I read the transcript later.) Payne quotes Judge Lord from one of the hearings:

> Certainly what I am attempting to do here and give herald to is a system whereby some 5,000 cases—which threaten to tie up the federal courts if they try each one of them for three months—can be resolved.

"That's not his charter," Payne tells the Eighth Circuit. "It's beyond his power."

Payne is no less agitated when he addresses discovery, the only issue that A. H. Robins raised in its appellate petition and therefore the only issue properly before the Eighth Circuit. He is particularly incensed about paragraph J of Judge Lord's February 8 order, which requires the production of studies of the Dalkon Shield conducted by experts retained for the litigation. "Can I ask you to think for a minute about paragraph J?" Payne says. "Lawyers are going to be afraid to go and get written reports from experts. . . . They want us to quit litigating simply because there may be somebody who gave us an adverse opinion." He is also beside himself when he talks about the special masters, or, as he puts it, "this master stuff that's going on down there."

He takes a shot at me, too. "A law clerk is here out of law school," he says. "She is going to go back and supervise the whole process."

"You wouldn't believe what's happening," he sums up for the panel.

One of the Eighth Circuit judges tries to focus Payne and asks him to be "very very specific now on exactly what it is you want us to do today."

Payne gets to the point. "Stop the discovery," he says.

When Payne sits down, Dale Larson, calm and collected, argues for the plaintiffs. He frames the issue simply: an attempt by A. H. Robins to overturn a preliminary discovery order. It would be virtually unheard of for an appellate court to take action at this juncture, he says, when no specific documents have been ordered produced.

But the Eighth Circuit judges pepper Larson with skeptical questions and comments. The judges point out that there was "prolonged discovery" in the MDL; they note that Judge Lord ordered discovery "that no other judge in this district has thought was even reasonably necessary"; and they wonder "why at this point in time do we expand [this discovery] beyond all comprehension." One of the judges on the panel—taking note of Judge Lord's damn-the-torpedoes reputation—assumes that the plaintiffs "probably didn't even ask" for the discovery. "Yes, Your Honor, we did," Larson tries to assure him.

The judges also seem concerned about the consolidated trial, even though that issue was not included in A. H. Robins's petition. They ask question after question about the trial and pick up on Payne's criticism of Judge Lord for trying to break the logjam. "None of the other judges have consolidated their cases," one judge points out.

In the end, it is impossible to tell how the Eighth Circuit will rule. The judges seem to recognize that the discovery issue is not ripe. At the same time, however, they are clearly not happy with Judge Lord and seem to want this whole mess to go away. At the close of the hearing, they request that the attorneys remain in the courtroom to try to settle the remaining cases.

The attorneys stay behind. Soon several more cases settle.

Two cases remain, however. They are the two women represented by RZLK, who continue to hold out.

On the same day as the Eighth Circuit argument, A. H. Robins also files its motion to disqualify Judge Lord, just in case nothing else works to extricate the company from its plight. The basis for the motion, A. H. Robins says, is the judge's bias against the company. (A. H. Robins also cites the judge's broadside against all corporations from his Council of Churches speech in 1981.) The motion is filed with Judge Lord, per the proper procedure. Everyone assumes that the judge will deny the request. But that could give A. H. Robins a second shot in the Eighth Circuit if the company is not successful as a result of today's hearing.

■ ■ ■ ■

As the week comes to an end, I fly back to Minneapolis for the weekend of February 18 and 19. I spend most of my time in chambers: I clean up work on other cases assigned to me, fill in Keith on the events in Richmond, and slap fluorescent green document labels all over my desk and chair. Then it's time to head back to Richmond on Monday morning, February 20.

We are moving at a snail's pace. The A. H. Robins lawyers are now polite and courteous but seem to be stalling for time, hoping that the Eighth

Circuit will pull the plug. As a result, Special Master Bartsh, on site this week, and I spend our days listening to A. H. Robins lawyers quibble about the minutiae of production. I'm amazed that partners from a major law firm would spend their time in these types of wearisome discussions: how to number the documents; how to staple or clip the documents; how to handle multiple folders within an expandable file; and, most of all, what constitutes a "document" (expense reports? court pleadings? duplicates?).

"A day-to-day and hour-by-hour process of definition, of redefinition, of defining and refining, further redefinition, and of discussions," as Magistrate McNulty describes it.

The special masters and I are supposedly there to insure the integrity of the process. (At one point, Schill asks how his team should proceed when the masters and I take a break to go to the bathroom.) But this seems to be a terribly wasteful effort. The A. H. Robins lawyers—at least one or more of them—presumably know where the hot documents are located. They could turn them over in minutes, I'm sure. And no matter how diligent the special masters and I are, we are not in a position to find documents that A. H. Robins wants to keep hidden. We don't even know where the documents are physically located: At A. H. Robins headquarters? In which departments? Or at A. H. Robins law firms? Which law firms of the one hundred or so? What if the documents have been moved to a warehouse who knows where, or to a lawyer's basement or garage, or someplace else? In the end, discovery is still an honor system. That is not to say there are no benefits to our presence in Richmond. In certain respects, we are playing a game of chicken. Our mere presence—and the spot checking—might be enough to prompt the lawyers into being more forthcoming.

Still, after a few more days of this, I've had enough. There's not much I can do here. I head back to Minneapolis the night of Wednesday, February 22, just in time for the ruling from the Eighth Circuit.

15

Election, 1968

The Democratic National Convention opened in Chicago on August 26, 1968. Hubert Humphrey had a commanding lead in delegates but was nervous. He worried that LBJ might swoop in and recant his withdrawal from the race. He worried that Edward Kennedy would also seek the nomination. He worried that Southern delegates would bolt from his camp.

The real threat, as it turned out, came from the streets.

An army of antiwar protesters converged on Chicago. Mayor Richard Daley, the old-time boss who ruled the city, prepared for battle. A combined force of thirty thousand—Chicago police, National Guardsmen, U.S. Army troops, and Secret Service agents—was mobilized and armed with mace, tear gas, flamethrowers, bazookas. The convention hall was surrounded by barbed-wire fences, its main doors bulletproofed. Thousands of antiwar protesters amassed in Grant Park, directly across from the convention headquarters of the Humphrey and McCarthy campaigns, both in the Conrad Hilton hotel.

Miles arrived at the Conrad Hilton.

On Wednesday, August 28, the night the nomination would be made, Miles went to Hubert's suite on the twenty-fifth floor of the hotel. He proposed that Hubert cross the street and talk to the demonstrators to ease the tensions. (Miles had done so himself, at the urging of his daughter Priscilla, and thought that most of the protesters seemed "rather amiable, decent, and ordinary, a little bit hippy-type but not excessively so.") The idea landed with "a thud," Miles would say. "Hubert's aides and the Secret Service contended my plan was too dangerous for the vice president, that it risked him getting killed."

As an alternative, Miles suggested setting speakers up on the outside of the hotel so Hubert could address the crowd from a safe distance. That went nowhere, too.

Miles had one final idea.

He asked Hubert if he could take the Humphrey children to meet with the protesters. Hubert agreed but requested that Miles also take along George McGovern's kids. Both Hubert and Miles were friends with the senator from South Dakota. (On occasion, McGovern joined Hubert and Miles on trips to the hunting lodge in Georgia.) McGovern was an outspoken dove and only two weeks before the convention had announced he was also seeking the nomination. He had no chance to win but thought he might be able to unite the feuding factions of the party, doves and hawks, at the close of the convention. When Miles found him in the hotel, he agreed with the plan to have his children cross the street.

But McGovern wanted Gene's kids to go along, too. Miles went to the twenty-third floor of the hotel and ran into Gene coming out of his room. Gene said no.

Miles was out of ideas.

He "damn near" went home to Minneapolis. "You didn't have to have much imagination to be able to foresee what was going to happen," he would say.

The first skirmish in the streets came not long before the nominations and balloting for president were set to begin. By 7:00 p.m., tear gas was seeping into hotel suites. Soon after, police charged the crowd in Grant Park, clubbed demonstrators to the ground, dragged them to patrol wagons, beat innocent bystanders, and pushed onlookers through the glass windows of the Conrad Hilton.

Demonstrators chanted: "The whole world is watching! The whole world is watching!" Newscasts played the scenes on television, over and over and over.

On the fifteenth floor of the hotel, the base of McCarthy's staff operations, volunteers set up an emergency first-aid center. Gene rushed there as the wounded—bruised, bleeding, dazed—were carried in. (Early the next morning, police also raided that floor and beat McCarthy supporters with billy clubs.)

On the twenty-fifth floor, Hubert wept.

Shortly before midnight, Hubert Horatio Humphrey went over the top on the first ballot—it wasn't even close—and became the first Minnesotan to ever receive the nomination of a major party for president.

Miles rode a bus with the Humphrey family entourage back from the convention hall that night. National Guard troops ringed the hotel. When Miles got off the bus to speak with the troops and walk across their line, a guardsman whacked him in the head with the butt of a rifle. Miles fell to the ground. As he staggered up, "one of the little hippies," as Miles called the demonstrators, "gave me the shoulder and knocked me on my duff again."

Once again, it was Miles in the middle, this time between the young soldiers and the young protesters.

Hubert accepted the nomination the following day and chose Senator Edmund Muskie from Maine as his running mate. George McGovern joined them on the platform in the convention hall in a show of party unity. Gene McCarthy declined to do so.

Instead, earlier that day Gene walked to Grant Park to address, as he called the crowd, "the government in exile."

It had been twenty years since Hubert, as a young upstart, had captivated the nation with his call at the Democratic National Convention in Philadelphia—*there will be no hedging and there will be no watering down*—for civil rights. Now Hubert was beholden to the establishment, and his fellow Minnesotan Gene McCarthy had assumed the mantle of the idealistic insurgent.

The Democratic Party was torn apart and in shambles. Hubert stood at a mere 30 percent in the polls. That put him closer to third-party candidate George Wallace, the former governor of Alabama—"segregation now, segregation tomorrow, and segregation forever"—than to Richard Nixon.

The general election was only a little more than two months away.

■ ■ ■ ■

Miles turned to a new mission: procuring Gene's endorsement of Hubert.

Miles implored Gene.

Gene was unmoved. He left for a vacation in the south of France. When he returned, he covered the World Series for *Life* magazine.

"No one completely understands Eugene McCarthy," wrote Theodore

White, in one of his classic *Making of the President* books. "He belonged to no one . . . and lived by truths and perceptions of his own soul."

Hubert, meanwhile, was absorbing unprecedented abuse on the campaign trail. Miles saw it firsthand, as he continued to travel with the candidate. On one trip, in Boston in September, Miles watched as Hubert—close to tears—tried to speak as hundreds of students screamed:

"Sellout! Sellout! Sellout!"

"Bullshit! Bullshit! Bullshit!"

"Dump the Hump! Dump the Hump! Dump the Hump!"

Everywhere Hubert went, it was the same. He was booed, heckled, jeered. Protesters threw urine on him, spit on his wife, and screamed obscenities. A "public humiliation that no major candidate had ever known," wrote White.

Hubert's position on the war was the most polarizing issue but not his only problem. His campaign organization had come out of Chicago in disarray. (There was some talk about turning over the organizational command to Orville Freeman, who had run Hubert's earliest campaigns in Minnesota, but in the end he was relegated to a lesser role.) Worst of all, Hubert had subjugated himself to an execrated, lame-duck president and lost his sense of self.

Miles pleaded with Hubert to resurrect his true self and, as Miles put it in one note, "show the people of America . . . your goodness glands."

On a campaign plane one day, Miles "shooed" away Hubert's staff. "Hubert, you're being taken over by position papers," Miles said. "All these professors and eggheads are trying to tell you how to run your campaign. . . . Quit reading those speeches. Go back to the days when you were first campaigning for the Senate and mayor of Minneapolis. Put some passion into it and talk about the little guy."

Hubert broke free, at last, in late September, in a speech in Salt Lake City, when he called for a halt to the bombing of North Vietnam and an immediate cease-fire and withdrawal of all troops. This single act changed everything. Overnight, the demonstrators virtually disappeared and stayed away for the rest of the campaign. "The goddam [speech] had a magical effect," said one aide. Instead of jeers, there were cheering crowds.

Hubert was liberated, his own man, and felt "good inside, for the first time," he told reporters. He found his voice—and began to rise in the polls.

■ ■ ■ ■

Miles doubled down on Gene.

Time and again, Miles would believe that Gene was ready to announce his support for Hubert. Time and again, it was false hope.

One day, Miles and Gene met for lunch. Gene brought along his psychiatrist friend (which irked Miles to no end), and laid out his ever-changing—and impossible—conditions for endorsing Hubert.

Miles tried every appeal. He told Gene that Hubert desperately needed his help, especially in California. He told Gene that the country deserved better "than to have him play any part" in electing Richard Nixon, who was breezing along in the campaign with his call for "law and order" and promise of a "secret plan" to end the war in Vietnam. He tried bonding with Gene over their shared annoyance with Orville Freeman, who had criticized Gene—attacking him as an appeaser—on the campaign trail. (Gene told Miles that "I was one of the better guys," Miles wrote to Hubert, "because anybody that didn't like Orville Freeman couldn't be all bad.") Miles even tried to induce Gene with money. "I suggested to him that now would be an appropriate time to pay his campaign deficit," Miles wrote Hubert.

Gene was unmoved.

The lunch ended, and, as they walked from the restaurant, Gene teased Miles about a federal judge being involved in politics. Miles replied that if Gene promised to support Hubert, "I would resign before we reached the next corner."

As October faded and the November 5 election loomed, Miles spoke with Gene again and again: on the phone, in person, in Minneapolis, in Washington. After starting the year with a grand vision of glory—Hubert and Gene together, on the campaign trail and in the White House—Miles was now begging one old friend to simply announce that he supported his longtime comrade against a Republican candidate who epitomized the antithesis of everything the three men had stood for all their lives. Miles's notes to Hubert were dire:

> The only possible endorsement he will give you is one which will hurt you more than it helps you.

> He foresees little opportunity for reconciliation.

Indeed, Miles told Gene that waiting for his endorsement of Hubert was "like waiting for the 'hang man.'"

One day, when Gene was in Minnesota, Miles and Gene met for breakfast and then spent a few more hours together, including an impromptu stop at Augsburg College, a small Lutheran school in Minneapolis. A reporter from the *Minneapolis Tribune* was at the gathering and reported, in the next day's paper, McCarthy's comments about efforts "to convince him that he should support the Vice-President." (The paper, however, failed to mention Miles.) The article described McCarthy as "aloof" and "with little apparent concern" about polls indicating a victory for Nixon in two weeks. Indeed, McCarthy declined to say whether he preferred Humphrey to Nixon, saying only that George Wallace was the least desirable of the three candidates.

Still, Miles never gave up. He tried psychoanalyzing Gene. (He thought Gene might be afflicted with "disassociative reaction." He also thought Gene was more perturbed by Hubert's failure to stand up to LBJ than by their differences on the war.) He tried scolding Gene. He told Gene that Minnesotans were directing "four-letter words at him." Miles tried a soft approach too, telling Gene in one conversation that he was going to visit Washington because "you need a friend to sweeten you up."

Miles finally reached the point, however, where he wrote Hubert that "I think he is dedicated to your destruction." Miles added that although Gene may endorse Hubert, "he will do it in such a manner as to cause you the maximum of harm and give you the least of help."

But Miles swung hopeful in one of his last conversations with Gene before the election. "Eugene is going to support you in a much better manner than I originally anticipated," Miles told Hubert. "I am getting kind of optimistic."

Miles's hope was misplaced. Gene did not endorse Hubert until October 29, only one week before the election. The announcement was late, and, as Hubert would write, "less than enthusiastic."

Others would call it "backhanded," "lukewarm," and "limp."

Indeed, although Gene announced that he would be voting for Hubert and recommended that his supporters do the same, he also declared that Hubert's position on the principal issues of the campaign—including ending the war in Vietnam and reforming the Democratic Party—"falls far short of what I think it should be." Gene also made it clear that his endorsement was "in no way intended to reinstate me in the good graces of the Democratic Party leaders, nor in any way to suggest my having forgotten or condoned the things that happened both before Chicago and at Chicago." He ended by announcing that he would not seek the nomination of the Democratic Party for president in 1972 and that, in fact, he would not seek reelection to the Senate when his term ended in two years.

■ ■ ■ ■

By election day, against all adversities, pollsters showed Hubert closing the gap and in one major poll even ahead of Nixon.

That night, as the voting booths closed, Hubert and his family and a few friends, Miles included, gathered in a fourteenth-floor suite at the Leamington Hotel in downtown Minneapolis. A crowd of well-wishers and campaign workers congregated downstairs in the Hall of States. The early returns were encouraging.

"By golly, we might do it!" Hubert exclaimed.

But by midnight, his dream was fading. By 2:00 a.m., Hubert knew all was lost. He held out hope for a miracle, however, and did not make a concession speech. He went to sleep.

By the time he awoke, the morning after election day, it was over.

Hubert went to address his supporters in the ballroom. He stood at the podium, Muriel by his side. His voice was flush with conviction, his eyes shimmered with tears, and his remarks were brief (especially for Hubert) and gracious: "I shall continue my personal commitment to the cause of human rights, of peace, and to the betterment of man," he said. He faltered, just a bit, when he neared the end.

"I have done my best . . . . I have lost."

The margin of defeat was less than one tiny percentage point: 43.4 percent for Nixon to 42.7 percent for Humphrey (and 13.5 percent for Wallace).

Many blamed Gene, saying that just the barest effort by him—an earlier and more robust endorsement, a little help in California and maybe one or two other states—would have made all the difference.

Hubert also thought that Gene could have "turned it." But he put much of the blame on himself. After four years as vice president, "I had lost some of my personal identity and personal forcefulness," he would say. "It would have been better that I stood my ground and remembered that I was fighting for the highest office in the land."

Gene, in the days after the election, placed the culpability squarely on Hubert for not breaking with the president earlier. Over time, however, Gene softened. He wrote a short essay, "Memories of Hubert," in which he blamed the defeat not on Hubert but on the office of the vice presidency, which, Gene wrote, had stripped Hubert of his political independence. Gene called Hubert "a politician too good to be vice president." In his memoir, he called Hubert's loss "just short of tragedy."

Indeed, Gene came to appreciate Hubert—who never faltered in his friendship, even as others would not be nearly as forgiving—as never before. "Hubert was loyal to his friends," Gene wrote, "to those who helped him, and those who hurt him."

Miles also remained loyal to Gene, even after Gene committed the ultimate sin of forsaking Hubert when Hubert needed him most. (Not so Maxine. Shortly after the election, when Gene visited their Christmas Lake home, "Maxine gave him a piece of her mind," Miles would say. "Gene was contrite," Miles remembered, "politely listening to Maxine vent.")

Perhaps Miles was following the lead of Hubert. "You'd think Hubert would call Gene a son-of-a-bitch or something," Miles said. "But Hubert had a capacity not to be bitter."

Miles, of course, was also indebted to Gene. He always remembered that Gene had stood by him—*steadfast*—when his appointments as U.S. attorney and federal judge were on the line.

Miles would also credit Gene with being right about the war.

But more than anything, perhaps, Miles admired Gene as a lone crusader who strode forward when no one else dared. It had also been what bonded Miles to Hubert decades before.

■ ■ ■ ■

The loss shattered Hubert. He had been defeated by a man who, he believed, lacked the requisite spirit and heart—and greatness—to be president. "In the eyes of the American people," Hubert would say, "I am not as good as Richard Nixon." And he had been deserted by so many in his own party, not only Gene McCarthy but also others whom he had thought of as allies and friends.

And he had come so close.

Miles took it upon himself to help Hubert through the pain of defeat. These days, especially, he believed that some good-natured ribbing was in order.

One day, Miles and Hubert and their wives went for a relaxing day-cruise down the St. Croix River, on the Minnesota-Wisconsin border, in a deluxe boat owned by a local businessman. Before boarding, Miles razzed Hubert. "Humphrey, you've been away for a long time," Miles said. "People have forgotten about you." Miles added that he—Miles Lord— was now more popular than Hubert and that they should put this to the test by seeing how many people recognized each of them as they floated downstream.

The shouts rang out from other boats: "Judge Lord!" "Judge Lord!" "Judge Lord!"

Finally, Miles leaned over the side of their boat and pulled up a large sign that he had asked the crew to hang before they left shore: "Miles Lord is on board, give him a hail."

Gradually, Hubert started to perk up.

One night, he invited Miles to accompany him to a speaking engagement in the Twin Cities. He introduced Miles to the audience and announced that he was going to take him to the opera that night. "The last time Miles had any culture was when he attended the Crosby Iron Range Glee Club Chorus in 1933," he told the crowd. After the speech, Hubert took Miles to a restaurant, where Hubert had arranged for opera and orchestra members to perform just for them and one other guest. The two friends stayed out until 4:00 a.m., which went over none too well at their respective homes. After that, Miles said, "Maxine and Muriel told us that we couldn't play together for six months."

For the first time in twenty-three years, Hubert was out of public office. He went back to Minnesota to teach but wanted to return to the Senate, a place he had always loved. And there should be an open seat soon, as Gene McCarthy had already announced he would not seek reelection when his term expired in 1970.

Except that Gene was now hedging.

He was not in a beneficent frame of mind. He was taking substantial abuse from party regulars for what he did—and didn't do—for Hubert during the presidential campaign. "If they keep yelling at me," Gene told Miles, "I will come back and run, just to beat them."

But although Gene held out for some months, he ultimately stepped aside. Hubert won the seat, to no one's surprise, and returned to Washington, joining Walter Mondale as Minnesota's second senator.

Gene commemorated his departure from the Senate at a gathering in Georgetown, where he read from his new book of poetry:

> *I am alone*
> *in the land of the aardvarks.*
> *I am walking west*
> *all the aardvarks are going east.*

He withdrew from mainstream politics—he no longer believed either party was worthy—and embarked on a succession of increasingly tenuous, and bewildering, runs for president as a third-party candidate. He separated from Abigail, his wife of more than two decades, moved to the foothills of the Blue Ridge Mountains, and spent his years teaching, lecturing, and writing.

But he would forever remain an enduring symbol of the peace movement and of the potency of grassroots politics.

And although many Democrats were disillusioned with Gene for his actions in 1968 and beyond, some of the core group of old DFLers—including Hubert and Miles—remained largely true. Walter Mondale also organized a farewell tribute in the Senate and praised Gene's 1968 insurgency: "For this act of singular courage, every member of this body, every citizen of the nation, and, indeed, virtually everyone in the world owes him an enormous debt."

Hubert also continued for years to invite Gene to lunch in the Senate, and they also met on occasion to drink and reminisce about the glory days of the DFL.

■ ■ ■ ■

After Hubert returned to Washington, Miles continued his involvement in politics, with Hubert calling him often, multiple times on some days. Before long, however, some of Miles's old friends in the FBI started to make comments that they knew about his private conversations.

Miles believed that Richard Nixon was tapping their phone calls.

He told Hubert that he didn't want to talk about politics over the phone anymore. Miles—and his judgeship—had escaped unscathed despite his daring-do in the 1968 presidential campaign, but he was no longer willing to so brazenly flout the ethical prohibitions.

Hubert continued the calls for a while, but Miles was adamant.

"The things Hubert was saying were not in themselves crooked, corrupt, or illegal," Miles said later, but "a federal judge shouldn't be in that kind of thing." So Miles stepped back from most—but not all, it was in his blood—of his active politicking.

Finally, he would turn his full attention to his courtroom.

Throughout the vortex of 1968, he had seen how Hubert was crushed by his failure to live up to the courage of his convictions. He also saw how Gene strode forward to claim his moment in history, much as Hubert had two decades earlier in 1948.

The path for him to take on the bench was clear.

16

The Brink of Settlement

The order issued by the Eighth Circuit on February 23 packs a jolt, and not in the way intended by A. H. Robins. The court finds that Judge Lord acted within his discretion and that, in any event, appellate review of his discovery orders would be premature since there are not yet any rulings on claims of privilege. The Eighth Circuit also directs that all discovery be completed.

Within fifteen days.

Judge Lord had never imposed a deadline for production of the documents, and the A. H. Robins lawyers, in turn, had been taking full advantage of that void. To date, not a single document has progressed through the pipeline. Not one page has been produced to the plaintiffs or even turned over to the special masters for review, even though mountains of documents need to be to be processed; laid end to end, Slaughter tells the press, the file drawers of potentially responsive documents would stretch more than a mile. Under normal circumstances, a production of this magnitude would take at least months and, more likely, much longer.

At the same time, however, the Eighth Circuit also displays its impatience with Judge Lord's approach to—and indefinite delay of—the trial. The appeals court orders the trial to start within thirty days, with a new jury due to concerns that the jurors-in-waiting have been exposed to too much publicity about the case. The court says it "neither condones nor disapproves" of a consolidated trial of all the cases at one time; it will rule on this issue only in any final review, in other words, only after trial. That raises the prospect of going through the entire trial, only to be ordered by the Eighth Circuit, after the fact, to start all over again.

Still, Judge Lord has prevailed on his discovery orders, the only issue directly before the Eighth Circuit at this time.

Do the Eighth Circuit judges—typically far removed from the nitty-gritty of discovery—know the implications of their fifteen-day deadline for documents?

Who knows? Who cares? Not Judge Lord.

After two weeks on the sidelines, he takes off like a shot. Within hours, he issues two orders of his own.

First, he denies the A. H. Robins motion to disqualify him in a single sentence: "Defendant's motion for disqualification and recusal of the undersigned judge is hereby denied as being insufficient and untimely."

Then he opens the door for the plaintiffs to depose any of the lawyers from the Richmond law firms with knowledge of the location of the documents. As practical as this seems to a layperson—the people who know where the documents are should fess up—this is virtually unheard of. Outside attorneys view their knowledge as sacrosanct, and this belief is rarely called into question, even though they often know more than anyone else (as they typically oversee the collection of documents in litigation). In the judge's view, this is factual information—not legal strategy or opinions—and not privileged.

The A. H. Robins lawyers think about their options. The judge's order for the depositions of outside counsel would be sure to raise eyebrows in the Eighth Circuit. But these depositions haven't started yet, and A. H. Robins was just slapped down for prematurely seeking review of other discovery. Another issue—the disqualification of Judge Lord—is procedurally ripe for appellate review now that the judge has denied A. H. Robins's motion for recusal. Still, the Eighth Circuit might not welcome another appeal so close on the heels of the first. And the lawyers may now be gun-shy, as A. H. Robins not only lost in its first foray to the Eighth Circuit but was also hit by the backfire of the fifteen-day deadline.

So A. H. Robins holds off—for now—on another petition for appellate review.

■ ■ ■ ■

Friday, February 24 is the first full day in the post–Eighth Circuit order world.

Special Master Bartsh (with a gaggle of lawyers on the phone with him in Richmond) makes multiple calls to Judge Lord (with another crowd of lawyers in his Minneapolis chambers) in an effort to arrive at a streamlined process for producing the documents. "My own view of discovery is that about 99 percent of documents produced are just an exercise in printing paper," the judge says. He asks Roger Brosnahan, who is arguing for the plaintiffs today, to list the documents he wants in order of importance.

"We want the wicking documents, we want the tests, we want the reports by consultants," Brosnahan says.

With the clock ticking, the judge doesn't want to play pin the tail on the donkey any more. The depositions of the lawyers have not yet been scheduled, so the judge tells Special Master Bartsh to ask Patricia Lashley—Forrest's paralegal—to locate these documents. Or, the judge says, just ask the A. H. Robins lawyers in Richmond. "It's not up to you to go around to the various parts of A. H. Robins," he says to Bartsh. "You have about seven lawyers sitting there, and at least one of them knows where every document is concerning wicking, and just ask them to produce those documents."

"I think it can be done," the judge says, "and I direct that it be done."

But by later that day, A. H. Robins pushes the settlement discussions to the brink of a deal.

Two lawyers—Dale Larson for the plaintiffs and Michael Berens for A. H. Robins, from the Oppenheimer firm in St. Paul—call on the judge in chambers on Friday afternoon to deliver the news that a final settlement is within reach.

Larson and Berens lay out the contours of the deal for the judge.

In most settlements, all discovery is halted and often any documents that have been produced must be destroyed or returned to the defendant. But here, the settlement agreement will require the ongoing production of documents per Judge Lord's order of February 8, although without a deadline and without the judge's supervision, as he will no longer have any cases before him. The newly produced documents will be placed in a library at A. H. Robins headquarters and made available for review by all plaintiffs' attorneys around the country.

The fact that A. H. Robins has agreed to these terms is an unmistakable indication of its desperation to break free from Judge Lord and gain some breathing room.

Earlier, when the judge was first getting into these cases, he would have been fine with this deal. Now, however, he has taken this litigation on as a personal crusade.

But the judge doesn't have the authority to nix the settlement even if he wants to, as that is typically a private matter between the parties. There are, however, some cases where judicial intervention is appropriate, for example, a class action, where a judge has an affirmative duty to approve or disprove the terms of any settlement in order to protect class members. Here, while the Dalkon Shield cases are not a class action, there are some similarities as there are thousands of women with claims. And the proposed settlement agreement includes provisions for the ongoing production of documents to benefit all of the women—somewhat akin to, but not formally, injunctive relief, which may also allow for judicial intercession.

At a minimum, Judge Lord wants to insure that A. H. Robins will not be able in the future to squirm out of the terms of the deal that require ongoing discovery. He tells Larson and Berens that he wants three top A. H. Robins officers to appear before him to ratify the agreement: E. C. Robins Senior, the chairman of the board; Skip Forrest, the general counsel; and Dr. Clark, the retired medical director. The judge's plan is to have these men sign the settlement agreement in open court, so there will be no opportunity to later renege. He's not sure that he has the authority to order them to appear, but he can at least try.

Larson and Berens call Slaughter from chambers and then leave to work out the final particulars of the deal. The judge calls the special masters to insure that they will continue the document search in Richmond—pushing the pace—over the weekend, in the few days left to advance the discovery.

Then the judge gets in his car to drive home.

He pulls out his pocket recorder—I've learned by now that he loves to dictate when he drives—and begins a speech to Senior and his retinue for when they appear in his courtroom.

He wants the officers to hear his view of the facts so they will not be able to claim ignorance—*what did they know? when did they know it?*—as the litigation continues in other cases. "I didn't want them ever again to say they did not know," he would say later. He also hopes to persuade them to abandon the company's fight-at-all-costs strategy and to recall the Dalkon Shield.

With one hand on the steering wheel and the other holding up his recorder, the judge lets loose. "Rise you sons of bitches," he growls, "and hear these words."

The judge plays the tape for Maxine when he gets home. She doesn't like the idea of a speech at all and certainly not this one.

But the judge is undeterred.

He meets with me in chambers Saturday morning to work on the draft. I listen to his recording. *Rise you sons of bitches.* . . . The judge looks at me. "Maybe we should tone it down a bit," I offer. We assume our familiar posts. I type away on Exxie; the judge paces over my shoulder. We hammer away all day.

The next day, Sunday, I drive out to the judge's house with a printout. We read over the draft and are pretty pleased with ourselves. Then Maxine takes a look. She shakes her head. She stares me down. She is clearly the keeper of propriety in this household—and looks the part with her conservative attire and bouffant hairdo—and has her hands full with the judge himself, let alone his new sidekick. There is no doubt she holds me responsible for encouraging the judge to tempt trouble once again.

The judge listens as Maxine vetoes some of the lines. But he won't be stopped. He tells me to head back to chambers and polish up the final version.

That same weekend, Special Master Bartsh is working fourteen-hour days, 8:00 a.m. to 10:00 p.m., at the A. H. Robins offices, with Special Master Thompson also joining him on Saturday. A full retinue of A. H. Robins lawyers—primarily young associates from McGuire Woods—is also on site reviewing documents. There is no question people are working very hard. But despite the judge's directive, the A. H. Robins lawyers are not forced to lead the way to the key documents. That, as I am learning, is easier said than done. Instead, there is a show of hubbub and bustle—"too many people running around in too many places," the judge says—while most likely the lawyers (and perhaps executives) with superior knowledge sit backstage.

Meanwhile, the top lawyers from both sides continue to hash out the terms of the final settlement over the weekend.

But they reach an impasse.

Larson and Ciresi do not believe that A. H. Robins is offering sufficient assurance that documents in the possession of the Richmond law firms—

and covered by the judge's order of February 8—will be protected from destruction.

In chambers on Monday morning, February 27, Slaughter tells the judge that the attorneys have given up on settlement. The judge says that's too bad because he and I worked over the weekend on some things he wanted to say to the three A. H. Robins executives. The judge looks at me; I smile and nod my head.

It's back into the courtroom and the business of the documents.

Larson comes out firing.

He and Ciresi are now more focused than ever on documents that may be in the possession of two key law firms: McGuire Woods (Slaughter's firm) and Mays Valentine (Cogar's). He asks the judge to direct the special masters—now at work in the A. H. Robins offices—to move their search to the law firms. He asks for the immediate depositions of Slaughter and Cogar, as well as Patricia Lashley. He also asks for a protective order to prevent the destruction of any documents.

The judge demands that only one lawyer from A. H. Robins respond. Socha steps to the fore.

Until now, Socha had taken a back seat on the document issues. In the division of labor, Socha, from Denver, is the trial specialist, while the Richmond lawyers have been in charge of the discovery. Slaughter, in particular, knows far more about the discovery than Socha. But today, Socha takes the lead. He is brazen and cocksure—a bit of a hotshot—in his midthirties, with stylish hair neatly combed over his ears.

Socha starts out indignant. "We do not destroy documents," he says. Even the request for a protective order, he says, is "an insult to the integrity of our lawyers."

This display of pique, real or feigned, peeves the judge. Protective orders are common, often entered as a matter of routine. Indeed, it is surprising that Larson and Ciresi did not ask for this order at the first hearing.

"It's no reflection on anybody," the judge says.

Socha ignores the hint. "Well, Your Honor, that does constitute a reflection, I believe, and I'm not—"

"I'll hear no argument on that," the judge says. "Next point."

Socha moves on. He argues that the relevant documents are in the MDL Source Files and long available for plaintiffs' attorneys to inspect.

The judge cuts to the chase. "Focus on the documents that were not produced," he says. "There is no sense in our talking about what's already been produced."

Socha tries another tack to shield the law firms. "Your Honor," he says at one point, "I don't believe that there is any basis for a finding that the documents within the parameters of the court's order have been removed from or kept out of Robins's physical possession and placed in the possession of the attorneys, with the exception of the Source File documents."

"Now let me ask you this," the judge says. "Do you know what the situation is with regard to these documents? Do you *personally* know?"

"Oh, no sir, not with respect to all of them," Socha says.

The judge digs deeper. "Do you know where the documents are, for instance, the wicking file?" the judge asks.

"Well, I don't believe there is any such thing as a wicking file, Your Honor," Socha says.

The judge tries to get beyond the word games. "You take the generic name—the tests and so forth we have referred to as the wicking files," the judge says. "Do you know what that sort of generic description means?"

Socha doesn't yield. "Well, I don't know what you mean by it," he says. "I try to avoid using those terms, Your Honor. I think they are too vague to really give us a real grasp or handle on what these documents refer to."

My head starts to hurt. What has everyone been arguing about for the past month or so, if not the wicking documents?

After a few more rounds, the judge gives up. "Take your seat," he barks at Socha. "You should make objections based on something that you know about."

Even the judge can't get to the bottom of this muddle, I think to myself.

But he instructs the special masters to start searching for documents at McGuire Woods tomorrow.

He also signs a protective order directing that "no party or their attorneys shall damage, mutilate or destroy any document having potential relevance to the consolidated actions."

And he orders more depositions to zero in on the documents:

Patricia Lashley, Tuesday (tomorrow), in Richmond.

Alexander Slaughter, Wednesday, in Minneapolis.

William Cogar, Thursday, in Minneapolis.

■ ■ ■ ■

With their own necks on the deposition chopping block, the A. H. Robins lawyers rush back to settlement negotiations. That night, an agreement appears to be back on.

There are two last demands by Larson and Ciresi.

The first is that the protective order remain in effect after the settlement under the auspices of another judge. The lawyers agree to ask Judge Renner in St. Paul, who has a group of Dalkon Shield cases assigned to him, to take over enforcement of the order to protect the documents from destruction.

The second, and last, issue is the appearance of the three A. H. Robins officers at a final settlement hearing. The judge had made this request on Friday but not in an order. To resolve any uncertainties about the judge's authority, Larson tells the A. H. Robins lawyers, "If Judge Lord wants those people to come up here, I'm not going to settle unless you do what Judge Lord wants."

The A. H. Robins lawyers dread the thought of the three officers appearing in Judge Lord's courtroom. But the company is frantic to settle.

"A. H. Robins simply did not care about anything," Larson would later say, "but stopping discovery."

With virtually no options, the A. H. Robins lawyers say that the three officers will appear at the hearing, on Wednesday, February 29. In view of health issues, however, everyone including the judge agrees that E. C. Robins Junior can substitute for his father, and Dr. Carl D. Lunsford, a PhD chemist who is in charge of the medical department, for Dr. Clark.

Except for housekeeping details, the deal is done.

■ ■ ■ ■

Under the terms of the settlement, A. H. Robins will pay an unprecedented amount—$4.6 million—to seven women: Brenda Strempke and Martha Hahn, whose verdicts are still being contested in post-trial motions by A. H. Robins; the last two holdouts in the Judge Lord cases; and three other women represented by Larson and Ciresi whose cases are not before Judge Lord. The amounts will far exceed the typical Dalkon Shield payouts and dwarf the $10,000 per woman from the days of Appert and Pyle.

By these comparisons, A. H. Robins is paying a small fortune to escape from Judge Lord and to achieve, in the words of the agreement, "the immediate departure of the Masters from Robins or the offices of its counsel."

The agreement provides that the RZLK attorneys may resume their pursuit of the documents. But that will be before other judges. And it will be after a hiatus of ninety days, during which time A. H. Robins will have a chance to regroup and entrench.

In the meantime, there is one day, Tuesday, and perhaps a few hours on the morning of Wednesday, February 29, for the discovery to continue in Judge Lord's cases.

Ciresi will take Lashley's deposition.

The special masters will continue their work in Richmond.

The A. H. Robins lawyers will try to run out the clock.

■ ■ ■ ■

On Tuesday, Patricia Lashley sits, nervous and uncomfortable, before Ciresi.

She has worked for general counsel Skip Forrest since 1974, first as his secretary, then his legal assistant. She is the minion, unused to the spotlight. Behind the scenes, however, Lashley has been the key in-house person at the hub of the A. H. Robins document collection efforts.

So here she sits.

She offers little insight into one of the central mysteries: the whereabouts of any expert analyses or opinions on the safety of the Dalkon Shield. Any such reports would have been sent to McGuire Woods, with Aetna footing the bills; the legal department at A. H. Robins, she says, is out of the loop. This testimony only confirms what Ciresi and Larson already believe, but will provide a better record of the need to search the law firms when they are in front of other judges down the road.

Lashley also provides an intriguing new lead. She testifies that just days after the first punitive damages verdict, in the Deemer trial in Wichita, Forrest called a meeting of top executives. The date was February 17, 1975. This was Presidents' Day, a legal holiday, but a dozen or so of the highest-ranking corporate executives gathered in the A. H. Robins offices.

This, of course, stokes Ciresi's interest. He suspects that the meeting was the genesis of the company's decision to turn over testing of the tail string to outside lawyers and Aetna to insulate A. H. Robins itself from any adverse results. "The subject matter of the meeting was to discuss the wicking of the tail string, wasn't it?" he asks.

Lashley's attorney, Thomas Kemp, interrupts. "Don't answer that question," he instructs her, claiming privilege.

Still, Ciresi is able to learn some key information. Lashley was also in attendance at the meeting and took shorthand notes, which she put in in a file folder labeled with the date: February 17, 1975.

"And where are those notes today?" Ciresi asks.

"In that file," Lashley responds.

Special Master Bartsh, meanwhile, is at ground zero on Tuesday: the law offices of McGuire Woods.

He spends the first couple of hours of the day trying to get a sense of how the files are organized. But he is overwhelmed by floor-to-ceiling paper. He has been working long hours and doesn't have much to show for his efforts. He is tired and, as he told the lawyers the day before, "a little cranky."

Roger Brosnahan, who is at McGuire Woods to provide input from the plaintiffs' perspective, tries to focus Bartsh on the wicking studies and other tests on the safety of the Dalkon Shield. "It would seem to us that somewhere in this law office there would be a file dealing with opinions; there would be a file dealing with tests," Brosnahan says.

Raymond Scannell—the lawyer who had led me through the in-house legal department a couple of weeks ago—tries a brushback. Any such documents would not be in one central location, Scannell insists, but in individual case files, in other words, strewn among the records of the thousands of women with claims against A. H. Robins.

"That is unfortunate," Scannell says, "but it simply doesn't match with your assumptions as to what we should be doing."

Brosnahan finds this hard to accept at face value. The wicking studies are relevant to generic liability issues, common to all cases, and there should be no reason to scatter them like fallen leaves throughout the individual case files.

Brosnahan presses Scannell.

Scannell hedges.

"It is *my understanding* that that is *essentially* correct," Scannell says, leaving himself some wiggle room. "I say essentially correct because in the context of where we are, with 10,000 cases, I cannot make any representation or warranty which is all-encompassing."

Now Duncan Getchell, who had argued so adamantly before Judge Lord in an attempt to cut off all discovery, enters the scrimmage. He complains that the reference to studies is too vague. But he admits that there are "individual things that we have asserted a claim of privilege over that reside in various places."

Brosnahan asks Getchell about the Source Files. Getchell says there are, in fact, documents in the Source Files not previously made available to plaintiffs' attorneys because A. H. Robins claims they are privileged.

"Fine," says Brosnahan. "Start there."

Getchell tries to slam the door by saying that Judge Theis ruled in the MDL that these documents are privileged. But Bartsh is not buying the MDL defense, and, even if so inclined, he has no authority to breach Judge Lord's directives. Produce the documents withheld in the Source Files, Bartsh says, and he and Judge Lord will rule on any claims of privilege.

But less than one day remains before the final settlement hearing.

■ ■ ■ ■

While Bartsh toils in Richmond, the judge and I drive to St. Paul to meet with Judge Renner. This puts the judge in a great mood. Robert Renner is a contemporary from small-town northern Minnesota and a prince of a man. His first federal appointment—in 1969, as the U.S. attorney for Minnesota—was by President Nixon. The story is that Nixon then sent John Dean, of later fame in Watergate, to tell Renner to rid the office of any holdover assistants who had served during Miles Lord's tenure as U.S. attorney. Renner refused, which no doubt burnished his bipartisan credentials. In 1980, President Jimmy Carter appointed him to the bench.

We spend a few minutes with Judge Renner in chambers. The two judges banter about a running prank they have going in Duluth, where they both use the same chambers when they hold court up north. For some time, they've been hiding small bottles of booze for each other to find, along with notes—poems in Judge Renner's case—with clues to the locations. Judge Lord (and his clerks, me included) have been unsuccessful in ferreting out the bottles that Judge Renner hid long ago. We get no helpful hints today, however, and soon it's time to get down to business. The judges take the bench.

Larson and Socha tell the judges about the status of the settlement. Larson says the deal is complete, with two remaining conditions to fulfill.

The first is Judge Renner entering a protective order, virtually identical to the one Judge Lord signed yesterday—*no party or their attorneys shall damage, mutilate or destroy any document*—once the agreement is signed tomorrow. Socha essentially acquiesces to this; he must do so if A. H. Robins wants the settlement to go forward. He tells Judge Renner that A. H. Robins objects to a protective order on the grounds previously argued before Judge Lord, "but we don't wish to argue it further."

The second condition is the appearance before Judge Lord tomorrow of the three A. H. Robins officers: Junior, Forrest, and Lunsford. "That is part of the settlement commitment that has been made by the defendant," Larson tells the judges.

Socha confirms that the three will appear. "The officers will be here tomorrow morning—not here, but in Minneapolis," he says.

Larson inquires whether Judge Lord wants to review the settlement agreement. The judge has been kept appraised of the terms but hasn't seen the actual agreement. But he tells Larson, "I don't think that technically I have authority to interfere with the settlement." He acknowledges that his run is ending. "I'll approve what you bring before me tomorrow," he tells the attorneys.

The settlement is done. The documents are protected by court order. A. H. Robins has agreed to bring in the three officers. The judge has stated he will approve the deal. Still, no one rests easy.

The final hearing, after all, will be before Judge Lord.

17

Bold on the Bench, 1969–1972

After the politicking of 1968, Miles launched into overdrive on the bench.

Among the first matters he confronted were an increasing load of draft-resister cases, as Minnesota became a hotbed of opposition to the war in Vietnam, and hundreds of young men were charged with violating Selective Service laws. The judge no longer had the shadow of Hubert Humphrey—and Hubert's plight—to impact his views. Still, perhaps suffering the aftershocks, he initially displayed little mercy in the wake of the 1968 election.

Though he did not show it, however, the judge was beginning to harbor his own doubts about the war and the draft, as more and more resisters appeared before him. "I'd see them come into my court . . . with pretty honest eyes and tell me they were going to jail rather than fight this goddam war," he would say later. "The more of those kids I saw, the softer I got."

Before long, the judge was announcing that anyone charged with a Selective Service violation could plead guilty and walk out of the courthouse sentenced to probation only. He was handing out the lightest sentences of any federal judge in Minnesota, and, for defendants who chose to go to trial without a jury, finding the fewest guilty.

He had turned 180 degrees, so much so that when a new law clerk came on board—John McShane, a Vietnam combat veteran with a hard-line view of draft resisters—they got into a fierce argument, with shouting on both sides. ("Oh God, John, you just screwed your entire career," John thought. But after they calmed down, the judge told his new clerk that he didn't have to work on draft cases if he felt that strongly, and, said John, they got along "marvelously after that.")

In the end, the young protesters had a bigger impact than they ever knew on the judge. He would talk about them for years to come and acknowledge that he had been late to see the light.

"The kids were right first, and then the public," he said, "and last the judges."

He didn't like being last. He wanted to go bold on the bench and make his mark.

■ ■ ■ ■

He did that when he helped to upend the state's system of financing public education.

It was a hot topic in Minnesota. At the time, the school districts were funded in large part through local property taxes, creating great disparities between tax-rich and tax-poor districts. Wendell (Wendy) Anderson, a rising star in the DFL's constellation, ran for governor on a pledge to overhaul school funding. He won the election in 1970—running on the same ticket as Hubert Humphrey, when Hubert took over Gene McCarthy's Senate seat—but once in office faced a legislative stalemate. Meanwhile, parents and students from a relatively poor district brought suit to challenge the existing financing as a violation of the U.S. Constitution's equal protection clause.

No one had to tell Judge Lord the value of a public school education or the need for poorer communities to tap funds from outside sources; Iron Rangers had learned early on to tax the mining companies to insure that their children went to the finest schools. In the case before him, the judge ruled in the fall of 1971 that the state law was unconstitutional. The current system in Minnesota, he wrote in his decision, "puts the state in the position of making the rich richer and the poor poorer."

Still, perhaps because this was the judge's first opinion of this magnitude, with weighty implications for every child—and taxpayer—in the state, he deferred ordering any relief to give the legislature one more chance to remedy the situation.

That was enough to spur the politicians. Within two and a half weeks, legislators passed a sweeping bill that shifted the primary source of education funding to state—not local—taxes and, to pay for this new state support, enacted one of the largest tax increases in Minnesota history: increasing the state income tax, increasing the state sales tax, increasing the state cigarette tax, and increasing the state liquor and beer taxes.

The formal name of this legislation was the Omnibus Tax Bill. But it would be known as the underpinning of the "Minnesota Miracle."

Despite the new taxes, this more equitable system of school financing proved to be a major source of Minnesota pride and helped gain the state national recognition for good governance. Governor Anderson, in fact, would land on the cover of *Time* magazine within two years—out on a lake, clad in a plaid shirt and proudly displaying a newly caught northern pike—in an effusive article titled, "MINNESOTA: A STATE THAT WORKS." And the judge's decision would be lauded as "a historical marker" that "helped change the concept of equality in financing education in the United States."

The "Miracle Case," one writer would call it.

■ ■ ■ ■

The judge also went looking for more action.

He had been assigned an antitrust case, filed by a group of Minnesota lawyers (the "Minnesota boys," he called them), that alleged price-fixing by pharmaceutical companies selling broad-spectrum antibiotics. But with scores of similar suits around the country, the Minnesota case, which focused on the agricultural market, was transferred to New York for consolidation in an MDL proceeding.

There, the case languished, with the MDL judge struggling to manage a deluge of filings.

Finally, the Minnesota lawyers, led by legend-in-the-making "Big John" Cochrane, requested that Judge Lord ask for their case to be sent back home. It would have been easy for the judge to say no. The standard operating procedure was that cases assigned to the MDL stayed in the MDL until ready for trial.

But Judge Lord said yes. He contacted the judge in charge of the MDL to make the request. That judge was quick to not only agree, but, with the approval of the chief justice of the U.S. Supreme Court, to also assign Judge Lord *all* of the pending antibiotics cases.

Judge Lord was now in charge of one of the largest and most complex collection of cases in the country.

The litigation had a long history, dating back to the 1950s.

Broad-based antibiotics (or tetracyclines) had come onto the market after World War II and, as their name implied, were effective against a wide range of organisms (as contrasted with penicillin, the first modern antibiotic, which was narrow-spectrum). Ultimately, the Justice Department charged three companies—Pfizer, American Cyanamid, and Bristol-Meyers—with committing fraud on the U.S. Patent Office in obtaining the tetracycline patent, monopolizing the market, and conspiring to fix prices, with two more companies named as co-conspirators. At the criminal trial, the Justice Department secured convictions, and, although the verdict would be overturned on appeal, that was enough to start an avalanche of copycat civil cases.

The lineup of plaintiffs was virtually endless, as the drugs were commonly used to treat all sorts of infections in humans and also used in animal medications and feed. Well over one hundred lawsuits were filed, many of them class actions covering millions of individual purchasers; there were also a wide range of institutional purchasers who sued, including federal, state, and local governments, wholesalers and retailers, hospitals, and insurance companies.

By late 1970, many of the cases in the MDL were settling. The nonsettling cases, with millions of plaintiffs still remaining, were sent to Judge Lord.

The cases were a morass of paper, motions, pleadings. The lawyers for the drug companies argued that the litigation was unmanageable. They argued that each one of the millions of plaintiffs who purchased antibiotics would need to testify at trial to prove when they bought the drugs, where they bought the drugs, how much they paid, etc., etc., etc. The judge asked the lawyers how long it would take to try the cases if they went round the clock.

"Eight thousand years," the defense lawyers said.

The judge was blunt in his reply. "There are no unmanageable cases," he would say, "only lazy judges."

In an early hearing on the cases, in New York, one of the defense lawyers invited Judge Lord to tour his Wall Street firm to demonstrate how hard they were working to produce the documents for discovery. It was an impressive operation, with dozens of young lawyers, paralegals, and secretaries stamping documents and filling boxes. As far as the judge could tell, however, the documents were inconsequential invoices and bills of lading, reams of meaningless paper, signifying nothing, to produce to the plaintiffs. The judge turned from the assembly line and walked over to a corner. There stood a stack of boxes about four feet high.

"Confidential Documents—Destroy Immediately," read the labels.

The judge walked away. He did not call the U.S. marshals or seize the documents, as he would have done, he often said, later in his career. He still considered himself "a relatively neophyte jurist."

But from this incident, among others, the judge was learning to be wary of out-of-town lawyers. He would much rather be dealing with the Minnesota boys, like Big John Cochrane, than the polished, big-city, big-firm lawyers, who to the judge were virtually indistinguishable: dressed alike, looked alike, acted alike.

Cochrane didn't look or act like any other lawyer.

He was described as "a refrigerator with eyebrows," weighing in at at least 250 pounds. A steamfitter by trade, he earned his law degree at a night school in order to collect on a $1,000 barroom bet. Indeed, Big John and bars made for many stories. After trials, he often headed to a favorite watering hole, Jimmy Hegg's, in downtown Minneapolis; "I'm going to Mass at St. Hegg's," he would announce.

"We understood each other," the judge would say of Cochrane and the other local lawyers.

As many as one hundred lawyers would attend the antibiotics pretrial hearings, with hundreds more churning—and billing—behind the scenes. For several years, discovery ground on: documents, more documents, more than one million all told ("a futile search for the smoking guns which I am morally certain were in those very boxes marked 'Destroy Immediately,'" the judge would say). There were also depositions—hundreds of depositions—taken throughout the United States as well as in Europe, Australia, and Hong Kong.

The judge was becoming more comfortable on the bench and, as a result, more active and outspoken. He began to display what would become the hallmarks in his self-professed "hands-on" approach to judging: taking an informal, waste-no-time role in discovery, appointing special masters, personally attending depositions, and offering brash proclamations of his views.

One deposition, in particular, had the judge boiling over. The judge thought that the witness was evasive and that the attorney for the United States, who was doing the questioning, was ineffective. Soon the judge took over, asking the questions himself and repeatedly chastising the witness and the defense lawyers. "At some point this witness is going to get pinned down and answer direct questions," he told them. "He is acting in a very devious manner."

The lawyers for the drug companies—from the most prestigious East Coast firms—were not accustomed to a judge like this.

The judge also asserted himself aggressively when attorneys for the United States, the largest of the plaintiffs before him, announced that the government had reached a tentative settlement of its claims.

This did not please the judge.

He believed that the United States was selling out and accused the government of attempting to enter into a deal that would permit the drug companies to "buy a monopoly." He phoned a top Justice Department lawyer in Washington to try to dissuade the government from accepting the deal. He also accused the Justice Department of having too cozy a relationship with the U.S. Patent Office, which, the more the judge learned in the litigation, the more he had come to distrust. "I think you ought to tell your attorney general, if he wants to look at something, he ought to look at that Patent Office," the judge told the government lawyers. "That has got to be the sickest institution that our government has ever invented."

The lawyers for the drug companies again took note. They believed that the judge was improperly trying to derail the settlement. They also believed that the judge's remarks about the Patent Office demonstrated that he could not impartially decide the issue of whether there had been fraud in obtaining the key patent.

Their petition to the Eighth Circuit was captioned, *Pfizer Inc., et al. versus Honorable Miles W. Lord, United States District Judge*. As the title suggested, this was personal.

The drug companies asked the Eighth Circuit to disqualify the judge for bias and prejudice. "Judge Lord," they wrote, "has improperly assumed the role of prosecutor and advocate against defendants and has increasingly become more aggressive and open in this role."

A panel of three Eighth Circuit judges, including Judges Myron Bright and Donald Ross (both of whom would later weigh in on the Reserve Mining case) considered the matter. They denied the petition of the drug companies, but with "a caveat." Judge Lord "misconceived his role" when he attempted to interfere with the settlement; the policy of the law, they wrote, is to encourage (not impede) the resolution of cases. The appeals judges also had harsh words for Judge Lord's comments about the Patent Office, which they called "totally injudicious." But, they added, since these remarks were based on the record of the proceedings, "we cannot say that they reflect an 'extrajudicial bias.'"

The Eighth Circuit did not remove the judge from the case. But the panel sent him a message:

> This record adversely reflects upon Judge Lord's conduct during the pre-trial proceedings. Reluctantly, we have pointed out his shortcomings in this case. We demand of Judge Lord, as we do of every trial judge in this circuit, a high standard of judicial performance with particular emphasis upon conducting litigation with scrupulous fairness and impartiality. We commend to Judge Lord the Socratic definition of the four qualities required of every judge: to hear courteously; to answer wisely; to consider soberly; and to decide impartially.

Judge Lord still had plenty to learn on the bench. He read the Eighth Circuit's admonition. He mulled it over. "A bunch of bullshit," he decided.

■ ■ ■ ■

While the antibiotic cases were pending—the litigation would last, on and off, for years—the judge also continued to juggle a full load of other assignments. One day, in 1972, when the judge was in the middle of a trial on another case, his son-in-law, Wayne Faris, dropped by to visit.

Wayne had heard about a new case, involving two high school girls who were barred from participating on boys' sports teams, that had been assigned to the judge. Wayne was interested, as a lawyer and an all-around jock, and engaged the judge in small talk about it.

The judge hadn't given much thought to the matter. "Oh, I might let them be on the wrestling team," he wise-assed.

Soon after, the judge was back on the bench when his secretary interrupted him for a call from his daughter Priscilla. He hurried into chambers and picked up the phone.

"Daddy, what did you say to Wayne about those girls?"

Priscilla had just given birth to her second baby—and Miles's first granddaughter; "a little female, feminine woman-person," he would call her—and was still in the hospital. But she was furious with what her father had said to her husband.

"You be careful, Dad!" Priscilla said. "You may have been kidding, but I don't like the words you used. Think about it now!"

Soon another call came in while the judge was still in chambers. This time, his sister Rilla was on the phone.

"Miles, what did you say to Wayne?"

Rilla reminded Miles of their school days in Crosby-Ironton. The girls would stand around the gym in their black bloomers, and, if they waited long enough, they would get to use the gym, but only when the boys took a break and only with an old wobbly ball. As soon as the boys were ready to return, Rilla told Miles, "it was, 'alright girls, off the court.'" Then the boys would trot out, in nice uniforms and woolen sweat suits, bouncing bright, new basketballs.

"'Girls, off the court,' came the order," Rilla remembered, "and off we went."

"Miles, you think about it!" she said.

The judge recessed his other trial and sent away everyone in the courtroom. Two of the women he loved most were forcing him to rethink his views. For the first time in his life, he realized that he was an "unthinking male supremacist" and that "chauvinistic blood had been coursing through my veins."

The case involved two girls: Peggy Brenden, who played tennis, and Antoinette (Toni) St. Pierre, who ran and skied cross-country. But their high schools had no teams for girls in those sports, so they wanted to compete against the boys. A Minnesota State High School League rule, however, barred their participation. Their lawsuit challenged that rule in one of the first cases in the country for gender equity in sports.

There was no jury; the trial was to the court with the judge himself deciding all issues.

The lawyers and witnesses for the High School League argued that there were substantial physiological differences between males and females that made it impossible for girls to compete with boys. Males were taller and stronger, the League argued, with greater muscle mass, larger hearts, and deeper breathing capacities, and, especially after puberty, ran more efficiently than women.

The judge was not impressed. This testimony, he said, had little relevance to the two plaintiffs before him, who were extraordinary athletes. And the League did not require any boy to demonstrate any skill to participate on the teams; the schools had a no-cut policy for boys, regardless of their talent or lack thereof.

The League also tried to argue that a male coach would not be able to treat an injured girl—even for a minor injury, like a charley horse—for fear of stirring up a storm. The judge offered up his own cure: just press on her knee and pull her heel without touching any forbidden part of her anatomy, the judge advised. And if the injury is serious, the judge said, call a doctor.

"Tennis courts aren't that far from civilization," he said.

By the time the trial ended, the judge's decision was a foregone conclusion. He found that the two girls were being denied an opportunity to join the boys' teams "solely on the basis of the fact of sex and sex alone" and that the League's prohibition, as applied to these two plaintiffs, was arbitrary, unreasonable, and in violation of the equal protection clause of the Fourteenth Amendment of the U.S. Constitution. He ordered that the two girls be declared eligible to compete on the boys' teams in their chosen sports.

"The League's forebodings of chaos are unjustified," he wrote.

It was hailed as a landmark ruling and, especially after being upheld on appeal by the Eighth Circuit, would help open doors for untold numbers of young women in high schools and colleges to participate both on boys' teams and on teams of their own as resources began to flow into girls' sports. (Title IX—the federal legislation that prohibited sex discrimination in education, including athletics—was also enacted shortly after the judge ruled.) In later years, the judge would consistently call the decision one of his proudest moments on the bench.

Indeed, he would often tear up when he spoke of the case, especially when he saw what it meant to his own family and, eventually, his four granddaughters. And he got no end of delight when he went to hockey rinks to watch his first granddaughter—that *little female, feminine woman-person*, as he continued to say—as she "slammed the boys around."

■ ■ ■ ■

There were other moments of personal joy in these years. In November 1972, the judge's younger son, Jim—who had made his political debut as a small child, asking his dad for a nickel on a campaign telecast—was elected to the Minnesota Senate, at the age of only twenty-three. The victory was made all the more sweet by the election at the same time of another young up-and-comer: Hubert H. (Skip) Humphrey III. No doubt, the famed last names—DFL gold—were of substantial significance in these electoral victories. Still, there was much to be proud of. The two rejoicing fathers didn't miss a chance to pose for a picture, Miles and Hubert with their two boys, as soon as their sons were sworn in at the state capitol.

■ ■ ■ ■

Meanwhile, the antibiotics cases continued to wind along.

By the fall of 1973, most of the plaintiffs had reached settlements (with the largest holdout, ironically, the United States). Now the most challenging—indeed unprecedented—issue was how to distribute tens of millions of settlement dollars to class members. The institutional purchasers with large claims, including hospitals and insurers, were relatively easy to identify and reimburse for the overcharges they had paid for the antibiotics. But individual purchasers—millions of them covered by the settlements—posed enormous administrative problems: not only their numbers but also the fact that each individual's claim was relatively small (an average of $23, it turned out). Other judges facing this type of situation had found the logistical difficulties insurmountable.

But Judge Lord plunged ahead. "Operation Money Back," he called it, the first time a settlement of this magnitude was distributed to such a massive class of consumers in an antitrust case.

The judge hired experts to conduct market research and authorized a multifaceted outreach effort: a media blitz, with ads in print and on radio and television; a direct mail campaign in English and Spanish to ten million households; and a school-based effort, with claims information distributed for kids to take home to their parents.

The scale—and success—of the effort brought the judge national praise.

Time magazine wrote that Operation Money Back defied the trend of judges who were dismissing large class actions due to the difficulty of rounding up class members. In the antibiotics cases, *Time* wrote, the drug companies had also hoped the courts would find the "whole morass" to be unmanageable.

"But they did not reckon with Judge Lord," the magazine said.

In the *Washington Post*, columnist Nicholas von Hoffman contrasted Judge Lord with his brethren: "The black sheet gang on the benches of the nation's courtrooms have generally ruled that it is too much trouble to stop big corporations from stealing nickels and dimes from large hordes of small customers." He added that "most judges wouldn't permit such a massive act of justice to take place in their courtrooms" and—von Hoffman was not known for his subtlety—that Judge Lord was "vulnerable to removal on the grounds of gross competence and excessive fairness."

With the antibiotics settlements came the task of awarding fees to the plaintiffs' lawyers. The judge had mixed feelings about this issue. He believed that awarding fees to lawyers who took big cases on a contingent basis—willing to put in years of time and money, with the risk of ending up empty-handed if they lost—was one of the few ways to even the playing field against bottomless-pit corporations. But the judge also could not help but envy plaintiffs' lawyers who reaped magnificent sums of money, well in excess of his own judicial salary (and truly exorbitant by his Iron Range standards).

Still, he would usually be generous in his fee awards. And when it came to Big John Cochrane, whom the judge liked as a person and admired as a professional, the decision was not difficult.

The judge, however, was going to get something, at least some entertainment, out of it for himself. He ordered Cochrane to don a bunny suit—his colleagues had one made for him somewhere along the line, as an inside joke—and hop around the courtroom if he wanted his payday. To commemorate the occasion, the judge posed for pictures: the judge in his black robe, side by side with Cochrane in his white bunny suit, complete with a hood and long pink ears.

Then Cochrane and his firm got a check for more than $4 million.

■ ■ ■ ■

The antibiotics cases were not over, with the United States and a few other plaintiffs moving toward trial. But even before Operation Money Back, the judge volunteered for more assignments.

Another federal judge in Minnesota, Philip Neville, privately told Miles that he had been diagnosed with leukemia. Miles agreed to help him with his caseload, starting in 1972. In particular, there was one new—and huge—case that had been filed in February of that year and assigned to Judge Neville.

The Justice Department, at the behest of the U.S. Environmental Protection Agency, had filed suit against Reserve Mining Company, which operated a humongous plant northeast of Duluth, along the shores of Lake Superior, that processed taconite, a low-grade iron ore. In the beginning, state officials had eagerly lured the operation, and its thousands of jobs, to northern Minnesota. But over the years, Reserve Mining's operation had morphed into a political hot potato, with environmentalists—concerned over the dumping of tons of waste "tailings" into the lake—clashing with one of the largest employers not only on the Range but in the entire state.

The judge was not eager to wade into this no-win, jobs-versus-environment debate. If anything, he was predisposed to favor Reserve Mining. He had grown up in an era when environmental purists were a rare breed; his own father-in-law, Emil Zontelli, with his family-owned mines, had discharged wastes into lakes near Crosby-Ironton, standard fare for the times. ("He leveled hills, filled swamps, dumped refuse into lakes," the judge would say, "and we never thought anything of it.") He also had no personal animosity toward Reserve. He considered one of Reserve's top lawyers, Robert Sheran, an old DFLer and former Minnesota Supreme Court justice, to be a good friend. (Sheran's law partner, Leonard Lindquist—an even closer friend and lifelong Republican—was serving as one of the judge's special masters in the antibiotics litigation.) The judge, along with Hubert and their wives, had vacationed up north as guests of a high-ranking Reserve executive. Most of all, the judge appreciated how much the good-paying jobs meant to Iron Rangers. These were his people: boys-now-men he grew up with, even family members, who worked at the plant.

In any event, the judge thought it best that a jurist from another state—immune to hometown pressures—take the case. He put out some feelers and called around to see if he could interest another judge. There were no takers.

Robert Sheran encouraged Judge Lord by assuring him that the case could be settled—Reserve's proposed solution was to pump the waste tailings to the bottom of the lake, where it said they would settle out of harm's way—and the judge would emerge as a hero.

The judge signed on. At a preliminary hearing in April 1972, he greeted Robert Sheran as "my friend, Bob Sheran here, whom I greatly respect and admire." He assured the attorneys that he would not force Reserve to close. He said that he had tried but was unable to find an out-of-state judge to take the case.

"I am pleased to hear that, Your Honor," said Edward Fride, another principal lawyer for Reserve.

In fact, it was the Justice Department lawyers who worried about the judge.

They feared that the judge would be too partial to Reserve. They also worried about the judge's close ties to DFL officials, many of whom, including Hubert Humphrey, had encouraged Reserve to build the taconite plant to aid the hard-pressed economy in northern Minnesota. Indeed, the Justice Department lawyers considered filing a motion to disqualify Judge Lord for bias. They held back, however.

Discovery and other pretrial proceedings got under way.

Then, as trial approached a year later, came the discovery that the waters of Lake Superior were swirling with microscopic fibers. According to government scientists, these fibers were identical to asbestos, a known human carcinogen.

18

The Speech

The A. H. Robins lawyers are plenty nervous in the hours before the final settlement hearing on February 29, 1984. Among themselves, they discuss the range of possibilities of what the judge might do—everything under the sun, no matter how extreme—and plan contingencies.

The judge takes the bench and scans the courtroom packed with attorneys, Dalkon Shield victims, journalists, and miscellaneous court watchers. To his surprise—he didn't think they'd show up—E. C. Robins Junior, Skip Forrest, and Dr. Lunsford are also there. Apparently, A. H. Robins was more afraid of the judge nixing the settlement if the executives failed to appear than of what the judge might do in court.

The judge calls on the three executives to take seats at the counsel table alongside the A. H. Robins attorneys: Slaughter, Socha, and Fribley. Larson is at the other counsel table. (Ciresi is still in Richmond.) The judge asks the attorneys if they want his formal approval of the settlement. He is now inclined to sign the agreement to affirm its terms, as agreed to by the parties, to insure that another judge, maybe Judge Renner, can enforce it as a court decree going forward.

Larson says that approval is not anticipated, but he has no objection to the judge doing so. Socha also does not voice any objection.

The three executives sign the agreement, and Socha delivers it up to the judge.

After some further preliminaries, the judge asks me to hand the three executives copies of his Council of Churches speech. He tells them to read the speech—"where I talked about corporate sin and individual responsibility for the acts of a corporation"—while they sit in the courtroom. He says that he also has a second speech he will give them to read later, with a personal appeal for the company to recall the Dalkon Shield. (He hasn't decided yet whether to hand it to the three executives to read to themselves, or to read it aloud in open court.) He tells Junior to open his eyes to what the company's lawyers have been doing in the name of A. H. Robins and urges him to prevail upon the company that bears his family name.

"I think your days on this earth and hereafter would be happier," the judge says.

Then he calls a recess and retreats into chambers, leaving the executives at counsel table to read the speech about corporate responsibility that he had delivered three years earlier:

> You need only take the scales off your eyes and see that it is the individual who would destroy, pillage, and ruin our earth and the people on it. It is up to you, for after all, when Cain asked God the question, we all had the answer: "Yes, we are our brother's keeper."

■ ■ ■ ■

Meanwhile, the special masters are in Richmond. The judge has instructed them to keep working until he tells them that the settlement is final.

Special Master Bartsh is trying to pick up the trail of documents that A. H. Robins withheld on claims of privilege in the MDL. He thinks this might be the most direct route to the smoking guns, as these documents were specifically pulled out of production by A. H. Robins lawyers. Bartsh had believed that these documents would be at the law firms but now finds out that many are instead (maybe) at A. H. Robins.

Pin the tail. . . .

Special Master Thompson, meanwhile, is spot-checking boxes that A. H. Robins lawyers say contain only nonresponsive documents and therefore will not be produced. He finds a box with correspondence from the A. H. Robins medical department responding to reports of injuries in Dalkon Shield users. These types of documents had been a focal point of the discovery—*what did they know? when did they know it?*—but it appears that relatively few had made their way into production in the MDL.

In chambers, on the break, the judge calls the masters for updated information and gets riled up by their reports.

He also looks over the settlement agreement. He asks Suze to type in

"So Ordered" on the last page, along with a signature line for him to sign his approval.

■ ■ ■ ■

The judge returns to the bench. He takes out his new speech.

"I have a fourteen-page document that I want to be sure you have read and understood," he says. "Would you rather have me read it aloud or would you rather have me hand it to you and let you read it?"

None of the three responds. Socha rises in their stead. "Well, if the court please, I think we would like to read it. Obviously counsel—"

The judge doesn't want to hear from Socha. He wants to converse with the three executives without attorneys running interference. "I was talking to the three gentlemen that I asked especially to come here," the judge says.

"Would you like to read it, Mr. Forrest?" the judge asks.

"Yes, sir, I would."

"Would you like to read it, Mr. Robins?"

"Yes, sir."

"Would you like to read it?" the judge asks Dr. Lunsford.

"Yes, sir."

"Very well," says the judge. He turns to me. "Hand it to them."

I hand copies of the new speech to the three executives and the A. H. Robins lawyers. They begin to read as the judge watches from the bench, interjecting occasional comments to break the silence.

"Please don't rush through."

"It is a very important, profound document."

"I hope it burns its mark into your souls."

As the reading nears its end, the judge—impatient—beckons Dr. Lunsford to stand for "just one question." Socha moves quickly. "Excuse me, Your Honor," he says. "I object to this procedure, and I would like to be heard."

"You put it in writing," the judge says.

"I would like to be heard now, if the court please," Socha says.

"You put it in writing," the judge says. He calls on the U.S. marshal in the courtroom.

"Yes, sir?" responds the marshal.

"This man is going to sit down now," the judge says. "Have a seat please."

Socha sits.

The marshal relaxes.

Lunsford stands. "Your Honor, with all due respect, I have been advised by my counsel not to answer questions of this nature," he says.

The judge picks up the settlement agreement in his two hands. "Does he answer or doesn't he?" he asks Socha.

"May the record reflect, Your Honor, that you are preparing to tear up the settlement agreement," Socha says.

"I don't intend to tear up anything," the judge says. "I'm just figuratively stating does he want this thing approved or doesn't he?"

"Well, Your Honor, it is not contemplated by us that it is necessary for you to approve that," Socha says. (But he still does not object.)

The judge again instructs Socha to sit. He tells the three executives to continue to read the speech. Then he calls another recess.

The judge gathers us—Keith, Jennifer, Suze, and me—in chambers.

He is agitated: from his phone call with the special masters; from Socha thwarting his conversation with the executives; from the thought of the curtain descending on his involvement in the Dalkon Shield cases; from the cumulative effect of the past three months.

Still, he hasn't decided whether he will read the speech aloud in open court. We have toned it down considerably from its *rise-you-sons-of-bitches* iteration. But the judge knows his words still pack a punch—that's the point—and may land him in hot water.

The judge asks us what he should do. The views are mixed. My vote is for him to deliver the speech out loud. In my mind's eye, I see Maxine. She was right about me as an instigator or, at least, enabler. I feel some guilt, but believe it is the right thing for the judge to do and don't believe I could stop him, even if I tried. Delivering his message in writing—in private to the three officers—is simply not in the judge's nature. He has too much on his mind, too much he wants to say. He has a big audience in the packed courtroom and a bevy of reporters to spread the word. He has Hubert's old advice that the duty of public officials is to educate the public. He has an opportunity to put on a show.

"Gung ho!" he says.

■ ■ ■ ■

We head back into the courtroom.

First, the judge decides that he should protect his record better, given what is about to transpire. He all but apologizes to Socha for cutting him off and gives him an opportunity to voice his objections in full.

"Step right up to the lectern," the judge says.

By now, Socha has read the speech. "And it is my judgment," Socha says to the judge, "that you have basically this morning made accusations against these men and their integrity." He says the judge is exceeding his jurisdiction and abusing his discretion and asks to halt the hearing "while we seek relief at a higher level."

When Socha winds up, the judge makes a few comments, maybe a little stall to gather his thoughts. Then he announces that he is going to read "the whole speech, my appeal, to these gentlemen." He begins:

Mr. Robins, Mr. Forrest, and Dr. Lunsford, after months of reflection, study, and cogitation, and no small amount of prayer, I have concluded it perfectly appropriate to make to you this statement, which will constitute my plea to you to seek new horizons in corporate consciousness and a new sense of personal responsibility for the activities of those who work under you in the name of A. H. Robins Company.

It is not enough to say, "I did not know," "It was not me," "Look elsewhere."

Time and time again each of you has used this kind of argument in refusing to acknowledge your responsibility and pretending to the world that the chief officers and directors of your gigantic multinational corporation have no responsibility for the company's acts and omissions.

In a speech I made several years ago—the document which I have just asked you to read—I suggested to hundreds of ministers of the gospel, who constitute the Minnesota Council of Churches, that the accumulation of corporate wrongs is in my mind a manifestation of individual sin.

You, Mr. Robins Junior, have been heard to boast many times that the growth and prosperity of this company is a direct result of its having been in the Robins family for three generations, the stamp of the Robins family is upon it, the corporation is built in the image of the Robins mentality.

You, Dr. Lunsford, as director of the company's most sensitive and important subdivision, the medical division, have violated every ethical precept to which every doctor under your supervision must pledge as he gives the oath of Hippocrates and assumes the mantle of one who would cure and nurture unto the physical needs of the populace.

You, Mr. Forrest, are a lawyer who, upon finding his client is in trouble, should counsel and guide him along a course which will comport with the legal and moral and ethical principles which must bind us all. You have not brought honor to your profession, Mr. Forrest.

Gentlemen, the result of these activities and attitudes on your part have been catastrophic.

Today, as you sit here, attempting once more to extricate yourselves from the legal consequences of your acts, none of you have faced up to the fact that more than 9,000 women have made claims that they gave a part of their womanhood so that your company might prosper. It is alleged that others gave their lives so you might prosper. And there stand behind legions more who have been injured but who have not sought relief in the courts of this land.

I dread to think what would have been the consequences if your victims had been men rather than women, women who seem through some strange quirk of our society's mores to be expected to suffer pain, suffering, and humiliation.

If one poor young man were by some act of his, without authority or consent, to inflict such damage upon one woman, he would be jailed for a good portion of the rest of his life.

And yet your company, without warning to women, invaded their bodies by the millions and caused them injuries by the thousands.

And when the time came for these women to make their claims against your company, you attacked their characters, you inquired into their sexual practices and into the identity of their sex partners.

You exposed these women and ruined families and reputations and careers in order to intimidate those who would raise their voices against you.

You introduced issues that had no relationship whatsoever to the fact that you planted in the bodies of these women an instrument of death, mutilation, and of disease.

The courtroom is hushed, except for the intermittent sound of women weeping; the judge can hear them as he reads. The three executives sit motionless. I hold my breath, and I don't think I'm the only one in the courtroom doing so. The judge continues:

> Gentlemen, you state that your company has suffered enough, that the infliction of further punishment in a form of punitive damages will cause harm to your ongoing business, will punish innocent shareholders and, conceivably, depress your profits to the point where you would not survive as a competitor in this industry.
>
> Well, when the poor and downtrodden in this country commit crimes, they too plead that these are crimes of survival and that they should be excused for illegal acts which help them escape desperate economic straits.
>
> On a few occasions when these excuses are made and a contrite and remorseful defendant promises to mend his ways, courts will give heed to such a plea.
>
> But no court would heed this plea when the individual denies the wrongful nature of his deed and gives no indication that he will mend his ways.
>
> Your company in the face of overwhelming evidence denies its guilt and continues its monstrous mischief. . . .
>
> Under your direction your company has in fact continued to allow women, tens of thousands of them, to wear this device, a deadly depth charge in their wombs, ready to explode at any time. . . . We simply do not know how many women are still wearing these devices, and your company, run by you three men, is not willing to find out.
>
> The only conceivable reasons you have not recalled this product are that it would hurt your balance sheet and alert women, who already have been harmed, that you may be liable for their injuries. . . . You have taken the bottom line as your guiding beacon and the low road as your route.
>
> This is corporate irresponsibility at its meanest. . . .
>
> Confession is good for the soul, gentlemen.
>
> Face up to your misdeeds. Acknowledge the responsibility that you have for the activities of those who work under you. Rectify this evil situation. Warn the potential future victims and recompense those who have already been harmed. . . .
>
> Were these women to be gathered together with their injuries in one location, this matter would be denominated a disaster of the highest magnitude.

To the judge, this whole affair is made even worse by the fact that it is being conducted in secret. The misconduct statute provides for confidentiality, presumably to protect the accused judge from the public airing of charges. But to Judge Lord, this seems like a modern-day star chamber. He wants the public—the people—to know what is going on. He tells Judge Lay that he will waive any confidentiality.

This will be the first judicial misconduct investigatory proceeding ever held in public.

With a high-profile case, a maverick judge, and two former U.S. attorneys general facing off, the press explodes. This, of course, brings even more publicity to the judge's speech, with newspapers, magazines, and, at some point, even the Congressional Record reprinting the entire text verbatim. The expression "going viral" is decades away, but that is exactly what happens.

A. H. Robins's move could not have backfired in a more dramatic fashion.

"A self-inflicted public relations debacle," Morton Mintz of the *Washington Post* will write. (In fact, the misconduct proceedings attract Mintz—a legendary journalist who has been uncovering corporate misdeeds since the thalidomide scandal of the 1960s—to Minnesota.)

More editorials also start to flow, virtually all favorable, if not laudatory, to Judge Lord (outside of Richmond).

In the *Washington Post,* a column by Pulitzer Prize–winner Mary McGrory frames the issue as "whether a judge may exercise moral authority at the expense of judicial etiquette." McGrory compares Judge Lord to Judge John Sirica—"Washington's most celebrated example of a federal judge leaning down from the bench"—whose judicial activism helped crack the Watergate case. (Judge Sirica didn't believe that the burglars caught in the office complex were acting alone and pressed to expose the complicity of high-ranking government officials, reaching up to the president.) McGrory also quotes Laurence Tribe, the noted Harvard University law school professor, praising Judge Lord for piercing the veil of corporate anonymity. "I wish the Supreme Court justices had some of his convictions and even passion," Professor Tribe says.

The *Minneapolis Star Tribune* reprints the judge's speech under the headline, "A DEADLY DEPTH CHARGE IN THEIR WOMBS," taking up almost an entire page, and runs an accompanying editorial:

The mere fact that these women are separated by geography blurs the total picture.

Here we have thousands of victims, present and potential, whose injuries arise from the same series of operative facts.

You three gentlemen have made no effort whatsoever to locate them and bring them together to seek a common solution to their plight.

If this were a case in equity, . . . I would order you now to take to the Food and Drug Administration a correct and proper report on what's happened with these devices. If I did that, they would order you to recall. So while governmental agencies are set up to protect the public, there is evidence here that you didn't tell the truth to the governmental agencies.

As the judge nears the end, he tries to break through the corporate and legal walls and reach out—and preach out—to the human decency of the three executives in urging them to recall the Dalkon Shield:

I must resort to moral persuasion and a personal appeal to each of you.

Would you believe it, gentlemen, I am not angry with you. I don't dislike you personally.

I am not happy with some of the things you have done.

I would really like to try to talk you into doing this. It's just awful, and you can't get hung up in that corporate thing, you can't worry about whether or not the stocks are going to drop.

You've got lives out there, people, women, wives, moms, and some who will never be moms. Can't you move in on this thing now? You are the people with the power to recall. You are the corporate conscience.

Please, in the name of humanity, lift your eyes above the bottom line.

You, the men in charge, must surely—I know you have hearts and souls and consciences—and I am not a great Bible pounder, but this almost takes you into Biblical reference, you can only explain it in that way.

The judge throws in an example from their own corporate family: born-again, lawyer-teacher-preacher Roger Tuttle:

If the thought of facing up to your transgressions is so unbearable to you—and I think it will be difficult for you—you might do as Roger

Graduation from high school, 1937, where Miles was known for schoolyard brawling.

Golden Gloves middleweight, 1939.

Maxine in 1940, at eighteen and ready to elope with Miles.

Miles with his children in the mid-1950s. *From left:* Priscilla, Miles Jr. (Mick), James, and Virginia. Photograph by Agar Photography, Minneapolis.

Campaigning for state attorney general in the late 1950s. Miles was one of a cadre of young men to follow Hubert H. Humphrey, who started as Minneapolis mayor, into politics. Courtesy of the Minnesota Historical Society.

To my good friend
Miles Lord
with appreciation
Gene McCarthy
U.S. Senate

Eugene McCarthy after his election to the U.S. Senate in 1958. McCarthy, along with Humphrey, was instrumental in Miles's eventual judicial appointment.

Miles often headed back to his northern Minnesota roots.

With his boss, U.S. Attorney General Robert F. Kennedy, in 1961; the two worked together on the prosecution of Jimmy Hoffa. Photograph by Earl Seubert, October 13, 1961, *Minneapolis Tribune.*

At the 1964 Democratic National Convention in Atlantic City after Hubert Humphrey (*center*) was selected as Lyndon B. Johnson's vice presidential running mate. Standing next to Miles is Karl Rolvaag, governor of Minnesota and another early Humphrey disciple.

Governor Rolvaag appointed the up-and-coming Walter Mondale to fill Humphrey's seat in the U.S. Senate. Courtesy of the Minnesota Historical Society.

Hunting with the vice president, whom Miles called "the Hubie," in 1965.

Swearing in the new U.S. district court judge in Minnesota in 1966. Photograph by Russell Bull, May 2, 1966, *Minneapolis Star.*

Flanked by Maxine *(left)* and Muriel Humphrey at his swearing-in ceremony. Against all odds—and against her family—Maxine believed in Miles from the start.

Relaxing up north, circa 1970.

'I Hear They're Thinking Of Changing The Name To Lake Inferior'

The Reserve Mining litigation was national news in 1974 after Miles ordered the massive taconite plant to halt discharges into Lake Superior. Illustration by Tom Engelhardt. Reprinted with permission.

Soaking in the public's adulation, circa 1977.

Miles at a naturalization ceremony, 1982. Photograph by John Croft. Copyright 1982, *Minneapolis Star Tribune.*

Miles's scorching speech to three A. H. Robins executives in February 1984 was reprinted verbatim in newspapers and magazines across the country. The editorial cartoonist from the *Minneapolis Star Tribune* also weighed in. Illustration by Craig MacIntosh. Reprinted with permission.

Miles and his law clerk hanging out in chambers.

Women wear pins shaped like oversized Dalkon shields at a protest during the
A. H. Robins bankruptcy proceedings. Courtesy of Bettman/Getty Images.

Contemplating retirement, post–Dalkon Shield. Photograph by Jim Welch for the *Rochester Post Bulletin*.

Still in fighting trim at eighty-five years old, 2005. Photograph by Larry Marcus.

Tuttle did and confess to your Maker and beg forgiveness and mend your ways. . . .

Please, gentlemen, give consideration to tracing down the victims and sparing them the agony that will surely be theirs.

The judge is spent. He delivers his last line impromptu: "And I just want to say I love you. I am not mad at you." He puts down the speech.

Socha is on his feet in a flash.

"Your Honor, on behalf of my client, I object to the court's remarks," Socha says. "It is apparent to me, Your Honor, with all respect, that you have become an advocate for the plaintiffs' position—"

The judge interrupts.

"I certainly have," he says. "At the end of this case, after reviewing thousands of documents, looking at the briefs, reading the depositions and studying the depositions, I have concluded that the plaintiffs are right and that the things I say are based—they are my judgment based on the record."

It is true, of course, that the judge is finished with his Dalkon Shield cases, and, as he says, his conclusions are based on the record of the proceedings before him. Still, even I am jolted by his choice of words as he dispenses with any pretense of judicial temperament.

"You don't have to argue that I am prejudiced at this point," the judge says. "I am."

Socha moves again to terminate the proceedings. He asks for return of the settlement agreement, which the judge has held onto. "It is not contemplated by us that you approve it—you may, if you wish—but we have a settlement," Socha says.

Finally, the judge says that having "bared my heart" and "begged" the A. H. Robins Company to "do right," he will approve the settlement and dismiss the last of the cases before him. He hands the settlement agreement—which he signed under Suze's "So Ordered" notation—back to the lawyers.

He offers some last words to the three executives. "Maybe you shouldn't listen too close to lawyers and insurance companies," he says. "You're in a tough spot all of you, but I hope you work it out."

"Thank you, folks. We'll stand in recess."

■ ■ ■ ■

The whole hearing lasted two hours or so, and the reading of the speech—or whatever else people come to call it: reprimand, rebuke, admonition, tongue-lashing, even a sermon—only about ten minutes.

I call Special Master Thompson at the A. H. Robins offices in Richmond and tell him it's over. Thompson calls Bartsh and passes on the word. The special masters retreat.

I also call Judge Renner's chambers and tell his clerk that the settlement is final. Judge Renner enters the protective order to prevent destruction of the yet-to-be-produced documents.

Judge Lord is ready to put the Dalkon Shield cases behind him and move on.

But while his days of presiding over the Dalkon Shield cases have ended—in only three months—his battle with A. H. Robins is far from over. The judge's speech, as it turns out, will set in motion a cascade of events that no one can foresee.

19

Judge Lord versus Reserve Mining, 1973–1974

The judge was stunned when government lawyers told him that Lake Superior was awash with asbestos-like fibers, presumably from Reserve Mining's taconite operation.

The magnitude of the situation was staggering.

Reserve was dumping 67,000 tons of waste tailings—every day—into the lake that supplied water—unfiltered—to more than two hundred thousand residents of Duluth and other towns along the shores of Lake Superior in Minnesota and Wisconsin.

The judge was overwhelmed. He called in lawyers from both sides of the case for several days of closed-door hearings. He interrogated the government scientists. Finally, he cut to the heart of the matter.

"Are you drinking Duluth water now?" the judge asked a scientist from the federal water quality lab in Duluth.

"Personally?" asked the scientist. "No, sir."

The news could not be kept under wraps for long. On June 15, 1973, a banner headline blared: "ASBESTOS-TYPE FIBER FOUND IN DULUTH WATER."

The U.S. Environmental Protection Agency (EPA), however, was careful not to overstate the issue. The agency announced it had found "high concentrations of asbestos fibers" in Lake Superior that were believed to be discharges from the Reserve Mining operation. (A corresponding statement from the Minnesota Pollution Control Agency called the fibers "asbestiform type" and noted they were also discovered in the plant's air exhaust.) The EPA stated "prudence dictates that an alternative source [of water] be found for very young children." But the agency added there was

233

"no conclusive evidence" that water from the lake was "unfit for human consumption."

Reserve Mining, for its part, said there was no asbestos—and nothing harmful—from its operations. And in the North Shore communities, many residents viewed the announcement as a false alarm or even a hoax. Bottled water was trucked in, but the mayor of Silver Bay, site of the plant, reported that only one half gallon had been purchased, and that, he said, "was to a lady who used it in her steam iron."

Trial would start in less than two months, on August 1, 1973.

The judge would be sitting without a jury and decide all issues by himself: the nature of the discharges; their health effects, if any; and whether Reserve Mining should be ordered to dispose of its wastes on land (in a contained site) or even shut down its taconite operation, a move that would throw thousands out of work and devastate the region's economy.

■ ■ ■ ■

When Reserve Mining had first come to northern Minnesota, after the end of World War II, the company had been hailed as the economic savior of the Iron Range. At the time, the region's once seemingly endless supply of high-quality iron ore was nearly exhausted. As with fur and lumber before it, this natural resource had been exploited to near depletion.

The hope for the future rested with taconite, a low-grade iron ore rock.

There was an abundance of taconite in the ground, but the problem was how to concentrate its iron to feed into steel-mill furnaces. The solution came in the 1940s with an engineering breakthrough led by E. W. Davis—"Mr. Taconite"—a professor at the University of Minnesota. State legislators also rewrote the tax laws as a further incentive to lure in new jobs (and voters later approved, in a landslide, a constitutional amendment for additional tax breaks for the taconite industry, with Hubert Humphrey and other DFLers leading the campaign for passage).

Reserve Mining was the first to respond. The company was a wholly-owned subsidiary of Republic Steel Corporation and Armco Steel Corporation, two of the largest corporations in the country, both based in Ohio. By 1946, the companies had their eyes on a site along the north shore of Lake Superior. But first they would need to find a way to dispose of the huge amounts of waste rock inherent in the beneficiating (concentration and enrichment) process and asked the state for permits to discharge these tailings into Lake Superior.

This was an audacious request.

Lake Superior—the biggest and purest of the Great Lakes—had been assiduously protected by government officials. No major industry anywhere along the lake, on its U.S. or Canadian shores, discharged *any* waste into its waters. But the economic future of the region was at stake. And Reserve Mining promised that its discharges would not damage the lake: the coarser tailings would form a land delta, and the finer would settle, out of harm's way, on the bottom of the lake in an area called the "Great Trough."

State officials issued the necessary permits in 1947, and Reserve built its sprawling plant, stretching a mile along the lake, some fifty miles northeast of Duluth, with a taconite mine forty-seven miles inland. As in the old days on the Iron Range, Reserve Mining also built towns for its workers: Silver Bay, on a hill above the plant, and Babbitt, near the mine, which combined would grow to a population of more than six thousand people, virtually all dependent, one way or another, on Reserve Mining.

Full-scale operations began in 1956. Tons of taconite were blasted out of the mine and hauled by rail to Silver Bay. At the plant, the rocks were crushed and ground into fine granules and the iron extracted by giant magnets, then formed into small pellets, which were loaded on ore freighters for shipment across the Great Lakes to Armco and Republic steel mills.

The wastes—a muddy slurry of tailings—were directed down concrete-and-steel chutes and cascaded in waterfalls fifteen feet wide into Lake Superior.

It did not take long for fishermen to begin reporting decreased catches. They also reported miles-long stretches of water, spreading out from near Silver Bay, where Lake Superior's ultrablue had turned a cloudy green.

Reserve attributed the "green water" to an illusion created by sediment from north shore streams. Some people thought it was algae.

But the "green water" attracted the attention of federal environmental officials. The green was not an illusion. It was not algae. It was caused by sunlight shining on suspended particles of taconite tailings.

Tons of tailings, as it turned out, were not sinking into the Great Trough but being carried by currents toward the population center of Duluth.

By this time, the modern environmental movement had begun its rise.

Rachel Carson's *Silent Spring,* published in 1962, had roused the public's consciousness; Congress was spurred to pass a series of new environmental laws; and a spate of government agencies sprang up, including the Minnesota Pollution Control Agency in 1967 and the U.S. Environmental Protection Agency in 1970, the year that also marked the first Earth Day celebrations.

To budding environmentalists, Lake Superior—immense and pristine—epitomized all they were fighting to preserve and protect. This was the legendary Gichigami, or Great Sea, as named by the Ojibwe: the largest body of freshwater by surface area on earth, roughly 350 miles long and 160 wide and holding 10 percent of the planet's fresh surface water, in many ways more ocean than lake, and during storms just as dangerous. ("The lake that never gives up her dead.") The lake was also among the world's most beautiful, with underwater visibility reaching seventy-five feet or more, and much of its shoreline ringed by wilderness and high, rocky cliffs. It was also considered so pure that Duluth and other North Shore towns did not filter their drinking water, although they did disinfect with chlorine.

The battle lines were drawn: a vast, unspoiled lake and a mammoth industrial plant that by itself produced as much as 15 percent of the nation's supply of iron ore.

Early government studies on the environmental impact of the discharges focused on the "green water" phenomenon, potential risks to fish and fauna, and the presence of heavy metals. There was no mention of asbestos. But there was enough information to intensify the pressure for action.

Federal officials attempted as early as 1969 to abate the discharges through administrative proceedings. That year, dueling lawsuits were also filed in Minnesota state courts. In 1970, a hometown judge in Lake County, site of the plant, ruled that Reserve's discharges had no adverse effects on water quality. But that judge also concluded that not all of the tailings reached the bottom of the lake, as Reserve had promised. And he was concerned that the discharges, over the long term, could be "a possible or potential source of pollution." In response, Reserve Mining offered a "Deep Pipe" plan that, it said, would pump all tailings down into the Great Trough.

On-land disposal, Reserve said, was simply not an option.

But the Deep Pipe did not satisfy the state of Minnesota.

By this time, Wendy Anderson—the DFL golden boy—had been elected governor. He was enormously popular: grandson of Swedish immigrants; a member of the 1956 U.S. Olympic hockey team; young, athletic, and photogenic (called "a Midwestern Kennedy"); and with a political philosophy described as "populist" and "anti-elitist." He and Judge Lord got along famously; the judge swore him into office, and the governor signed a picture of the two together: "To Miles, dear friend, great liberal, outstanding judge and public servant."

Once in office, and joined by the governor of Wisconsin, Anderson began pressuring federal officials to force Reserve Mining to switch to on-land disposal.

In opposition, officials from Reserve and its Big Steel parent companies stepped up their lobbying efforts in Washington. Many of the corporate executives were big-time Republican Party fund-raisers. With Richard Nixon in the White House—defeating Hubert Humphrey in 1968 and George McGovern in 1972—they were not lacking for friends in high places. Newspapers noted the lobbying onslaught:

"POLLUTER OF LAKE SEEKS WHITE HOUSE RELIEF"

"LOBBYISTS SWARM ON CAPITOL TO HEAD OFF POLLUTION ORDER"

Still, the EPA was able to convince the Nixon administration to file suit against Reserve Mining in February 1972, the biggest pollution case ever brought by the federal government.

Later, the states of Minnesota, Wisconsin, and Michigan joined as plaintiffs, as did several environmental groups and, eventually, the cities of Duluth and Superior, Wisconsin. On the other side, some of the smaller North Shore towns, including the village of Silver Bay, and organizations like the Duluth Area Chamber of Commerce—and also the steelworkers union—intervened as defendants on behalf of Reserve.

■ ■ ■ ■

When the trial started, in August 1973, Judge Lord warned Reserve that the company should prepare a contingency plan for on-land disposal in case the evidence led him to conclude, in the end, that disposal into the lake created a public health hazard. (With disposal on-land, the waste—and fibers—could be contained within specially constructed sites.)

Few people tried to predict how the judge would rule. The case was too complicated; the judge was too unpredictable, and his loyalties too divided. He and the lawyers dug in for the longest and most complex environmental trial in U.S. history.

In phase one of the trial, expert after expert, including virtually every asbestos expert in the world—"a seemingly endless string of scientists," one reporter wrote—trooped through the courtroom.

There was no dispute that Reserve Mining was discharging tons of waste into the lake and air.

There was also no dispute that a major component of the waste was cummingtonite-grunerite, a member of the same mineral family—amphiboles—as asbestos.

The plaintiffs argued that these fibers were substantially identical in morphology (shape and form) and in chemistry to amosite asbestos; Reserve Mining argued that the fibers were, in fact, distinguishable.

Much of this testimony was technical and deadly dull: electron microscope analysis of morphology, X-ray diffraction analysis of crystal structure, laboratory analysis of chemical composition. There was also testimony about geology, lake currents, lake sediments, air sampling—and on and on.

In the beginning, the courtroom was jammed with spectators: press, lawyers, environmental activists, corporate observers, luminaries of one sort or another. But as the days drained into weeks and then months, the audience trickled out. Soon, only a couple of tenacious reporters remained as regulars, Dean Rebuffoni from the *Minneapolis Tribune* and Don Boxmeyer from the *St. Paul Pioneer Press,* both sitting in the jury box (where they could hear better). Boxmeyer wrote that while the trial might be the most important environmental case in the country, it also was "probably the most boring." Another reporter, not one of these regulars, fell fast asleep one day. The judge stopped the testimony, walked down from his bench, stood over the dozing journalist, and smacked his gavel on the rail of the jury box, close to the man's head. The reporter woke with a start and fell out of his chair. The judge, without a word, walked back to his bench.

As the witnesses droned on, the judge paced behind the bench or walked the courtroom in his robe and stocking feet. "A rather small, tightly coiled figure," Boxmeyer wrote, "a fighter in a black robe."

Reserve Mining proffered an endless circle of defenses. The company's lawyers and witnesses argued that much of the cummingtonite-grunerite in the lake was naturally occurring from tributary streams and not coming from its plant; that Reserve's tailings were not only harmless but actually helped purify the lake water; that even if the fibers from its plant were asbestos-like, the levels in the water and air were too low—and the fibers too short—to pose a health risk; and that studies among asbestos workers of asbestosis (an often fatal scarring or fibrosis of the lungs) and cancers (including mesothelioma, a particularly lethal cancer of the lining of the lungs or abdominal cavity) were not relevant to a nonoccupational setting.

And then there was Reserve's bottom-line defense: there was no evidence of an increase in the incidence of cancers in the North Shore communities. Or as would be paraphrased—or stated verbatim—at various points in the case: "Show me one dead body."

In many ways, the trial tested the frontiers of science. There was no question that exposure to asbestos—at high levels, through inhalation, in the workplace—caused deadly diseases of the lung. But little was known about inhalation outside of an occupational setting or exposure from ingesting water. The question for the judge, and the judge alone, was how much unknown risk to accept before taking action to protect hundreds of thousands of North Shore residents, including children, who would be ingesting and inhaling the fibers, around the clock, for their entire lives.

In truth, despite the lengthy testimony, it did not take long for the judge to conclude that the taconite tailings were virtually indistinguishable from asbestos. It was testimony on the health effects of asbestos, and not the esoteric evidence on morphology, that set off the fireworks.

A biophysicist from Mount Sinai School of Medicine in New York City took the stand for the government. He testified that there was often a decades-long lag between exposure to asbestos and manifestation of disease, which made it difficult to prove causation. But he emphasized that, even without conclusive evidence, precautionary steps must be taken. Duluth tap water, he testified, showed concentrations of up to seventy-four million amphibole fibers—per liter—under an electron microscope.

This risk was compounded, he said, by the fibers in the air, particularly in Silver Bay.

Robert Sheran—the judge's old friend, now representing Reserve Mining—stood to cross-examine the biophysicist. Sheran was a true gentleman, with wavy gray hair and a dignified manner, as befitting his prior years as a justice on the Minnesota Supreme Court. (In fact, Sheran would soon return to the court as its chief justice, ending his involvement in the case.) But he minced no words with this witness:

> Wouldn't you say that it's a reasonable proposition that before you characterize an activity as constituting a serious public health hazard, that somebody, somewhere, should establish that one death or serious illness is attributable to the activity?

The biophysicist replied that they should not wait "until we see the bodies in the street."

The star witness for the government came soon after: Dr. Irving Selikoff.

Dr. Selikoff was a chest physician, also from Mount Sinai, and widely considered the country's leading authority on asbestos-caused disease. In the early 1950s, he had begun a pioneering study of insulation workers with long-term exposure to asbestos. At that time, the causal link between asbestos and lung cancer was not considered established. (Later, the disclosure of internal documents in the asbestos litigation would reveal that industry insiders were well aware, decades before Dr. Selikoff's work, of the deadly consequences.) Dr. Selikoff's study, published after years of follow-up, provided the first solid public evidence that asbestos—widely used by an array of industries for fireproofing—was a major industrial cause of cancer.

Dr. Selikoff was not one to shy from controversy and did not temper his words when he first appeared on the witness stand. He testified that the Reserve discharges created "a distinct public health hazard." He testified that drinking the lake water was "a form of Russian roulette" and that the risks were compounded by the fibers in the air. A sign should be hung along U.S. Highway 61 entering Silver Bay, he said: "Please Close Your Windows Before Driving Through."

The next day, however, Dr. Selikoff—concerned by alarmist press reports on his testimony—qualified his statements. He said that his statements about closing car windows were "facetious" and "not meant to be taken literally." He testified that by stopping the exposure, "we can look forward, with some good confidence, to the future."

Reserve and its allies pounced. Along the North Shore, in the company towns, residents loudly proclaimed that they were "perfectly healthy" and lambasted the renowned scientist as "Dr. Sillycough."

The testimony of the government witnesses, however, was having a cumulative impact. There was a growing consensus, in the press and in the public, that it was simply untenable to allow the daily dumping of 67,000 tons of industrial waste into a beauteous lake, even if there were no proven health effects. Bold action would be needed, but Reserve Mining was still unyielding. This made politicians, even Wendy Anderson, increasingly nervous. By October 1973, *Time* magazine reported that the trial had become "a political whirlpool" and "savvy politicians like Minnesota Governor Wendell Anderson are trying to swim clear."

There was no cover, however, for the judge.

Later in the year, he took a break from the courtroom to clear his head. He traveled north to tour the taconite operation, accompanied by a few lawyers and reporters. As he walked through the plant, he noticed a welder, overalls covered with grime, working on a front-end loader. Without a word, the judge broke away from his official entourage. He tossed off his coat, knelt by the welder, picked up the welding rods, and—relying on the skills he had learned as a young man—executed a near-perfect weld, the rods arcing brilliantly. He handed back the equipment and shook hands with the welder.

He was ready to face the weeks and months of controversy ahead.

■ ■ ■ ■

With the start of 1974, the trial shifted into its second phase. Now the focus would be on the feasibility of alternative methods of waste disposal. Over and over, the judge pressed Reserve for a plan to move to on-land disposal. Over and over, Reserve repeated its refrain that its Deep Pipe plan—pumping the tailings to the bottom of the lake—was the only feasible alternative.

The judge searched for ways to pressure Reserve off its entrenched position and took direct aim at the parent companies. He issued an order that Armco and Republic—separate legal entities under the law—be joined as defendants in the litigation, which would put their deep-pocket assets, a combined net worth of more than $2 billion, on the line.

The judge viewed this as "an insurance policy" for the people of the North Shore. To him, Reserve Mining was nothing more than a corporate shell created by Armco and Republic to limit their liabilities.

But Armco and Republic ran straight to the Eighth Circuit.

With notable speed, a three-judge panel—including Judges Bright and Ross (from the *Pfizer versus Lord* decision in the antibiotics case), as well as Judge William Webster (who would later head the FBI)—reversed Judge Lord before the month was out.

Some observers were surprised that the Eighth Circuit would act at all, let alone so fast, on an interlocutory order before a final judgment or any order for relief against the parent companies. The Eighth Circuit did leave the door open for Judge Lord to join Armco and Republic again, after further evidence at trial. Still, it was a disconcerting signal.

Meanwhile, the judge was growing increasingly skeptical of Reserve's protestations that on-land disposal was not feasible. In fact, there were now a half dozen other taconite plants in northern Minnesota, *all* of which disposed their tailings on land. And the judge believed that any prudent businessmen at Reserve, with the future of the plant on the line, would plan for the possibility of a court order compelling on-land disposal.

Repeatedly, the judge requested that Reserve produce any contingency plans it had developed for on-land disposal.

Repeatedly, Reserve said it had none.

True, on-land disposal was more expensive than lake dumping. But it was certainly achievable. Where were Reserve's plans?

The judge thought he knew. He told one of his law clerks to tell the government lawyers to slap a subpoena on Armco and Republic, which as nonparties had not been subject to prior discovery requests.

The Justice Department attorneys viewed this idea as a waste of time. They had already served wide-ranging discovery requests on Reserve. And while the judge had been unsuccessful in joining Armco and Republic as parties, it seemed inconceivable that any engineering documents in the files of the two parents would not also be in the possession or control of Reserve.

Still, the Justice Department lawyers did not want to antagonize the judge by rejecting his suggestion. They served subpoenas on Armco and Republic and continued to slog on through trial in the weeks awaiting a response.

There were three months of testimony left to go. The judge kept warning Reserve of the stakes. On February 5, in open court, he declared that the government had made "a *prima facie* case of a public health threat." Unless he heard "dramatic testimony" that changed his mind, he said that he would issue an order at the end of trial for on-land disposal.

"If at the end of this case I am still as concerned about the public health as I am now," he said, "I will consider closing the plant immediately."

Still, Reserve remained fast.

Then, on March 1, the day the judge had set aside for response to the subpoenas on the parent companies, lawyers for Armco and Republic arrived in court carrying stacks of documents never before produced.

One document—dated more than a year before trial had started—contained a report from an engineering task force, whose members included representatives from Reserve, Armco, and Republic. The task force had concluded that there were "serious questions about the technical and economic feasibility" of the Deep Pipe plan—which Reserve was still promoting in courtroom proceedings—and that it should not be pursued any further. "Total on-land disposal appears to be the only reasonable method," the report concluded.

A second document was a plan for on-land disposal of tailings at a site near Silver Bay.

A third was a more fully developed on-land plan, accompanied by a raft of engineering documents.

Document after document, hundreds of them—many of which had also been in Reserve Mining's files—were produced in the ensuing days.

Reserve's attorneys, unabashed, had reasons aplenty why the documents had not been previously produced. The attorneys argued that there were no on-land "plans," as called for in discovery requests and the judge's orders, but only "ideas" and "concepts"; that the on-land "concepts" did not provide for "complete" or "total" on-land disposal; and that there was no on-land plan "approved" by Reserve's board of directors. The attorneys also argued that the task force rejection of the Deep Pipe plan was only an interim engineering report.

The title of the report read: "Reserve Mining Company—Tailings Disposal—Alternate Studies—*Final Recommendation.*"

With Reserve unmasked, the stage was set for settlement. Throughout the month of March, the two sides tried to agree on a site and other terms for on-land disposal.

But the settlement talks bogged down. The end of the trial loomed.

By now, the judge could not contain his anger. He threatened to fine Reserve $60,000 each day—an amount equal to the company's daily profits, he said—if the company continued to withhold information.

He also issued an order rejoining Armco and Republic as defendants. "I had to do it twice," he said later, "but it finally stuck."

One of the last witnesses to testify was Dr. Arnold Brown, from the Mayo Clinic in Rochester. The judge had appointed Dr. Brown before trial started as the court's own expert, not aligned with either side, to provide an unbiased view of the evidence. Dr. Brown testified that amphibole asbestos was only one of fifteen or twenty substances proven to cause cancer in humans (not only in experimental animals); that the discharges from Reserve were indistinguishable from amphibole asbestos; and that "if there are some means of removing that human carcinogen from the environment that should be done." But Dr. Brown also qualified his testimony—too much for the judge's liking (by this point in the trial, the judge felt that he no longer needed Dr. Brown, given all the other testimony in the case)—and stated that there was insufficient evidence to conclude that the discharges from Reserve, in the water and in the air, would or would not increase the cancer rates.

The doctor left that ultimate question of whether the fibers would more probably than not cause irreparable harm—the standard for issuing an injunction—for the judge alone.

By mid-April, the settlement talks were dead. Any day now, the judge would issue his ruling. In chambers, the judge told reporters that he would order Reserve to switch to on-land disposal, but with a grace period of up to two years to avoid a shutdown during the conversion.

Throughout the week of April 15, the judge and his law clerks worked to finalize his order. The judge had two last issues on his mind.

The first was clean water. On an interim basis, the judge directed the U.S. Army Corps of Engineers to supply free filtered water to the affected cities. The judge had in mind that he would ultimately order Reserve Mining to pick up the tab, but he wouldn't address that issue until later in the year. Meanwhile, he wanted filters installed in schools, hospitals, fire stations, and other government buildings, where people could fill up bottles to take home.

Next, the judge turned to the top officers of the parent companies in one last effort to resolve the case. He ordered C. William Verity Jr., president and chairman of Armco, and William DeLancey, president and CEO of Republic, to appear in court. Both also sat on Reserve's board of directors.

But the officers, especially Verity, were unyielding.

Verity—a blue-blooded corporate titan (who would later serve as President Reagan's secretary of commerce)—was not used to being pushed around. It was an epic showdown: "the populist judge versus the corporate aristocrat," one author wrote.

Verity asserted that top corporate management had never accepted the conclusion of its own task force that the Deep Pipe plan was not viable. "Your Honor," he said, "I believe that the underwater deposition would work and would solve the problem," he said.

"Well," said the judge, "we don't have any of your engineers who say that."

As the normal workweek came to a close, the judge recessed for the day at 5:50 p.m. on Friday.

Nearly nine months of trial had passed.

The judge had heard from more than one hundred witnesses. He had reviewed more than sixteen hundred exhibits. He had tried everything he could think of to get Reserve Mining and its parent companies to agree to a resolution.

Tomorrow would be the day of reckoning.

William Verity was back on the witness stand at 9:00 a.m., Saturday, April 20, 1974.

He stuck to his guns—and his attitude.

The judge lashed out. He called the Deep Pipe plan "a joke." He accused Armco and Republic of "hold[ing] out for the last dollar of profit and to the last point of time." He berated the companies for promoting the Deep Pipe plan through months of trial, knowing that the "inevitable day" would come for on-land disposal. "That's six months later, and ten million dollars profit later, and fifty billion fibers later down the throats of the children in Duluth," he said.

About one hour into the hearing, the judge directed Verity and the other corporate officials to confer and report back later in the day on whether they would agree to on-land disposal. Then the judge would issue his order. "The time is running short," he said.

The judge reconvened at 1:40 p.m.

Verity took the stand. "It is our considered judgment that Reserve's discharges do not constitute a health hazard," he began. He went on to state, however, that Reserve was prepared to convert to an on-land system.

But his offer was conditioned. Verity demanded a five-year grace period to complete the conversion; government financial assistance; a guarantee that the necessary government permits would be issued for the anticipated life of the plant, no matter what future health hazards might be discovered; and "a satisfactory court resolution of the alleged health hazard issues."

The judge was stunned.

He called Verity's demand to dictate the court's conclusions on the health risks—or "for a capitulation," as one reporter would write—"shocking and unbecoming in a court of law."

"I am afraid I have hoped for miracles," the judge said.

He took one last recess at 4:15 p.m.

The courtroom, packed to full house, waited for the judge to return.

A few reporters gathered for a scrum. "All bets are off now, guys," said one. Another reporter would call Verity's performance "the most amazing display of arrogance I've ever seen," akin to "giving [the judge] the finger right in his face."

Back in chambers, the judge and his clerks—Peter Thompson and John McShane—worked furiously to revise the order.

The judge returned to the bench a half hour later. The courtroom was silent. The judge began to read.

The first part of his order confirmed what the judge had been saying for months: that fibers from Reserve's discharges were identical to amosite asbestos and had the potential to cause great harm to the exposed popu-

lations. He said that Armco and Republic had the means to switch to on-
land disposal and "that it was their choice whether they should make the
investment or abandon their employees in the state of Minnesota." He
ruled that the discharges violated federal water pollution laws and created
a common law nuisance. His words grew more harsh:

> Under no circumstances will the court allow the people of Duluth to be
> continuously and indefinitely exposed to a known human carcinogen in
> order that the people in Silver Bay can continue working at their jobs.

It was now 5:15 p.m. The judge read the last two paragraphs of his order,
newly typed:

> Therefore, it is ordered:
> One, that the discharge from the Reserve Mining Company into Lake
> Superior be enjoined as of 12:01 a.m., April 21, 1974.
> Two, that the discharge from the Reserve Mining Company into the
> air be enjoined as of 12:01 a.m., April 21, 1974.

That would be in less than seven hours.

At one minute after midnight, the giant Reserve Mining complex at Silver
Bay shut down, along with its mine at Babbitt. More than three thousand
employees were out of work. Local residents in Silver Bay and Babbitt de-
rided the "holy Miles Lord." As one said, "It seems strange that one man
could have all this power."

No other judge in the country had ever ordered a major industrial plant
to cease operations in order to protect the environment.

"A courageous decision," wrote the *New York Times*.

On Monday morning, April 22, the judge was back on the bench. There
were additional issues yet to decide, including continuing water filtration,
civil fines, and potential sanctions for discovery abuse.

Foremost on the judge's mind, however, were the laid-off workers. "The
people who suffer, I fear, will not be the corporation at all but the workers involved," he said, "and my heart goes out to them." He told Reserve
Mining that he was ready to entertain a motion to immediately reopen the

plant, as long as there was a commitment to abate the pollution within a reasonable period of time.

But Reserve's attorneys had other plans. They asked the judge to stay his injunction while they sought relief in the Eighth Circuit.

"The motion is denied," said the judge.

A government lawyer inquired whether Reserve had already scheduled an emergency hearing with the appeals court. The judge looked around the courtroom. One key member of the defense team—attorney Edward Fride—was missing.

"Is Mr. Fride on the airplane now?" the judge asked.

20

A. H. Robins Fires Back

Calls pour into chambers in the aftermath of the judge's speech to the three A. H. Robins executives.

I man (*woman-person?*) the phones, especially calls from the national press. The *New York Times, Washington Post, Wall Street Journal,* and *Chicago Sun-Times* blast headlines: "JUDGE CASTIGATES COMPANY CHIEFS IN SUIT OVER INTRAUTERINE DEVICE"; "U.S. JUDGE ASSAILS OFFICERS OF DALKON SHIELD MAKER"; "JUDGE SCOLDS FIRM"; "IUD FIRM SEARED BY WRATH OF LORD." Editorials follow. The Richmond papers stand by their hometown company. (An editorial in the *Richmond Times-Dispatch* begins: "One of the most persuasive arguments against lifetime tenure for federal judges can be found in Minneapolis . . . . His name is Miles W. Lord.") But outside of Richmond, most editorials offer support, even acclamations. In the *Washington Post,* a column by Colman McCarthy quotes much of the speech verbatim and calls it "beautiful anger":

> The beauty of Judge Lord's anger is that for once the corporate infrastructure of lawyers, public-relations men, boards of directors, and balance sheets was penetrated. Three culpable human beings were uncovered. For a moment, the Robins men were unincorporated. Responsibility was assigned individually.

Colman McCarthy is well known as "the liberal conscience" of the *Washington Post.* In many respects, he is the judge's soul mate. (In a later column, he says of the judge: "His love is for justice, truth and action.") But McCarthy is also widely respected, and his column is reprinted in other papers around the country.

All of the publicity and the speech itself also galvanize plaintiffs' attorneys—and other judges—to take up the torch on discovery. A. H. Robins may have bought time with its settlement of the consolidated cases, but soon a new push begins in other courtrooms to uncover what become known coast-to-coast as "the Judge Lord documents." Other judges begin to order production of these documents and also further depositions of A. H. Robins personnel.

The tide is turning.

■ ■ ■ ■

Meanwhile, our chambers returns to other work. Among other things, the judge has a backlog of cases in Duluth, which gives us a chance for a group road trip to the judge's northern habitat.

The mood is set when we arrive at the Duluth courthouse and find a poem left by Judge Renner with new clues in verse to the hidden stash of liquor. Judge Lord leads our search party. We scour every inch of chambers, then begin to dismantle the room. We find one pint of liquor behind a large wall clock. Three more pints are behind false panels in a bookshelf. The judge gathers us for a picture; we pose proudly holding the bottles as if we are federal agents who just busted a backwoods moonshine operation. Then it's our turn. We cut out a large hollow in one of the hundreds of hefty law books in chambers—this volume holds parts of Title 42 of the U.S. Code—and insert a pint of tequila.

The rest of the week in Duluth is a combination of work by day—motion after motion and a personal injury trial in a slip and fall case—and play after hours. We smoke cigars (at least the judge and I do) and drink margaritas. One night our crew gathers in the judge's hotel room to watch the NCAA basketball finals, hyped as the battle of the giants, Patrick Ewing of Georgetown versus Hakeem Olajuwon of Houston; the judge tells us the game isn't as intense as the old Iron Range high school rivalries and promptly falls asleep in his chair in his suit and tie. Much more interesting to the judge is a broomball tournament that he tows us to on another night. To me, the judge's pure joy in the stands is loads more entertaining than the men sweeping ice with brooms. (I grew up in New Jersey, not the northern reaches of Minnesota.)

Another night we pile into the court reporter's old Cadillac to drive to dinner. Keith and I are in the backseat; as Motown music comes on the radio, we start a hand jive and come up with a routine that ends with a thumbs up or down, to grant or deny a make-believe motion. We name our group "The Enforcers" and adopt a motto: "Settle or Die." The judge, sitting in front, loves the act and promises he'll give us a chance to use it. Sure enough, after some attorneys argue a motion the next day in chambers, the judge turns to us and asks for a decision. We perform in a line, ending with thumbs down. "Motion denied," says the judge. The attorneys stare straight ahead. They look as if they are trapped in a room with a bunch of crazies who might do who knows what if anyone moves an inch. To add to the scene, the bottles of contraband booze are in full display on a bookshelf. Finally, one of the attorneys, from out of town, states the obvious. "You run a loose ship, judge," he says.

■ ■ ■ ■

But while Judge Lord is decompressing from his time in the ring with A. H. Robins, elsewhere more problems start to emerge for the company, one after another.

At the top of the list is the issue of document destruction.

Several weeks after the settlement of Judge Lord's cases, A. H. Robins files a curious motion with Judge Renner. The title is a mouthful: "Alternative Motion to Vacate or Modify and Clarify Order of February 29, 1984 and to Extend Time for Filing Notice of Appeal." More directly put, this is a full-fledged attack on the protective order signed by Judge Renner. Back in February, when Judges Renner and Lord had appeared side by side on the bench, Socha all but acquiesced to Judge Renner entering the order; the plaintiffs had demanded that as a condition of settlement. But now that the settlement is done, A. H. Robins threatens to appeal to the Eighth Circuit if Judge Renner does not vacate or modify the order.

The A. H. Robins lawyers argue in their motion that they do not understand the "meaning and requirements" of the protective order.

In fact, the order is broad and sweeping.

The order prohibits the destruction of *"any document"* that *"in any way relates"* to Judge Lord's discovery order of February 8. The order also requires that A. H. Robins make reasonable efforts to notify *"all its attorneys . . . and other persons"* who have access to any of the documents of the directive to preserve them.

But the A. H. Robins lawyers say they do not understand which documents are covered by the protective order and who must be notified of its terms. In their motion, the lawyers postulate a series of hypothetical scenarios that take the language of the order—"read literally," they write—to extremes. ("The Order *read literally* would prevent use of a magnetic typewriter for this memorandum because editing of any draft would 'damage' a 'tape' or 'disk' 'related' 'in any way' to the documents covered by the February 8 order"; "*Read literally,* an argument could be made that every scrap of paper, together with dictaphone tapes and automatic typewriter disks, generated by any hundreds of lawyers in thousands of cases are covered by the Order.")

A. H. Robins knows, of course, that no one is interested in whether a disk from an electronic typewriter used to type a brief for Judge Renner is destroyed. There is, however, intense interest in the documents as defined in Judge Lord's order of February 8, including the secret tail-string studies, as A. H. Robins very well knows.

Yet on the very same day that A. H. Robins files this motion before Judge Renner, as many as twenty boxes of Dalkon Shield documents—many relating to the secret studies—are thrown into a dumpster in Columbus, Indiana.

The documents had been in the basement of Harris Wagenseil, an attorney who represented A. H. Robins from 1978 to 1983, while he lived in San Francisco. During that time, Wagenseil secretly arranged for studies of the Dalkon Shield, including tests of bacterial migration along the tail string. Indeed, Wagenseil, a Rhodes scholar and Harvard Law School graduate, was a "point man" for the studies and "a key figure and architect" of A. H. Robins's defense strategy, the plaintiffs' lawyers would later say.

In 1983, Wagenseil took a job as in-house counsel for another company and relocated to Indiana. Even though Wagenseil no longer worked for A. H. Robins, he moved fifteen to twenty boxes of his Dalkon Shield documents and stored them in the basement of his new home. The boxes contained lab reports, memoranda, and Wagenseil's notes on the studies, among other things. (He later says that other lawyers representing A. H. Robins would have copies of some of these documents but not all, such as his notes.)

In March 1984—shortly after Judges Lord and Renner entered their protective orders—Wagenseil's wife, who was cleaning out the basement, asked if he had any problem with her hiring neighborhood boys to take the boxes to the local dump. "No, go ahead," he said.

The documents were destroyed on March 22 and 23.

When A. H. Robins discloses this destruction to Judge Renner and plaintiffs' attorneys, its lawyers pooh-pooh the incident, describing it as merely part of "general spring cleaning."

The A. H. Robins lawyers also say that Wagenseil was never informed of the need to preserve documents since, in their view of the protective order, *all its attorneys* means only current, not former, attorneys. And *other persons*, in the words of the protective order, also does not, according to A. H. Robins, include the person of Harris Wagenseil.

Then, on March 30, A. H. Robins files another peculiar request for relief, this time with the Eighth Circuit. The company files an appeal seeking to strike Judge Lord's signature and his "So Ordered" notation from the settlement agreement, which would mean, among other things, that the terms of the agreement could not be enforced as a court order. Socha hadn't objected to Judge Lord signing the agreement on February 29. (*You may, if you wish.*) And, of course, A. H. Robins had agreed to all terms of the settlement. But as with its post-hoc attack on the protective order, A. H. Robins is now trying to batten down the hatches, after the fact.

More problems, however, keep popping up.

Patricia Lashley presents the newest problem.

Her deposition resumes on April 19 in Richmond under the auspices of a Minnesota state court judge, with Ciresi picking up his questioning about her shorthand notes from the 1975 Presidents' Day meeting. Lashley testifies that after her deposition in February, she had gone back to the collection of Dalkon Shield documents at A. H. Robins, kept in a locked room that her attorney calls "Fort Knox" but that is officially known as the library. The last time she had looked in the file folder—she can't remember when—her notes were there.

The manila folder labeled "February 17, 1975" is still there. But the folder is empty.

Ciresi pounces.

He asks Thomas Kemp, representing A. H. Robins at the deposition, to preserve the empty folder in a cellophane bag until it can be produced to him for testing. "I want to try to get fingerprints off it," Ciresi says.

Kemp says he needs to make sure that removing the folder from the library, even to preserve it, does not violate any previous agreements or orders, including the final settlement agreement. "I'm not going to agree to something here," Kemp says, "that is contrary to what was provided for in your agreement between Judge Lord and McGuire Woods."

Ciresi offers to call Judge Lord—"right now"—to ask him if that would be a violation of his order.

The last thing A. H. Robins wants is to face Judge Lord again. Ultimately, Kemp agrees that, even though Ciresi's request is "rather ridiculous," he will put the folder in a protective covering and place it in a secure area.

Ciresi never calls the judge. But the threat alone—the specter of Judge Lord rising from the ashes, as well as the repercussive impact of the judge's words (in his speech) and actions (in his discovery orders)—make it clear that A. H. Robins needs to do something more to try to stop the hemorrhaging.

■ ■ ■ ■

Five days after the Lashley deposition, on April 24, 1984, A. H. Robins turns again to the Eighth Circuit. This time, however, it is not an appeal but two extraordinary complaints—filed in secret and under seal—with identical titles: "IN RE: COMPLAINT OF JUDICIAL MISCONDUCT."

One of the complaints is filed on behalf of the company and the other on behalf of the three executives—Robins Junior, Forrest, and Lunsford—who had appeared at the final settlement hearing. Both are signed by Griffin Bell, who had served as a judge on the Fifth Circuit Court of Appeals and later as U.S. attorney general under President Jimmy Carter (the two had grown up just miles apart in west-central Georgia), but who is now on the payroll of A. H. Robins as a partner in a large Atlanta law firm.

The complaints accuse the judge of "grossly abusing" his office; of showing "open disdain" for the company from the outset of his involvement in the Dalkon Shield cases; and of assuming "the role of an advocate for the plaintiffs" and "directing the prosecution of their cases." But the main focus of attack is the judge's speech at the settlement hearing, which the complaints call "defamatory" and "a scathing condemnation" based not on adjudicated facts but, they say, the judge's personal opinions. The three executives say that they "were unaware that such opprobrium awaited them"; that the speech subjected them "to public scorn and ridicule" and "methodically destroyed their personal and professional reputations"; and that they were "deprived of all their constitutional rights to due process of law." Both complaints cite the Colman McCarthy column from the *Washington Post—Three culpable human beings were uncovered. . . . Responsibility was assigned individually*—as an example of the harm that has flowed from the judge's remarks. The complaints also state that the speech was designed to—and will—impact pending and future Dalkon Shield cases:

> With approximately 4,000 Dalkon Shield cases now pending in courts across the country, the adverse ramifications of Judge Lord's acts are immeasurable.

A. H. Robins does not contest the truth of any specific statement by the judge. Nevertheless, the complaints ask for "a judicially fashioned remedy of comparable notoriety" to be imposed upon Judge Lord. They also ask that his speech be expunged—erased, obliterated, purged—from the record.

While sealed to the public, the complaints are sent to Judge Lord.

He thought he'd seen everything in his years of controversy and battles, but he has never had a misconduct complaint filed against him. Initially, he is filled with excitement and pride that his words packed the power to provoke this extraordinary attack by a Fortune 500 company.

"I'm up to my ass in crocodiles!" he shouts in chambers.

But his mood soon turns serious.

On May 1, Chief Judge Lay issues an order, also under seal, appointing a committee of five judges, including himself, to investigate the complaints against Judge Lord and to file a report with the Judicial Council of the Eighth Circuit. (Each circuit has a Judicial Council, composed of appellate and district court judges.)

Judge Lord is grim as he reads the order.

He darkens even more when we learn that this is the first time Judge Lay has ever appointed an investigatory committee under the Judicial

Conduct and Disability Act. Judge Lay had summarily dismissed any previous complaints outright, without further ado, as either frivolous or directly related to the merits of a case, in which event the proper remedy is an appeal (which A. H. Robins already has pending on the "So Ordered" notation), not a complaint of judicial misconduct. In fact, we cannot find any record of *any* judge *ever* having been disciplined under this statute, anywhere in the country.

There is no doubt in Judge Lord's mind that he is being dragged through this opprobrium because he has enemies on the Eighth Circuit and because A. H. Robins is a large and powerful corporation, which demands—and receives—preferential treatment. This, of course, confirms his view of the legal system.

"One kind of justice for the mighty," the judge says, "and one for the meek."

■ ■ ■ ■

I start to research the Judicial Conduct and Disability Act. It's a fairly new statute, enacted in 1980 and born in controversy. Many viewed it as an unparalleled—and unconstitutional—infringement on the independence of the federal judiciary.

Under the Constitution, impeachment by Congress is the only punishment provided for a federal judge and only for "Treason, Bribery, or other high Crimes and Misdemeanors." Proponents of the new statute believed that the impeachment process was too limited and unduly cumbersome (of course, that is what the founders intended in drafting the constitutional protections) and sought a new procedure for disciplining federal judges by other judges, instead of by Congress. The statute provided two bases for discipline: first, if a judge engages in "conduct prejudicial to the effective and expeditious administration of the business of the courts," or second, if the judge is unable to discharge his duties "by reason of mental or physical disability." The penalties for violation may be severe: public or private censure or reprimand, cutting off the assignment of future cases, a certification of disability, or a request that the judge voluntarily retire. The Judicial Councils can also recommend, but not impose, impeachment by Congress.

Opponents of the new statute argued that it would intimidate judges and threaten their independence by exposing them to personal attacks for unpopular decisions. One respected appellate judge, Irving Kaufman of the Second Circuit, called it an "unprecedented intrusion into our federal judges' traditionally inviolate sphere" that "invites dissatisfied litigants to harass judges who rule against them." (Judge Kaufman knew quite a bit about controversial cases: he was the judge who sentenced the Rosenbergs to the electric chair after their espionage trial; he was also the first judge to order the desegregation of a public school in the North.) The appropriate remedy if a judge commits error—or demonstrates bias, impropriety, or even irrationality—should be through the appellate process, not personal reprobation, Judge Kaufman wrote.

Indeed, the A. H. Robins complaints embody the worst fears of the statute's opponents about how the law might be misused: an activist judge in the center of a controversial case.

"A very visible target," as one commentator would write of Judge Lord.

■ ■ ■ ■

The judge needs a lawyer.

A. H. Robins has Griffin Bell, a former U.S. attorney general. It just so happens that the judge knows another former U.S. attorney general himself: Ramsey Clark.

Ramsey Clark had served as LBJ's attorney general, appointed in 1967. The judge knew him even before that, back when Clark was a high-ranking official in the Justice Department and in the loop on the judge's appointment to the bench. Ramsey Clark also has exemplary ideological credentials, as far as the judge is concerned. Among other things, Clark had served as a chief advisor to Supreme Court Justice William O. Douglas when he faced an impeachment challenge. (Justice Douglas—appointed to the Supreme Court in 1939 by FDR and serving until 1975—was one of Judge Lord's heroes: bold and independent, a liberal icon.) Now Ramsey Clark is in private practice in New York City, practicing "poor people's law," as he likes to say, and creating more than his share of controversies with left-wing causes and clients.

"He's cut from the same cloth as me," the judge says. "He's a born rescuer."

The judge calls Clark's office in New York.

His words were strong and his message simple: Issue a recall and try to do something for the victims, known and unknown, injured in the course of company business. . . . While Lord lacked legal authority, his position as a judge and his research into Dalkon Shield cases gave him moral authority to make his case. We hope the judges' panel investigating the incident finds no merit to the company's charges against him. It would be sad and perverse to find that judges must be constrained from making speeches in the cause of justice.

The *Star Tribune* also runs a prescient editorial cartoon. In the drawing, the judge—black-robed and with an oversized gavel in hand—glares at the three A. H. Robins executives. A company lawyer, standing by their side, is saying, "Shame on you, Judge Lord. My clients felt bad enough without your lecturing them." The executives are wearing suits and ties but depicted as crocodiles—and shedding tears.

Melodramatic tears. Crocodile tears.

The judge, in real life, smiles at the coincidence. *Up to my ass.* . . . He takes out a pen and autographs a copy of the cartoon: "Roberta Walburn done put me up to it," he writes, then signs his name.

Indeed, we soon learn how apt that cartoon is.

"I didn't think that was so bad," Robins Junior had reportedly said when he left the courtroom after listening to the judge's speech.

Junior's remarks are recounted by Dr. Lunsford when his deposition is taken in late April by Dale Larson. And while Dr. Lunsford testifies that he himself had been upset by the speech, he nevertheless took no heed of the judge's pleas for action. Dr. Lunsford testifies that after he left the courtroom on February 29, he made no effort to find out whether the judge's charges were true; he did not review any of the evidence from the Minnesota trials; he did not ask anyone else to review the evidence concerning the safety of the Dalkon Shield (he relied on the medical department, which reported to him, to do so); and he had no intention of discussing with anyone how many women might have been, or in the future might be, injured by the Dalkon Shield.

Even the death of another woman—who died *after* the judge's speech and *after* the judge's plea for a recall—was not enough to move Dr. Lunsford to action. The woman died in a Los Angeles hospital despite all-out efforts to save her life, including surgery to remove her uterus, fallopian tubes, and ovaries. Her doctor sent notice of her death directly to Dr. Lunsford. (She would be one of at least twenty reported deaths from the Dalkon Shield in the United States alone.) Still, Dr. Lunsford—the highest-ranking A. H. Robins official responsible for the safety of the Dalkon Shield—did not take a look at any evidence himself or check to see what the experts had to say.

"I have not done that personally, no, sir," he testifies.

■ ■ ■ ■

Through Ramsey Clark, who is now officially on board, the judge asks the Eighth Circuit investigatory committee to allow him to serve interrogatories and document requests on A. H. Robins. But the committee denies the judge's request as "unauthorized" and "inappropriate" since, it rules, the only issue is "the propriety of respondent's conduct"—that is, Judge Lord's (and not A. H. Robins's)—"particularly on February 29, 1984." It also schedules a two-day hearing, for July 9 and 10 in St. Paul.

In private, the judge is more agitated—angry and anxious—than I have ever seen him. He starts calling the misconduct proceedings a kangaroo court. And by now, he has taken to calling A. H. Robins "mass murderers."

■ ■ ■ ■

While the Eighth Circuit is fixated on Judge Lord, elsewhere the focus continues on A. H. Robins.

In St. Paul, Judge Renner assigns Magistrate McNulty to supervise the ongoing discovery and appoints Peter Thompson and Tom Bartsh, who had both served under Judge Lord, as his special masters. Judge Renner also formally adopts Judge Lord's order of February 8 for production of the Judge Lord documents, which will provide an extra safeguard if the terms of the settlement agreement—which also call for production of these documents—cannot be enforced. Judge Theis, in Wichita, also issues an order for the Judge Lord documents to be produced in the MDL proceedings. And Ciresi opens a new offensive by accusing A. H. Robins of violating the protective order, citing the Wagenseil "spring cleaning" and the missing Lashley shorthand notes, among other things.

There also is bad news for A. H. Robins from Denver. The Colorado Supreme Court issues a decision upholding a verdict of $6.8 million—the largest so far and most of it for punitive damages—for a woman who had

suffered a life-threatening septic abortion, with the court finding sufficient evidence that A. H. Robins acted with "a conscious disregard of life
threatening hazards" to sustain the jury's extraordinary award.

But perhaps the worst news for A. H. Robins comes out of Tulsa. Roger
Tuttle is about to resurface.

His bar journal article, "The Dalkon Shield Disaster," had created quite
a stir, with a number of plaintiffs' lawyers trying to persuade him to agree
to a deposition. Tuttle resisted. But in late December, the RZLK lawyers
tried their hand. Brosnahan called Tuttle, and it was the first time, Tuttle
would say, that a plaintiffs' lawyer was courteous to him. As a result, Tuttle
agreed to meet face-to-face with Ciresi; they met in Tulsa in early January, in Tuttle's law school office—where the books on display included
On Being a Christian and a Lawyer and *The Conscience of a Lawyer*—and
walked around the Oral Roberts University campus. Tuttle told Ciresi he
would think about whether to appear for a deposition. He was fearful that
if he testified, A. H. Robins would accuse him of improperly breaching
attorney-client confidences from his years in the company's legal department and haul him before the state board of professional responsibility.

Later, Ciresi mailed Tuttle a copy of Judge Lord's speech. Tuttle read
over the lines that referred to him:

If the thought of facing up to your transgressions is so unbearable . . . , you
might do as Roger Tuttle did and confess to your Maker and beg forgiveness
and mend your ways.

Tuttle showed the speech to his wife and they talked it over. He also
prayed.

Finally, Roger Tuttle decided that he should exhibit the same courage
as Judge Lord. He sends Ciresi a letter:

After giving the matter much prayerful consideration, and in light of
Judge Lord's recently reported comments to several of Robins' officials, I
am now prepared to submit to an oral deposition.

The deposition will take place in Minneapolis, in late July.

■ ■ ■ ■

Back on the misconduct front, both sides gear up for the hearings on July 9 and 10. The judge hires a prominent Minneapolis attorney, Joe Walters, to assist Ramsey Clark. Walters is known as "the toughest litigator between Chicago and California," but, just as important for the judge, is a trusted friend. Still, the judge is increasingly frustrated that he must leave his defense to others, especially since he knows so much more, from hard-gained experience, about A. H. Robins and the Dalkon Shield.

In chambers, a few friends and supporters stop by from time to time to offer the judge encouragement. One day, Big John Cochrane pays a visit. When I walk into the room, there he is, all 250 pounds of him stuffed into a bright (almost neon) plaid jacket, not as outlandish as the bunny pictures I've seen from the antibiotics litigation, but shocking nonetheless.

"Hello, my little chickadee," he bellows out to me. "My, you're looking mighty summery today."

I look down at my jacket and skirt, very much the bland lawyer uniform today. I take another look at Cochrane and his jacket.

I laugh. The judge laughs.

There hasn't been much of that for a while, so unlike the earlier months of my clerkship, when the judge's high spirits filled the air.

21

Reserve Mining versus Judge Lord, 1974–1976

Reserve Mining's attorney, Edward Fride, was indeed headed for a rendezvous with the Eighth Circuit to seek an order to reopen the Reserve Mining plant before the day was out on Monday, April 22, 1974.

The government attorneys scrambled to catch up. At first, they were thinking St. Louis. Then they learned that the appeals judges were at a judicial conference in Springfield. It took awhile to sort out whether that was Illinois or Missouri. Before long, they were on a chartered Learjet, headed for Springfield, Missouri.

The Eighth Circuit wasted no time.

That very night, a panel of three Eighth Circuit judges held a hearing at the unusual hour of 9:30 p.m., in the hotel where they were staying for their conference. The three judges entered the room dressed in business suits and sat behind a dinner table covered with a green cloth; the lawyers sat at card tables. The scene looked like "an impromptu board meeting of your American Legion post," one reporter said.

These were the same judges who had so quickly reversed Judge Lord's first order joining the parent corporations as defendants: Judges Bright, Ross, and Webster.

Myron Bright and Judge Lord had walked parallel paths: both born in the same year, 1919, on the Iron Range (Bright in the town of Eveleth); both attending law school at the University of Minnesota in the 1940s; both owing their judgeships to close friendships with Democratic U.S. senators (in Bright's case, Senator Quentin Burdick of North Dakota); and both appointed to the bench by LBJ (in 1968 for Bright). But there was no love lost between the two, which, in Miles's mind, dated back to when Bright was seeking his judgeship and Miles, in conversations with Hubert, had supported someone else for an open Eighth Circuit seat.

On this night in Springfield, however, Judge Lord (or, more precisely, his injunction; the judge was not at the hearing) faced a bigger problem from another panel member, Judge Ross.

Donald Ross, from Nebraska, had a distinguished background, skewing conservative and corporate: a bombardier twice awarded the Distinguished Flying Cross in World War II; the U.S. attorney for Nebraska; vice chairman of the Republican National Committee; general counsel at a large corporation; and, in 1971, appointed by President Nixon to the Eighth Circuit Court of Appeals.

Judge Ross's children called him "Peaches."

Reporters who were at the hotel that night called him "scornful" and "openly contemptuous."

He complained to the government lawyers that there was "no proof that any individual has been harmed" and not "one shred of evidence of anyone getting sick." Yet, he scolded, "you would close down a giant industry."

"Show me one dead body," Judge Ross reportedly said.

Judge Lord had presided over a trial of nearly nine months, with a transcript of more than eighteen thousand pages.

That night in Springfield, the Eighth Circuit judges spent about a half hour in a hearing and fifteen minutes in deliberations. Then, on the spot, they granted Reserve's request to stay Judge Lord's injunction, at least until a more formal hearing could be held the following month.

The plant and mine quickly reopened. The injunction had lasted less than forty-eight hours.

■ ■ ■ ■

By this time, however, public opinion and the media (except along the North Shore) had moved solidly behind Judge Lord. "The nation can no longer tolerate the profoundly irresponsible and anti-social behavior of corporations, sometimes supported by unions, that use lakes, rivers, and the surrounding air as their private sewer system," wrote the *New York Times*. In a later editorial, the *Times* lauded Judge Lord for "set[ting] an example of social conscience" and berated Reserve Mining for "put[ting] profits above the public health." In view of the judicial record, the *Times*

wrote, "it is appalling that the company should want—much less be allowed—to continue its depredations even temporarily."

Still, the Eighth Circuit held fast. The same three judges held another
hearing in mid-May and, in a written opinion on June 4, extended their
stay of Judge Lord's injunction for seventy days. The appeals judges con-
ceded that the state's original decision to allow Reserve Mining to dump
its waste into Lake Superior was, in retrospect, "a monumental environmental mistake." But they stressed the many unknowns, saying that the
government's allegations of harm were "simply beyond proof."

In this order, the appeals judges did not reach any final conclusions, as
this was an interim decision on whether to continue their stay while Reserve Mining appealed on the merits. But they acknowledged that the lake
discharges would have to stop—eventually—and ordered the company to
submit a proposal for on-land abatement, sending the case back to Judge
Lord to assist the parties in reaching an "appropriate settlement."

By now, however, Judge Lord was in no mood for seeking out a compromise. He was itching for a fight.

He believed that Reserve had misled him—"lied to me at every turn,"
he would say—and had been using the litigation as a means to delay the
shift to on-land disposal. He had spent month after month in a grueling
trial, only to have the Eighth Circuit betray him with, he believed, scarcely
a glance at the thousands of pages of trial transcripts. He believed that he
now knew more than anyone in the world about the issues. Yet here he
was stripped of any meaningful authority, as the Eighth Circuit's order
relegated him to a mere advisory role in trying to settle the case.

Reserve Mining—buoyed by the Eighth Circuit's extended stay—was
in no mood for compromise either. If the company was forced to move to
on-land disposal, it would be on a site of its choosing.

In response to the Eighth Circuit directive, Reserve submitted a plan
for disposal in an area called Palisades Creek. As Reserve well knew, this
location, a spectacular wilderness, was not acceptable to the state. Nevertheless, Judge Lord, as directed by the Eighth Circuit, held hearings and
headed up to inspect the site. He took along a retinue of thirty people
and—wearing old tennis shoes, with a hole in one toe—explored the wilds
of the Palisades: a land of high hills, bluffs, and bogs; of trout streams,
lakes, and waterfalls; of deer, moose, beaver, wolves, grouse, and pine mar-
ten. He walked for miles, inspected fresh moose tracks, and gazed at a

hundreds-years-old white pine, a vestige of the magnificent species that had drawn his bloodlines to the north woods so many years before.

When the judge returned to Minneapolis, he called the Palisades area "a unique environmental treasure" and recommended that the site be rejected. He also recommended that the appeals court end its stay and immediately halt the dumping into Lake Superior.

The ball passed back to the Eighth Circuit.

Throughout August 1974, the appeals judges tried to move the parties to resolution. By the end of the month, with no success, they extended their stay again, this time until their final resolution of Reserve's appeal on the merits.

In other words, indefinitely.

Indeed, the Eighth Circuit's hearing on the merits—only a step on the road to its decision—would not be held for several months. The urgency of the past April—with the same-day, makeshift hotel-room hearing in Springfield—had turned to May, to June, to July, to August, to September, to October, to November, to December, with no resolution, the *monumental environmental mistake* notwithstanding.

■ ■ ■ ■

Meanwhile, Judge Lord steered his energies into other matters, including his remaining antibiotics antitrust cases.

While most of these cases had settled, the United States and a few other plaintiffs were now ready for trial. Even with all the prior settlements, this trial would be a huge production. "One of the most massive trials in U.S. history," the press called it.

The judge decided that he needed not one but two juries and two jury boxes. "The courtroom," wrote one local columnist, "resembles the floor of the New York Stock Exchange in its congestion of attorneys."

The trial would continue, off and on, through the judge's remaining days on Reserve Mining—and beyond.

There were also fleeting moments of reprieve—and gratification—for the judge outside of the courtroom that fall.

His son, Jim, who had already been elected to the Minnesota Senate, ran in his first statewide race and was elected treasurer; at twenty-five, he was the youngest constitutional officer in the history of the state. (Skip

Humphrey, son of Hubert, was still in the state senate but in future years would also ascend to statewide office, serving multiple terms as Minnesota attorney general.)

In November, the judge turned fifty-five and celebrated with a party. Hubert was out of the country but sent his regrets. "Dear Miles," he wrote:

> Now listen, old buddy—you're not as young as you used to be, so take it easy. A man of your age can get over excited, if you know what I mean. No more pinching—no more ogling—and take it easy on you know what!!

But on the bench, at least, there was no slowing down: antibiotics (in trial) and Reserve Mining (on hold, but far from over), two of the largest cases in the country before him at the same time, along with the rest of his docket, including a historic trial involving logging in the virgin forests of northern Minnesota's Boundary Waters Canoe Area, which the judge ultimately banned.

By the end of 1974, he was the obvious choice for Minnesota newsmaker of the year.

■ ■ ■ ■

The Eighth Circuit finally held its hearing on the merits of Reserve's appeal on December 9, 1974, in St. Louis. This time, five judges were on the bench.

By now, as one reporter wrote, the judges had clearly "done some deep reading" of the transcripts from Judge Lord's trial. The appellate judges questioned Reserve's attorneys, carefully and sometimes skeptically. But there would be no quick decision. When the hearing ended, the appeals court took the case under advisement.

December turned to January turned to February turned to March 1975.

Finally, on March 14, 1975, the Eighth Circuit issued its decision.

In an opinion authored by Judge Bright, the Eighth Circuit ruled—just as Judge Lord had—that Reserve's discharges into the air and water contained fibers that "cannot be meaningfully distinguished from amosite asbestos"; gave rise to "a reasonable medical concern for the public health"; and violated federal and state law and created a public nuisance. But the Eighth Circuit stated that the risk to the public health was "potential, not imminent or certain." Thus, while the court affirmed Judge Lord's injunction, it was on substantially modified terms.

Most importantly, there would be no immediate shutdown.

Instead, the Eighth Circuit ruled that Reserve Mining should be given "a reasonable time" to convert to on-land disposal. This would include time for state agencies to act on Reserve's application for permits—by now, Reserve had ditched the Palisades area and was pushing a site further inland, called Milepost 7—or come to an agreement for another site. Beyond that, the Eighth Circuit was hardly clear or firm on a deadline, other than suggesting there could be a year or so just to choose a site.

(The Eighth Circuit viewed the discharges into the air as a more significant health risk and directed Reserve to take "reasonable immediate steps" to comply with state requirements, which Reserve had said it was prepared to do.)

The appeals court also made it clear that the selection of an on-land site would be left up to state administrative agencies and the state courts, not the federal courts—and most definitely not Judge Lord. In fact, the court restricted Judge Lord's ongoing jurisdiction to ensuring that filtered water remained available and keeping abreast of any new scientific studies.

In Washington, D.C., many government attorneys were perplexed. The Eighth Circuit, they believed, had ruled for them on the law but failed to award any meaningful relief. "It read as though there were a page missing," one government lawyer would write. Reserve Mining, with no deadlines, could continue to discharge into the lake in violation of federal and state law (as the Eighth Circuit had found), well into the open-ended future.

Gerald Ford was now president and Robert Bork the solicitor general. Bork made the decision that the United States would not seek U.S. Supreme Court review of the Eighth Circuit's ruling. Indeed, by the spring of 1975, according to a government attorney, federal officials in Washington were attempting to "withdraw gracefully" from the fight.

The state administrative proceedings—a long, drawn-out process—began in June 1975.

Reserve threatened to shut down its entire operation if its Milepost 7 site was not approved. The word on the street was that Governor Anderson also favored Milepost 7, for reasons of "political expediency," his critics said.

Judge Lord may have been under orders from the Eighth Circuit to steer clear of the siting decision. But that didn't stop him from speaking out. His early ambivalence when he started the case—three years before in 1972—was long gone. He made it clear that he opposed Milepost 7; among other reasons, he believed that Reserve's plan—which called for the construction of huge impounding dams—raised too many safety concerns. (His preferred solution was for Reserve to return the wastes to its mine pit at Babbitt.)

In public, he stood against two Big Steel corporations; he stood against the governor—his onetime friend and ally—and other officials from his own DFL Party who he believed were too "cozy" with Reserve; he stood against the Eighth Circuit Court of Appeals. He also stood against many local government officials who, he believed, had been remiss in their responsibilities to safeguard the public health.

The public-at-large saw the judge as fighting a lonely battle, and he surged in popularity (except in the North Shore communities). Letters from everyday citizens poured into the judge's chambers.

"You remind me of the story of the little Dutch boy with his finger in the dike [with] your efforts to hold back the sea of powerful interests," wrote one Minneapolis man. "Win or lose, thanks from all of us."

■ ■ ■ ■

By November 1975, the judge, by his standards—although not, by a long shot, the Eighth Circuit's—had restrained himself for an interminable duration, in the face of what he believed was a lethal threat. In the meantime, not much had changed, except for the worse. The water filtration program was failing miserably, with no quality control and many filters simply not working, and the U.S. Army Corps of Engineers was making noises that it would no longer participate at all. Dr. Selikoff's group of scientists was also ready to report ominous new findings. Both of these issues—filtered water and new health studies—were still within his jurisdiction.

The *holy Miles Lord* was ready to explode.

He instructed U.S. marshals to serve letters on a bevy of public officials requesting their attendance at a hearing. The letter was a request, not an order—"I urge that you be present"—but the combination of delivery by a U.S. marshal and the signature of a federal judge had the desired effect. The courtroom was full on Friday morning, November 14.

"Good morning, ladies and gentlemen," the judge said, as he took the bench. "This is what will be termed as an unusual session of the federal court."

And unusual it was, even for Judge Lord.

He demanded a roll call. One by one, seventy people stood and gave their names and affiliations: officials from multiple state agencies (Pollution Control Agency, Department of Health, Department of Natural Resources, Attorney General's office); from federal agencies (EPA, Corps of Engineers, Justice Department); from affected counties (including health officers); from the city of Duluth (the city attorney and the director of the Department of Water and Gas). The state administrative officer who was conducting the hearings on Milepost 7 was there. So were superintendents from the area schools. There were, of course, also representatives from Reserve Mining, as well as Armco and Republic.

The judge knew that the Eighth Circuit would soon read every word of the transcript. He didn't care.

"As long as I am the judge," he announced, "I am going to be a judge from head to toe, and from the tippy tip of each finger to the tippy tip of the other."

Indeed, he was not only a judge but also a virtual one-man show. He called the witnesses. He conducted the questioning. He offered his own testimony and his own monologue, extolling his knowledge of the case and chastising the public officials and the Eighth Circuit:

> I know that what I am saying and doing here may not be very popular in some circles and with the Court of Appeals, but I am saying to you that I apprehend the danger much more than the Court of Appeals does. I heard this evidence, word for word. I cross-examined. We were at it for months. . . . I want you folks to learn, those of you who have in your hands the health and the welfare of the children up there. I have had less than what I conceive to be an adequate response by the local officials who seem in a large part to be dependent in one way or another on Reserve Mining Company. . . . I address all of you and admonish you, that you are playing with fire. . . . Sometimes I feel like a voice in the wilderness. . . . I am the repository of almost every bit of scientific evidence that has ever been adduced on the subject. . . . I'm not comparing myself to Moses, but in this respect that it has all been here, it is all indelibly written in the record in this court.

The star witness—if there was a star this day, other than the judge— was Dr. William Nicholson, a colleague of Dr. Selikoff's at Mount Sinai, who testified about new studies on the dangers of even low-level exposure to asbestos.

The judge turned to his audience. "You may wonder why I asked you to come here," he said. "You have just heard it."

He told the officials that he was going to put together a packet of information for every schoolteacher in the affected area to be designated as required reading. "I don't want you to scare the kids," he said, "you just teach them about the precautions they can take."

And then the judge touched the Eighth Circuit's third rail: the issue of an on-land site.

He left no doubt that he opposed the Milepost 7 site and intimated that he might jump back into this forbidden territory, if state officials did not do the right thing. "I just want to make it clear that I do not *as of this time* propose to assert any jurisdiction whatsoever over this aspect of it," he said. "However, I believe that it may properly be reviewed *at the appropriate time.*"

The hearing picked up the next day, a Saturday. The judge pressured the city of Duluth to make a formal request for Reserve Mining to pay for an adequate filtration program. He thought that the city's reluctance was due to pressure from the local business community, solidly in Reserve's camp, and urged the city "to throw off its shackles."

"If Duluth will move to do so, I will have Reserve lay $50,000 on the doorstep of City Hall Monday morning," the judge said.

The Duluth city attorney hesitated. The judge prodded. The city attorney finally made the motion.

"Granted," the judge said in a flash. He waved his fist in the air. "The people of Duluth have been invited to drink poisoned water," he said. "That will no longer go on."

Then the judge remembered that Edward Fride, Reserve's attorney, had not been given an opportunity to speak. Fride stated Reserve's objections.

The judge responded by upping the stakes. "Reserve Mining Company, as of Monday morning at 10:00 o'clock, shall hand to the city treasurer of the city of Duluth, a check in the amount of $100,000," the judge said. The money, he said, would serve as an initial deposit—a "token," he later called it—for the costs of water filtration.

The judge also had a message for the Eighth Circuit. "It may appear in reviewing this," he said, that he was "going beyond the traditional role of a court." And that, he said, "is the exact truth." He was taking action, he said, to "save the lives of a good many of the children in Duluth who might otherwise die."

Just before 10:00 a.m. on Monday, November 17, Reserve Mining deposited $100,000 with the city of Duluth—and dashed back to the Eighth Circuit. Once again, when the company came knocking, the Eighth Circuit acted quickly. A three-judge panel—Judges Ross, Bright, and Lay—held a hearing that same week.

At the hearing, the company made an additional request for relief: remove the judge from the case altogether. An attorney for the state of Minnesota, Byron Starns, who was taking on more responsibility as the federal lawyers decamped, admitted that Judge Lord's actions had been "unusual" but asked the appeals judges to concentrate on substance—what the judge had done—rather than on his style.

Judge Bright asked whether "the ends justify the means."

"Yes," replied Starns.

(He was a fairly young lawyer and unusually frank.)

The arguments lasted about two hours, then the Eighth Circuit said it would consider the matter further at its next hearing, on December 18, 1975, in St. Louis. Until then, Judge Lord was ordered to stand down.

The judge's closest confidants warned him not to attend the St. Louis hearing or, if he did go, to merely observe the proceedings. It would be unusual—if not unheard of—for a federal judge to appear and argue on his own behalf at a disqualification hearing like this.

"You know the old adage," said one friend. "Don't be your own lawyer."

"Bite your tongue," urged another.

The judge flew to St. Louis.

The morning of the hearing, he had breakfast with Robert Mattson Sr., an old friend (who had served as an assistant to the judge in the attorney general's office and was later appointed to the post himself), as well as Byron Starns, the young lawyer representing the state, who would argue against disqualification. The judge confirmed to them that he would not address the court but only listen to the proceedings.

Six grim Eighth Circuit judges took the bench.

Byron Starns did his best. He argued that this was "an extraordinary case which has demanded and deserved extraordinary judicial action." He began to recount the Eighth Circuit's own far-from-ordinary conduct, starting with the motel hearing in Springfield, where—only days after the conclusion of Judge Lord's long trial and without the appeals judges reviewing the voluminous record—"demands for dead bodies were made," Starns said.

This was perhaps not the best way for Starns (again, unusually frank) to sway the Eighth Circuit.

"From whom?" asked Judge Webster.

"Yes, I am interested in that, too," said Judge Ross. "Who made the demands for dead bodies?"

"The court," said Starns, without singling out the angry judge before him.

Judge Ross pressed. "Who?"

"You did, Your Honor," said Starns.

"I did not," said Judge Ross. "That is a falsehood."

Soon all of the attorneys' arguments were over. Judge Lord, despite his promises, stood and began to make his way to the front of the courtroom. Bob Mattson leaned over to the law clerk sitting next to him in the peanut gallery.

"Yell 'fire!'" Mattson whispered.

But nothing would have been able to stop the judge.

He spoke of his duty as a judge "and as a human being." He spoke of the health risks, especially for children, "those little bodies." He spoke of the delays in the legal process; while the proceedings dragged on, "carcinogenic fibers continue to be disbursed, exposing thousands to a potential health risk," he said. He spoke of the need to inform the public of the hazards; "at what point," he asked, "is this court going to enable me or any other judge to tell the people of Duluth what is happening to them?" He spoke of Reserve Mining's misdeeds in court: "the hiding of documents, the misrepresentations."

He admitted that he had become "something of an advocate." That, he said, is "something I can't change."

He repeatedly invited the Eighth Circuit judges to ask him questions. The only response was a brusque reply from Judge Lay. The record—"the full transcript," said Judge Lay—is "the only basis upon which we can decide this case." Otherwise, the appeals judges sat silent and stony.

Judge Lord wrapped up after about fifteen minutes. The Eighth Circuit judges took the matter under advisement and left the bench.

Their decision was issued two and a half weeks later, on January 6, 1976, under the caption *Reserve Mining Company et al. versus Honorable Miles W. Lord, United States District Judge.*

The Eighth Circuit tallied Judge Lord's transgressions. Judge Lord demonstrated "a gross bias" against Reserve Mining. Judge Lord "acted in defiance" of the Eighth Circuit's order to steer clear of the on-land siting decision; his summoning of public officials in November showed "a purposeful intent to influence the state officials to reject the Milepost 7 site." Judge Lord failed to afford Reserve proper notice or an opportunity to be heard before ordering the deposit of $100,000, thereby denying Reserve due process of law.

One sentence of the opinion, in particular, would ring through time:

Judge Lord seems to have shed the robe of the judge and to have assumed the mantle of the advocate.

That the judge had become an advocate was never in doubt. He had admitted as much in St. Louis. But to see these words in an appellate opinion in such memorable—and sure-to-be-quoted—language was still a striking blow.

And the Eighth Circuit also removed the judge—completely—from the case.

Knocked off, but not by a tree.

■ ■ ■ ■

A new judge took over. It was Edward Devitt—the judge from central casting—who ten years before had officiated at Miles's swearing-in ceremony.

The contrast between the two judges was stark.

Judge Devitt was a rock-ribbed Republican. He had been elected to the U.S. House of Representatives from St. Paul in 1946; two years later, he lost his reelection bid to another young Irish Catholic more suited to the heavily Democratic district, the up-and-coming Gene McCarthy. (McCarthy painted Devitt as a reactionary who favored the rich and opposed the New Deal.) In 1954, Devitt was appointed by President Eisenhower to the bench, where the accolades piled up year after year: "one of the most respected district court judges in the nation"; "revered as the embodiment of the classic and ideal federal judge"; "role model to countless judges."

If Miles Lord was the judge for "the little guy," Edward Devitt, very much the patrician, was his opposite number for the established order of society. Even their chambers reflected their differences, with Judge Lord's plain and unadorned and Judge Devitt's resplendently ornate, furnished with antiques and hung with photographs of Republican luminaries, including Richard Nixon and Strom Thurmond, many with Judge Devitt by their side.

Still, Miles and Judge Devitt got along just fine.

Miles called him "Eddie."

Judge Devitt, in fact, picked up where Judge Lord had left off.

First, Judge Devitt held Reserve liable for the interim costs of providing filtered water. The amount was to be determined later, but the estimate was as high as $6 million, far above the $100,000 down payment ordered by Judge Lord. Reserve's arguments against this payment—including that it would be an unconstitutional taking of private property—were, Judge Devitt wrote, "fatuous" and "without merit."

Next, Judge Devitt hit Reserve with penalties, totaling more than $800,000, for violating its discharge permits.

Judge Devitt also sanctioned Reserve for "bad faith in the conduct of the defense of this lawsuit" and for "failure to truthfully and fully comply with discovery requests and court orders." This was for failing to produce documents, while the case was before Judge Lord, that revealed the company's hidden plans for on-land disposal. Judge Devitt gave Reserve's justifications—the standard dog-ate-my-homework excuses—short shrift, dismissing them as "no more than a belated rationalization" and "frivolous." As a sanction, he ordered Reserve to pay $200,000 of the plaintiffs' litigation expenses.

A sanction is a rarity in litigation, no matter how egregious the conduct.

But Judge Devitt's sanction was only a fraction of the amount spent by the government in the long-running case and a mere slap on the wrist for Reserve's billion-dollar parent companies.

More importantly, on the issue of setting a deadline for Reserve to cease dumping into Lake Superior, Judge Devitt and Judge Lord were markedly apart.

For several months, Judge Devitt held out hope that the state of Minnesota and Reserve Mining could reach agreement for an on-land site. Finally, Judge Devitt gave Reserve a midnight deadline, but for July 1977—another year away.

The Eighth Circuit, which would affirm all of Judge Devitt's orders on the case, affirmed this one as well but with a "caveat." The deadline could be modified—in other words, extended—if warranted by "changed circumstances."

Which is, of course, what happened.

By now, more than one commentator was writing that the Reserve Mining case seemed right out of a Charles Dickens novel, with, as Dickens wrote in *Bleak House,* lawyers "appearing, and disappearing, . . . and interrogating, and filing, and cross-filing, and arguing, and sealing, and motioning, and referring, and reporting . . . and equitably waltzing ourselves off to dusty death."

And the odyssey was not nearly over.

The state examiner, after hearings that lasted the better part of a year, recommended the rejection of Reserve's proposed Milepost 7 site and urged a location farther away from population centers. Reserve appealed to a panel of three state court judges in Lake County, who, after taking additional evidence, reversed and ordered the state to issue permits for the company's preferred site. The battle then moved to the Minnesota Supreme Court. There, the justices found "undisputed evidence" that Reserve's discharges contained carcinogenic fibers. But they also ruled that there was only "unsubstantial and inconclusive" proof of any detriment to the public health and ordered the state to issue permits for Milepost 7, subject to stringent conditions for protection of the environment and the public health.

That was in the spring of 1977.

Then Judge Devitt extended his deadline . . . three more years.

Finally, in March 1980, Reserve Mining completed one of the largest environmental projects in history, at a cost of $370 million, and halted its discharge of taconite tailings into Lake Superior.

More than eight years had passed since the government filed suit in federal court.

Seven years had passed since the discovery of asbestos-like fibers.

Six years had passed since Judge Lord's midnight injunction.

Virtually everyone—even Reserve Mining—had acknowledged for much of this time that it was intolerable to dump 67,000 tons of waste, every day, into a Great (in every sense of the word) Lake that was not only a beauty to behold but also served as the source of drinking water to North Shore residents.

Yet Reserve had been able to play the courts and stall the inevitable.

For year . . . after year . . . after year.

Still, many would credit Judge Lord with having saved Lake Superior.

For the judge, however, the battle would never end. For years, he continued to press—unsuccessfully—for an accounting of the health hazards not only from Reserve but also the entire taconite industry on the Iron Range. He would call the failure "to determine scientifically, once and for all, the degree of danger of mining tailings . . . one of the greatest disappointments of my life."

He would also be consumed—forevermore—by his death match with the Eighth Circuit. He believed that the appellate judges would look at his future decisions with, he said, "a more jaundiced eye." He believed that would bring nothing but trouble.

22

The Judge Stands Accused

The judicial misconduct proceedings are set to begin on the complaints filed by A. H. Robins. On the morning of July 9, 1984, a crush of people swarms into the courtroom in the federal building in St. Paul. Extra folding chairs have been carted in for the overflow; forty seats are reserved for reporters, and the national media, including all three television networks, show up in force.

"A media circus of grand proportions," one journalist will write.

Judge Lord enters, not from behind the bench—he is the accused, not the presiding judge for these two days—but from the back doors, where the general public comes in.

Still, his entrance is grand.

The judge is tense, but when he sees the crowd, many of whom are well-wishers, turn in their seats—Miles! they shout—his showmanship takes over. He proceeds down the aisle, shaking hands and looking every bit the politician he was (and still is). With all eyes on him, he takes his seat in the front row, flanked by Maxine and their two sons and two daughters. I watch from nearby, sitting with Keith.

The five judges on the investigatory panel take the bench, all gray-haired men in long black robes. Judge Lay opens the hearings. The issue before the panel, he says, is the propriety of Judge Lord's conduct, particularly on February 29. The conduct of A. H. Robins—"the alleged legal or moral responsibility of the A. H. Robins Company," he says—is not relevant.

I look over at Judge Lord. He sits still, without expression.

Judge Lord feels "squeezed out" by his own lawyers. He had wanted to address the investigatory panel, but his lawyers vetoed the idea. The judge thought he could convince Ramsey Clark—"I think Ramsey would have gone for it," he says later—but Joe Walters, who had lived through Reserve Mining as a friend and confidant of the judge, was adamantly opposed.

But his two lawyers agree to the judge offering a written statement. Clark stands and reads the judge's remarks about why he reprimanded the three A. H. Robins executives. In large part, this ignores Judge Lay's opening admonition, but it is simply not possible to consider Judge Lord's conduct without also examining the actions of A. H. Robins (at least not in the real world). In his statement, Judge Lord, through Clark, speaks of the litigation strategy of A. H. Robins to keep corporate officials "totally insulated" from information that would show the "widespread disability and death" caused by the Dalkon Shield; of how this blurred the line "between defensive litigation tactics and normal medical and pharmaceutical practice . . . with fatal results"; and of how if he had not acted, "this would have implicated the courts of this country as an accessory to the continuing improper medical and pharmaceutical practices of A. H. Robins and continued injuries that this caused."

Clark and Walters then call two expert witnesses, both professors of law, who testify about the history and meaning of the Judicial Conduct and Disability Act, the nature of due process, and the need to preserve the independence of the judiciary. The testimony is drab and academic; at least one person in the audience falls asleep. Griffin Bell conducts short cross-examinations for A. H. Robins, which are also none too exciting. The high point comes when Bell asks one of the professors if litigants are entitled to a neutral judge. "Yes, an objective judge," the professor replies, but then adds, "there's a difference between objective and being ignorant."

The next witness for the judge is Robert Sheran, the former Minnesota Supreme Court justice. He gets right to the point: judges should not be disciplined, he says, for statements made in good faith and in the course of litigation. The most interesting aspect of Sheran's appearance, given his role in Reserve Mining, is simply the fact that he is here to support Judge Lord. (The judge, in turn, believes that Sheran acted honorably in Reserve Mining and was not implicated in any misdeeds; in the judge's view, it is possible to represent corporations—even ones that act disreputably—in an upright fashion.)

Two of the judge's colleagues on the federal bench in Minnesota—Judges Renner (naturally) and Magnuson (who tried the Martha Hahn case)—also offer support in a written submission, which Walters reads into the record:

> It is often our duty to take difficult and controversial action. We understand and accept this responsibility. However, we can perform the duties of this office effectively only if we may act without fear of retaliation directed at us by litigants or others who are dissatisfied with our actions. We understand this to be the essence of judicial independence. . . .
>
> We must be free to act untrammeled by fear, answerable only to the Constitution and to our consciences.

This statement by two of the judge's brethren—a class act—is immensely appreciated by Judge Lord. No doubt, neither of these judges would ever consider giving a speech like Judge Lord's. But they defend his right to do so. ("Regardless of whether you agree with him or disagree with him, there is a place and time for Judge Lords in the federal judiciary," Judge Renner says later, "although," he adds, "I don't know that we want too many.") To me, however, it is all too noticeable that, other than Judges Renner and Magnuson, no other federal judge in Minnesota adds his or her voice in support. But I am more disheartened by this than Judge Lord. He is used to, and accepts, the desire of other judges to avoid controversy.

One more judge, however, does come to Judge Lord's defense: Judge Theis, who has been presiding over the MDL litigation in Wichita for eight and a half years.

Personally, Judge Theis disagrees with Judge Lord for having delivered the speech. But he holds dear the right of a federal judge to speak freely. In an affidavit, Judge Theis writes about A. H. Robins's "pattern of repetitive and dilatory tactics" in the MDL; he states that, based on the reports of Special Masters Thompson and Bartsh, it appears that A. H. Robins's representations about the completeness of the MDL discovery "are open to serious question"; and he concludes with a sentence that hedges but still hits hard:

> Without knowing all of the details it appears that under the circumstances known, Judge Lord's remonstrance to the responsible company officials was mild punishment indeed considering the strong possibility

that such apparent misrepresentations and trial tactics seem to permeate the proceedings here and elsewhere.

This is the boldest statement Judge Theis has made in all of his years in the Dalkon Shield litigation. Later, A. H. Robins will point to this affidavit in an unsuccessful effort to disqualify Judge Theis from the MDL, arguing that he too lost his impartiality by speaking out in support of a fellow judge.

When it comes time for A. H. Robins to present its case, the company calls only one witness: Alexander Slaughter. This seems to me an odd choice—to put the company's lead attorney on the witness stand—as it opens the door for his cross-examination; but what do I know, I think, compared to A. H. Robins's high-powered lawyers. Griffin Bell introduces Slaughter as the person who knows more about the document discovery than anyone else, then turns the direct examination over to his law partner, Charles Kirbo (another close friend of Jimmy Carter, who served as the former president's personal attorney). Slaughter attempts to deflect the growing allegations in courtrooms across the country that documents have been concealed by testifying about what he calls the "massive searches" for documents in the MDL. In the end, however, Slaughter sheds little light on the issues at hand: "I don't recall," he says; "I'm not certain"; "I'm doing this from hearsay"; "preliminarily, it appears"; "I can't speculate"; "I can't go into the details."

And these are his answers to questions from Kirbo, his own attorney, who does little but toss Slaughter big, fat softballs.

Joe Walters then starts the cross-examination. He gets Slaughter to admit that at one of the hearings before Judge Lord in February, Slaughter believed that representations made by one of his partners about the completeness of the MDL discovery were not accurate. "You didn't stand up and tell the court, did you, that your partner, Mr. Getchell, was in error when he was telling the court that everything's been produced except what's privileged," Walters asks.

"I didn't correct Mr. Getchell," Slaughter says.

Walters also gets Slaughter to admit that there are "clearly" documents covered by Judge Lord's orders that were not turned over in the MDL.

Maybe my instincts about what a bad idea it is for Slaughter to testify aren't half-bad, I start to think. But that's as far as Walters gets. He has extracted a couple of nuggets but simply does not have sufficient background in the Dalkon Shield litigation to penetrate further.

Judge Lord all but squirms in his seat. He wants to jump up and take over the cross-examination. But he sits.

After about five hours, the hearing wraps up for the day. All that's left are closing arguments set for tomorrow. The A. H. Robins case against the judge hasn't amounted to much.

The judge unknots.

He is not much impressed with the A. H. Robins legal talent. Bell and Kirbo remind him of the old days when horses were let loose in the spring after being locked up all winter: "their knees would be a little stiff and their joints would be stiff and they'd kick up their heels and fall down," he says later. "That's the way these guys looked in court."

The next morning, the closing arguments pit Griffin Bell and Ramsey Clark—two former U.S. attorneys general with little in common but that office—against each other, head-to-head.

Despite Judge Lord's view, Bell is reputed to be a skillful advocate, described as a "Southern gentleman of the law," and, even in this Northern courtroom, he tries a few homespun stories in his deep Southern tones. His folksiness, however, is overshadowed by vitriol: he calls Judge Lord "an accident waiting to happen"; says the judge's speech was more outrageous than anything he's heard "in my entire career as a lawyer"; and grumbles that A. H. Robins "paid a lot of money to get out of Judge Lord's hands" by settling the cases before him, only to have the speech live on through its impact on other judges across the country.

I even get a cameo in Bell's catalog of complaints; he gripes that the judge called on not one but two special masters—"one wasn't enough"—and "then sent his law clerk over to Richmond to help out," even though there had already been "all sorts of discovery" in the MDL.

Bell also complains that the Dalkon Shield litigation cost the A. H. Robins Company "forty cents a share" last year.

"So they're suffering," he says, "they're suffering."

(The company, he means, not the women.)

But Bell's main argument is that A. H. Robins and the three executives were denied due process—"No person shall be . . . deprived of life, liberty, or property, without due process of law," the Fifth Amendment states—when Judge Lord issued his reprimand without a trial and, Bell says, without notice or an opportunity to be heard.

To me, this argument seems far-fetched. The seminal due process case—cited by Bell and well known to every first-year law student—is *Goldberg versus Kelly,* where the Supreme Court held that welfare recipients are entitled to prior notice and the opportunity to be heard before their benefits can be terminated. This seems to me to have little bearing in this case, where a Fortune 500 company was represented up the wazoo by dozens of lawyers who had the opportunity to appear in hearing after hearing before Judge Lord, and where the judge didn't fine or sanction or terminate any benefits—or order a recall of the Dalkon Shield—or take any other tangible action against A. H. Robins, but only spoke his mind.

A columnist for the *St. Paul Dispatch* at the hearing is also unimpressed with the due process argument. His column pierces the "legal mush" and boils A. H. Robins's grievances down, in plain English, to the company's gripe that the judge "didn't warn the executives . . . that he was going to yell at them." The judge "didn't put those executives in jail, he didn't take any more of their money than was agreed to, he didn't deprive them of life, liberty or property," the columnist writes. "He yelled at them."

Ramsey Clark—a contrast in style, tone, and message—follows Bell to the podium. He stands tall and Texas lanky and speaks in a soft-spoken drawl as he implores the panel to champion the independence of the judiciary ("the judiciary has an affirmative obligation to achieve justice"); discusses the ability of large corporations to corrupt the promise of equal justice ("it's no irony that the first case that comes before this council is brought by a powerful corporation"); stresses that the statements in Judge Lord's speech were based on what the judge had learned during the proceedings before him, not on improper extrajudicial sources ("they are documented in the records"); and reminds the panel of judges that it is the women—not A. H. Robins—who are suffering.

"You haven't heard A. H. Robins say anything about the women," Clark says.

Clark calls the due process argument "bizarre." Like Judge Lord, he sees one type of justice for the rich, one for the poor. In Clark's own law practice, he represents poor people and unpopular causes—not corporate America—and routinely sees judges who are none too hesitant to harangue his clients. He is accustomed to judges saying "things that at the time really burn me up," he tells the panel. But, he says, "I respect their right to say it." Judges have the right—indeed, the obligation—to comment on cases, he says, and there is no due process violation where, as here, there was no adjudication of rights, no legally binding findings of fact, and no order to pay sanctions or fines.

In the end, Clark pounds on one theme: the truth. "We've been told what outrageous statements the judge made," he tells the panel. "They're true." He points to an annotated version of the judge's speech: fifty-one pages, single-spaced, of footnotes documenting the bases for the judge's remarks. "Overwhelming factual evidence in the record," Clark says.

Bell, by contrast, makes little effort to controvert the substance of the judge's speech. "Not that we're trying to prove that we're right on any of these issues," he says, "but that if we had a hearing we would have been able to show some countervailing evidence."

Bell, however, does not ask for an evidentiary hearing.

Instead, he says that the speech must be expunged because it is causing "big problems" for A. H. Robins in courts "all over the country." He asks the panel to "put us back to the status quo . . . where we were before that happened." Then, he says, "we can go ahead and put all the pieces back together again."

23

Fire and Brimstone, 1976–1981

The Reserve Mining case had taken four years of the judge's life. But at age fifty-six, when the Eighth Circuit removed him, he was still in fighting trim. The disqualification left him angry and bitter; for a time, he considered leaving the bench and returning to the private practice of law. But he also viewed his unceremonious dethroning as "a badge of honor."

Many in the public agreed.

His actions in the case earned him "the adulation of many Minnesotans," wrote one reporter, and, said another writer, "had the effect of making him a hero to many."

Indeed, he was a full-blown celebrity. Walking down streets or through downtown skyways, in restaurants and bars, at gas station pumps, in corner shops, out on fishing boats, riding in elevators in office buildings or on escalators in department stores, everywhere he went, so many people, from so many walks of life, hailed him with handshakes, waves, pats on the back, hugs, and shout-outs to "Miles!"

He loved the attention and yakked and joked with one and all.

Public opinion polls skewed strongly in his favor. In one, conducted for the *Minneapolis Tribune,* the judge scored an enviable 55 percent favorable rating, with unfavorables of only 11 percent. (The remaining 34 percent were somehow undecided.) By contrast, only 21 percent of Minnesotans approved of the Eighth Circuit's removal of the judge from the case. There was no correlation with party affiliation; the judge seemed to have transcended partisan politics.

Despite these glowing numbers, the poll still rankled the judge. How could anyone—other than Eighth Circuit judges and Reserve Mining executives and lawyers—not love him? he wondered. He went to a bar near his home, eyed a group of men standing around with drinks, and pounded his fist on the bar. "Fifty-five percent of the people like me, 34 percent don't give a damn, but there's 11 percent that don't like me," he yelled. "I want to know right now whether there are any such bastards among your number."

Filled with "fire and brimstone," the judge hit the speaking circuit. He spoke to attorneys, to teachers, to environmentalists, to college students, to scientists, to church groups, to journalists, and to groups as disparate as bird-watchers and firemen, often to standing ovations.

He embraced the cause of the environmentalists.

"Our earth is not here to be desecrated and destroyed. . . . We have captured the earth. We have subjugated it and we must now set upon a course of carefully preserving it, lest in the end we all die in one giant manmade cesspool."

He lambasted corporations.

"The system is set up so that a man in a large corporation cannot let his heart or soul or concerns get away with him. The only thing there is to stop corporate misconduct is the law, and the law narrows down to the judge."

He upbraided the churches.

"Even the churches, I submit, have not seen the light. The whole thrust of our religious training is that we're here in preparation for another world and that some day some kind of giant spiritual spacecraft will come, lift us off, and take us away to that other place where we need not worry about the mess we left behind."

And he beseeched his audiences to heed their better selves.

"I believe that you believe we are our brother's keeper, so I implore you to let your feelings be known."

The judge also went out of his way to attack and antagonize the high and mighty. He scolded politicians who were beholden to and "blackmail[ed]" by the mining interests; "if a politician speaks out against the mining companies, he's helpless, a beached whale," he told the press. He engaged in a public falling out with Governor Wendy Anderson, who, the judge believed, had done his best to convince the Eighth Circuit that the judge had "lost my marbles." He went a few rounds with the *Duluth News-Tribune*; the publisher—facetiously (or not)—said he couldn't figure out whether the judge believed North Shore people were "going to start dropping like flies"; the judge responded in a guest column. "Cancer victims don't die like flies," he wrote, "they die in the arms of their loved ones slowly and painfully."

And, of course, the judge carried on his feud with the Eighth Circuit.

He made it clear that the Eighth Circuit had upheld all of his essential findings in Reserve Mining—that the taconite fibers could not be distinguished from asbestos and created a potential public health hazard—and only differed on the timing of the conversion to on-land disposal by giving the company a virtual free hand.

"I don't have any problem justifying my behavior," he said. "I think it would be the appeals judges' problem to justify their behavior."

He was especially piqued at Judge Heaney, another of his contemporary DFLers. Gerald Heaney was born in 1918 in a small farming town in southeastern Minnesota (high school class of five); graduated from the University of Minnesota law school, where he was fraternity brothers with Orville Freeman; made a name for himself in Duluth as a prominent community leader and political operative (called northeastern Minnesota's "unofficial political boss"); and was nominated to the Eighth Circuit by LBJ in 1966 (the same year Miles was named a trial judge). Judge Heaney was a staunch liberal—renowned for his role in major school desegregation cases—and saw eye to eye with Miles on most issues of substance. But Miles believed that Heaney was too close to the corporate interests in northern Minnesota, especially the mining companies. "You don't want to monkey around with a mining company when he is around," Miles said. Judge Heaney had recused himself from Reserve Mining and was not on the Eighth Circuit panel that removed Miles from the case. But the two men, with their shared (but complicated) history, still spoke to each other about the matter. Reportedly, Judge Heaney was also advising Governor Anderson and the mayor of Duluth on the case. Miles, ever distrustful, wondered what else Heaney may have been up to.

One of the few public officials to escape the judge's wrath was Hubert, even though it was public knowledge that as senator he had been working to achieve an acceptable compromise with Reserve. Indeed, a Reserve official had testified in the judge's own courtroom that Senator Humphrey was supporting financial assistance for the company to convert to on-land disposal; the judge lashed out, unable to bear the thought of such blasphemy, and declared that the testimony "be stricken as hearsay, incompetent, immaterial, and not consistent with the truth."

■ ■ ■ ■

The judge also sparred again with the Eighth Circuit in the antibiotics litigation.

He had been presiding over that trial—for the United States and other nonsettling plaintiffs—for more than a year, on and off, throughout the Reserve Mining tempest. By the end of 1975, the United States was the last remaining plaintiff. The trial seemed to be moving in slow motion. Even the lawyers for the United States seemed in no particular hurry.

Finally, the judge had enough.

He called in the pharmaceutical company lawyers and asked for their best settlement offer. Seventy-six million dollars, they said. The judge thought that was fair. It was multiples of what the Justice Department attorneys had been ready to accept several years before, only to be impeded by the judge himself. But now they wanted more. The judge tried his best to persuade the government attorneys to change their minds—these were difficult cases to win at trial and sustain on appeal—but to no avail.

He had been working on the antibiotics cases for more than five years and saw no end in sight. The combination of both antibiotics and Reserve Mining had taken its toll. He was no longer in his *no-unmanageable-cases, only-lazy-judges* mind-set. "I couldn't stand it any longer," he said later. "Damn near killed me."

He called a halt to virtually all proceedings, and, in the spring of 1976, after several months in limbo, the pharmaceutical company defendants moved for a mistrial. The judge seemed inclined to grant the request. Before he could rule, however, the Justice Department attorneys filed an emergency petition with the Eighth Circuit to prohibit the judge from discharging the jurors.

This was another case where the judge himself made the marquee: *United States of America versus Honorable Miles W. Lord.*

This time, however, the Eighth Circuit—with Judges Lay, Heaney, and Roy Stephenson presiding—did not remove Judge Lord. In fact, the exact opposite. The appeals court ordered that Judge Lord complete the case himself: either finishing the current trial or starting all over again with new jurors.

Judge Lord promptly declared a mistrial. He said that that the length and complexity of the trial had "tired and confused" the jurors and that the "barrage of publicity" surrounding the case—especially about the large settlements for other plaintiffs—made a fair trial impossible. For another year, the case languished without meaningful action and then, despite the Eighth Circuit's admonition, was transferred to U.S. District Judge Charles Weiner in Philadelphia, who volunteered for the assignment. Ultimately, Judge Weiner tossed out all of the government's remaining claims, a ruling that was affirmed on appeal.

After more than a decade of litigation, the government ended up with nothing.

■ ■ ■ ■

This period of time also brought the judge back into politics, when Walter Mondale joined the national ticket in 1976 as Jimmy Carter's vice presidential running mate. Mondale phoned Miles early on, and, after that, Miles was a fairly regular buttinsky, offering all kinds of advice. (Miles had been particularly fixated for a couple of years on President Gerald Ford's pardon of Richard Nixon—he didn't like the smell of that—and thought it was a great issue to use against the incumbent.) Miles was not nearly as active as he had been in 1968. Still, there was no question he could be a nuisance. "Oh yeah!" Mondale laughed, years later.

Mondale followed his mentor Hubert Humphrey's path to the second highest office in the land—and would become widely credited with redefining the vice presidency with his influential role in the administration—when the Carter-Mondale ticket won that fall.

Miles was thrilled.

(Gene McCarthy, not so much. "He had contempt for the vice presidency as an office," Mondale would say, "and, based on my experience, most of its occupants.")

Now Mondale's Senate seat in Minnesota was open. This time around, unlike when Humphrey had ascended to the vice presidency and Karl Rolvaag was governor, Miles's views were not welcome. The appointment would rest in the hands of Governor Wendy Anderson. And Wendy Anderson appointed . . . himself. (He resigned as governor with the understanding that his successor would officially appoint him to the Senate.) This infuriated Miles (and many others), an added provocation to their ongoing feud over Reserve Mining. Miles further fanned the flames by threatening to run against Anderson in the next Senate election. "That prospect of me running against Wendy Anderson must just scare the living hell out of him," he told the press, laughing and slapping his knee.

■ ■ ■ ■

Meanwhile, the judge's speaking tour was taking him near and far.

One speech was to a gathering of the New York Academy of Sciences in Washington, D.C. The event was to honor Dr. Irving Selikoff, the star witness from the Reserve Mining trial. The judge urged his audience to follow the lead of Dr. Selikoff, a man, he said, who "sacrificed personal gain for the integrity of his beliefs."

"Let's face it, ladies and gentlemen," the judge said, "changes cannot be made by the meek, the humble, the reticent."

The judge also spoke of the power of publicity—as Hubert had taught him—because, in the end, he said, "the power lies with the people and the people are frequently the last to hear."

Indeed, Hubert was much on his mind as he spoke. "The reason I'm going so long," the judge explained as he wound on, "is because Humphrey said, 'Miles, give them an extra few minutes from me.'"

The judge had visited Hubert in his old friend's Washington apartment just before this speech. Hubert scrawled a note for Miles to take to Selikoff: "Dear Irving: I have appointed my friend, Miles Lord, to bring you greetings."

Hubert's hand shook as he wrote.

It was December 1977. Hubert was dying of cancer. He had been through surgery and chemotherapy, and it was now clear that all was lost.

The two men were alone.

"How are you doing, Slim?" Miles asked.

"I'm cheating the damn undertaker," Hubert said. "I'm just going to hang on as long as I can."

Hubert asked Miles to regale him with the well-worn tales of the fun and pranks they had pulled over the years. Then their thoughts turned to the future. Hubert asked whether after his death, Miles would take his seat in the Senate.

"No way," Miles said. "Maxine would kill me. Besides, you're still swinging."

But they both knew the end was near.

As he contemplated his friend's impending death, Miles thought about what he'd recently read about new advances in the science of cloning. He thought to himself how "an entire heredity is in one cell." He wondered if he could get "just get a slice" of the Hubie. One slice, one cell, to clone.

Hubert made his rounds of farewells as his health allowed. He saw Gene McCarthy one last time at a banquet in Washington. Hubert spoke to the gathering about the future of America. He still radiated optimism. As he was helped back to his table, Gene stood to greet him. Hubert and Gene faced each other. "We embraced, spoke each other's name—that was all," Gene said later.

No words could convey all that had passed between them.

Hubert went home to Minnesota.

His family installed a toll-free 800 number in his home so he could reach out to friends and colleagues and say good-bye.

Days before his death, Hubert called Richard Nixon, the man who had vanquished his presidential dreams by the thinnest of margins. "Dick, I'm not going to be around much longer," Hubert said. "There's going to be a memorial service for me in the Capitol rotunda. I want you to attend."

Nixon balked. He was living in seclusion after having resigned the presidency in the wake of Watergate. But Hubert won out—"You must attend"—with his insistence.

"Civility, decency, and rising above party defined his dreadful last days," wrote two Humphrey aides.

Miles visited the Humphrey home in Waverly, Minnesota, one last time, on January 13, 1978. By then, Hubert had slipped into a coma. He died that evening, at sixty-six years of age.

There was a nationwide outburst of appreciation for his life and for his spirit. "He was mourned with a display and depth of feeling that few politicians—particularly one who had never been president—have ever aroused," wrote *Newsweek*. "He was always a happy warrior, an un-abashed liberal who loved the politics of small towns and the power of Big Government. . . . He never lost his sense of optimism, his personal warmth or his joy in public life."

For Miles, a friend of thirty years was gone.

"He was more brilliant, he was more fun, he had more compassion, he was more practical, he had more foresight, he had more understanding, he had more everything than anybody I ever knew," Miles would say. "And nobody even comes close."

Miles was on the short list for appointment to Hubert's Senate seat. He didn't want the job, but he did want to get in his two cents on the choice. The new governor of Minnesota—Rudy Perpich, who succeeded Wendy Anderson—would make the pick. Miles (and others) had the perfect person in mind to stand in for Hubert: Muriel Humphrey, Hubert's wife.

Miles counseled Muriel and the Humphrey family. He met with Perpich, a fellow Iron Ranger, at the governor's house. Muriel got the appointment, to widespread acclaim.

Her special term in the U.S. Senate would last only the rest of the year. That fall, in the election of November 1978, Muriel passed on a run. The DFL-endorsed candidate for the seat was trounced. So was Wendy Anderson in the race for the second Senate seat, essentially ending his meteoric political career with the public soured by his self-serving appointment two years earlier.

The DFL domain was shrinking.

Mondale was still vice president. But he would be voted out of office when Ronald Reagan defeated Jimmy Carter in 1980. Four years later, in 1984, Mondale again followed in Humphrey's footsteps by capturing the Democratic nomination for president, only to take a historic shellacking. True to his DFL roots, Mondale ran as a classic liberal: he chose as his running mate Geraldine Ferraro, the first woman to run as a vice presidential candidate on any major party ticket; supported a nuclear freeze and the Equal Rights Amendment; and declared that, if elected, he would *raise* taxes. "Mr. Reagan will raise taxes and so will I," Mondale said. "He won't tell you. I just did." The country, however, was more interested in Reagan's optimistic "Morning in America" message. On election day, Mondale carried only his home state, Minnesota, as well as the District of Columbia.

This was a resounding defeat for not only Mondale but also, by proxy, the original band of DFLers. There had been cracks before—in 1966, Republicans won all but one of the state constitutional offices—and now, after decades of dominance, the DFL was a shadow of its heyday self: both U.S. Senate seats occupied by Republicans; Mondale defeated; Humphrey dead and even his legacy much diminished. Indeed, after the initial outpouring upon his death, and despite his achievements (especially but not only on civil rights), Hubert Humphrey became a "forgotten man," as one historian would lament in the *New York Times*. "Poor Humphrey could never catch a break," he wrote. "That such a figure in American history is largely ignored today is sad."

■ ■ ■ ■

Judge Lord, however, was still going strong.

The judge's next blockbuster case after Hubert's death would be Dalkon Shield, a few years down the road. In the interim, he still made headlines, both on and off the bench. He was praised in some quarters. He was blistered in others. In other words, he was Miles Lord.

One of his bigger cases in this interlude involved the University of Minnesota as the defendant. A chemistry professor, Dr. Shyamala Rajender, sued the university for discrimination on the basis of sex (and national origin). The judge certified a class action—exponentially increasing the potential scope of the suit—and after eleven weeks of trial, the university was astute enough to head for the settlement table. Ultimately, the judge signed a ground-breaking consent decree, which established an affirmative action program at the university and set up a mechanism to resolve hundreds of claims. This was one of the earliest suits involving promotion and tenure in the academic world and, as other schools followed its model, was praised for having "more impact on a university's personnel practices than any other case in the nation's history."

The judge also issued another decision involving the Boundary Waters Canoe Area Wilderness, this time restricting the use of motorboats and snowmobiles in the lake-studded wilderness along the Canadian border. "Bring in the cameras," he said, as he called a press conference to announce his decision. "This is a historic moment."

On smaller matters, the judge enjoyed himself as much as possible, which was quite a bit. In one case, he rented a bus, loaded up the jurors, and moved the trial up north to the home of the injured plaintiff, who was not in good shape to travel, in Brainerd. The local paper reported on the whole affair, praising the "former Cuyuna Range lad" for not having grown too big for his britches. The judge also made quite an impression on the jurors. "Isn't he just a great man," said one.

And the judge continued to meddle a bit in politics. In one incident, he attended a fund-raising event for Skip Humphrey, who was running for state attorney general. The judge introduced Hubert's son at the event and endorsed his candidacy for the office the judge had once held himself. When Republicans complained about a federal judge engaging in politics, the judge pled to the deed. He reminded the Republicans of his long friendship with the Humphrey family.

"I will vote for Skip Humphrey," he said. "My wife will vote for him. . . . All my kids will vote for him. . . . All my cousins, too."

The judge also let his mouth run on another matter that attracted more attention.

A suspected murderer, John Hartmann, escaped from a state security hospital in the spring of 1979. Hartmann had been committed years before as mentally ill and dangerous after being accused, but not convicted, of killing a man. In the ensuing years, he was suspected of three additional murders: one of a fellow inmate and two in New Mexico after an earlier escape. Hartmann had been before Judge Lord on several occasions with various unsuccessful habeas corpus petitions. During one of those cases, a man identifying himself as Hartmann had called the judge and said, "I'll be out one way or another, and when I do I'm coming out there to see you."

Now Hartmann was on the loose again. Maxine picked up the phone to find a man with a deep voice on the line. The judge believed it was Hartmann. There had not been any explicit threat, but "as far as I'm concerned," the judge said, "the calling is threat enough."

The hunt for Hartmann was hampered, however, because he had no formal conviction on his record, which prevented the FBI from entering the case. The judge was put under the protection of armed U.S. marshals, while days passed with no sign of the fugitive. The judge lashed out. "There is something wrong with a system that allows a civilly insane person to escape without being able to call in the appropriate law enforcement agencies," he said.

The judge also called Hartmann "a mass murderer." "Give him his rights," he said, "when you've got him in irons."

Eventually, the bureaucratic snags were resolved, and Hartmann was found hiding out in Missouri. The scare was over. But the judge's comments had attracted widespread headlines and, in some circles, a lingering furor.

■ ■ ■ ■

Indeed, the judge's profile—for better and for worse—was sky-high.

A year after the Hartmann affair, in July 1980, the *American Lawyer,* a national legal publication, named him one of the worst federal judges in the country. There were about five hundred federal judges at the time. The magazine picked the worst from each of the (then) eleven judicial circuits; Judge Lord was the selection from the Eighth Circuit.

The magazine focused on three matters: Reserve Mining, the antibiotics trial (the judge pulling the plug), and his comments about "mass murderer" John Hartmann. Several lawyers were quoted in the article, none identified by name, all critical of the judge. The judge "loves a good fight," said one lawyer. "And that's exactly what makes him such a bad judge."

The judge called the article "a hatchet job." In fact, in a follow-up by the *St. Paul Pioneer Press,* a reporter interviewed more than twenty-five local lawyers who frequently appeared before the judge and found that none had been contacted by the national magazine, in a town where federal court practitioners were a fairly confined community. Only two of the local lawyers agreed with the magazine's portrayal of the judge. One lawyer suspected that the magazine's sources may have been out-of-town corporate types, "probably a bunch of Eastern silk-stocking civil lawyers who represent big business," he said. "When these guys come into court, they expect the judge to roll over and play dead." The *Pioneer Press* reported that the local lawyers were "genuinely fond of Lord as a person"; "greatly respect his acuity and incisiveness"; and believed he was "a very sharp customer" with "a knack for quickly peeling away layers of legal mumbo jumbo to get at the hard core of truth." Even the criminal defense attorneys had praise: "As well as a mind, he has a heart" . . . "He is extremely bright and quick" . . . "He tries to cut through a lot of the bullshit and get right down to the heart of the matter." But the hometown lawyers, especially from the criminal defense bar, also criticized the judge's penchant for picking sides. "He fills in all the holes in the prosecutor's case," said one defense attorney. "The son of a bitch is a very astute examiner."

The next year, in July 1981, the Association of Trial Lawyers of America (ATLA)—with some forty-two thousand members nationwide—named the judge the country's "outstanding federal trial judge."

As examples of the judge's finest work, ATLA pointed to the same cases that the *American Lawyer* had cited for opposite effect—Reserve Mining and antibiotics (particularly Operation Money Back)—along with his decision that opened up high school sports to girls. Summing up, ATLA lauded the judge as "a staunch protector" of the rights of consumers and the environment and for being "in the forefront of judicial innovation to insure that substantive rights are . . . not forfeited or lost in a procedural morass."

As one might guess, the members of ATLA were overwhelming plaintiffs' lawyers. The judge recognized that. Still, an accolade was an accolade. He was touched.

■ ■ ■ ■

All the while, the judge had been thinking more and more about the nature of corporations. For years, especially during Reserve Mining, he had been sounding out his reflections, in bits and pieces, before various audiences. ("Where is Reserve's heart?" he had asked at one hearing. "Does it have a soul?") But his most memorable remarks came in November 1981, in his speech before the Minnesota Council of Churches.

He titled his speech "The Church's Claim on the Corporate Conscience: Toward Redefinition of Sin." In the eyes of the law, he said, a corporation was "a person," with "the rights and privileges and immunities that are accorded to natural-born people." But, he said, "the corporation has no soul, it has no heart, it has no conscience." And, he said, corporations are not held accountable in the same way as individuals: *Many people denounce crime in the street, but few examine crime in the skyscraper.*

He spoke about the pressures on corporations to achieve "a maximum return on the investment—not next year, not the year after, not ten years from now, but today." He added:

> Now is that a very good system to turn loose to control the long-term destiny of mankind? Having selfishness and greed control our environment, control our workplaces, decide that which we are going to breathe, what we are going to eat, what we are going to drink, whether or not we go to war?

He decried the "cost-benefit analysis, where you weigh how much a human life is worth." That analysis, he said—echoing a phrase from Dr. Selikoff—led to a game of Russian roulette, where there is "no clear plan as to . . . which individual will be sacrificed." This led to some of the judge's most controversial comments:

> You know, even if a group of people were alone in a lifeboat and had to sacrifice one person to save water and get a little raw meat, it would probably pick on some old doodler, who had lived beyond his time anyway. Even Hitler, when he was butchering people, articulated a reason to his madness. We don't even do that.

He spoke of how corporate officials are "in the main decent people":

> It seems that the system they get caught up in causes them the trouble. They are kind and honorable in their personal relationships, their personal mores. They attend church, they do charitable deeds. Almost any corporate president or official would walk miles to help a little child who is hungry or injured or who is hurting. But he or she could then walk back to the office and approve a plan that would dump tons of poison into the drinking water of that same child.

He returned to the overriding lesson of his boyhood. "It is up to you, for after all, when Cain asked God the question, we all had the answer," he said. "Yes, we are our brother's keeper."

And he called on the church leaders in the audience—"the pastor, the confident, the trusted friend"—to take a stand against the sins of corporate officials. "It occurs to me," he said, "that the church might develop an ethic which would say that pollution, contamination, and desecration of our environment are sins and that we should not look to the Second Coming immediately, but should plan for future generations." He added more specific advice:

> The corporate officer or official sits in the front pew of your church. . . . You, as church leaders, can change the nation's way of thinking. You can raise their ideals and shame the wrongdoer. Every religious person should know that the church holds that person individually responsible for participating in group wrong. The old concept of individual responsibility should be applied. . . . They are acting against God's wishes; they

cannot morally justify their actions by saying that they were ordered to do it, even if others are doing it in concert with them.

The judge knew that his words shook some in the audience. "You're probably saying to yourself right now, 'What kind of a bird is this speaker? He's really anti-corporation, isn't he?'" But, he said, he was not opposed to all corporations, only the bad actors. "What is being denounced here are those people and institutions that are doing wrong."

24

Endgame

Griffin Bell's plea notwithstanding, it is too late for A. H. Robins to *put all the pieces back together again.*

Despite the hoopla, the judicial misconduct proceedings have been a sideshow. Indeed, on the very day after the hearings, Chief Judge Lay issues an order that puts the A. H. Robins complaints on hold, pending resolution of the company's "So Ordered" appeal. This is a strong sign that the Eighth Circuit now realizes, after the fact, that the extraordinary procedures of a disciplinary tribunal should never have been invoked.

Meanwhile, the main event—the ongoing Dalkon Shield litigation—continues to crescendo as a direct result, everyone seems to agree, of what Judge Lord started. More judges issue orders for the production of the secret tail-string studies. (A. H. Robins lawyers, however, continue to resist with repeated delays, motions for reconsideration, emergency petitions for appellate review, and settling cases where the orders have been entered.) Some judges also follow Judge Lord's lead by entering orders barring the dirty questions. And in Judge Renner's cases, Magistrate McNulty denies A. H. Robins's motion to vacate or clarify the protective order. He rules that the language of the order—requiring that A. H. Robins notify *all its attorneys . . . and other persons* to preserve relevant documents—should be read "reasonably and in good faith." He questions whether the company has done that and schedules evidentiary hearings on Ciresi's allegations of document destruction.

Then comes Roger Tuttle.

■ ■ ■ ■

Tuttle's deposition starts on July 30, 1984, in a courtroom down the hall from us, under the auspices of Judge Renner and Hennepin County Judge

Jonathan Lebedoff, who is presiding over the Minnesota state court cases. Another U.S. magistrate, J. Earl Cudd, will be presiding, primarily to rule on the bevy of attorney-client privilege objections that are sure to arise. (Magistrate Cudd and Judge Lord go back a long ways: friends since the early 1960s, when the judge was the U.S. attorney and hired Cudd as one of his assistants.)

The judge sends me over to watch. I welcome the opportunity to check out this man Tuttle, whom we have been puzzling over for months. It's also a chance to see Ciresi, always entertaining, back in action.

Tuttle enters the courtroom dressed in a powder-blue jacket and looking mild mannered, even meek (to use the judge's vernacular): receding hair, pinched face, pursed lips, flushed cheeks, and small eyes behind large aviator glasses.

The questioning starts slowly. Ciresi covers the standard queries about Tuttle's background and other relatively benign topics. Then Ciresi turns to his binder of A. H. Robins documents. He points Tuttle to a memo from 1970 that discusses the paucity of premarket testing for the Dalkon Shield. He asks whether Tuttle was aware of that fact.

The attorney defending the deposition is Thomas Harlan Sloan Jr., from San Francisco. He is another of the seemingly interchangeable lawyers from the A. H. Robins stable: smart and with a blue-chip résumé. He speaks in a formal and precise clip. "Objection, Your Honor," he says. "That invades the attorney-client privilege."

Ciresi counters that he is only asking for facts, not Tuttle's legal opinions or mental impressions. But Magistrate Cudd is leaning over backwards to protect the privilege. "I'll sustain the objection," he rules.

Ciresi tries a number of other questions about the memo and the testing of the Dalkon Shield. Sloan continues to object. Magistrate Cudd continues to rule for Sloan.

Ciresi turns to a few other documents in his binder and gets another flurry of objections and mostly the same rulings from Magistrate Cudd.

"I'll sustain the objection."

"I'll sustain it for the time being."

"Sustained."

And so it goes. The deposition is going nowhere, slowly. "Let's go on to something else," Magistrate Cudd says to Ciresi at one point.

After the lunch break, Ciresi turns in his binder to the "Dalkon Shield: Orientation Report." He reads the key sentence—*The string or "tail" situation needs a careful review*—and asks Tuttle for his reaction when he first saw the report.

"Your Honor, I object," says Sloan.

Then Tuttle also objects, separate and apart from Sloan, based on the work-product doctrine. I start to wonder which Tuttle has shown up today: the lawyer who had zealously defended the company and counseled against taking the Dalkon Shield off the market, or the born-again Christian who appeared ready to confess his sins when he wrote his bar journal article.

Magistrate Cudd sustains Tuttle's objection. Ciresi tries his best to change the ruling. Sloan argues back. The clock ticks on.

A bit later, Ciresi turns to the August 1974 memo from then-president William Zimmer III and reads his favorite part out loud:

> *You are requested to immediately search your pertinent files for any letters, memos or notes on oral or written communications relating in any way to the thread utilized for the tail for the Dalkon Shield and send them to Ken Moore. Of particular interest are any references to "wicking" of the tail.*

Tuttle says he has never before seen this memo. Still, Ciresi wants to pursue the whereabouts of this collection of documents, as well as other disappearing-document issues. He takes a flier. "Have there ever been documents destroyed by the Robins Company concerning the Dalkon Shield?" Ciresi asks.

Tuttle pauses a beat. He nods his head. "Yes, sir," he says.

Ciresi repeats his question to make sure there has been no misunderstanding. "You're aware of documents that have been destroyed by the Robins Company concerning the Dalkon Shield?" he asks.

Tuttle nods his head again. "Yes, sir," he says.

Ciresi turns to his associate, Marti Wivell, sitting at counsel table. "Can you fucking believe this?" he says softly.

Under questioning by Ciresi, Tuttle gives his account.

It was early 1975, around the end of the Deemer trial in Wichita. Skip

Forrest (who, as general counsel, was Tuttle's boss) believed that Dr. Clark's trip report, noting the discrepancies in pregnancy rates and produced to plaintiffs in discovery, had badly hurt the company at trial. With the litigation still in its early stages, there would in all likelihood be continuing demands from plaintiffs' attorneys for additional documents. And that is when, Tuttle testifies, Forrest told him to collect problematic documents from the files of eight top corporate executives—and destroy them.

Tuttle wasn't sure if this would be legal or illegal. In his mind, it was not a clear-cut issue. There were pending lawsuits but no protective order from any court requiring the preservation of documents. Tuttle did believe, however, that the destruction would be morally wrong. He struggled with the conflict between his duties to his employer (his client) and his "duties to the Lord." But he had a wife and two children in private school and did not want to lose his job.

"Do it," Forrest ordered.

Tuttle complied.

He gave the directive to several A. H. Robins employees, who collected hundreds of documents and, after review by Tuttle, burned them in a forced-draft furnace that was otherwise used to destroy bad lots of product.

Afterwards, Tuttle took out a notepad and, in a red pen, titled the page, "Records destruction." He wrote the initials of the eight executives whose files were searched, starting with chairman E. C. Robins Senior ("ECR Sr.") and president William L. Zimmer III ("WLZ III").

Sloan showers objections as Tuttle testifies.

But now Magistrate Cudd, although he still sustains some objections, is viewing the assertions of privilege from a markedly different vantage.

"The witness may answer."

"It's a subject matter question. He may answer."

"Objection's overruled."

"Same ruling. He may answer."

"I'll overrule the objection and direct the witness to answer."

As the deposition continues, Tuttle testifies that the documents selected for destruction demonstrated "guilty knowledge" of the company's "highest command levels."

Ciresi seizes on the issue. "Are you aware that the top management of the A. H. Robins Company has testified in the consolidated proceedings before His Honor, Judge Lord, that most of them just don't recall what they knew at a given point in time or they don't know if they received a memorandum even if their name was on the distribution list?" he asks.

"No, sir," says Tuttle.

"But you do know that you were told to search these top management individuals' files and get sensitive documents out which may show they had some knowledge of direct involvement in the Dalkon Shield, correct?" asks Ciresi.

"Correct," says Tuttle.

Tuttle also testifies that he made the decision to appear for this deposition despite A. H. Robins threatening him—and his good standing in the bar—for breaching the attorney-client privilege.

"Has Robins threatened to bring action against you?" asks Ciresi.

"Yes, sir," says Tuttle.

"Have they threatened to go to the board of professional responsibility in Oklahoma?" asks Ciresi.

"Yes, sir," says Tuttle.

"Have you put your own job at jeopardy by coming here to testify?" asks Ciresi.

"There's no question about it," says Tuttle.

"Why did you come?" asks Ciresi.

Tuttle lists several factors, including his confidence in Ciresi (and the courtesy shown by Ciresi and his partner, Roger Brosnahan, in contacting him prior to the deposition) and the presence of a federal magistrate to protect legitimate claims of privilege.

"I guess the final thought that struck me," Tuttle testifies, "was Judge Lord's courage."

He is speaking, of course, of the judge's speech.

"So Judge Lord gave you the courage to come here?" Ciresi repeats.

"Yes, sir," says Tuttle.

A. H. Robins fights back against Tuttle's accusations. The company calls his testimony "false," "absurd," and "the product of the imagination of a disgruntled former employee." Skip Forrest—"I did not give Mr. Tuttle any instructions to destroy any documents"—and everyone else at A. H.

Robins implicated by the testimony also deny any knowledge or participation in the destruction.

Sloan suggests that Tuttle is trying to get even with the company for firing him.

"No, sir, that's not my province," Tuttle replies. "It's in the hands of a higher being than you and I both."

Sloan also points out that Tuttle didn't witness the employees burn documents, so he has no firsthand knowledge of what happened. He calls the destruction, if it even occurred, "a meaningless act," since, he argues, many (but not all) of the allegedly destroyed documents were later produced in the MDL. (Presumably, those documents had been sent to additional recipients not included in Tuttle's search-and-destroy mission.) Sloan also falls back on a tried-and-true A. H. Robins argument, despite its lack of relevance on this occasion. "A majority of these lawsuits tried around the country have resulted in defense verdicts," Sloan says to Magistrate Cudd. "That is a fact."

But A. H. Robins's arguments gain no traction.

Tuttle's sensational story produces coast-to-coast headlines: a former in-house lawyer and born-again Christian, drawing courage from a renegade judge, reappears after almost a decade to accuse a Fortune 500 company, besieged by litigation, of burning up documents that would implicate its top brass. Reporters rush to the courthouse as Tuttle continues to testify over several days and, on breaks in the deposition, pilgrimage down the hall to our chambers. Judge Lord declines to comment on the record. That's not to say, however, that he tries to conceal his feelings. Local journalist David Carr writes that the judge was overheard "expressing wonderment at what his handiwork had wrought."

The rest of us exult along with the judge.

"His chambers," writes Carr, "have the undeniable aura of a winning locker room."

Carr—who writes for the *Twin Cities Reader,* a local weekly (and later goes on to a famed career at the *New York Times*)—sums up the situation as well as anyone:

> [Judge Lord's] accomplishment can hardly be overstated. After ten years
> of inchworm progress in the litigation, Lord used a combination of

fireball rhetoric and wily legal strategy to build enough momentum to move the cases in Minnesota, and perhaps the rest of the nation, toward resolution. . . .

Robins lawyers, most of whom came in from Virginia, have been stripped of the cockiness they initially brought to Minnesota. A legal strategy which served them very well over the past decade has apparently lost all relevance in the hostile climate of the Minnesota courts.

Indeed, document destruction (or disappearance) changes everything. First, there were the missing Zimmer-memo documents. Then Lashley's shorthand notes and Wagenseil's "spring cleaning." And now, far more dramatic, Tuttle's revelations.

The endgame will soon be in play.

■ ■ ■ ■

Although the litigation is steamrolling—and the judicial misconduct complaints are on hold—Judge Lord continues to obsess about his fate and his antagonists on the appellate bench. For much of the summer, we don't see him much in chambers. When he does come in, he talks more and more about retiring. (He'll turn sixty-five in the fall.)

The media attention, however, continues unabated, which the judge loves.

In August, *60 Minutes,* the CBS program, shows up to film a segment on him. The judge takes the producer—the warm-up for correspondent Mike Wallace—up to Crosby-Ironton with her film crew to tour the old haunts and visit friends and family. Later, Mike Wallace arrives. For the formal interview, he sits with the judge at a counsel table in the courtroom. Wallace is no-nonsense, brusquely reading off prepared questions. The judge gives a hard-edged performance with some over-the-top comments about A. H. Robins. (He talks about A. H. Robins poisoning women and killing babies and calls the Eighth Circuit judges "those birds.") But the judge figures that the producer will smooth over his interview in the editing room and that the program will be a feel-good, poor-boy-from-the-Range-does-good profile, with lots of B-roll footage of him hobnobbing in the northland.

■ ■ ■ ■

Back in Richmond, Ciresi and Larson start on additional depositions authorized by other judges, now taking place in the Commonwealth Park Hotel. The scent of A. H. Robins blood—spilled by Tuttle—attracts a small crowd, with some attendees lucky to find a spot to sit on the floor.

In one particularly combative affair, Ciresi has at William Zimmer III, tempers flaring. Ciresi, in his usual form, asks the former president the how-many-women questions—*one hundred? one thousand?*—and whether Zimmer would want his daughter to use a Dalkon Shield. "None of your business," replies Zimmer. ("Mr. Ciresi," he says later, "you're a most irritating sort of fellow.") Ciresi also probes Zimmer about the whereabouts of the tail-string and wicking documents—*of particular interest*—collected pursuant to Zimmer's memo of August 1974. Zimmer says he doesn't know.

Patricia Lashley, Skip Forrest's paralegal, also appears for her continuing deposition. After an argument about whether "shorthand notes" are "documents"—Lashley claims they are not—Lashley gives bewildering testimony. In February, she had testified that she filed the notes away in a folder. In April, she testified that the folder was mysteriously empty. Now, she testifies that her April testimony was not true (perhaps because there were unrelated documents, but not her notes, in the file). Larson presses. "Was your testimony accurate?" he asks. "I don't remember," Lashley says. Finally, she pulls off the microphone clipped to her dress and storms out of the room. Her attorneys, citing her "emotional condition," say she will not be returning.

Lashley also fails to show for the hearings on document destruction that Magistrate McNulty holds in Minneapolis in August. Once again, Judge Lord sends me down the hall to listen. There's a fair share of excitement— Griffin Bell is making another command appearance (he calls Judge Renner's protective order "ambiguous in the extreme"), and Harris Wagenseil testifies about his "spring cleaning"—but not much new light is shed on the missing documents. McNulty takes the issues under advisement.

On the document front, several thousand pages have now been produced in response to Judge Lord's order of February 8. But the smoking-gun documents—most importantly, those on which A. H. Robins claims privilege—remain secreted. As late as September, the sweep for documents at the law firms, including McGuire Woods and Mays Valentine, has not even begun.

But there is a growing sense that the litigation has reached the tipping point. "JURIST'S TACTICS HASTEN THE PACE OF LITIGATION IN DALKON SHIELD CASES," headlines a story in the *Wall Street Journal,* with the "jurist," of course, being Judge Lord. ("When Robins declared that it had nothing else to produce," the *Journal* wrote, "nearly everybody accepted the assertion—except, eventually, Judge Lord.") And Tuttle's testimony, videotaped and available to all plaintiffs and their attorneys, is taking on a life of its own. The first jury to see the tape—in September, at a trial in Miami—awards $4.5 million, one of the largest Dalkon Shield verdicts to date.

■ ■ ■ ■

On October 29, 1984, in a striking sign of the turn of the tides, A. H. Robins announces a recall of the Dalkon Shield.

The company had adamantly resisted this for so many years. But now, with much fanfare, the company unveils a multimillion-dollar advertising blitz, in print and on TV, urging women to see their doctors to have the devices taken out, with A. H. Robins footing the bill. (The company, however, still doesn't use the word *recall*.) Thousands of phone calls stream into A. H. Robins's toll-free hotline. More than four thousand women will have their devices removed. E. C. Robins Junior calls the program "unprecedented in American medical history."

A. H. Robins, however, does not admit to any defects in the Dalkon Shield or that the device poses a higher risk to women than other IUDs. Instead, the company stresses that any woman still wearing the device presumably had it inserted at least ten years ago, before the cessation of sales in 1974, and that continued long-term use may be hazardous.

Indeed, the recall is not an entirely altruistic move by A. H. Robins. Judge Lord and some plaintiffs' lawyers believe that the company is taking this action, at least in part, with an eye toward cutting off future litigation. The company, they say, will argue that the extensive publicity surrounding the recall will start the statute of limitations—the time period for filing suit—running against all women who have not yet filed in court.

The press seeks out the judge for comment. He is not in a charitable mood. He dismisses the company's "belatedly developed concern for the women whose health it purports to protect." He says the company's actions are merely "an attempt to save them money in future." He revisits a line from his speech: "I fear," he says, "that the eyes of the company executives have not lifted above the bottom line."

Still, the recall is seen as a near-final act of desperation by the company.

■ ■ ■ ■

A. H. Robins, however, does gain a brief respite.

Four days after announcement of the recall, on November 2, 1984, the Eighth Circuit issues its decision on A. H. Robins's pending appeal and rules straight down the line for the company.

The appeals court—the three-judge panel is Donald Lay, Myron Bright, and Richard Arnold—finds that Judge Lord had no authority to sign the settlement agreement since it was a private contract among the parties and strikes the judge's signature and his "So Ordered." The court also finds that Judge Lord violated the due process rights of A. H. Robins and its officers when he gave his speech without, it says, proper notice or an opportunity to be heard by an impartial tribunal—and orders that the speech be stricken from the record. "*Judge Lord,*" the Eighth Circuit writes, reprising the line from its decision in Reserve Mining, "*seems to have shed the robe of the judge and to have assumed the mantle of the advocate.*"

The Eighth Circuit in its decision once again expresses no interest in the merits of the claims against A. H. Robins:

> We do not evaluate the truth or falsity of any allegations made during this litigation. . . . The truth or falsehood of plaintiffs' claims, and the propriety, legal or ethical, of the actions of Robins and its employees are not the point here.

The appeals court is concerned, however, about the harm that the speech is causing A. H. Robins:

> The reprimand has been used against Robins in other Dalkon Shield cases across the country, resulting in potential prejudice to Robins' litigation posture in those cases. The adverse publicity Robins has received from the public reprimand could conceivably have caused Robins other forms of property damage as well.

The Eighth Circuit does not mention that A. H. Robins's litigation posture might also be damaged by the fact that, after all these years, the truth is finally emerging.

A. H. Robins officials are elated. "Justice has been done," says a company spokesman.

Judge Lord is incensed.

"The truth of it," as he later says about his speech, "nobody ever questioned one single statement."

He would expect a decision like this from Judge Bright. But he had held out hope for Judge Lay; for some reason, he feels no personal animus even though Judge Lay participated in the rebuke in Reserve Mining. And Judge Arnold, a widely respected jurist from Arkansas (who would nearly make it to the U.S. Supreme Court), was untarnished in Judge Lord's eyes.

Judge Lord does not take solace from the fact that the Eighth Circuit judges give an unmistakable signal that the misconduct complaints—which are still being held in abeyance—will ultimately be dismissed. "It is far more desirable for this issue to be addressed in the normal appellate process than in the extraordinary context of a disciplinary proceeding," the court writes in its decision. Why, the judge grumbles, did it take the Eighth Circuit so long to wake up to this realization?

Nor is he assuaged by the fact that the practical effect of the Eighth Circuit's ruling is minimal. With other judges issuing orders for production of the Judge Lord documents, the "So Ordered" notation has become superfluous. And the speech, of course, has already left an indelible mark on the landscape of the litigation and the public consciousness.

"It is the speech . . . and not the ruling," Morton Mintz will write, "that will be remembered."

Indeed, the Eighth Circuit's decision—so out of step with the march of events and so perplexing to laypersons, to the press (*he yelled at them*), and to at least one newly minted lawyer—is only a momentary blip in A. H. Robins's free fall.

■ ■ ■ ■

The judge hits his sixty-fifth birthday.

On November 6, the given day, he is in the middle of a product-liability trial. The jurors—enchanted by the judge, as usual—bring in two cakes at lunchtime; one juror, an opera singer, breaks into song. "It doesn't quite measure up to my idea of judicial decorum," the judge would say. "But it was my sixty-fifth birthday. What was I to do?"

As he passes this milestone, retirement is much on his mind.

"I'm getting too old for this sort of thing," he soon tells the press. "I'd just like to get out to some calm water, where I can think about what has happened."

But he is not done courting controversy.

Just days after the judge's birthday, two peace activists who had smashed military equipment at a Sperry Corporation plant in suburban Minneapolis appear for sentencing. (This is the same Sperry Corporation that had earlier pled guilty, and gotten a sweet deal in the judge's view, for overcharging on defense contracts.) The judge had given the two defendants great leeway during their trial—he thought the young man and woman were "cute," especially the way they held hands in the courtroom—and, over the objections of the prosecutor, let them present their moral arguments about the indiscriminate use of weapons of mass destruction. Still, the jury quickly convicted the two. Now at their sentencing, John LaForge and Barb Katt face ten years in prison and fines of $10,000.

LaForge and Katt come into court carrying toothbrushes and prepared for prison.

The judge comes into court carrying a three-page speech.

(I helped with some light editing and encouraged him to speak his mind. Sorry, Maxine.)

It gives the judge no pause that he is fresh off his latest Eighth Circuit rebuke. He pulls out his new speech and echoes the pleas of Katt and LaForge to stop the "military madness." "Why do we condemn and hang individual killers while extolling the virtues of warmongers?" he asks. "What is that fatal fascination which attracts us to the thought of mass destruction of our brethren in another country?"

Then the judge announces the sentences. No prison time. No fines. Nothing except a suspended sentence and six months of probation.

Spectators gasp and cheer. Many weep.

"Lord is a human being first," says Katt," a servant of the state next."

"What a judge," says LaForge, "he was beautiful."

And in the headlines once again, sparking both praise—and outrage.

Then two days later, on Sunday night, November 11, CBS airs its *60 Minutes* profile, which it titles "The Prairie Judge." It is not, as the judge had let himself anticipate, a puff piece.

Indeed, Mike Wallace goes so far as to pose the question of whether the Eighth Circuit will try to remove the judge from the bench (despite the fact that the disciplinary proceedings no longer appear to be a threat). Wallace calls the judge's speech to the A. H. Robins executives "a tongue lashing" and the resulting Eighth Circuit opinion "blistering." He reads from the judge's speech:

Today, as you sit here . . . none of you has faced up to the fact that more than 9,000 women claim they gave up part of their womanhood so that your company might prosper.

"That was pretty tough talk?" Wallace says to the judge.

"It wasn't as tough as what I should have done," says the judge.

"Oh, come on!" Wallace says, egging the judge on. "That's tough talk."

"I should have put 'em in jail," says the judge.

Wallace reads more of the speech:

If one poor young man were, without authority or consent, to inflict such damage upon one woman, he would be jailed for a good portion of the rest of his life.

"And that's the truth," the judge says. "They go to jail, but these people can sneak up and plant something in their womb that'll poison them, kill their babies, give 'em retarded babies, and that's in the name of profit and that's America?" The judge's gaze is fixed. He looks like a hard-bitten preacher-man. "Forbid it, almighty God!" he says.

Wallace notes that "it's hard to stay neutral" about the judge. "You will either applaud his conduct on the bench, or you will deplore it."

He says the judge's candor and style have earned him "respect" and "affection." He shows an interview with a woman who had nine operations after using the Dalkon Shield and received a settlement of $75,000 but says her vindication came more from the judge's speech than the payment. "The words meant more than the money?" Wallace asks. "Oh, definitely," she says. There's footage of the judge being greeted by lawyers at an ATLA convention in Seattle. "Give them hell!" says one. "I really admire your guts," says another. There's also film of the judge walking through Crosby-Ironton, shaking hands and greeting old-timers with hugs and kisses.

But Wallace also notes that some have called the judge the "most reckless" in the country. He interviews a bow-tied law professor (and former New York City judge), who says, "on the basis of sort of street talk," that most judges would tend to say that Judge Lord "goes over the line." He interviews a criminal defense attorney, who complains that the judge usually decides "before we walk into the courtroom" that his clients are guilty.

And Wallace, of course, brings up Reserve Mining and the judge's other run-ins with the Eighth Circuit. "You've been removed?" says Wallace. "You've been reprimanded?"

The judge cuts him off. "Why don't we put it this way," he says. "I don't get along with some of those birds on the Court of Appeals." He lashes out at the Eighth Circuit for its actions that, he says, have intimidated the federal judiciary and says he does not put much stock in what the appellate judges have to say about him. "Is it the appearance of impropriety to judges or to the people of this world?" the judge asks.

He answers his own question: "I'll take the people."

At home, as the judge watches the broadcast, he sinks farther and farther down in his chair, until he is almost on the floor. To his mind, he looks "a little bit rocky." For a short while, he is uncharacteristically embarrassed.

Soon, however, *the people of this world* let their voices ring.

Fan mail floods into chambers and into the CBS studios in New York. The *60 Minutes* producer sends the judge a bundle of letters, written by men and women, young and old, from across the country. "As you will see," she writes, "the large majority of the viewers were fascinated by the broadcast and cheered your independence and integrity."

Indeed, many viewers were deeply affected, as person after person literally thanked the Lord: "I thank God for Miles W. Lord." . . . "God Bless Judge Lord! We are proud of his righteous indignation." . . . "Thank God for judges like him that still put people's safety ahead of corporate and individual profit!" . . . "God bless him and more power to him."

The more secular writers also profess their admiration, affection, gratitude, and even love:

"Right on, Miles!"

"Go for it Miles!"

"Bravo to Judge Lord!—some integrity and justice not up for sale."

"This man! He is something else!"

"He is not afraid to confront the corporate outlaws who use the American public like guinea pigs in their greedy quest for profit."

"In his courtroom money doesn't talk. . . . It seems predictable that Big Money wouldn't like him."

"Hooray for Minnesota's Judge Miles Lord! Shades of Harry Truman—tell it like it is!"

"I haven't got as excited about a man since I saw [the] 'Gandhi' film. What a courageous person."

"A dozen red roses for judge Miles Lord."

"I think I am in love. . . . He has the gratitude of women all over the United States. May his tribe increase."

"Long live Judge Lord! There's hope for America with the likes of him!"

"The Court of Appeals has just confirmed my life-long suspicion that victims have NO constitutional rights—the corporations have them all."

"The judiciary in the United States has always been owned by wealth and power and in my opinion doesn't deserve the term honorable. As for

Judge Miles Lord, "Your Honor," doesn't go far enough to describe this great man."

Some letters come from Dalkon Shield victims: from a woman who had twelve surgeries ("The doctor told my mother I was lucky to be alive, my female organs were 'so infected, so unrecognizable, that it was like scraping them out with a spoon.'"); from a woman who cried as she heard the judge's reprimand of A. H. Robins ("Let those hollow-hearted chair<u>men</u> suffer as thousands of we women have."); and from the parents of a young woman who write that Judge Lord's words and deeds pulled their daughter out of depression and gave her a renewed interest in life ("she is now a 2nd-year law student . . . with a deep dedication to make this a safer, better world.").

One letter comes from a former classmate of the judge's ("Graduating Class of 1937, Crosby-Ironton High School," she writes). She takes *60 Minutes* to task for confusing the prairie with the Iron Range and heralds the judge as one of their own:

> Judge Lord is not a Prairie Judge. We are products of the Cuyuna Iron Range . . . whose lives and characters of strong principles were literally molded by miners of the bowels of the earth. Feisty fighters for "right over might," we are proud to claim Miles as our friend as well as watchdog of our rights as human beings and United States citizens.

There also are the inevitable letters—but not many—harshly critical of the judge, calling him "intemperate," "vindictive," and "a contemptible little wretch."

And a few letter writers lash out at Mike Wallace, asking "how much stock" he owns in A. H. Robins, calling his "confrontation demeanor disgusting," complaining that he failed to look "at the hard, operative facts" against A. H. Robins, and questioning why he had to "denigrate this man when Judge Lord is interested in bringing out the truth."

■ ■ ■ ■

With his message resonating with the public—and the misconduct complaints sure to be dismissed—the judge begins to plan his retirement in earnest.

But his legacy continues to haunt A. H. Robins.

The situation is so ominous that some fear the viability of the company itself. Before the year is out, Larson and Ciresi settle all of their firm's remaining Dalkon Shield cases—at amounts averaging nearly four times the norm—to protect their clients against any eventualities. (A. H. Robins attributes the extraordinary amounts to "Judge Miles Lord's public attacks and utterances [that] have so inflamed and prejudiced potential jurors that a fair and impartial trial for Robins in Minnesota is no longer possible.") This settlement agreement does not forbid Larson and Ciresi from taking on additional Dalkon Shield clients, although the two lawyers say that, after spending years on the cases, they expect to move on. Before they do, their firm puts together a 150-page catalog of its Dalkon Shield litigation materials—trial transcripts and exhibits, deposition videotapes, briefs and court pleadings—and makes it available to all plaintiffs' attorneys for the cost of copying.

Which, of course, further fans the flames engulfing A. H. Robins.

■ ■ ■ ■

In the new year, 1985, the situation becomes more dire.

The publicity from A. H. Robins's recall campaign—far from insulating the company from future litigation—seems to have resulted in a surge of new claims.

Tuttle's testimony also continues to plague the company. "When your own in-house attorney, a born-again Christian, says this," Bill Cogar tells the press, "well . . . we have been buffeted and kicked in the ass by every judge."

And, he might add, by every jury.

In Wichita, after a nine-week trial in the spring of 1985—with blown-up pages of the Tuttle deposition on prominent display—a jury returns a verdict of $9.2 million, with $7.5 million in punitive damages, the largest yet.

The pressure to produce the documents also continues. The pace is slow; A. H. Robins is still the master of delay. But in two extraordinary developments, the special masters (still working for Judge Renner) and Judge Theis (still presiding over the MDL) take actions that shake the foundation of A. H. Robins's claims of privilege. First, in an advisory report, the special masters find *prima facie* evidence, sufficient to raise a presumption unless rebutted, that A. H. Robins perpetrated "a massive fraudulent scheme . . . with the knowledge and assistance of in-house counsel" by

misrepresenting the safety and efficacy of the Dalkon Shield and destroy-
ing or withholding evidence. (The masters' report implicates the company's in-house counsel, not the outside lawyers whose documents have not
yet been reviewed.) Next, Judge Theis issues a similar decision, writing that
the *prima facie* evidence includes attempts "with the assistance of counsel,
to devise strategies to cover up Robins' responsibilities and lessen its liability." Judge Theis stresses that his order, as with the report of the special
masters, is only for purposes of discovery in the civil cases and is not to
be taken as a ruling on the merits of the underlying litigation. Still, these
rulings have far-reaching ramifications as they open the door for striking
down even otherwise legitimate claims of privilege. (The privilege "takes
flight," in the words of the Supreme Court, when a client consults an attorney to further an ongoing or future, as opposed to a past, crime or fraud.)
Judge Theis also appoints two special masters for the MDL to examine the
"voluminous amount" of privileged documents in light of his ruling.

By August 21, 1985, Judge Theis's special masters are closing in on the
documents in Richmond.

On that day, however, the A. H. Robins Company files for bankruptcy.

Afterword

The A. H. Robins bankruptcy petition stopped the Dalkon Shield litigation in its tracks. All discovery was halted. All trial dates were canceled.

A. H. Robins did not claim that it was insolvent. Instead, the company cited the continuing burden of litigation and asked to reorganize under Chapter 11 of the Bankruptcy Code so it could receive protection from lawsuits while it formulated a plan, subject to court approval, to pay Dalkon Shield claimants.

As a result, a new—and long—legal chapter began, with all claims consolidated in federal bankruptcy court in Richmond, presided over by Judge Merhige. Initially, about five thousand lawsuits were pending. But with publication of the required notices of bankruptcy, in newspapers and on television, tens of thousands more victims surfaced. In the end, more than two hundred thousand valid claims were filed, far more than A. H. Robins could pay on its own, forcing the Robins family to seek a corporate suitor. Eventually, American Home Products, a huge conglomerate, agreed to buy out the A. H. Robins Company and finance a $2.3 billion fund, called the Dalkon Shield Claimants Trust, to compensate the victims. Aetna contributed an additional $425 million. It took four years—until 1989—for the battles over the bankruptcy plan to end; another seven years—until 1996—for most of the claimants to be paid; and another four years—until 2000—for all claims to be resolved.

That was almost thirty years after the first lawsuits had been filed.

The Robins family lost control of their company in the bankruptcy but fared well—extremely well—receiving about $300 million in the American Home acquisition but ordered to make a payment to the claimants, by E. C. Robins Senior and Junior, of a combined total of only $10 million. With that, the company and all individuals connected with A. H. Robins were absolved of any further liability.

(Senior would die in 1995—eleven years after the proceedings before Judge Lord—and not from a heart condition but from pancreatic cancer.)

Some plaintiffs' attorneys called the bankruptcy "unjustified" and "a sham." But many others supported the reorganization as a way to stop the litigation warfare. Indeed, 94 percent of the women who filed claims voted in favor the bankruptcy's final payout plan, under which most women received compensation without the need for trial (or even an attorney), with payments ranging from several hundred to several million dollars, depending on the severity of injuries. One plaintiffs' attorney called the result "the most successful settlement from any product liability case in history."

Judge Lord had mixed emotions about the bankruptcy. He acknowledged that many women received significant payments through the Claimants Trust. No amount of money, however, could restore the fertility and health—or the lives—of so many women. And, said the judge, "I didn't teach corporate America that crime does not pay."

Things would have been different if he had remained in charge. "I would have taken their buildings apart brick by brick," the judge said, "and handed them out to the victims."

■ ■ ■ ■

While the bankruptcy proceeded, a federal grand jury was convened in Wichita to investigate the A. H. Robins Company and its attorneys for allegations of criminal and fraudulent activities, including obstruction of justice and perjury. But the Justice Department abandoned its probe after five years, without bringing charges and without explanation.

No attorney for A. H. Robins was ever disciplined by any board of professional responsibility.

At least one was appointed to the federal bench as a U.S. district court judge in Richmond.

■ ■ ■ ■

I decided to have a go at practicing law.

But I still had that threat from A. H. Robins hanging over my head: that it would take "appropriate action" if I joined a law firm that had any cases against the company. I asked the judge for help. He pressed the local A. H.

Robins lawyers, who passed the judge's request up the chain of command. Before long, Griffin Bell himself wrote a letter that put the matter to rest:

> Neither A. H. Robins Company nor any of its counsel will make any objection to Ms. Walburn practicing law with any firm whatsoever.

Originally, I had signed up for a one-year clerkship with Judge Lord. I stayed on an extra few months to see the misconduct proceedings and A. H. Robins appeal through to the end. When the time came to leave, my decision was easy after all I'd seen in the Dalkon Shield litigation: I ended up at Robins, Zelle, Larson & Kaplan (by that time, all of the firm's Dalkon Shield cases had settled anyway), working alongside Mike Ciresi. As I started out practicing law—and through the years ahead—I would be fortunate to be able to rely on the advantages of lessons learned during my clerkship. (I could play pin the tail on the donkey with the best.) Still, there were many days when I wished for a judge to slash through the subterfuges of big-time litigation and pierce to the heart of the matter.

Like the one-and-only Miles Lord.

■ ■ ■ ■

Judge Lord formally stepped down in September 1985—the month after A. H. Robins filed for bankruptcy—after nineteen years of *romping and stomping* on the bench.

He was ready to leave his judgeship, he said, but not retire. He hung out his shingle, opened a small law office, and set out to represent people who "are aching and hurting and wanting and needing some kind of help." He found clients while driving around the state (tooting his horn at cows, no doubt), strolling through the skyways, and through advertisements on television and in the Yellow Pages. Calls flooded his office, sometimes dozens a day. Not all were seeking legal counsel; many called just to find a sympathetic ear. That they found, as the judge spent endless hours on the phone with people from all walks of life.

He had a ball. He looked and felt younger. His spirits were further boosted by the companionship of his children, all four of whom worked at his law office at some point. (The only non-lawyer, Mick, was the office manager.)

He stirred up controversy too, of course. In particular, critics took aim at his advertising, accusing the judge of "ambulance chasing" and "selling his judgeship." The judge shot back. He offered no apologies for "trying to beat insurance agents to my clients" and for "let[ting] injured people know that they have some place to go for help."

He hadn't accomplished all that he had hoped for in the Dalkon Shield cases. The darkest secrets of A. H. Robins never saw the light of day. No individuals were held accountable. But Judge Lord's actions had led to the downfall of a Fortune 500 company, the recall of a deadly product, and the recompense of its victims.

In the end, he simply spoke his mind, and the public listened.

And while the Eighth Circuit's words had been a stinging admonition, its actions—expunging the judge's speech and striking his signature from the settlement agreement—were inconsequential. "They hatched out a mouse," Judge Lord would later say. As expected, the misconduct complaints also fizzled in the end, with the Judicial Council dismissing them, eventually, as "moot."

Indeed, throughout his years on the bench, even when he was overturned or disqualified, rebuked or expunged, he had been the one, against all odds, who was left standing in the ring. It was Judge Lord—bolstered by *the people of this world*—who ultimately prevailed.

He had his detractors, of course, and those who questioned his straight-line route to the bottom line. Certainly, his exploits raise provocative questions—that still resonate—about the appropriate role of a judge. But from my perspective today, looking back on my years in private practice, I have come to an even greater appreciation of Judge Lord and his ways, no matter if the usual decorum and formalities of the law be sacrificed in the process. We cannot, of course, abide judges who run amok. But the law itself is not inflexible; it cannot, as Oliver Wendell Holmes wrote more than a century ago, "be dealt with as if it contained only the axioms and corollaries of a book of mathematics." The fact is, justice will not be served in many cases unless a judge is willing to intervene to help those in need.

The judge himself had no regrets about the path he took. As an Iron Ranger who came from nothing and as the comrade of a generation of men dedicated to the common good (whose legacies are also well worth remembrance), his road was forged long before ascending to the bench.

He was born and bred to take on bullies, from the schoolyards and pool halls of the Range to the boardrooms of corporate America. He had fought his battles, he would say, because of his love for the little guy. Not lawyers, not his fellow judges, not society's big shots. But the man—and woman-person—on the street.

He dreamed of writing a memoir and, while he never saw the project through, started drafts and even fashioned an ending to one. "This is a great country filled with great people," he wrote. "Each one of us can do his or her part." And he quoted his favorite poem, which he had often used throughout his life to exhort his audiences to reach out to their brothers and sisters—and to the extended family of man—who were in need of help:

I am only one,
But I still am one.
I cannot do everything,
But I can do something;
And because I cannot do everything
I will not refuse to do the something that I can do.

"That applies to me," he said. "And, my friends, it applies to you."

Acknowledgments

First and foremost, I owe endless thanks to Judge Lord for affording me not only the wondrous experience of serving as one of his law clerks but also the freedom to tell this story by making it clear that nothing in his chambers required secrecy once a case had concluded. The judge died in December 2016 at age ninety-seven; he was predeceased by his wife, Maxine, and sons, Jim and Mick. His two daughters, Priscilla Lord and Virginia Lord, were of invaluable assistance in my efforts, for which I am deeply grateful.

I am also indebted to the following people who gave assistance or advice along the way: Sylvia Ahlgren, Michael Ciresi, Joe Daly, Dale Herron, Denise LaMoreaux, Josephine Marcotty, Munir Meghjee, Amy Melchert, Peter Pringle, Todd Rapp, Elizabeth Stawicki, Doug Stone, and Randall Tietjen. My thanks also to Ron Rosenbaum, a no-holds-barred sounding board and one-of-a-kind friend, who left us too soon.

Finally, deep appreciation to the team at the University of Minnesota Press—including Erik Anderson, Douglas Armato, Emily Hamilton, Daniel Ochsner, Heather Skinner, Kristian Tvedten, and Laura Westlund, and copy editor Mary Keirstead—for their vision and thoughtfulness in bringing this book into being.

Notes and Sources

In addition to my firsthand experiences with Judge Lord during the Dalkon Shield litigation, this book is based on thousands of pages of court records: transcripts of trials, hearings, and depositions (many of them videotaped); trial exhibits and other internal A. H. Robins Company documents; and a mountain of pleadings. I retained some of these materials through the years and accessed more at the Robins, Zelle, Larson & Kaplan warehouse. (The firm has gone through various alterations in name since its involvement in Dalkon Shield.) Collections at the Harvard Law School Library, with Dalkon Shield litigation materials donated by James Szaller of Brown & Szaller, and at the University of Virginia Law Library, with its special collection from the Dalkon Shield Claimants Trust, were particularly helpful. Several books were also written in the immediate aftermath of the Dalkon Shield litigation, as cited in the selected bibliography and notes; most notable, in my mind, was *At Any Cost* by the incomparable Morton Mintz, formerly of the *Washington Post*, a muckraking hero to a generation and more of journalists.

For the biographical chapters, I relied on a robust historical record, including oral histories, interviews, diaries, letters, and other source material at the Minnesota Historical Society; court records from old cases, including the Reserve Mining litigation; countless newspaper and magazine articles; and memoirs and other books.

I was not able to interview Judge Lord for this book due to his deteriorating health. However, he had regaled me endlessly during my clerkship with his old-time stories, many of which I was able to confirm in interviews and/or the historical record. In addition, the judge's daughters granted me unrestricted access to a family storage unit filled with a treasure trove of documents chronicling his life: dozens of boxes of public and private records, letters, old newspaper clips (how he loved to be in the headlines!), photographs, and other memorabilia. With his ever-handy pocket recorder, the judge also left a lifetime of dictation of contemporaneous thoughts and historical recollections. Some of this was with hope of writing his own memoir, and he started various drafts with the help of at least two writers, Scott Carlson and David Gidmark, which provided further source material.

I also interviewed many individuals, including former Judge Lord law clerks, his friends and former colleagues, and attorneys who appeared in his courtroom. Special thanks to Walter Mondale, who graciously gave of his time. None of the national counsel for the A. H. Robins Company whom I contacted agreed to be interviewed, but I did meet with two of the company's local counsel in Minnesota and, of course, had an extensive record of statements and actions by the company and its lawyers during the Dalkon Shield litigation and my own contemporaneous observations.

Given the volume of research materials and considerations of space, I have not cited every source in these notes but instead tried to include the most important and useful. Regardless of whether specifically cited or not, it is the entirety of my research that informs this book.

Quotations have been lightly edited, for example, for grammar, length, and clarity. Generally, I have not included an endnote if the quoted remarks were made in my presence; in some instances I provided a third-party source—for example, from the judge's dictation or a draft manuscript, interview, or newspaper article—for a statement that I heard myself at another time if that source provided a more precise account than my recollection (the judge often repeated himself verbatim with his philosophizing and favorite stories).

Some newspaper articles cited here were preserved in Judge Lord's scrapbooks without complete publishing information; for some of these, this information was typed or handwritten on the clips or could be ascertained (for example, from a reporter's byline), but in a few cases the information in the endnotes is incomplete.

Abbreviations

Cases

The Dalkon Shield proceedings before Judge Lord were consolidated under various case names and numbers in the U.S. District Court for the District of Minnesota, including: *Grudem v. A. H. Robins Co.*, No. 3–80–256; *Dean v.*

A. H. Robins Co., No. 3–82–698; *Junkermeier v. A. H. Robins Co.*, No. 3–82–1811; and *Gardiner v. A. H. Robins Co.*, No. 3–83–1025. In most instances, the end-note citations use the generic "consolidated *Dalkon Shield* proceedings."

For clarity, citations to Dalkon Shield cases before other judges have been standardized in certain respects, for example, citing the defendant as the A. H. Robins Company (or Co.). In some instances, I have also short-ened the headings of motions and briefs to eliminate unnecessary verbiage.

The multidistrict litigation proceeding before Judge Theis, *In re: A. H. Robins Company Dalkon Shield IUD Products Liability Litigation*, MDL No. 211, U.S. District Court, District of Kansas, is cited as the "*Dalkon Shield MDL*."

The judicial misconduct proceedings, *In re: Complaint of A. H. Robins Company* and *In re: Complaint of E. Claiborne Robins Jr.*, JCP 84–001 and JCP 84–002, U.S. Judicial Council of the Eighth Circuit Court of Appeals, are cited as the "judicial misconduct proceedings."

Strempke v. A. H. Robins Co., No. 3–80–168, U.S. District Court, District of Minnesota, is cited as "*Strempke*."

Hahn v. A. H. Robins Co., No. 3–80–594, U.S. District Court, District of Minnesota, is cited as "*Hahn*."

Bonlender v. A. H. Robins Co., No. 3–80–341, U.S. District Court, District Minnesota, the lead Dalkon Shield case before Judge Renner, is cited as "*Bonlender*."

The Reserve Mining litigation before Judge Lord, *United States v. Reserve Mining Company*, No. 5–72–19, U.S. District Court, District of Minnesota, is cited as "*Reserve Mining*."

Manuscripts and Interviews

Miles Lord's unfinished manuscript with Scott Carlson is cited as "MWL manuscript (Carlson)."

Miles Lord's unfinished manuscript with David Gidmark is cited as "MWL manuscript (Gidmark)."

Miles Lord's 1987 interview with Tom Downs, located in the Bentley Historical Library at the University of Michigan as well as the Minnesota Historical Society, is cited as "MWL interview (Downs)."

Other Sources

The Guide to the Dalkon Shield Claimants Trust Collection, Special Collections, University of Virginia Law Library, http://ead.lib.virginia.edu, which provides an index to the collection and also an informative narrative about the litigation, is cited as the "Guide to the Dalkon Shield Claimants Trust Collection, University of Virginia."

"The Dalkon Shield Litigation: Revised Annotated Reprimand by Chief Judge Miles W. Lord," *Hamline Law Review* 9 (1986): 7, is cited as "'Annotated Reprimand,' *Hamline Law Review*."

Hubert H. Humphrey, The Art of the Possible, South Hill Films (2010), which aired on PBS, is cited as "*The Art of the Possible,* PBS."

The Minnesota Historical Society is cited as "MHS."

Other Abbreviations

MWL   Miles W. Lord
HHH   Hubert H. Humphrey

Prologue

Page 1   "It is the unpopular": *Gay Pride Comm. v. Mpls.*, No. 4–81–208 (D. Minn. May 20, 1982).

Page 1   "The federal courts": Roberta Walburn, "Judge Again Orders City to Allow Gay Pride to Stage Block Party," *Minneapolis Star Tribune,* May 22, 1982.

Page 1   At lunch: The colleague was Jim Parsons.

Page 3   In the end: Guide to the Dalkon Shield Claimants Trust Collection, University of Virginia; ranking: Dan Oberdorfer, "The Tangled Saga of the Dalkon Shield," *Minneapolis Star Tribune,* September 15, 1985; "one of the most": Morton Mintz, "The Pro-Corporate Tilt," *Nieman Reports,* Fall 1991.

Page 4   "Judge Lord . . . seems to have shed": *Reserve Mining Co. v. Lord,* 529 F.2d 181, 185 (8th Cir. 1976).

Page 5   "They broke": author interview, James Rubenstein (former law clerk).

Page 5   "An unforgiving": Austin C. Wehrwein, "Judge Lord Throws the Book at Corporate Irresponsibility," *Minneapolis Star,* December 10, 1981; "live-wire": David Carr, "Heaven Can Wait," *Minnesota Monthly,* January 1990; "a Mark Twain": Bruce Marshall, "Judge Lord Raps Business for Lack of Conscience," *St. Cloud Daily Times,* May 9, 1985; "Trumanesque"; "folksy": Barry Siegel, "Miles Lord: Champion or Zealot?," *Los Angeles Times,* June 28, 1984; "feisty": M. Howard Gelfand, *Washing-*

ton Post, "'Activist' Judge Admired," May 23, 1976; "impulsive": Larry Millett, "Judge Miles Lord: Champion of the Underdog, or Misguided Judicial Zealot?," *St. Paul Pioneer Press*, September 14, 1980.

Page 5   "Oz-like": Jacqui Banaszynski, "Judge Miles Lord Leaving Bench," *St. Paul Pioneer Press Dispatch*, May 20, 1985; "the land of Miles": David Carr, "The Shield The Power and The Lord," *Twin Cities Reader*, February 15–21, 1984 (quoting court observer); "where the unexpected": Millett, "Judge Miles Lord."

Page 5   "A disgrace": Carr, "Heaven Can Wait" (quoting civil defense attorney); "an out-of-control": Siegel, "Miles Lord: Champion or Zealot?"; "reckless": *60 Minutes*, CBS, November 11, 1984; "an embarrassment": Steve Berg and Doug Stone, "The Lord of Federal Court and His Life of 'Intrigue,'" *Minneapolis Tribune*, December 9, 1976; "Miles God": Banaszynski, "Judge Miles Lord."

Page 5   "A World War II mine": John J. Oslund, "Is Lord Anti-business?," *Minneapolis Star Tribune*, November 25, 1984.

Page 6   "Robins feels": Janet Bamford, "Dalkon Shield Starts Losing in Court," *American Lawyer*, July 1980.

Page 7   "The hard questions": *Dalkon Shield MDL*, 575 F. Supp. 718, 724 (D. Kan. 1983); "shell game": *A. H. Robins Co. v. Devereaux*, 415 So.2d 30, 32 (Fla. App. 1982); "continually thwarted": *Thoma v. A. H. Robins Co.*, 100 F.R.D. 344, 348 (D. N.J. 1983).

Page 8   "Judges tend": Posner, *Reflections on Judging*, 13, 106.

1. Boyhood on the Range

For background on Miles Lord's childhood and family, this chapter relies generally on the judge's recollections as dictated over the years; draft manuscripts of memoirs he prepared with Scott Carlson and David Gidmark; family ancestry charts; third-party interviews with the judge (particularly the Tom Downs oral history); and what I learned from the judge during my clerkship and from his daughters during research for this book. For background on the Iron Range, I relied generally on Aulie and Johnson, *Cuyuna Country;* Brown, *Overburden;* Lamppa, *Minnesota's Iron Country;* Larson, *The White Pine Industry;* Lass, *Minnesota;* Nemanic, *One Day for Democracy;* and "A Timeline of Minnesota's Iron Range," Minnesota Public Radio, May 2006.

Page 9   "Hard, loud": Brown, *Overburden*, 89; "a deep distrust": ibid., 124; "never forget": Wilson, *Rudy!*, 32.

Page 11   "Class warfare": Nemanic, *One Day for Democracy*, 85.

Page 11   "Do away": ibid., 68.

Page 11   "Solidarity Forever": Industrial Workers of the World, www.iwworg/history/icons/solidarity_forever.

Page 11   "Our Past": Brown, *Overburden,* 133.

Page 11   "Milesy": MWL manuscript (Carlson undated).

Page 12   "We ate"; "She seemed": ibid.

Page 12   On February 5, 1924: On the Milford Mine disaster, see Aulie, *The Mil-
              ford Mine Disaster;* Curt Brown, "Milford Mine Disaster Was State's
              Worst," *Minneapolis Star Tribune,* October 10, 2015; Renee Richardson,
              "Milford Mine Disaster," *Brainerd Dispatch,* January 5, 2006.

Page 12   "Relatives and friends": Aulie, *The Milford Mine Disaster,* 57.

Page 13   "Second to none": Hansen, *Cuy-Una!,* 40.

Page 13   One-bag-of-candy: Sam Newlund, "Christmas with the Lords Judged
              an Utter Delight," *Minneapolis Star Tribune,* November 24, 1982.

Page 13   "My parents": Ellen Tomson, "Lord's Justice," *St. Paul Pioneer Press,* May
              1, 1994.

Page 13   "In every conceivable": MWL manuscript (Gidmark 1988).

Page 13   "I never": ibid.

Page 14   "Take me in": MWL manuscript (Carlson undated).

Page 14   "A few blood lines"; "I was": ibid.

Page 14   "You pay": Ron Drevlow, "Judge Calmly Deals with Stormy Cases,"
              Rochester Post-Bulletin, February 2, 1985; "Those kids"; "Maybe mom";
              "poor"; "They had": MWL interview (Downs).

Page 14   "I thought": MWL dictation (1987).

Page 14   "Don't say": MWL manuscript (Carlson 2007).

Page 14   "Miles, you have": ibid.

Page 15   "Everybody was afraid": ibid.

Page 15   "I never thought": Doug Hennes, "Lord Likes Fight for 'The Right,'" *St.
              Paul Pioneer Press,* December 24, 1977.

Page 15   "The People's Governor": Mayer, *The Political Career of Floyd B. Olson,*
              xi. For additional discussion of Olson, see Haynes, *Dubious Alliance,*
              11, 28; Mitau, *Politics in Minnesota,* 13–16; Roberts, *Minnesota 150,* 133;
              Walter W. Liggett, *Radical or Racketeer?, The Mid-West American* (1935).

Page 15   "I am not": Mitau, *Politics in Minnesota,* 15.

Page 15   Even 5 percent: ibid., 153.

Page 15   "Capitalism has failed": Solberg, *Hubert Humphrey,* 59.

Page 15   "Great voice"; "beloved person": MWL interview (Downs).

Page 16   The first Communist mayor: Aulie and Johnson, *Cuyuna Country,* vol. 2,
              151–52, 159–60. The Range was also the birthplace of famed Commu-
              nist Gus Hall, born Arvo Kusta Halberg in 1910 in the Mesabi town of
              Cherry (where the Communists were known as "Cherry Reds"). Hall
              left school after the eighth grade to work in a logging camp, where the
              hardships—working from sunup to sundown in below-zero winters
              (like Frank Lord) and bunking next to the corpse of a man who died on
              the job—further radicalized him. He eventually rose through the ranks

to become the most prominent Communist in the country, leaving the
Range for New York City.

Page 16   "Pretty good food"; "We Little": MWL interview (Downs).

Page 16   "All the things"; "We would have": MWL manuscript (Gidmark 1988).

Page 16   "Made it his business": MWL interview (Downs); "I was the little guy":
author interview, Virginia Lord.

Page 16   "Some mean bastards": MWL manuscript (Gidmark 1988); "I would go":
MWL dictation (undated).

Page 16   "Beautiful sense"; "fascinating wink": Crosby-Ironton High School
graduation brochure, 1937.

Page 17   "We all sprang": MWL dictation (1987).

Page 17   "You know"; "I felt": MWL interview (Downs).

2. The Dalkon Shield Quagmire

For background on the Dalkon Shield litigation, this chapter relies generally on
Mintz, *At Any Cost;* Perry and Dawson, *Nightmare;* and Engelmayer and Wagman,
Lord's Justice, all written in the immediate aftermath of the Minnesota litigation,
as well as transcripts, court pleadings, judicial decisions, internal A. H. Robins
documents, and the Guide to the Dalkon Shield Claimants Trust Collection, University of Virginia.

Page 19   "Thoroughly condemned": Hilliard Dubrow and Alan Guttmacher,
"The Present Status of Contraception," *Mt. Sinai Journal* 26 (1959): 118.

Page 20   In January 1970: This account of Davis's testimony is based on Perry
and Dawson, *Nightmare;* Michael Ollove, "Destroyed by His Own Invention, Hugh Davis Had It All," *Baltimore Sun,* October 25, 1998.

Page 20   "A superior modern": Hugh J. Davis, "The Shield Intrauterine Device:
A Superior Modern Contraceptive," *American Journal of Obstetrics and
Gynecology* 106 (February 1970): 455.

Page 20   "Learn on-the-job": *Tetuan v. A. H. Robins Co.,* 738 P.2d 1210, 241 Kan.
441, 447 (1987) (quoting internal A. H. Robins memo).

Page 20   What the company learned: *Tetuan,* 241 Kan. at 446 ("[P]rior to its purchase of the Dalkon Shield, Robins had information which indicated
that the Dalkon Shield's rate of pregnancy was *nearly five times worse*
than Davis' purported 1.1 percent rate, at a minimum.").

Page 21   "The string or 'tail'": A. H. Robins memo from R. W. Nickless, June 29,
1970.

Page 21   Best-known speech: "The Church's Claim on the Corporate Conscience: Toward a Redefinition of Sin," MWL speech, Minnesota Council of Churches, November 12, 1981.

Page 21   No safety testing: *Tetuan,* 241 Kan. at 446 ("no pre-marketing testing");

Mintz, *At Any Cost,* 69 (A. H. Robins did not test "for safety in either women or animals").

Page 22   "For the express": A. H. Robins memo from W. Roy Smith to C. E. Morton, June 10, 1970.

Page 22   "No excuses": Telegram from A. H. Robins division sales manager, February 26, 1971.

Page 22   "Gruesome looking"; "veritable instrument": Mintz, *At Any Cost,* 101.

Page 22   "A law enforcement": Guide to the Dalkon Shield Claimants Trust Collection, University of Virginia; "a butterfly": deposition of Angela Piper, *Piper v. A. H. Robins Co.,* No. 3–80–6616, D. Minn., May 27, 1982; "a fishing lure": Mintz, *At Any Cost,* 138; "a skeleton": deposition of Brenda Strempke, *Strempke,* August 25, 1982.

Page 23   "The most traumatic": Mintz, *At Any Cost,* 99.

Page 23   "Bacterial garden"; "similar to the mouth": Deposition of Dr. Gerald Zatuchni, *In re: N. Dist. Cal. Dalkon Shield IUD Prod. Liab. Litig.,* No. C-80–2213, April 11, 1983.

Page 23   "I'm not anti-corporation:" Miles W. Lord, "Corporate Irresponsibility: The Sin with No Sinners," *Hamline Law Review* 9 (February 1986): 53.

Page 23   "In a contaminated field": Roger L. Tuttle, "The Dalkon Shield Disaster Ten Years Later—A Historical Perspective," *Oklahoma Bar Journal* 2501 (1983): 54.

Page 24   "With the physicians who pushed"; "They told me": Barry Siegel, "One Man's Effort to Tell Dalkon Story," *Los Angeles Times,* August 22, 1985.

Page 24   "We'll smite": Perry and Dawson, *Nightmare,* 224.

Page 24   "Only the courts": "Judgment Day: An Interview with Miles Lord," *Multinational Monitor,* May 1987.

Page 25   "If this product": A. H. Robins memo from Stuart Petree, May 24, 1974 (quoting Tuttle).

Page 25   "You are requested": A. H. Robins memo from William L. Zimmer III, August 15, 1974.

Page 26   "Demanded my scalp": deposition of Roger Tuttle, *Bonlender,* July 30, 1984.

Page 26   Aetna took charge: Morton Mintz, "The Dangers Insurance Companies Hide," *Washington Monthly,* January 1991.

Page 27   In addition: On the secret studies and the role of defense lawyers and Aetna, see Mintz, *At Any Cost,* 198; Mintz, "The Dangers Insurance Companies Hide."

Page 27   In the MDL: Multidistrict litigation bears some similarities—and some differences—to a class action. In an MDL, each plaintiff maintains his or her own separate case, but certain issues, such as discovery common to all plaintiffs, are handled on a consolidated basis. See 28 U.S.C. §1407. By contrast, in a class action all plaintiffs are joined in a single case; class actions are generally considered inappropriate for personal injury claims given the unique issues, including causation and damages, in each person's case. See Fed.R.Civ.P. 23, cmt. subd. (b)(3)(1966). In the Dalkon Shield litigation, a federal judge in California attempted to certify a nationwide class for punitive damages and a statewide class for liability, but was reversed by the Ninth Circuit Court of Appeals. *In re N. Dist. Cal. Dalkon Shield IUD Prod. Liab. Litig.*, 693 F. 2d 847 (9th Cir. 1982), *cert. denied,* 499 U.S. 1171 (1983).

Page 28   "A copy of all files": Order for Production of Documents, *Dalkon Shield MDL,* June 8, 1976.

Page 28   "You never go": Barry Siegel, "Miles Lord: Champion or Zealot," *Los Angeles Times,* June 28, 1984.

Page 28   "A boom town": "Tale of Two Firms," *American Lawyer,* July 1980.

Page 28   "At what age": All quotes are from the *Strempke* deposition, August 25 and October 18, 1982.

Page 29   If a strong case: A. H. Robins also used its winning percentage to defeat attempts by plaintiffs to invoke "collateral estoppel." Under this doctrine, where multiple cases involve similar claims (for example, the same product), the plaintiff may preclude the defendant from relitigating an issue decided in previous cases and thus eliminate the need to reprove generic issues over and over again (for example, whether the Dalkon Shield was defective by reason of its design). By contrast, the case-specific issues—including causation and the extent of each woman's injuries—could still be contested in future trials. In the Dalkon Shield litigation, however, judges declined to apply collateral estoppel; Judge Alsop, for example, would rule that collateral estopped would be "unfair" to A. H. Robins "in light of the prior judgments it has obtained." *Alcorn v. A. H. Robins Co.*, No. 3–78–356 (D. Minn. August 22, 1983).

Page 29   The woman is: The account of this trial and quotes are based on the *Strempke* trial transcript, April 6, 13, and 18; May 25 and 31; and June 3 and 6, 1983.

Page 30   Proper "foundation": "Annotated Reprimand," *Hamline Law Review;* "highly inflammatory"; "irrelevant and prejudicial"; "clearly collateral": A. H. Robins Brief in Support of Motions for Judgment Notwithstanding the Verdict, *Strempke,* July 5, 1983.

Page 33   "Excessive," "shocking," "unconscionable": A. H. Robins Brief in Support of Motions for Judgment Notwithstanding the Verdict, *Strempke,* July 5, 1983.

Page 33   "Something has got": Jacqui Banaszynski, "Judge Moves to Hasten Dalkon Shield Trials," *Minneapolis Star Tribune,* June 10, 1983.

Page 33   "I want to see": *Strempke* trial transcript, May 26, 1983.

3. Young Man in the Cities

For Miles Lord's young adult years, this chapter also relies generally on the sources cited in the introductory note to chapter 1.

Page 35 "Go sign up": MWL interview (Downs).

Page 35 "A clean rural": Beale Cormack, *Aaron Slick from Punkin Crick,* Walter H. Baker and Co., 1919.

Page 35 Emil Zontelli: On the Zontelli businesses, see Aulie and Johnson, *Cuyuna Country,* vol. 2, 71–73, 184; Hansen, *Cuy-Una!,* 71.

Page 35 "Citizen-miners": Hansen, *Cuy-Una!,* 71.

Page 36 "A little guy": Philly Murtha, "Fat Guys vs. Teeny Guys," *Twin Cities,* December 1981.

Page 36 "Took quite a fancy": "Jack Dempsey Took Fancy to Crosby Glover," unnamed and undated local newspaper.

Page 36 "Tough nut": MWL manuscript (Carlson undated).

Page 36 "Beautiful left hook": MWL dictation (1987).

Page 37 "But he got up": Dick Cullum, *Minneapolis Tribune,* June 5, 1974.

Page 37 "You think"; "But that": ibid.

Page 37 "I would now have to work": MWL manuscript (Gidmark undated).

Page 37 "Expelled": MWL interview (Downs).

Page 37 "A hell of": MWL manuscript (Gidmark 1988).

Page 38 "I married Miles!": author interview, Virginia Lord.

Page 38 "All I had": MWL interview (Downs).

Page 39 "We are going": author interview, Priscilla Lord.

Page 39 "Bright-eyed": MWL speech, University of Minnesota Law School, May 1983.

Page 39 "A big, spooky": MWL manuscript (Carlson 2007).

Page 39 "Little high heels"; "I'll just": MWL manuscript (Gidmark 1988).

Page 39 "My young friends": MWL interview (Downs).

Page 39 "He inspired": MWL interview (HHH Oral History Project, MHS, 1978).

Page 40 "Old men": MWL dictation (1986).

Page 40 "Dropping bombs"; "shooting down": ibid.

Page 40 "Real live"; "scorching love"; "I was so": ibid.

Page 40 Humphrey seized: On the merger of the parties, see Humphrey, *The Education of a Public Man,* 53–56; Mitau, *Politics in Minnesota,* 24–25; Solberg, *Hubert Humphrey,* 94–96.

Page 40 "Diaper brigade": *The Art of the Possible,* PBS.

Page 41 "Boy wonder": "The Humphrey Image," *The New Republic,* March 21, 1960.

Page 41 By the 1920s: Dara Moskowitz Grumdahl, "Minneapolis Confidential," *City Pages,* October 11, 1995; Paul Maccabee, "Alias Kid Cann," *Mpls.St. Paul,* November 1991.

Page 41   "Poison spot": Gordon Schendel, "How Mobsters Grabbed a City's Transit Line," *Collier's,* September 29, 1951.

Page 41   "Wide-open": Humphrey, *The Education of a Public Man,* 50–51.

Page 41   "I have the city": Maccabee, "Alias Kid Cann."

Page 41   Mayor Humphrey named: On Humphrey cleaning up the city, see Eisele, *Almost to the Presidency,* 58; Humphrey, *The Education of a Public Man,* 63–68; Solberg, *Hubert Humphrey,* 107.

Page 41   "The capital of anti-Semitism": Eisele, *Almost to the Presidency,* 58.

Page 41   "Out in front": Solberg, *Hubert Humphrey,* 134; "He lit": *The Art of the Possible,* PBS (quoting Arthur Naftalin).

Page 42   "Fascist"; "warmonger": Eisele, *Almost to the Presidency,* 61.

Page 42   Humphrey and his band: On the battle for control of the DFL, see Eisele, *Almost to the Presidency,* 61–66; Haynes, *Dubious Alliance,* 6–7; Sandbrook, *Eugene McCarthy,* 46, 52–53; Solberg, *Hubert Humphrey,* 116–17.

Page 42   "Intense"; "highly competitive": Humphrey, *The Education of a Public Man,* 37.

Page 42   "Hubert's strong-arm": Gerald Heaney interview (HHH Oral History Project, MHS, 1978).

Page 42   "Brain group": MWL interview (Downs).

Page 43   "Outright war": Solberg, *Hubert Humphrey,* 116.

Page 43   "Grubby": Orville Freeman interview (HHH Oral History Project, MHS, 1978).

Page 43   The "commies": Sandbrook, *Eugene McCarthy,* 46.

Page 43   "We campaigned": MWL interview (Downs).

Page 44   Mayor Humphrey had gone: On the Philadelphia convention, see Caro, *Master of the Senate,* 439–45; Eisele, *Almost to the Presidency,* 66–70; Solberg, *Hubert Humphrey,* 11–19.

Page 44   "I got it": *The Art of the Possible,* PBS.

Page 44   "This pipsqueak": Solberg, *Hubert Humphrey,* 14.

Page 44   Greatest speeches: *Almost to the Presidency,* 68; Rick Perlstein, "America's Forgotten Liberal, " *New York Times,* May 26, 2011.

Page 44   "He was on fire": Eisele, *Almost to the Presidency,* 68.

Page 44   "No. 1": Solberg, *Hubert Humphrey,* 133.

Page 45   "Those who are in": "The Happy Warrior," *Newsweek,* January 23, 1978.

4. Courtroom No. 1

Page 48   "He is a natural": Larry Millett, "Judge Miles Lord: Champion of the Underdog, or Misguided Judicial Zealot?," *St. Paul Pioneer Press,* September 14, 1980.

Page 49   "As I tell my clerks": Peppers and Ward, *In Chambers,* 393.

Page 51   "Like taking": Mark D. Streed, "Miles Lord: A Warrior Fighting for Justice," *Minnesota Trial,* Summer 2009.

Page 51   Allowing girls: *Brenden v. Ind. School Dist. 742,* 342 F. Supp. 1224 (D. Minn.
             1972), *aff'd,* 477 F.2d 1292 (8th Cir. 1973).

Page 51   Historic sex-discrimination case: *Rajender v. Univ. of Minn.,* 546 F. Supp.
             158 (D. Minn. 1982).

Page 52   "I don't go bouncing": Deborah Schoenholz, "The Dissenting Opinion:
             An Interview with District Court Judge Miles Lord," *Tenant Inquirer,*
             March/April 1985.

Page 53   "We have more money": Affidavit of Dale Larson, judicial misconduct
             proceedings, July 2, 1984.

Page 53   Tobacco and asbestos: Pringle, *Cornered* (tobacco litigation); Brodeur,
             Outrageous Misconduct (asbestos litigation).

Page 53   "The aggressive posture": Internal tobacco industry memorandum,
             quoted in *Haines v. Liggett Group, Inc.,* 814 F. Supp. 414, 421 (D. N.J. 1993).

Page 54   "A bulldog": Deposition of Roger Tuttle, *Bonlender,* August 1, 1984.

Page 54   In his deposition: All quotes are from the deposition of E. C. Robins
             Junior, *Renaldo-Lee v. A. H. Robins Co.,* No. 82-C-940, W.D. Wis., Sep-
             tember 19 and 20, 1983.

Page 55   "The poorest": Sam Newlund, "Disability Benefits Battle Jams Court-
             rooms," *Minneapolis Star Tribune,* November 30, 1983.

Page 55   "Respect the role": *U.S. v. Singer,* 710 F.2d 431, 437–38 (8th Cir. 1983) (Lay,
             J., concurring).

Page 57   Temporarily suspended: *In the Matter of the Application for the Discipline
             of George C. Gubbins Jr.,* C3–85–61 (Minn. February 6, 1986).

Page 57   "Grind me down": Affidavit of George Gubbins Jr., consolidated *Dalkon
             Shield* proceedings, January 6, 1984.

Page 58   Ciresi's client: The account of this trial and quotes are based on the
             Hahn trial transcript, October 24, November 17, and December 12, 1983.

5. Hotshot Prosecutor

Page 60   He set out: Miles's early days practicing law are discussed in MWL
             manuscript (Carlson 2007); MWL letter to Clarence Landrum, October
             26, 1950.

Page 60   "The howl": Annette M. Larson, "Miles Lord: The Case of the Eclectic
             Judge," *Minnesota Alumni,* Spring 1985.

Page 61   "There is not": MWL letter to Clarence Landrum, October 26, 1950.

Page 61   "By some strange quirk": ibid.

Page 61   "It sounded like": MWL interview (HHH Oral History Project, MHS
             1978).

Page 61   "Splendid race": Letter from HHH to MWL, December 15, 1950.

Page 61   Miles seized: MWL interview (HHH Oral History Project, MHS 1978).

Page 61   Not long after: The St. Cloud Reformatory scandal is discussed in

MWL dictation (undated) and multiple contemporaneous newspaper articles.

Page 62　"Our Minnesota penal": Letter from MWL to HHH, September 18, 1951.

Page 62　Hubert Humphrey: On Humphrey and the racketeers, see Paul Maccabee, "Alias Kid Cann," *Mpls.St. Paul,* November 1991.

Page 62　"Most notorious": Gordon Schendel, "How Mobsters Grabbed a City's Transit Line," *Collier's,* September 29, 1951.

Page 62　"Nerve center": Maccabee, "Alias Kid Cann" (quoting *True* magazine).

Page 62　Another longtime gangster: On Tommy Banks, see Schendel, "How Mobsters Grabbed a City's Transit Line"; Jim Klobuchar, "A Legend from the City's Checkered Past Dies," *Minneapolis Star Tribune,* September 12, 1985.

Page 62　A political enemy: FBI report on Fred Gates, November 26, 1962 (MHS).

Page 63　First "net worth": George Johnson, "Lord Fights On," *Duluth News-Tribune,* November 4, 1973.

Page 63　"Is your Dad there": author interview, Priscilla Lord.

Page 63　Miles got a visit: MWL interview (HHH Oral History Project, MHS, 1978); MWL manuscript (Carlson 2007).

Page 63　"A poor boy": Wit and Wisdom from Hubert H. Humphrey, http://lgi .umn.edu/about/HHHquotes.html.

Page 63　He was born: On Humphrey's early life, see Eisele, *Almost to the Presidency,* 11, 15, 20, 50–51; Solberg, *Hubert Humphrey,* 38.

Page 64　Inscribed by Hubert Humphrey's biographer: All quotes are from Solberg, *Hubert Humphrey,* 12, 18, 134, 257, 466–67, 469.

Page 64　"I felt very humble"; "If he hadn't been": MWL interview (Downs).

Page 64　"Hubert Humphrey stood": Philly Murtha, "Fat Guys vs. Teeny Guys," *Twin Cities,* December 1981; "Being with Hubert": MWL interview (Downs).

Page 65　"Go talk to Miles": author interview, Hubert H. (Skip) Humphrey III.

Page 65　"I have never seen": Letter from HHH to MWL, June 24, 1958.

Page 65　"Hubert's concept": MWL dictation (undated).

Page 65　"A fifty-eight holer": ibid.

Page 65　"My, this doorknob": ibid.

Page 65　One time: This account is based on Humphrey, *The Education of a Public Man,* 361; Solberg, *Hubert Humphrey,* 229–30.

Page 66　On one trip: author interview, Walter Mondale.

Page 66　In private: MWL interview (HHH Oral History Project, MHS, 1978).

Page 66　"The power": MWL speech, New York Academy of Sciences, December 1977.

Page 66　"Miles," said Hubert: MWL interview (Downs).

Page 66　"Too much static": Brian Lambert, "Independently Speaking, Conversations with Miles Lord," *Twin Cities Reader,* September 24–October 1, 1980.

Page 66   "I would rather": Frank Wright, "The Long Road to Nomination," *Minneapolis Tribune*, August 27, 1964.

Page 67   One of the greatest legislators: *The Art of the Possible*, PBS; "the art of the possible": ibid.

Page 67   "He was a terrific fighter": Solberg, *Hubert Humphrey*, 469.

6. Meeting the Enemy

Page 68   Another, short matter: *U.S. v. Sperry Corp.*, CR 4–83–94, D. Minn., December 9, 1983.

Page 69   The first matter of business: All quotes from this hearing are from the transcript of consolidated *Dalkon Shield* proceedings, December 9, 1983.

Page 70   "I don't know": Transcript of consolidated *Dalkon Shield* proceedings, January 26, 1984.

Page 70   "Stupid sons": author interview, Michael Ciresi.

Page 71   "How can you represent": ibid.

Page 71   The "big city": author interview, Jack Fribley.

Page 71   Oppenheimer Wolff: The full name of the firm was Oppenheimer, Wolff, Foster, Shepard & Donnelly.

Page 71   "You're a fine": Transcript of consolidated *Dalkon Shield* proceedings, February 2, 1984.

Page 73   "The biggest lawsuit": Gwenyth Jones, "'Biggest Suit' to Be Tried Here," *Minneapolis Star,* June 5, 1971.

Page 74   The A. H. Robins attorneys have argued: For discussion of A. H. Robins arguments on document admissibility, see generally *Dalkon Shield MDL,* 575 F. Supp. 718 (D. Kan.1983).

Page 74   "If they pulled": Deposition of E. C. Robins Senior, consolidated *Dalkon Shield* proceedings, January 26, 1983 (ruling of Judge Lord).

Page 74   "Mummy up": MWL dictation (March 1987).

Page 74   A key factor: See Minn. Stat. §549.20 (listing the factors for punitive damages, including "the number and level of employees involved in causing or concealing the misconduct").

Page 75   Charles Osthimer: All quotes from the closing arguments of Osthimer and Ciresi are from the *Hahn* trial transcript, December 15, 1983.

Page 76   Judge Lord issues: Initial Pretrial Order, consolidated *Dalkon Shield* proceedings, December 13, 1983.

Page 78   "Do you have": All quotes from this hearing are from the transcript of consolidated *Dalkon Shield* proceedings, December 20, 1983.

Page 78   Alexander Slaughter and William Cogar: Slaughter represented both A. H. Robins and Aetna; Cogar was retained by A. H. Robins alone.

Page 79   Another judge in Oregon: See *Coursen v. A. H. Robins Co.*, 764 F.2d 1329 (9th Cir. 1985).

Page 79   Refusal to recall: In 1980, A. H. Robins sent a second "Dear Doctor"

letter recommending removal of the Dalkon Shield due to the duration of use and potential for a rare fungus infection, called actinomyces
israelii, only thirty-one cases of which had been reported anywhere
in the world. A. H. Robins emphasized that this letter was not "to be
construed as a 'recall' . . . of a defective and potentially life-threatening
product." *Tetuan v. A. H. Robins Co.*, 738 P.2d 1210, 241 Kan. 441, 452–53
(1987).

Page 80   "We have three rooms": Kay Miller, "15 Face Charges in Protest at Honeywell," *Minneapolis Star Tribune,* December 29, 1983. (The headline
was in reference to other protesters arrested that day at Honeywell.)

Page 80   "When do I get": All quotations from this hearing are from the transcript of consolidated *Dalkon Shield* proceedings, January 5, 1984.

Page 82   He issues his opinion: *Sierra Club v. Clark,* 577 F. Supp. 783 (D. Minn.
1984).

Page 82   "A nationwide cause celebre": Dean Rebuffoni, "Coalition Sues Federal
Agency to Stop Proposed Wolf Trapping," *Minneapolis Star Tribune,* December 12, 1983.

Page 83   A Dalkon Shield order: Order for Depositions, consolidated *Dalkon
Shield* proceedings, January 9, 1984.

7. Political Wunderkind

Page 84   "Covetous eyes": MWL dictation (September 1976).

Page 85   Even one of Freeman's: Gerald Heaney interview (HHH Oral History
Project, MHS, 1978).

Page 85   "Free-swinging": Jim Parsons, "Miles Lord Nominated as U.S. Judge,"
Minneapolis Tribune, February 11, 1966.

Page 85   "Quick"; "just a trifle": William Swanson, "Fire on the Bench," *Corporate
Report,* July 1976.

Page 85   "Why donate": MWL dictation (November 1985); "a breeding ground":
MWL campaign TV script, August 26, 1954; "hanky panky": MWL dictation (September 1976); "Pretty profitable": MWL and congressional
candidates campaign TV script, undated; "hardened, habitual"; "How
much humanity": MWL campaign TV script, September 11, 1954; "my
dear old mother": MWL dictation (September 1976).

Page 85   "Small, oppressed"; "Well, I have": MWL campaign TV script, September 11, 1954.

Page 86   "People who need"; "wealthy, powerful": ibid.

Page 86   "An earthquake": Solberg, *Hubert Humphrey,* 168.

Page 86   "Wunderkind": Larry Millett, "Judge Miles Lord Champion of the
Underdog, or Misguided Judicial Zealot?," *St. Paul Pioneer Press,* September 14, 1980.

Page 86   "A brilliant"; "charming": Miriam Alburn, "Has Miles Lord Quit Politics for Good?," *Minneapolis Tribune,* May 6, 1960; "uncanny": "Miles Lord Resigns," *Worthington Globe,* May 6, 1960; "a genuine compassion"; "forgot to think": John McDonald, "Lord's Reason for Quitting Simple, Best Sources Say," *Minneapolis Tribune,* May 8, 1960; "intemperate"; "not in keeping": "Intemperate Official," *Minneapolis Star,* October 25, 1956; "a positive genius": Alburn, "Has Miles Lord Quit Politics for Good?"

Page 86   "Two-bit raid": "Miles Lord Likes Dramatics," *Granite Falls Tribune,* September 1, 1955.

Page 87   "Rotten, pregnant": MWL interview (Verna Corgan 1988).

Page 87   "Miles Lord Likes Dramatics": *Granite Falls Tribune,* September 1, 1955.

Page 87   Adoption of prepaid health care: *The Pulse,* Group Health Plan annual meeting report, April 1977.

Page 87   "I didn't worry"; "All they had to do": MWL interview (Downs).

Page 87   "He has compiled": "Maybe Lord?," *Valley News,* August 15, 1957.

Page 87   He was lampooned: "Guildsmen Roast Public Figures," *Minneapolis Star,* April 10, 1956.

Page 88   It came in the prosecution: On the Connelly trial, see Sam Romer, "Connelly Gave Bomb Orders, Lord Tells Jury," *Minneapolis Tribune,* April 12, 1956; Hal Seymour, "Connelly Trial Hangs in Balance," *Minneapolis Star,* April 30, 1956; Sam Romer, "Judge Frees Connelly in St. Paul Bombing Trial," *Minneapolis Tribune,* May 1, 1956.

Pages 88   Only such loss: William Martin, "Miles Lord Calls Kline Minnow Caught in Net for Big Fish, Koolishes," *St. Paul Dispatch,* April 15, 1964.

Page 88   "Get rough": Clark Mollenhoff, "Witness Says He Lied in Connelly Bomb Trial," *Minneapolis Tribune,* undated.

Page 89   In the late 1950s: On the DST controversy, see Citizens League Report No. 101, February 1959; Session Weekly, Minnesota House Public Information Office, 1991; "Here's How Time 'Crisis' Developed—Hour by Hour," *Minneapolis Tribune,* April 26, 1959; "Won't Be Swayed by Hysteria, Says Dell," *Minneapolis Star,* April 27, 1959.

Page 89   "Death knell": Session Weekly, Minnesota House.

Page 89   "One of the greatest": ibid.

Page 89   "Dropped with": "Off Again, On Again," *Minneapolis Tribune,* April 27, 1959.

Page 89   A questionable view: The writ stated that the counties "shall cease and desist from attempting to promulgate, order and impose or otherwise attempt to put into effect any order, decree, resolution or directive attempting to change the time other than central standard time." See "Court Blocks DST, Entire State Is Thrown into Confusion," *St. Paul Dispatch,* April 25, 1959.

Page 90   "We do not intend": "Judge Dell Warns DST 'Violators,'" *St. Paul Dispatch,* April 27, 1959.

Page 90   "A three-and-a-half hour": J. C. Wolfe, "High Court Airs DST Fight,"

St. Paul Pioneer Press, May 7, 1959; "hammered": Russell Hurst, "Court Delays Its Ruling in Daylight Case," *Minneapolis Tribune,* May 7, 1959; "gave as good": "Legislature May Beat Court to Punch on DST," *Minneapolis Star,* May 7, 1959.

Page 90   "Am I on trial": Hurst, "Court Delays Its Ruling in Daylight Case."

Page 90   "Professional conduct": *In re Lord,* 97 N.W.2d 287, 255 Minn. 370, 371 (Minn. 1959).

Page 90   "A serious infringement": Letter from Orville Freeman to MWL, May 26, 1959.

Page 90   "We do not intend": Russell Hurst, "High Court Plans Action against Lord," *Minneapolis Tribune,* May 28, 1959.

Page 90   "Severe censure": All quotes in this paragraph are from *In re Lord,* 355 Minn. 370, 380, 382, 382.

Page 91   In October 1959: On the meatpackers strike, see *Wilson and Co. v. Freeman,* 179 F. Supp. 520 (D. Minn. 1959); Harry Hite, "200 Guardsmen Patrol Streets with Bayonets," *St. Paul Pioneer Press,* December 12, 1959; "Spectators Crowd Federal Courthouse," *Minneapolis Tribune,* December 17, 1959.

Page 91   In private: MWL dictation (March 1987); Confidential Report to Subcommittee Re Appointment of Miles W. Lord (by U.S. Senate Judiciary Committee investigator), 1966.

Page 91   "A free people": *Wilson,* 159 F. Supp. at 526.

Page 92   Ornery: Solberg, *Hubert Humphrey,* 167; "for timidity": Martin, "Miles Lord Calls Kline Minnow."

Page 92   Miles had secured: MWL dictation (1987); Parsons, "Miles Lord Nominated."

Page 92   His former law partner: Trudi Hahn, "Lee Loevinger 1913–2004: Jurist, Regulator, Trustbuster Dies," *Minneapolis Star Tribune,* May 1, 2004.

Page 92   "What a travesty": "Lord's Balloon Deflated," *Minneapolis Tribune,* March 4, 1960.

Page 92   "I hadn't been": MWL dictation (March 1987).

Page 93   "The rotten business": MWL manuscript (Carlson 2007).

Page 93   "Who comes out": MWL dictation (January 1978).

Page 93   "Maxine didn't want": MWL dictation (1987).

Page 93   "An amateurish": Eisele, *Almost to the Presidency,* 142.

Page 93   "I had kids": MWL interview (Downs).

Page 94   Three times: MWL manuscript (Carlson 2007).

Page 94   "An impartial": "Lord Resigns," *Shakopee Argus Tribune,* May 3, 1960.

Page 94   "Few tears": "The Departure of Lord," *Minneapolis Tribune,* May 3, 1960.

Page 94   "It is a pleasant": Alburn, "Has Miles Lord Quit Politics for Good?"

Page 94   His father: Mondale, *The Good Life,* 7–8.

Page 94   He entered the office: David Harris, "Understanding Mondale," *New York Times,* June 19, 1983.

Page 94   A list of enemies: author interview, Walter Mondale.

Page 95   "Take a look": Mondale, *The Good Life,* 15.

Page 95   "Why are you": author interview, Virginia Lord.

Page 95   "I heard"; "It came": author interviews, Priscilla Lord and Virginia Lord.

Page 96   "They think": Letter from Luvan Troendle, April 27, 1979.

Page 96   In the 1960 presidential primaries: On the West Virginia primary, see Caro, *The Passage of Power,* 84–87; Eisele, *Almost to the Presidency,* 144–47.

Page 96   Orville Freeman: On the 1960 Democratic National Convention and Freeman's quest for the vice presidency, see Eisele, *Almost to the Presidency,* 150–57; Humphrey, *The Education of a Public Man,* 170; Orville Freeman diary, August 30, 1968 (MHS); MWL interview (Downs).

Page 96   "They love": MWL interview (HHH Oral History Project, MHS, 1978).

Page 96   "The elder statesman"; "the most impressive": "The Humphrey Image," *The New Republic,* March 21, 1960.

Page 97   "My merit": Price, *Judge Richard S. Arnold,* 127.

8. Lawyers Objecting, Witnesses Stonewalling

Page 98   "Doctor, assume": All quotes from the deposition of Ellen Preston are from the deposition transcripts of January 18 and 20, 1984, in the consolidated *Dalkon Shield* proceedings.

Page 99   The whole premise: See *Grimshaw v. Ford Motor Co.,* 119 Cal. App.3d 757, 810 (1981), a landmark case involving a Ford Pinto that burst into flames when rear-ended. ("Punitive damages thus remain as the most effective remedy of consumer protection against defectively designed mass produced articles. They provide a motive for private individuals to enforce rules of law and enable them to recoup the expense of doing so which can be considerable and not otherwise recoverable.")

Page 100   Two other plaintiffs' lawyers: Unless otherwise indicated, this account of Appert and Pyle is based on Paul Blustein, "How 2 Young Lawyers Got Rich by Settling IUD Liability Claims," *Wall Street Journal,* February 24, 1982.

Page 100   The U.S. Supreme Court: *Bates v. State Bar of Ariz.,* 433 U.S. 350 (1977).

Page 100   Only $10,000: Perry and Dawson, *Nightmare,* 175.

Page 100   "Harassed": Austin Wehrwein, "Minn. Firm Withdraws from Dalkon Shield Suits," *National Law Journal,* October 26, 1981.

Page 100   Temporarily suspend: *In the Matter of the Application for the Discipline of Robert J. Appert,* C9-85-243 (Minn. 1985); *In the Matter of the Application for the Discipline of Gerald G. Pyle,* CO-85-244 (Minn. 1985).

Page 101   A. H. Robins was demanding: Affidavit of Dale Larson, judicial misconduct proceedings, July 2, 1984.

Page 101   This was a condition: Mintz, *At Any Cost,* 197–98; Barry Siegel, "Miles

Lord: Champion or Zealot?," *Los Angeles Times,* June 28, 1984; Josephine Marcotty, "Attention Focuses on Review of Lord," *Minneapolis Star Tribune,* July 9, 1984.

Page 101   "That restricts": The provision in effect was DR2–108(B) of the Code of Professional Responsibility.

Page 102   "Yes, I am": author interview, Michael Ciresi.

Page 102   "Mr. Attorney": All quotes in this chapter from the deposition of Dr. Frederick Clark Jr. are from the deposition transcripts of January 19, 20, and 25, 1984, in the consolidated *Dalkon Shield* proceedings.

Page 104   Senior's grandfather: On the history of A. H. Robins, see *A Guide to the A. H. Robins Company Records, 1885–2004,* Virginia Historical Society; Mintz, *At Any Cost,* xv, 45–48.

Page 104   "Most Generous": Mintz, *At Any Cost,* xv.

Page 105   Larson starts: All quotes in this chapter from the deposition of E. C. Robins Senior are from the deposition transcripts of January 23 and 24, 1984, in the consolidated *Dalkon Shield* proceedings.

Page 108   We start the day: All quotes from this hearing are from the transcript of consolidated *Dalkon Shield* proceedings, January 25, 1984.

9. Persecutor of Organized Crime

Page 111   Hubert suggested: MWL interview (Downs).

Page 111   "A stepping stone": ibid.

Page 112   "Hubert has been clocked:" Mondale, *The Good Life,* 11.

Page 112   "By-gosh": "The Happy Warrior," *Newsweek,* January 23, 1978.

Page 112   "Can you imagine": Caro, *Master of the Senate,* 448.

Page 112   "Dark days": ibid., 450.

Page 112   "One of the mightiest": ibid., xiii.

Page 112   "Firebrand Senator Cools Down": *Business Week,* June 1963, quoted in Eisele, *Almost to the Presidency,* 187.

Page 112   "The idea factory": *The Art of the Possible,* PBS (quoting *Washington Post*); The Peace Corps: ibid.

Page 113   "The epicenter": Eisele, *Almost to the Presidency,* 179.

Page 113   Gene was: On McCarthy's early years, see Eisele, *Almost to the Presidency,* 27–39; Sandbrook, *Eugene McCarthy,* 13, 20; White, *The Making of the President 1968,* 88.

Page 113   "Too handsome": Kaiser, *1968 in America,* 48.

Page 113   He had served: On McCarthy's view of JFK, see Eisele, *Almost to the Presidency,* 148.

Page 114   "A very small list": author interview, Walter Mondale.

Page 114   "With a marked lack": Charles W. Bailey, "Lord Given U.S. Job—Reluctantly," *Minneapolis Tribune,* March 24, 1961; Bobby Kennedy took: ibid.

Page 114   "So that you may": Letter from HHH to MWL, April 14, 1961.

Page 114   At the White House: Bailey, "Lord Given U.S. Job—Reluctantly."

Page 115   "Uncle Sam Shows"; "compassion"; "pathetic": *Minneapolis Star,* December 27, 1963.

Page 115   "If Lord isn't": William Martin, "Miles Lord Calls Kline Minnow Caught in Net for Big Fish, Koolishes," *St. Paul Dispatch,* April 15, 1964.

Page 115   Kennedy told Miles: MWL manuscript (Carlson 2007).

Page 116   "Bob Kennedy Tells Lord": *Daily Herald,* May 1, 1962.

Page 116   "I know where": MWL manuscript (Carlson 2007).

Page 116.   "Clad in mink": Unnamed and undated newspaper photo and caption.

Page 116   The FBI: On Dranow's escape and capture, see Larry Fitzmaurice, "Nationwide Manhunt Launched for Dranow," *Minneapolis Star,* October 17, 1962; "Dranow Return Order Speeded, Caught in Luxurious Miami Home," *Minneapolis Star,* November 29, 1962.

Page 116   "I am being": "Dranow in Court Again, Sparks Fly," *Minneapolis Star,* January 3, 1963; "He laughs": Al McConagha, "Dranow Appears as Witness at Competency Test," *Minneapolis Tribune,* January 20, 1963.

Page 117   "You get me the goods": MWL interview (Downs).

Page 117   Ossanna agreed: This account is based on MWL interview (Downs); MWL dictation (1987); Martin, "Miles Lord Calls Kline Minnow."

Page 117   "I suppose": MWL interview (Downs).

Page 117   In June 1963: *U.S. v. Hoffa,* 367 F.2d 698 (7th Cir. 1966).

Page 117   "Rumpled and dispirited": Clark Mollenhoff, "Dranow Is a Broken but Key Figure in Hoffa Fraud Trial," *Minneapolis Tribune,* May 24, 1964.

Page 117   "Hoffa Trial Figure Testifies": *Chicago Sun-Times,* July 14, 1964; "Enraged at Presence of Miles Lord": *St. Paul Pioneer Press,* July 14, 1964; "Hoffa Assails U.S. Attorney": David Halvorsen, unnamed and undated newspaper.

Page 118   On a break: This account is based on MWL dictation (1987); MWL interview (Downs).

Page 118   "So here I am" through "So I wiped": MWL interview (Downs).

Page 118   Miles's other big splash: On the Sister Kenny case, see *U.S. v. Kline,* 221 F. Supp. 776 (D. Minn. 1963); *Koolish v. U.S.,* 340 F.2d 513 (8th Cir. 1965), *cert. denied,* 381 U.S. 951 (1965); Roberts, *Minnesota 150,* 96–97.

Page 118   "Minnow"; "big fish": Martin, "Miles Lord Calls Kline Minnow."

Page 119   "The sweetest": MWL interview (Downs).

Page 119   "Mammoth production": Richard Conlon, "'Cast' Dwindles Somewhat as Kenny Fraud Trial Nears End," *Minneapolis Tribune,* May 19, 1963.

Page 119   "Overzealousness": *Koolish,* 340 F.2d at 532.

Page 120   A dozen or so names: On the vice presidential speculation, see Eisele, *Almost to the Presidency,* 200–203.

Page 120   "The Minnesota Twins": ibid., 204.

Page 120   Senator Humphrey at the helm: *The Art of the Possible,* PBS; Norman

Sherman, "Civil Rights 1964: How a Bill Became an Act," *Minneapolis Star Tribune,* June 6, 2014.

Page 121   "Senator, it strikes": Transcript, *Meet the Press,* NBC, August 23, 1964.

Page 121   "An A-plus": Eisele, *Almost to the Presidency,* 210.

Page 121   "You're my candidate": ibid., 210.

Page 121   On the second day: ibid., 215; Solberg, *Hubert Humphrey,* 246, 254.

Page 121   Conflicting accounts: MWL manuscript (Carlson 2007) (Humphrey told Lord); MWL interview (HHH Oral History Project, MHS, 1978) (Humphrey didn't tell Lord).

Page 121   Went for a car ride: This account is based on MWL interview (Downs); MWL manuscript (Carlson 2007).

Page 121   "It is my opinion": Eisele, *Almost to the Presidency,* 216.

Page 122   "If you go": MWL manuscript (Carlson 2007).

Page 122   "I asked Maxine": Letter from MWL to Karl Rolvaag, September 1, 1964.

Page 122   Rolvaag could channel: Rolvaag's father, Ole Edvart, was the author of *Giants in the Earth,* the epic Norwegian novel about immigrant home-steaders on the Dakota plains.

Page 123   "Appoint somebody": MWL interview (Downs).

10. Judge Lord Goes to Richmond

Page 124   "Integrate"; "restore": Sheryl Gay Stolberg, "For Bachmann, God and Justice Were Intertwined," *New York Times,* October 13, 2011.

Page 124   The Dalkon Shield Disaster: Roger L. Tuttle, "The Dalkon Shield Disas-ter Ten Years Later—A Historical Perspective," *Oklahoma Bar Journal* 2501 (1983): 54.

Page 125   Before he goes to sleep: The Judge was well known for working around the clock. "He regarded sleep," one columnist wrote, "as a Republican conspiracy." Jim Klobuchar, "Miles Lord: Judicial Godfather to Troubled Environment," *Minneapolis Star,* December 9, 1974.

Page 126   "And I think": All quotes in this chapter from the hearings in Richmond are from hearings transcripts in the consolidated *Dalkon Shield* pro-ceedings, January 26 and 27, 1984.

Page 126   Senior arrives: All quotes in this chapter from the deposition of E. C. Robins Senior are from the deposition transcripts in the consolidated *Dalkon Shield* proceedings, January 26 and 27, 1984.

Page 127   Slaughter and one of his colleagues: Slaughter also argued that the Tut-tle reports were not addressed to the board as a whole but to individual board members and senior executives, a difference that the judge found to be without distinction.

Page 128   The deposition of Dr. Clark: All quotes in this chapter from the depo-sition of Dr. Frederick Clark Jr. are from the deposition transcripts in the consolidated *Dalkon Shield* proceedings, January 26 and 27, 1984.

Page 128   On an insurance dispute: See Agreement between A. H. Robins and the
            Aetna Casualty and Surety Company, February-March 1977.

Page 129   Aetna will later be named: Sobol, *Bending the Law,* 116.

11. The People's Judge

Page 136   "Former flamboyancy": "Lord's Appointment," *St. Paul Pioneer Press,*
            February 13, 1966.

Page 136   "Coolness": Jim Parsons, "Miles Lord Nominated as U.S. Judge," *Minne-
            apolis Tribune,* February 11, 1966.

Page 136   A contentious fraud case: Frank Wright, "American Allied Case Political
            Factors Puzzling," *Minneapolis Tribune,* August 8, 1965.

Page 136   "A wild ass"; "Miles understands": Sherman, *From Nowhere to Some-
            where,* 274–75.

Page 137   "You are okay": Letter from HHH to MWL, January 26, 1966.

Page 137   "Ramsey Clark": Letter from HHH to MWL, December 2, 1965.

Page 137   "Fritz is trying": Letter from HHH to MWL, January 26, 1966.

Page 137   "McCarthy was steadfast": MWL interview (Downs).

Page 137   "The primary consistent": Draft letter from MWL to Steve Rubin, Oc-
            tober 4, 1985; "A true friend": MWL interview (Downs).

Page 137   "Miles is the kind": David Carr, "Heaven Can Wait," *Minnesota Monthly,*
            January 1990; "break trail"; "take chances": Ellen Tomson, "Lord's Jus-
            tice," *St. Paul Pioneer Press,* May 1, 1994.

Page 138   "I will be the last": Donald Giese, "Magnusson Enters DFL Governor
            Race, Calls Lord Unfit for Judgeship," *St. Paul Pioneer Press,* February 21,
            1966. In the end, the insurance commissioner was acquitted in a trial
            handled by other prosecutors after Miles's appointment to the bench.

Page 138   "Obvious lack"; "Would not": Letter from George Thiess to Senators
            Mondale and McCarthy, with copy to Senate Judiciary Committee,
            April 18, 1966.

Page 138   "An iron hand": Marjorie Hunter, "James O. Eastland Is Dead at 81;
            Leading Senate Foe of Integration," *New York Times,* February 20, 1986.

Page 138   "Ridiculous": Confidential Report to Subcommittee re Appointment of
            Miles W. Lord (by U.S. Senate Judiciary Committee investigator), 1966.

Page 138   "Natural enemies": Al Eisele, "Miles Lord Hearing Has Third Delay, Ju-
            diciary Unit Told Charges Are Baseless," *St. Paul Pioneer Press,* March 29,
            1966.

Page 138   "A very able"; "a man of impeccable": Confidential Report to Subcom-
            mittee re Appointment of Miles W. Lord.

Page 139   "Wild West": author interview, Walter Mondale.

Page 139   "One of the most remarkable:" David Rubenstein, "True Tales of the
            Legend of Miles Lord," *Minnesota Law & Politics,* April/May 2005.

Page 139   "The people's judge": Larry Millett, "Judge Miles Lord: Champion of the

Underdog, or Misguided Judicial Zealot?," *St. Paul Pioneer Press,* September 14, 1980.

Page 139   "Going to heaven": MWL manuscript (Carlson 2007).

Page 140   "My *own*-laws": All quotes from this ceremony are from the transcript of Induction of Miles W. Lord as U.S. District Judge, May 2, 1966.

Page 140   "Jesus Christ": author interview, Virginia Lord.

Page 140   "Judge from central casting": Congressional Record, 113th Congress, H5890, September 27, 2013.

Page 141   "Don't let me frighten": MWL speech, Minnesota Bar Association, June 1966.

Page 141   He instructed: author interview, John Weeks (Judge Lord's first law clerk).

Page 141   "Rather naïve": MWL dictation (February 1987).

Page 142   "Independent of heaven": Bruce A. Ragsdale, "The Federal Courts in Our Constitutional Democracy," *Insights,* American Bar Association, Fall 2011 (quoting antifederalist "Brutus").

Page 142   "Dullsville": MWL interview (Gidmark 1988).

Page 142   "The freedom": Corgan, *Controversy, Courts, and Community,* 36.

12. On the Trail of Secret Documents

Page 143   "Stampede pace": A.H. Robins Supplement to Petition for Writ of Mandamus, *In re A. H. Robins Co.,* 84–5028, Eighth Circuit, February 14, 1984.

Page 143   "Good morning": All quotes from this hearing are from the transcript of consolidated *Dalkon Shield* proceedings, February 1, 1983.

Page 146   "Pin the tail" through "charade": On Judge Lord's views of discovery, which he often repeated verbatim, see Miles W. Lord, "Discovery Abuse: Appointing Special Masters," *Hamline Law Review* 9 (1986): 66.

Page 146   The process relies on defense attorneys: All attorneys are "officers of the court" with an obligation to aid in the administration of justice, but attorneys must also zealously represent their clients—and the balance is often not easily drawn.

Page 147   Not going to stick to the rules: Rule 34 of the Federal Rules of Civil Procedure generally governs document discovery; Judge Lord, however, often cited Rule 16, which allows for special procedures in difficult cases.

Page 147   Three motions: All quotes in this paragraph are from A. H. Robins motions and memoranda in the consolidated *Dalkon Shield* proceedings filed on January 31, 1984.

Page 148   "Mishmash" through "a fog surrounded by a mystery": Transcript of consolidated *Dalkon Shield* proceedings, February 2, 1984.

Page 148   "Hit-and-run treatment" through "a little oath": Transcript of consolidated *Dalkon Shield* proceedings, February 1, 1984.

Page 149 At the hearing on February 2: All quotes from this hearing are from the transcript of consolidated *Dalkon Shield* proceedings, February 2, 1984.

Page 150 "To the bare walls": Lord, "Discovery Abuse."

Page 151 "Some mischievous gnome"; "jumping up": MWL dictation (March 1987).

Page 151 "Maybe women": MWL manuscript (Gidmark undated).

Page 151 "If this is the way" through "Neither do the plaintiffs": Transcript of consolidated *Dalkon Shield* proceedings, February 2, 1984.

Page 152 "We actually have a doctor": All quotes from this hearing are from the transcript of consolidated *Dalkon Shield* proceedings, February 3, 1984.

Page 153 "Indulge us" through "an appropriate day": ibid.

Page 154 "No, oh no": All Slaughter quotes in this paragraph are from the transcripts of consolidated *Dalkon Shield* proceedings, February 6 and 7, 1984.

Page 154 "Great guy"; "wonderful": ibid., February 6, 1984.

Page 154 "We basically" through "So there is no problem there": ibid.

Page 155 Nothing personal: All quotes from this hearing are from the transcript of consolidated *Dalkon Shield* proceedings, February 6, 1984.

Page 155 The next morning, Tuesday: All quotes from this hearing are from the transcript of consolidated *Dalkon Shield* proceedings, February 7, 1984.

Page 156 Copies of the order: *Dean v. A. H. Robins Co.*, 101 F.R.D. 21 (D. Minn. 1984).

Page 156 "Any stay": All quotes from this hearing are from the transcript of consolidated *Dalkon Shield* proceedings, February 8, 1984.

Page 157 "Here to hell": MWL dictation (undated).

13. Presidential Politics

For background on the 1968 presidential campaign, this chapter relies generally on Eisele, *Almost to the Presidency;* Humphrey, *The Education of a Public Man;* Kaiser, *1968 in America;* McCarthy, *1968: War and Democracy;* Mitau, *Politics in Minnesota;* Sandbrook, *Eugene McCarthy;* Solberg, *Hubert Humphrey;* White, *The Making of the President, 1968;* and *The Art of the Possible*, PBS.

Page 158 "Stained with blood": *The Making of the President, 1968,* 301.

Page 158 "Unofficial envoy": MWL manuscript (Carlson 2007).

Page 158 "Cut his balls off": Solberg, *Hubert Humphrey,* 240; "Took him captive": ibid., 469; "he was Johnson's": ibid., 274.

Page 159 "He was eternally optimistic": MWL interview (Downs).

Page 159 "Candidate-martyr": White, *The Making of the President 1968,* 8.

Page 159 "And in my judgment": Tim Pugmire, "Eugene McCarthy, Who Galvanized a Generation of War Opponents, Dies," Minnesota Public Radio, December 10, 2005.

Page 160] "Teeny-boppers": MWL memo to HHH, April 22, 1968; "hippies": MWL manuscript (Carlson undated).

Page 160   "Get a taste": Tilsen, *Judging the Judges,* 33–34.

Page 160   "What you're saying": MWL interview (Downs).

Page 160   "He is very pessimistic": All quotes in this and the following two para-
            graphs are from MWL memo to HHH, February 5, 1968.

Page 160   Miles often reported: Copies of these memos were located among the
            judge's papers in the Lord family storage unit; most were also found
            among the collection of Humphrey papers at MHS.

Page 161   "Dear Miles": Letter from HHH to MWL, February 5, 1968.

Page 161   "No matter how mean": MWL interview (Downs).

Page 162   In Minnesota: Kaiser, *1968 in America,* 92; Mitau, *Politics in Minnesota,*
            49.

Page 162   "A triumph": Jon Wiener, "Eugene McCarthy: 1916–2005," *The Nation,*
            May 3, 2004 (quoting *Newsweek*).

Page 162   Plenty of animosity: Kaiser, *1968 in America,* 8–9 (noting the "hatred"
            between LBJ and RFK); Sandbrook, *Eugene McCarthy,* 191 (McCarthy
            "extreme contempt" for RFK); White, *The Making of the President 1968,*
            9 (RFK bitterness toward LBJ); Jack Newfield, "Kennedy's Search for a
            New Target," *Life,* April 12, 1968 (RFK hostility toward McCarthy).

Page 162   "Dear Hubert": MWL letter to HHH, March 21, 1968.

Page 163   "I am therefore pessimistic": MWL memo to HHH, March 21, 1968.

Page 163   LBJ showed Hubert: HHH dictation (MHS undated).

Page 164   "Here we are": Eisele, *Almost to the Presidency,* 330.

Page 164   He concluded: MWL memo to HHH, April 22, 1968; see also Jon Green-
            berg, "Can the President and the Vice President Be from the Same
            State?," www.politifact.com, April 16, 2015.

Page 164   "I suggested": All quotes from this meeting are from MWL memo to
            HHH, April 22, 1968.

Page 165   "Definitely received": Sandbrook, *Eugene McCarthy,* 205.

Page 165   "Tithing": "So You Want to Buy a President?," *Frontline,* PBS, January
            1996.

Page 165   "I'd hop": MWL interview (Downs); "I never trumpeted": MWL manu-
            script (Carlson 2007).

Page 165   "From a friend": MWL memo to HHH, October 17, 1968; "This mes-
            sage": MWL memo to HHH, August 7, 1968.

Page 166   On one occasion: MWL interview (HHH Oral History Project, MHS,
            1978).

Page 166   "Someone needed": author interview, Walter Mondale.

Page 166   The two candidates: McCarthy, *1968: War and Democracy,* 171; Mem-
            orandum for the Record From the Vice President, June 7, 1968 (MHS).

Page 166   "Honest, happy": William Connell interview (LBJ Library 1985); "a very
            human": White, *The Making of the President 1968,* 324.

Page 166   "Rancor": Larry Adcock, "Hubert Horatio Humphrey: Some Parting
            Notes," *Minneapolis Star,* January 28, 1978.

Page 166   "A scholar": White, *The Making of the President 1968,* 88.

Page 166   "A loner"; "an aesthetic": MLW interview (Downs).

Page 167   "Subservience": Sandbrook, *Eugene McCarthy,* 116.

Page 167   "He does that"; "in style"; "different kinds": Humphrey, *The Education of a Public Man,* 281.

Page 167   Party kingpins still controlled: Solberg, *Hubert Humphrey,* 336; Kaiser, *1968 in America,* 168, 221. By contrast, after 1968 most states adopted either primaries or caucuses for selecting presidential delegates.

Page 167   "My wattles": Solberg, *Hubert Humphrey,* 368.

Page 167   "He would speak": William Connell interview (LBJ Library 1985).

Page 167   "A Poet's Voice": Shana Alexander, *Life,* April 12, 1968.

Page 167   Miles stayed: MWL interview (Downs).

Page 167   "Tell Gene": This account and quotes are based on MWL manuscript (Carlson 2007).

Page 168   The first electoral defeat: White, *The Making of the President 1968,* 159.

Page 168   "Deeply": ibid., 316; "unhinged": Solberg, *Hubert Humphrey,* 341.

Page 168   "Trying to find": Eisele, *Almost to the Presidency,* 339.

Page 168   "Enigmatic"; "Erratic": White, *The Making of the President 1968,* 311–12.

Page 169   "To abandon": All quotes from this meeting are from MWL memo to HHH, July 12, 1968.

Page 169   "I was always": MWL interview (Downs).

Page 169   Andreas would be: "So You Want to Buy a President?," *Frontline,* PBS, January 1996. Four years later, a contribution by Andreas of $25,000 to the 1972 Nixon campaign was traced to a Watergate burglar. Kurt Eichenwald, "Top Archer Daniels Midland Executive Steps Down," *New York Times,* January 26, 1999.

Page 170   "Not an impossibility": Eisele, *Almost to the Presidency,* 342.

Page 170   "You didn't say": All quotes from this meeting are from MWL memo to HHH, August 7, 1968.

Page 171   Hubert and Gene met: This account is based on Eisele, *Almost to the Presidency,* 343.

14. Sweeping Corporate Headquarters

Page 172   The papers A. H. Robins filed: Motion for Temporary Stay of All Proceedings and Petition for Writ of Mandamus, February 9, 1984.

Page 173   Issues an order: *In re: A. H. Robins Co.,* No. 84–5028 (8th Cir. February 9, 1984).

Page 174   The judge signs: Order, consolidated *Dalkon Shield* proceedings, February 10, 1984.

Page 175   Ciresi steps: All quotes in this section are from the deposition of William Forrest Jr., consolidated *Dalkon Shield* proceedings, February 10, 1984.

Page 176   In coming years: *Jenson v. Eveleth Taconite Co.*, 130 F.3d 1287 (8th Cir. 1997), *cert. denied*, 524 U.S. 953 (1998).

Page 177   "Was she having": All quotes in this section are from the Forrest deposition, February 13, 1984.

Page 179   "Not to my knowledge"; "I don't recall": ibid., February 14, 1984.

Page 180   "They have acted": Transcript of consolidated *Dalkon Shield* proceedings, February 29, 1984.

Page 181   The call starts: All quotes from this hearing are from the transcript of consolidated *Dalkon Shield* proceedings, February 16, 1984.

Page 182   "We're now in the law department": ibid.

Page 183   Around the same time: All quotes from this hearing are from an unofficial transcript of *In re: A. H. Robins Co.*, No. 84–5028, Eighth Circuit, February 16, 1984.

Page 183   "Unapologetic liberal": Dennis Hevesi, "Donald P. Lay, 80, Federal Judge Notable in Rights Cases, Dies," *New York Times*, May 2, 2007.

Page 185   A. H. Robins also files: The motion for disqualification was based on 28 U.S.C. §455, which, among other things, applies to a judge whose "impartiality might reasonably be questioned."

Page 185   "A day-to-day": Order, consolidated *Dalkon Shield* proceedings, February 16, 1984 (Magistrate McNulty).

15. Election

On the 1968 election, this chapter also relies generally on the sources cited in the introductory note to chapter 13.

Page 187   Miles arrived: This account and quotes are based on author interviews with Walter Mondale and Priscilla Lord, as well as MWL interview (HHH Oral History Project, MHS, 1978), MWL dictation (undated), and MWL manuscripts (Carlson 2007 and undated).

Page 188   "Damn near"; "You didn't": MWL dictation (undated).

Page 188   Hubert wept: Solberg, *Hubert Humphrey*, 365.

Page 189   "One of the little hippies": MWL manuscript (Carlson undated).

Page 189   "The government in exile": Solberg, *Hubert Humphrey*, 370.

Page 189   "No one"; "He belonged": White, *The Making of the President 1968*, 88, 90.

Page 190   On one trip: MWL interview (Downs 1987).

Page 190   A "public humiliation": White, *The Making of the President 1968*, 398.

Page 190   "Show the people": MWL memo to HHH, October 17, 1968.

Page 190   "Shooed"; "Hubert"; "All these": MWL interview (Downs); "Quit reading": MWL manuscript (Carlson 2007).

Page 190   "The goddam [speech]": William Connell interview (LBJ Library 1985).

Page 190   "Good inside": Kaiser, *1968 in America*, 249.

Page 191   One day: This account and quotes are based on MWL memo to HHH (undated).

Page 191   "The only possible": MWL memo to HHH, October 23, 1968.

Page 191   "He foresees": MWL memo to HHH, October 27, 1968.

Page 192   "Like waiting": ibid.

Page 192   One day: This account is based on MWL memo to HHH, October 22, 1968.

Page 192   "To convince": Sam Newlund, "McCarthy Still Spurns HHH," *Minneapolis Tribune*, October 22, 1968.

Page 192   "Disassociative reaction": MWL memo to HHH, October 27, 1968.

Page 192   "Four-letter words": MWL memo to HHH, October 22, 1968; "you need": MWL memo to HHH, October 27, 1968.

Page 192   "I think": MWL memo to HHH, October 23, 1968.

Page 192   "Eugene is": MWL memo to HHH, Oct 27, 1968.

Page 192   "Less than": Humphrey, *The Education of a Public Man*, 282.

Page 192   "Backhanded": Kaiser, *1968 in America*, 252; "lukewarm"; "limp": Eisele, *Almost to the Presidency*, 393, 398.

Page 192   "Falls far short"; "in no way": Transcript, McCarthy's statement to the press, October 29, 1968.

Page 193   Pollsters showed: Kaiser, *1968 in America*, 252 (Humphrey ahead in Harris poll).

Page 193   "By golly": Eisele, *Almost to the Presidency*, 391.

Page 193   "Turned it": Humphrey, *The Education of a Public Man*, 282; "I had lost": Solberg, *Hubert Humphrey*, 407.

Page 194   "Memories of Hubert": McCarthy, *Gene McCarthy's Minnesota*, 131.

Page 194   "Just short": McCarthy, *Up 'Til Now*, 95.

Page 194   "Hubert was loyal": McCarthy, *Gene McCarthy's Minnesota*, 134.

Page 194   "Maxine gave"; "Gene was": MWL manuscript (Carlson 2007).

Page 194   "You'd think": MWL interview (Downs).

Page 194   Miles admired Gene: See MWL interview (HHH Oral History Project, MHS, 1978) ("There wouldn't even have been an opening in '68 if McCarthy hadn't done the unthinkable and taken on Lyndon Johnson and raised heck about the Vietnam War.").

Page 194   "In the eyes": Berman, *Hubert*, 232.

Page 195   One day: This account and quotes are based on MWL manuscript (Carlson 2007).

Page 195   One night: This account and quotes are based on MWL interview (HHH Oral History Project, MHS, August 10, 1978).

Page 196   "If they keep": MWL memo to HHH, May 16, 1969.

Page 196   Gene commemorated: "Eugene McCarthy; "Candidacy Inspired Antiwar Movement," *Los Angeles Times*, December 11, 2005.

Page 196   *I am alone*: ibid., quoting "The Aardvark," by Eugene McCarthy.

Page 196   He withdrew: On McCarthy's post-1968 life, see Bart Barnes and Pa-
            tricia Sullivan, "Gentle Senator, Presidential Hopeful Empowered U.S.
            Antiwar Movement," *Washington Post,* December 11, 2005; Tim Pug-
            mire, "Eugene McCarthy, Who Galvanized a Generation of War Oppo-
            nents, Dies," Minnesota Public Radio, December 10, 2005.

Page 196   "For this act": Sandbrook, *Eugene McCarthy,* 240.

Page 196   Hubert also continued: ibid., 259, 277.

Page 196   Before long: This account is based on MWL interview (Downs).

Page 197   "The things Hubert": ibid.

16. The Brink of Settlement

Page 198   The order: *In re: A. H. Robins Co.*, 732 F.2d 161 (8th Cir. 1984).

Page 198   Slaughter tells: Dave Anderson, "IUD Firm Must Turn Over Docu-
            ments," *Minneapolis Star Tribune,* February 24, 1984.

Page 199   Two orders: Orders, consolidated *Dalkon Shield* proceedings, February
            23, 1984.

Page 200   "My own view": All quotes from this hearing are from the transcript of
            consolidated *Dalkon Shield* proceedings, February 24, 1984.

Page 201   "I didn't want": Barry Siegel, "Miles Lord: Champion or Zealot?," *Los
            Angeles Times,* June 28, 1984.

Page 202   "Too many people": Transcript of consolidated *Dalkon Shield* proceed-
            ings, February 27, 1984.

Page 203   Larson comes out: All quotes from this hearing are from the transcript
            of consolidated *Dalkon Shield* proceedings, February 27, 1984.

Page 204   He also signs a protective order: Order, consolidated *Dalkon Shield* pro-
            ceedings, February 27, 1984.

Page 205   "If Judge Lord wants": Testimony of Alexander Slaughter, judicial mis-
            conduct proceedings, July 9, 1984.

Page 205   "A. H. Robins simply": Affidavit of Dale Larson, judicial misconduct
            proceedings, July 2, 1984.

Page 206   Patricia Lashley sits: All quotes in this section are from the deposition
            of Patricia Lashley in the consolidated *Dalkon Shield* proceedings, Feb-
            ruary 28, 1984.

Page 206   February 17, 1975: Lashley originally testified that the meeting was
            in 1977 but corrected that error in the April 19, 1984, session of her
            deposition.

Page 207   "A little cranky": Transcript of consolidated *Dalkon Shield* proceedings,
            February 27, 1984.

Page 207   Roger Brosnahan: All quotes from this hearing are from the transcript
            of consolidated *Dalkon Shield* proceedings, February 28, 1984.

Page 208   Larson and Socha: All quotes from this hearing are from the transcript of *Bertler v. A. H. Robins Co.*, No. 3–83–1028, D. Minn., February 28, 1984.

17. Bold on the Bench

Page 210   Among the first matters: On draft resisters in Minnesota and Judge Lord's record, see Tilsen, *Judging the Judges*.

Page 210   "I'd see them": Jim Klobuchar, "Miles Lord: Judicial Godfather to Troubled Environment," *Minneapolis Star,* December 9, 1974; "The more": MWL interview (Downs).

Page 210   "Oh God": author interview, John McShane; "marvelously": David Rubenstein, "True Tales of the Legend of Miles Lord," *Minnesota Law & Politics,* April/May 2005.

Page 211   "The kids": Klobuchar, "Miles Lord: Judicial Godfather."

Page 211   It was a hot topic: On education funding and the "Minnesota Miracle," see *Minnesota School Finance History, 1849–2011,* https://education.state.mn.us; *Public Education—The Minnesota Miracle,* MHS, www.libguides.mnhs.org/publiced; Patrick Coolican and Paul Walsh, "Wendell Anderson, Former Minnesota Governor, Dead at 83," *Minneapolis Star Tribune,* July 18, 2016.

Page 211   His decision: *Van Dusartz v. Hatfield,* 334 F. Supp. 870, 876 (D. Minn. 1971).

Page 212   "Minnesota: A State That Works": *Time,* August 13, 1973.

Page 212   "A historical marker"; the "Miracle Case": Glen Dawursk Jr., *Minnesota's Miracle Case: Van Dusartz v. Hatfield, www.yuthguy.com/classroom/super/vandusartzhatfield.htm.* The legislation endured until 2002, when the legislature again revised the property tax structure. *Public Education—The Minnesota Miracle,* MHS.

Page 212   He had been assigned: Judge Lord's quotes about the antibiotics litigation are from MWL dictation (March 1986), unless otherwise indicated. For additional background on this litigation, see *Pfizer Inc. v. Lord,* 456 F.2d 532 (8th Cir. 1972), *cert. denied,* 406 U.S. 976 (1972); *U.S. v. Lord,* 542 F.2d 719 (8th Cir. 1976); Bartsh et al., *A Class-Action Suit That Worked.*

Page 213   "There are no": "The $175 Million Rx," *Time,* March 4, 1974.

Page 213   In an early hearing: This account and quotes are based on MWL dictation (March 1986) and MWL manuscript (Carlson 2007), as well as Miles W. Lord, "Discovery Abuse: Appointing Special Masters," *Hamline Law Review* 9 (1986): 63; and author interview, John Cochrane.

Page 214   "A refrigerator": "Longtime St. Paul Lawyer John Cochrane Dies," *St. Paul Pioneer Press,* October 15, 2015.

Page 214   "I'm going": "Minnesota Legal Hall of Fame, John Cochrane," *Minnesota Law & Politics,* 2007.

Page 214   "We understood": MWL dictation (December 1970).

Page 214   "A futile": MWL dictation (March 1986).

Page 214   "Hands-on": MWL interview (Verna Corgan 1988).

Page 215   "At some point"; "He is": *Pfizer v. Lord,* 456 F.2d at 538.

Page 215   "Buy a monopoly": All quotes in this paragraph are from *Pfizer v. Lord,* 456 F.2d at 536, 542.

Page 215   *Pfizer Inc.*: All quotes from this opinion are from *Pfizer v. Lord,* 456 F.2d at 538, 542, 543.

Page 216   "A bunch": MWL dictation (March 1986).

Page 216   One day: This account and quotes are based on MWL dictations (undated and November 1985) and author interview, Priscilla Lord, unless otherwise indicated; for additional background on the case, see *Brenden v. Ind. School Dist.* 742, 342 F. Supp. 1224 (D. Minn. 1972), *aff'd,* 477 F.2d 1292 (8th Cir. 1973).

Page 217   "Unthinking": Klobuchar, "Miles Lord: Judicial Godfather"; "chauvinistic": MWL manuscript (Carlson 2007).

Page 218   "Tennis courts": Bob Lundegaard, "Injured Girl Athletes Pose No Dilemma, Judge Says," *Minneapolis Star,* April 27, 1972.

Page 218   "Solely on the basis"; "The League's forebodings": *Brenden,* 342 F. Supp. at 1234.

Page 218   It was hailed: Jackie Crosby, "She Blazed the Trail for Girls' Sports," *Minneapolis Star Tribune,* February 17. 2013; "The Prairie Judge," *60 Minutes,* CBS, November 11, 1984.

Page 220   "Whole morass"; "But they": "The $175 Million Rx," *Time.*

Page 220   "The black sheet": Nicholas von Hoffman, "Operation MoneyBack: Of Price Fixing and Antibiotics," *Washington Post,* May 10, 1976.

Page 221   Privately told: MWL interview (Downs).

Page 221   "He leveled": MWL speech, New York Academy of Sciences, December 1977.

Page 222   Robert Sheran encouraged: MWL dictation (November 1975).

Page 222   "My friend": Bastow, *"This Vast Pollution,"* 75; "I am pleased": ibid.

Page 222   They feared: ibid.

18. The Speech

Page 223   Among themselves: Testimony of Alexander Slaughter, judicial misconduct proceedings, July 9, 1984.

Page 223   The judge calls: All quotes from this hearing are from the transcript of consolidated *Dalkon Shield* proceedings, February 29, 1984.

Page 224   Bartsh had believed: Report to the Court of Thomas Bartsh Regarding Dalkon Shield Production, June 15, 1984.

Page 224   He finds a box: Report to the Court on Dalkon Shield Production by

Peter Thompson, June 18, 1984; These types: Affidavit of Judge Theis, judicial misconduct proceedings, July 3, 1984.

Page 232   Judge Renner enters: Order, *Bertler v. A. H. Robins Co.*, No. 3–83–1028, D. Minn., February 29, 1984.

19. Judge Lord versus Reserve Mining

For background on the Reserve Mining case, this chapter relies generally on Bastow, *"This Vast Pollution";* Bartlett, *The Reserve Mining Controversy;* and Lass, *Minnesota,* as well as transcripts, court pleadings, judicial decisions, and contemporaneous newspaper articles.

Page 233   "Are you drinking"; "Personally": *Reserve Mining* transcript, June 15, 1973.

Page 233   "Asbestos-Type Fiber": *St. Paul Dispatch,* June 15, 1973.

Page 233   "High concentrations": All quotes in this paragraph are from Bastow, *"This Vast Pollution,"* 112; Bartlett, *The Reserve Mining Controversy,* 123.

Page 234   "Was to a lady": Jane E. Brody, "Iron Ore Company vs. the Changing Times: U.S. Court Will Decide on Right to Pollute," *New York Times,* August 8, 1973.

Page 236   "A possible": Bartlett, *The Reserve Mining Controversy,* 265 (quoting decision by Lake County Dist. Court Judge C. Luther Eckman).

Page 237   "A Midwestern Kennedy"; "populist"; "anti-elitist": "Minnesota: A State That Works," *Time,* August 13, 1973.

Page 237   "Polluter of Lake"; "Lobbyists Swarm": Bastow, *"This Vast Pollution,"* 68.

Page 238   "A seemingly endless": Don Boxmeyer, "Taconite Trial on Last Lap," *St. Paul Pioneer Press,* December 14, 1973.

Page 238   There was no dispute: On the position of the parties, see generally *Reserve Mining Co. v. U.S.,* 498 F.2d 1073 (8th Cir. 1974).

Page 238   "Probably the most": Boxmeyer, "Taconite Trial on Last Lap."

Page 238   Fell fast asleep: This account is based on Don Boxmeyer, "Still the Maverick," *St. Paul Pioneer Press Dispatch,* December 10, 1989.

Page 239   "A rather small": ibid.

Page 239   A biophysicist: This account of the biophysicist's testimony and quotes are based on Bastow, *"This Vast Pollution,"* 115–17.

Page 240   Dr. Selikoff: On Dr. Selikoff's background and the history of the asbestos industry, see Paul Brodeur, "Casualties of the Workplace," *The New Yorker,* October 29, 1973; Brodeur, *Outrageous Misconduct,* 6, 180, 200, 210–11, 216.

Page 240   He testified: All quotes of Dr. Selikoff's testimony are from the *Reserve Mining* transcript, September 20 and 21, 1973.

Page 241   "Perfectly healthy"; "Dr. Sillycough": Thomas R. Huffman, "Enemies of the People: Asbestos and the Reserve Mining Trial," *Minnesota History,* Fall 2005.

Page 241   "A political whirlpool"; "savvy politicians": "Crisis in Silver Bay," *Time,*
           October 22, 1973.

Page 241   Later in the year: This account is based on "Judge Brings Wide Experi-
           ence to Tough Case," *Milwaukee Journal,* November 11, 1973.

Page 241   Over and over: *U.S. v. Reserve Mining Co.,* 412 F. Supp. 705, 710–712 (D.
           Minn. 1976), *remanded,* 498 F.2d 1073 (8th Cir. 1974); *U.S. v. Reserve Min-
           ing,* 380 F. Supp. 11, 64–67, 84–85 (D. Minn. 1974), *aff'd and remanded,*
           498 F.2d 1073 (8th Cir. 1974).

Page 241   He issued an order: See *Armco Steel Corp. v. U.S.,* 490 F.2d 688 (8th Cir.
           1974). The two parent companies each owned 50 percent of Reserve
           Mining's stock and together controlled all major management deci-
           sions and reaped all of Reserve's profits.

Page 242   "An insurance policy": MWL dictation (February 1977).

Page 242   Reversed Judge Lord: *Armco Steel,* 490 F.2d 688.

Page 242   He told: This account is based on Bastow, *"This Vast Pollution,"* 147–48.

Page 243   "A *prima facie*": All quotes from this hearing are from the *Reserve Mining*
           transcript, February 5, 1974.

Page 243   One document: These documents are detailed in *Reserve Mining,* 380 F.
           Supp. at 67–68; see also Bastow, *"This Vast Pollution,"* 148–49.

Page 243   "Plans"; "ideas"; concepts": *Reserve Mining* transcript, April 20, 1974;
           "complete" or "total"; "approved: ibid., March 29, 1974; only an interim:
           Reserve Mining, 412 F. Supp. at 712.

Page 244   "I had to": MWL dictation (February 1977).

Page 244   Dr. Brown testified: The account of this testimony and quotes are
           based on Bastow, *"This Vast Pollution,"* 136–39.

Page 244   In chambers: author interview, Dean Rebuffoni.

Page 244   Throughout the week: author interview, Peter Thompson (former law
           clerk).

Page 245   "The populist judge": Huffman, "Enemies of the People."

Page 245   "Your Honor"; "Well": *Reserve Mining* transcript, April 19, 1974.

Page 245   Verity was back: All quotes from this hearing are from the *Reserve Min-
           ing* transcript, April 20, 1974.

Page 246   "For a capitulation": Don Boxmeyer, "Reserve Ordered Shut Down," *St.
           Paul Pioneer Press,* April 21, 1974.

Page 246   "All bets": author interview, Dean Rebuffoni.

Page 246   "The most amazing": Bastow, *"This Vast Pollution,"* 159.

Page 246   Back in chambers: author interviews, Peter Thompson and John
           McShane (former law clerks).

Page 247   The "holy": Huffman, "Enemies of the People"; "It seems strange": Peg
           Meier, "Workers Contemplate Reserve-less Future," *Minneapolis Tri-
           bune,* April 22, 1974.

Page 247   No other judge: Stephanie Hemphill, "The Legacy of the Reserve Min-
           ing Case," Minnesota Public Radio, October 29, 2003.

Page 247   "A courageous decision": "Showdown at Superior," *New York Times,*
            April 28, 1974.

Page 247   On Monday: All quotes from this hearing are from the *Reserve Mining*
            transcript, April 22, 1974.

20. A. H. Robins Fires Back

Page 249   "Judge Castigates Company Chiefs": *New York Times,* March 2, 1984;
            "U.S. Judge Assails Officers": *Washington Post,* March 2, 1984; "Judge
            Scolds Firm": *Wall Street Journal,* March 2, 1984; "IUD Firm Seared":
            Chicago Sun-Times, March 2, 1984.

Page 249   "One of the most": "Broadside from the Bench," *Richmond Times-
            Dispatch,* March 7, 1984.

Page 249   "Beautiful anger": Colman McCarthy, "Judge Lord's Beautiful Anger
            Penetrates the Corporate Shield," reprinted from *Washington Post* in
            Minneapolis Star Tribune, April 2, 1984.

Page 249   "Liberal   conscience":   http:/medlibrary.org/medwiki/Colman_
            McCarthy (quoting *Washingtonian* magazine).

Page 249   "His love": Colman McCarthy, "Vindication for Judge Lord," reprinted
            from *Washington Post* in *Minneapolis Star Tribune,* January 6, 1985.

Page 251   "Alternative Motion": Filed in *Bertler v. A. H. Robins Co.,* No. 3–83–1028,
            D. Minn., March 22, 1984.

Page 251   The protective order: Order, *Bertler,* February 29, 1984.

Page 252   As many as twenty boxes: This account of document destruction and
            quotes are based on Morton Mintz, "IUD Maker Fighting Court Sanc-
            tions," *Washington Post,* August 25, 1984; Dan Oberdofer, "Ex-Robins
            Aide Admits Dumping Documents," *Minneapolis Star Tribune,* Au-
            gust 24, 1984; Mintz, *At Any Cost,* 218–21; Letter from Michael Berens,
            counsel for A. H. Robins, to Judge Renner, May 25, 1984.

Page 252   "Point man": Oberdofer, "Ex-Robins Aide Admits"; "key figure": Plain-
            tiffs' Memorandum in Support of Motion for Sanctions, *Bonlender,*
            July 2, 1984.

Page 253   Files an appeal: *Gardiner and Michalik v. A. H. Robins Co.,* Nos. 84–5061,
            84–5062 (8th Cir.)

Page 253   Her deposition: All quotes in this section are from the deposition
            of Patricia Lashley, *Abeln v. A. H. Robins Co.,* No. 804999, Hennepin
            County Dist. Court, April 19, 1984.

Page 254   Two extraordinary complaints: *In re: Complaint of A. H. Robins Com-
            pany* and *In re: Complaint of E. Claiborne Robins Jr.,* JCP 84–001 and JCP
            84–002 (8th Cir. Jud. Council, April 24, 1984).

Page 255   Judicial Conduct and Disability Act: The statute in effect was 28
            U.S.C. §372 (1980) (subsequently amended and recodified as 28 USC
            §§351–364).

Page 256   Impeachment by Congress: U.S. Const., art. II, §4 and art. III, §1. In addition to life tenure, subject only to impeachment, federal judges are further protected by the compensation clause of Article III, section 1, which prohibits any diminution in pay during their time in office.

Page 257   "Unprecedented intrusion": Irving R. Kaufman, "The Essence of Judicial Independence," *Columbia Law Review* 80 (May 1980): 671, 699–700.

Page 257   "A very visible": Drew E. Edwards, "Judicial Misconduct and Politics in the Federal System," *California Law Review* 75 (1987): 1071, 1080.

Page 257   "He's cut": MWL manuscript (Carlson 2007).

Page 258   "A self-inflicted": Mintz, *At Any Cost,* 234.

Page 258   "Whether a judge": Mary McGrory, "Sirica Set the Precedent for Morality Outweighing Manners," *Washington Post,* July 10, 1094.

Page 258   "A Deadly Depth Charge": *Minneapolis Star Tribune,* May 18, 1984.

Page 259   "His words were": "Miles Lord's Speech in the Cause of Justice," *Minneapolis Star Tribune,* May 18, 1984.

Page 259   "Shame on you": Editorial cartoon, *Minneapolis Star Tribune,* May 17, 1984.

Page 259   "I didn't think": All quotes in this section are from the deposition of Carl Lunsford, *Dean v. A. H. Robins Co.,* No. 3-82-698, D. Minn., April 23-24 and June 12-13, 1984.

Page 260   Highest-ranking: Lunsford testified that as head of the research and development division at A. H. Robins, which included the medical department, "I have responsibility for safety of all products." Lunsford deposition, April 23, 1984.

Page 260   "Unauthorized"; "inappropriate"; "the propriety": Orders, judicial misconduct proceedings, June 21, 1984.

Page 260   "Mass murderers": Jacqui Banaszynski, "Judge Miles Lord Leaving Bench," *St. Paul Pioneer Press Dispatch,* May 20, 1985.

Page 260   Judge Renner assigns; Judge Renner also: Order, *Bonlender,* July 27, 1984.

Page 260   Judge Theis: Order, *Dalkon Shield MDL,* May 21, 1984. A Minnesota state court judge, Jonathan Lebedoff, also ordered production of the secret study documents in *Laughlin v. A. H. Robins Co.,* No. 776868, Hennepin County Dist. Court, on March 21, 1984. Judge Lebedoff had issued a similar order on February 10, 1984.

Page 260   The Colorado Supreme Court: *Palmer v. A. H. Robins Co.,* 684 P.2d 187 (Colo. 1984).

Page 261   "After giving": Barry Siegel, "One Man's Effort to Tell Dalkon Story," *Los Angeles Times,* August 22, 1985.

Page 262   "The toughest litigator:" Trudi Hahn, "Joe Walters, HHH Attorney, Dies at Age 85," *Minneapolis Star Tribune,* May 20, 2005.

21. Reserve Mining versus Judge Lord

On the Reserve Mining case, this chapter also relies generally on the sources cited in the introductory note to chapter 19.

Page 263   "An impromptu": Bastow, *"This Vast Pollution,"* 165.
Page 263   No love lost: MWL dictation (March 1986).
Page 264   "Peaches": Sue Story Truax, "Retired Judge Donald Ross of Omaha Lived by a Simple Rule: Do What's Right," *Omaha World-Herald,* December 21, 2013.
Page 264   "Scornful": Sally Bixby Defty, "Arguments Concluded Here in Minnesota Mine Dumping Case," *St. Louis Post-Dispatch,* December 10, 1974; "openly contemptuous": Bastow, *"This Vast Pollution,"* 166.
Page 264   "No proof": Defty, "Arguments Concluded Here"; not "one shred": "Lord's Order Is Stayed," unnamed St. Paul newspaper, April 23, 1974; "you would close": Defty, "Arguments Concluded Here."
Page 264   "Show me one dead body": Thomas R. Huffman, "Enemies of the People: Asbestos and the Reserve Mining Trial," *Minnesota History,* Fall 2005; Bastow, *"This Vast Pollution,"* 166; author interview, Byron Starns.
Page 264   "The nation": "Showdown at Superior," *New York Times,* April 28, 1974.
Page 264   "Set[ting] an example"; "it is appalling": "Superior, Private Dump?," *New York Times,* July 7, 1974.
Page 265   In a written opinion: All quotes from this opinion are from *Reserve Mining Co. v. U.S.,* 498 F.2d 1073 (8th Cir. 1974).
Page 265   "Lied to me": Brian Lambert, "Independently Speaking, Conversations with Miles Lord," *Twin Cities Reader,* September 24–October 1, 1980.
Page 266   "A unique": *U.S. v. Reserve Mining Co.,* 380 F. Supp. 11, 82 (D. Minn. 1974), *remanded,* 498 F.2d 1073 (8th Cir. 1984).
Page 266   "One of the most massive": Linda Picone, "Historic Trial of 5 Drug Firms Begins," *Minneapolis Tribune,* November 19, 1974.
Page 266   "Resembles the floor": Jim Klobuchar, "Miles Lord: Judicial Godfather to Troubled Environment," *Minneapolis Star,* December 9, 1974.
Page 267   "Dear Miles": Letter from HHH to MWL, November 1, 1974.
Page 267   Logging in the virgin forests: *Minn. Public Interest Research Group v. Butz,* 401 F. Supp. 1276 (D. Minn. 1975). On appeal, the Eighth Circuit called Judge Lord's opinion "exhaustive," but nevertheless reversed. 541 F.2d 1292, 1295 (8th Cir. 1976), *cert. denied,* 430 U.S. 922 (1977).
Page 267   Five judges: The full court decided to hear the appeal en banc, but two judges recused themselves.
Page 267   "Done some deep:" Don Boxmeyer, "Reserve Case in Appeals Court," *St. Paul Pioneer Press,* December 9, 1974.
Page 267   The Eighth Circuit issued: All quotes from this opinion are from *Reserve Mining v. U.S.,* 514 F.2d 492 (8th Cir. 1975).

Page 268 "It read": Bastow, *"This Vast Pollution,"* 182. By contrast, a law school professor would praise the appeals court for its "pioneering" approach and "sensitivity to environmental risks with realism about economic costs." Daniel A. Farber, "The Legacy of Reserve Mining," *Minnesota Law Review* 83 (1998): 299.

Page 268 "Withdraw gracefully": Bastow, *"This Vast Pollution,"* 182.

Page 268 "Political expediency": William E. Farrell, "Six-Year Dispute on Dumping by Reserve Mining Aired Again in Minnesota," *New York Times,* June 25, 1975.

Page 269 "Cozy": MWL dictation (February 1977).

Page 269 "You remind me": Postcard from Glenn McGann to MWL, August 23, 1975.

Page 269 "Good morning": All quotes from this hearing are from the *Reserve Mining* transcript, November 14, 1975.

Page 271 The hearing picked up: All quotes from this hearing are from the *Reserve Mining* transcript, November 15, 1975.

Page 271 A "token": Hearing transcript, *Reserve Mining Co. v. Lord,* No. 75-1867, Eighth Circuit, December 18, 1975.

Page 272 At the hearing: All quotes from this hearing are from Dean Rebuffoni, "Appeals Court Tells Lord to Halt Further Reserve Hearings," *Minneapolis Tribune,* November 21, 1975.

Page 272 "You know:" author interview, Lewis A. Remele Jr. (former law clerk); "Bite": MWL manuscript (Carlson 2007).

Page 272 The judge confirmed: author interview, Byron Starns.

Page 273 Six grim: All quotes from this hearing are from the Eighth Circuit hearing transcript of December 18, 1975. An additional judge had been appointed to the Eighth Circuit since the five-judge hearing on the case.

Page 273 "Yell 'fire'": author interview, Byron Starns.

Page 274 Their decision: All quotes from this decision are from *Reserve Mining Co. v. Lord,* 529 F.2d 181 (8th Cir. 1976).

Page 274 Removed the judge: Reserve Mining's request for disqualification was procedurally deficient because the company had not brought a motion for recusal in the trial court (before Judge Lord) or even requested disqualification in its appellate papers. Instead, Reserve had belatedly raised the issue in oral argument in November. Thus, the Eighth Circuit took the action *sua sponte,* it said, of its own accord.

Page 275 "One of the most"; "revered"; "role model": Congressional Record, 113th Congress, H5890, September 27, 2013.

Page 275 First, Judge Devitt; "fatuous"; "without merit": *U.S. v. Reserve Mining Co.,* 408 F. Supp. 1212, 1214, 1216 (D. Minn. 1976).

Page 275 Next, Judge Devitt: *U.S. v. Reserve Mining Co.,* 412 F. Supp. 705 (D. Minn. 1976), *aff'd and remanded,* 543 F.2d 1210 (8th Cir. 1976).

Page 275   Judge Devitt also sanctioned: *Reserve Mining,* 412 F. Supp. at 707, 711, 713.

Page 275   A sanction is a rarity: The legal system is built largely on trust, and even if an attorney is caught in an improper act by his adversary, the accused can cloud the issue—with piles of paper and endless word games—to escape the consequences. A judge often doesn't know which attorney to believe and, with hundreds of cases on his calendar, doesn't have the time to unravel the competing arguments. Particularly if the attorney at issue is a member of an establishment law firm—influential in the community and the bar, which is usually the case for defense lawyers in big civil lawsuits—a judge will give him the benefit of the doubt. Judge Lord didn't believe much in monetary sanctions and rarely imposed them, but for different reasons; he believed that a sanction, virtually no matter the amount, could be too easily paid and was therefore meaningless to a large corporation.

Page 276   A midnight deadline: *U.S. v. Reserve Mining Co.,* 417 F. Supp. 789 (D. Minn. 1976), *aff'd and remanded,* 543 F.2d 1210 (8th Cir. 1976).

Page 276   A "caveat"; "changed circumstances": *Reserve Mining,* 543 F.2d at 1212.

Page 276   More than one commentator: "Deadline for Pollution," *St. Louis Post-Dispatch,* July 9, 1976; "The Reserve Scandal," *New York Times,* January 10, 1976.

Page 276   The odyssey: On the continuing litigation, see Attorney General: Natural Resources Division, An Inventory of Its Reserve Mining Company Case Files, MHS, www.mnhs.org/library/findaids; *Reserve Mining Co. v. Herbst,* 256 N.W.2d 808 (Minn. 1977).

Page 276   The justices found: *Reserve Mining,* 256 N.W.2d at 812–13, 841, 845–46.

Page 276   In March 1980: Huffman, "Enemies of the People"; Lass, *Minnesota,* 263.

Page 277   "To determine scientifically": Statement of MWL, February 22, 2005.

Page 277   "A more jaundiced": MWL manuscript (Carlson 2007).

22. The Judge Stands Accused

Page 278   "A media circus": David Carr, "Heaven Can Wait," *Minnesota Monthly,* January 1990.

Page 278   Judge Lay opens: All quotes from these two days of hearings are from the transcript of judicial misconduct proceedings, July 9 and 10, 1984.

Page 278   "Squeezed out": MWL manuscript (Carlson 2007); "I think Ramsey": MWL interview (Gidmark 1988).

Page 280   "Regardless of": David Shaffer, "Friends, Critics Say They'll Miss Lord," *St. Paul Pioneer Press Dispatch,* May 20, 1985.

Page 280   Judge Theis disagrees: *Dalkon Shield MDL,* 602 F. Supp. 243, 252 (D. Kan. 1985).

Page 280   In an affidavit: Affidavit of Judge Theis, judicial misconduct proceedings, July 3, 1984.

Page 281   Later, A. H. Robins: *Dalkon Shield MDL,* 602 F. Supp. at 244.

Page 282   "Their knees": MWL interview (Gidmark 1988).

Page 282   "Southern gentleman": Patrick J. Lyons, "Griffin Bell, Ex-Attorney General, Dies at 90," *New York Times,* January 6, 2009.

Page 283   *Goldberg versus Kelly:* 397 U.S. 294 (1970).

Page 283   "Legal mush": Joe Soucheray, "Skip Legal Mush; Lord Spoke Mind," *St. Paul Dispatch,* July 11, 1984.

23. Fire and Brimstone

Page 285   "A badge": MWL manuscript (Carlson 2007).

Page 285   "The adulation": Howard Gelfand, "'Activist' Judge Admired," *Washington Post,* May 23, 1976; "had the effect": Lass, *Minnesota,* 263.

Page 285   In one [poll]: "Poll Shows Approval of Judge Miles Lord," *Minneapolis Tribune,* April 11, 1976.

Page 286   "Fifty-five percent": MWL dictation (April 1976).

Page 286   "Fire and brimstone": Bob Tucker, "Federal Judge Miles Lord Lets Fly with 'Fire and Brimstone,'" *Bemidji Pioneer,* November 15, 1977.

Page 286   "Our earth": Lee Egerstrom, "Lord Confesses Own Role as Polluter," *Duluth News-Tribune,* December 6, 1977.

Page 286   "The system": James Winterer, "Judge Lord Sums Up the Reserve Battle," *Rainy Lake Chronicle,* March 28, 1976.

Page 286   "Even the churches": MWL speech, New York Academy of Sciences, December 1977.

Page 286   "I believe": *The Pulse,* Group Health Plan annual meeting report, April 1977.

Page 286   "Blackmail[ed]"; "if a politician": Don Boxmeyer, "Lord: Mining Firms Are Able to 'Blackmail' State," *St. Paul Pioneer Press,* April 23, 1976.

Page 286   "Lost my marbles": MWL dictation (1987).

Page 286   "Dropping like flies": John McMillion, "Lord: An Environmental Moses?," *Duluth News-Tribune,* December 5, 1976; "Cancer victims": Miles W. Lord, "Judge Lord Rebuts Criticism," *Duluth News- Tribune,* December 12, 1976.

Page 287   Upheld all: See Bartlett, *The Reserve Mining Controversy,* 175 ("all of Judge Lord's essential findings of fact and key conclusions of law had been upheld").

Page 287   "I don't have": Dean Rebuffoni, "Reserve Sends Lord Quotes to Court," *Minneapolis Tribune,* May 8, 1976.

Page 287   "Unofficial political boss": Bob von Sternberg, "Judge Was Behind-Scenes DFL Power," *Minneapolis Star Tribune,* June 22, 2010.

Page 287   Especially the mining companies: MWL interview (Downs); see also Bastow, *"This Vast Pollution,"* 125 (Heaney had served as a lawyer for Reserve, although not in the pollution case, "and other mining interests").

Page 287   "You don't": MWL interview (Downs).

Page 287   Still spoke: *Reserve Mining* transcript, June 15, 1973; MWL dictation (October 1976 and February 1977); "Judge Lord Rebuts Criticism," *Duluth News-Tribune.*

Page 287   Reportedly: Bastow, *"This Vast Pollution,"* 125.

Page 287   "Be stricken": *Reserve Mining* transcript, April 23, 1974.

Page 288   "I couldn't stand": MWL speech, Association of Trial Lawyers of Iowa, November 1, 1984.

Page 288   *United States of America versus Honorable Miles W. Lord:* 542 F.2d 719 (8th Cir. 1976).

Page 288   "Tired"; "barrage": Doug Stone, "Mistrial Declared in Antitrust Suit," *Minneapolis Tribune,* August 17, 1976.

Page 289   Judge Weiner tossed: See *In re Antibiotic Antitrust Actions,* 498 F. Supp. 28 (E.D. Pa. 1980), *aff'd,* 676 F.2d 51 (3d Cir. 1982).

Page 289   "Oh, yeah": author interview, Walter Mondale.

Page 289   "He had contempt": ibid.

Page 290   "That prospect": Steve Berg and Doug Stone, "The Lord of Federal Court and His Life of 'Intrigue,'" *Minneapolis Tribune,* December 9, 1976.

Page 290   One speech: All quotes from this speech are from MWL speech, New York Academy of Sciences, December 1977.

Page 290   "Dear Irving": ibid. (MWL read note during his speech).

Page 290   "How are you doing": This account and quotes are based on MWL interview (Downs).

Page 291   "We embraced": McCarthy, *Gene McCarthy's Minnesota,* 131.

Page 291   "Dick": This account and quotes are based on Norman Sherman and John Stewart, "Hubert Humphrey and the Lost Art of Unity," *Minneapolis Star Tribune,* May 12, 2012.

Page 291   "He was mourned": "The Happy Warrior," *Newsweek,* January 23, 1978.

Page 292   "He was more": MWL interview (Downs).

Page 292   "Mr. Reagan will": Mondale, *The Good Fight,* 294.

Page 293   "Forgotten man"; "Poor Humphrey": Rick Perlstein, "America's Forgotten Liberal," *New York Times,* May 26, 2011.

Page 293   One of his bigger cases: See *Rajender v. Univ. of Minn.,* 546 F. Supp. 158 (D. Minn. 1982).

Page 293   "More impact": E. R. Shipp, "The Litigious Groves of Academe," *New York Times,* November 8, 1977.

Page 293   Another decision involving the Boundary Waters: *Nat'l Ass'n of Prop. Owners v. U.S.,* 499 F. Supp. 1223 (D. Minn. 1980), *aff'd,* 660 F.2d 1240 (8th Cir. 1981), *cert. denied,* 455 U.S. 1007 (1982).

Page 293　"Bring in": Dean Rebuffoni, "Judge Lets Cameras Roll for 'History,'" *Minneapolis Tribune,* July 25, 1980.

Page 293　"Former Cuyuna Range lad": "Miles Lord," *Brainerd Daily Dispatch,* March 2, 1980; "Isn't he": Les Sellnow, "Judge Lord Brings Court to Brainerd," *Brainerd Daily Dispatch,* March 22, 1978.

Page 294　"I will vote": "IRs Protest Judge Lord's Humphrey Endorsement," unnamed and undated newspaper.

Page 294　"I'll be out": Doug Stone, "Hospital Escapee Charged with Crime," *Minneapolis Tribune,* April 13, 1979.

Page 294　"As far as": "Armed Guards Protect Lord After Call," *Minneapolis Star,* April 10, 1979.

Page 294　"There is something wrong": Doug Stone, "Search for Hospital Escapee Is Hampered by Legalities," *Minneapolis Tribune,* April 11, 1979.

Page 294　"A mass murderer"; "Give him": ibid.

Page 295　The *American Lawyer*: "The Best and Worst Federal Judges," *American Lawyer,* July 1980.

Page 295　"A hatchet job:" Jim Klobuchar, "Gunsmoke in Miles' Corral," *Minneapolis Star,* July 25, 1980.

Page 295　In a follow-up: Larry Millett, "Judge Miles Lord: Champion of the Underdog, or Misguided Judicial Zealot?," *St. Paul Pioneer Press,* September 14, 1980.

Page 295　"Outstanding federal": Doug Stone, "U.S. Lawyers Select Lord as Top Trial Judge," *Minneapolis Tribune,* July 18, 1981.

Page 296　"A staunch protector"; "in the forefront": ibid.

Page 296　"Where is": Don Boxmeyer, "Lord Raises Moral Issue," *St. Paul Pioneer Press,* April 25, 1974.

Page 296　He titled his speech: All quotes are from MWL speech, Minnesota Council of Churches, November 12, 1981.

24. Endgame

Page 299　A. H. Robins lawyers, however: See *Dalkon Shield MDL,* 107 F.R.D. 2, 13–14 (D. Kan. 1985).

Page 299　Magistrate McNulty denies: Orders, *Bonlender,* July 20 and August 9, 1984.

Page 300　The questioning starts: All quotes in this section from the deposition of Roger Tuttle are from his deposition in *Bonlender* and *Abeln v. A. H. Robins,* No. 804999, Hennepin County Dist. Court, July 30–August 2, 1984.

Page 303　"False"; "absurd"; "the product of": A. H. Robins statement to the press, July 31, 1984.

Page 303　"I did not give": Don Finefrock, "Robins Lawyers, Foe Clash on Status of Documents," *Richmond News Leader,* August 17, 1984.

Page 304   Many (but not all) of the allegedly destroyed documents: Tuttle testified that he saved several documents from destruction and kept them
at his home for years. One of these documents—not produced in the
MDL, but marked as Tuttle Exhibit 10 at his deposition—was an A. H.
Robins memorandum from June 1970 that discussed the addition of
copper to the Dalkon Shield "for the express purpose of improving
effectiveness" and "getting an added 'drug effect.'" If this information
had been disclosed to the FDA, history might have been rewritten with
the Dalkon Shield classified as a drug, not a device, and subject to premarket testing and regulatory approval. Special Masters Thompson
and Bartsh found that Tuttle's disclosure of this "key document" at his
deposition, when it had not been produced despite years of prior litigation, "substantially corroborates the essence of his story that Robins
lawyers have culled documents from files so that they would not be
produced." The masters also stated that "[s]ubstantial questions remain
as to what other documents were destroyed or withheld." Report (II)
of Special Masters, *Hewitt v. A. H. Robins Co.*, No. 3-83-1291, D. Minn.,
February 21, 1985.

Page 304   "Expressing wonderment" through "hostile climate of the Minnesota
courts": David Carr, "Robins Faces Burning Issue," *Twin Cities Reader,*
August 8, 1984.

Page 306   One particularly combative affair: All quotes in this paragraph are from
the deposition of William Zimmer III, *Bonlender,* August 14–16, 1984.

Page 306   Patricia Lashley: All quotes in this paragraph are from the deposition
of Patricia Lashley, *Bonlender,* August 17, 1984.

Page 306   "Ambiguous": Morton Mintz, "IUD Maker Fighting Court Sanctions,"
Washington Post, August 25, 1984.

Page 306   Several thousand pages: Report on Activities of the Masters Regarding
Dalkon Shield Litigation, *Bonlender,* September 1984.

Page 307   "Jurist's Tactics": Mary Williams Walsh, *Wall Street Journal,* September
14, 1984.

Page 307   "Unprecedented": Mintz Morton, "Maker Pays for IUD Removal,"
Washington Post, October 30, 1984.

Page 307   "Belatedly developed concern" through "the bottom line": ibid.

Page 308   The Eighth Circuit issues: All quotes are from the opinion in *Gardiner
v. A. H. Robins Co.*, 747 F.2d 1180 (8th Cir. 1984).

Page 309   "Justice has been": Morton Mintz, "Rebuke of A. H. Robins Stricken
from Record," *Washington Post,* November 3, 1984.

Page 309   "The truth": MWL interview (Gidmark 1988).

Page 309   "It is far more": *Gardiner,* 747 F.2d at 1192.

Page 309   "It is the speech": Mintz, *At Any Cost,* 236.

Page 310   "It doesn't quite": Julie Anne Hoffman, "Lord's Fete Draws Fire," *St. Paul
Pioneer Press Dispatch,* April 2, 1987.

Page 310   "I'm getting too old": Jim George, "Lord Irked over Slant of TV Inter-view," *St. Paul Dispatch,* November 12, 1984.

Page 310   Appear for sentencing: *U.S. v. LaForge and Katt,* CR. 4–84–66 (D. Minn.).

Page 310   "Lord is": Dan Oberdofer, "Judge Lord Assails 'Warmongers,'" *Minneapolis Star Tribune,* November 9, 1984; "What a judge": "Judge Miles Lord on the Arms Race," *City Pages,* November 14, 1984.

Page 311   "The Prairie Judge": All quotes in this section are from a transcript of *60 Minutes,* November 11, 1984.

Page 312   "A little bit rocky": MWL interview (Gidmark 1988).

Page 312   "As you will see": Letter from Marion Goldin to MWL, December 5, 1984.

Page 314   There are also the inevitable letters: The judge also received a postcard from a crank he had heard from on a number of occasions in the past. All of these cards had started the same—"Just a few lines to comment on . . ."—and time and again returned to the same subject: "shameless," "godless," and "two legged females." After the *60 Minutes* program, the postcard man wrote again to condemn the judge for having been "brainwashed" by "sex crazy females." (Interestingly, I had received a couple of similar cards at the newspaper after I reported on eight women who went on strike to protest discriminatory practices at a small bank in Willmar, Minnesota: "Just a few lines to comment on . . . crazy trouble making females.")

Page 315   "Judge Miles Lord's public": Mintz, *At Any Cost,* 241.

Page 315   "When your own": Barry Siegel, "One Man's Effort to Tell Dalkon Story," *Los Angeles Times,* August 22, 1985.

Page 315   In Wichita: *Tetuan v. A. H. Robins Co.,* 738 P.2d 1210 (Kan. 1987).

Page 315   The special masters find: Report (II) of Special Masters, *Hewitt,* February 21, 1985.

Page 316   Judge Theis issues: *Dalkon Shield MDL,* 107 F.R.D. 2, 14–15, 16 (D. Kan. 1985). Generally, *prima facie* evidence establishes a presumption of fact if not refuted. As Judge Theis stated in his order: "The Opinion is *not* a finding that Robins is guilty of perpetrating a crime or fraud; this is merely a discovery order which holds that plaintiffs have made out a *prima facie* case with respect to the application of the crime or fraud exception to the work product doctrine and the attorney-client privilege."

Page 316   "Takes flight": *Clark v. United States,* 289 U.S. 1, 15 (1933).

Page 316   "Voluminous amount": Order, *Dalkon Shield MDL,* May 31, 1985.

Afterword

Page 317   Reorganize under Chapter 11: In this respect, A. H. Robins was following the playbook of Manville Corporation, which, seeking refuge from asbestos litigation, had filed for bankruptcy protection the previous year.

Page 317   As a result: On the bankruptcy proceedings, see Sobol, *Bending the Law;* Kenneth R. Feinberg, "The Dalkon Shield Claimants Trust," *Law & Contemporary Problems* 53 (1990): 79; Guide to the Dalkon Shield Claimants Trust Collection, University of Virginia.

Page 318   Senior would die: Milt Freudenheim, "E. Claiborne Robins, 84, Dies; Executive and Philanthropist," *New York Times,* July 7, 1995.

Page 318   "Unjustified"; "a sham": Mintz, *At Any Cost,* 245.

Page 318   94 percent: Malcolm Gladwell, "Robins Plaintiffs Caught in Million-Dollar Waiting Game," *Washington Post,* October 20, 1988.

Page 318   "The most successful": Malcolm Gladwell, "To Alan Morrison, Justice Falls Short in Robins Case," *Washington Post,* September 19, 1989.

Page 318   "I didn't teach": MWL interview (Gidmark 1988).

Page 318   "I would have taken": David Carr, "Heaven Can Wait," *Minnesota Monthly,* January 1990.

Page 318   A federal grand jury: Sobol, *Bending the Law,* 220; Morton Mintz, "The Pro-Corporate Tilt," *Nieman Reports,* Fall 1991; Malcolm Gladwell, "Supreme Court Refuses to Block Dalkon Shield Probe," *Washington Post,* July 3, 1989.

Page 318   At least one: The Honorable Robert E. Payne, U.S. Dist. Court, E. D. Va.

Page 319   "Neither A. H. Robins": Letter from Griffin Bell to Joe Walters, September 11, 1984.

Page 319   "Are aching": MWL speech, Roseville/Falcon Heights Chamber of Commerce, April 1987.

Page 320   "Ambulance chasing": Dan Oberdofer, "Miles Lord Happily Switches from Arbiter to Advocate," *Minneapolis Star Tribune,* April 2, 1987; "selling his judgeship": Don Boxmeyer, "Still the Maverick," *St. Paul Pioneer Press Dispatch,* December 10, 1989.

Page 320   "Trying to beat": Ellen Tomson, "Lord's Justice," *St. Paul Pioneer Press,* May 1, 1994; "let[ting] injured people": Boxmeyer, "Still the Maverick."

Page 320   "They hatched": MWL interview (Gidmark 1988).

Page 320   "Moot": Order, *In re: Complaint of A. H. Robins Co.,* JCP 84–001 and 84–002 (8th Cir. Jud. Council, December 26, 1984). In addition, the Eighth Circuit summarily dismissed, without the fanfare of a hearing or an investigatory committee, three additional judicial misconduct complaints that had been filed after Judge Lord's performance on *60 Minutes* and sentencing and speech in the Sperry case. (One of the complaints was filed by a conservative legal foundation and the other two by individuals.) In one of these orders of dismissal, Chief Judge Lay even seemed to atone for having used the misconduct statute in Dalkon Shield by offering an ode to the independence of the federal judiciary: "The Judicial Conduct and Disability Act should not be invoked so as to chill the independence of a trial judge in a judicial proceeding. A trial judge should not fear that because of comments he or she makes from the bench, which the judge feels are related to the proceeding before the court, he or she ultimately may be subject to a disciplinary sanction by the Judicial Council." *In re Petition of Lauer,* 788 F.2d 135, 138 (8th Cir. Jud. Council 1985).

Page 320 "Be dealt with": Oliver Wendell Holmes, *The Common Law,* 1 (1881).

Page 321 "This is a great country"; "Each one"; "applies to me"; "applies to you": MWL manuscript (Carlson 2007).

Page 321 "*I am only one*": Edward Everett Hale, reprinted in John Bartlett, *Familiar Quotations* (Boston: Little, Brown and Company, 1968), 14th edition.

Selected Bibliography

Aulie, Berger. *The Milford Mine Disaster*. Virginia, Minn.: W. A. Fisher Company, 1994.

Aulie, Berger, and Beverly Mindrum Johnson, eds. *Cuyuna Country: A Peoples' History*. 2 vols. Ironton, Minn.: Cuyuna Country Heritage Preservation Society, 2000, 2002.

Bartlett, Robert V. *The Reserve Mining Controversy: Science, Technology, and Environmental Quality*. Bloomington: Indiana University Press, 1980.

Bartsh, Thomas C., Francis M. Boddy, Benjamin F. King, and Peter N. Thompson. *A Class-Action Suit That Worked: The Consumer Refund in the Antibiotic Antitrust Litigation*. Lexington, Mass.: Lexington Books, 1978.

Bastow, Thomas F. *"This Vast Pollution . . .": United States of America v. Reserve Mining Company*. Washington, D.C.: Green Field Books, 1986.

Berman, Edgar. *Hubert: The Triumph and Tragedy of the Humphrey I Knew*. New York: G. P. Putnam's Sons, 1979.

Bingham, Clara, and Laura Leedy Gansler. *Class Action: The Story of Lois Jenson and the Landmark Case That Changed Sexual Harassment Law*. New York: Anchor Books, 2002.

Brodeur, Paul. *Outrageous Misconduct: The Asbestos Industry on Trial*. New York: Pantheon Books, 1985.

Brown, Aaron. *Overburden: Modern Life on the Iron Range*. Duluth, Minn.: Red Step Press, 2008.

Caro, Robert A. *The Years of Lyndon Johnson: Master of the Senate*. New York: Vintage Books, 2003.

———. *The Years of Lyndon Johnson: The Passage of Power*. New York: Alfred A. Knopf, 2012.

Corgan, Verna C. *Controversy, Courts, and Community: The Rhetoric of Judge Miles Welton Lord*. Westport, Conn.: Greenwood Press, 1995.

de Kruif, Paul. *Seven Iron Men: The Merritts and the Discovery of the Mesabi Range*. Minneapolis: University of Minnesota Press, 1929.

Eisele, Albert. *Almost to the Presidency: A Biography of Two American Politicians*. Blue Earth, Minn.: Piper Company, 1972.

Engelmayer, Sheldon, and Robert Wagman. *Lord's Justice: One Judge's Battle to Ex-*

pose the Deadly Dalkon Shield I.U.D. Garden City, N.Y.: Anchor Press/Doubleday, 1985.

Hansen, Arvy, ed. *Cuy-Una! . . . a Chronicle of the Cuyuna Range.* Cuyuna Range Bicentennial Committee, 1976.

Hayes, John Earl. *Dubious Alliance: The Making of Minnesota's DFL Party.* Minneapolis: University of Minnesota Press, 1984.

Humphrey, Hubert H. *The Education of a Public Man: My Life and Politics.* Minneapolis: University of Minnesota Press, 1991.

Kaiser, Charles. *1968 in America: Music, Politics, Chaos, Counterculture, and the Shaping of a Generation.* New York: Grove Press, 1988.

Kennedy, Robert F. *The Enemy Within.* New York: Harper and Row, 1960.

Lamppa, Marvin G. *Minnesota's Iron Country: Rich Ore, Rich Lives.* Duluth, Minn.: Lake Superior Port Cities, 2004.

Larson, Agnes M. *The White Pine Industry in Minnesota: A History.* Minneapolis: University of Minnesota Press, 1949, 2007.

Lass, William E. *Minnesota: A History.* 2nd ed. New York: W. W. Norton and Company, 1998.

Manuel, Jeffrey T. *Taconite Dreams: The Struggle to Sustain Mining on Minnesota's Iron Range, 1915–2000.* Minneapolis: University of Minnesota Press, 2015.

Mayer, George H., *The Political Career of Floyd B. Olson.* St. Paul: Minnesota Historical Society Press, 1951, 1987.

McCarthy, Eugene J. *1968: War & Democracy.* Red Wing, Minn.: Lone Oak Press, 2000.

———. *Gene McCarthy's Minnesota: Memories of a Native Sun*, Minneapolis: Winston Press, 1982.

———. *Up 'Til Now: A Memoir.* San Diego: Harcourt Brace Jovanovich, 1987.

Mintz, Morton. *At Any Cost: Corporate Greed, Women, and the Dalkon Shield.* New York: Pantheon Books, 1985.

Mitau, Theodore G. *Politics in Minnesota.* 2nd ed. Minneapolis: University of Minnesota Press, 1970.

Mondale, Walter F. *The Good Fight: A Life in Liberal Politics.* New York: Scribner, 2010.

Nemanic, Mary Lou. *One Day for Democracy: Independence Day and the Americanization of Iron Range Immigrants.* Athens: Ohio University Press, 2007.

Pennefeather, Shannon M., ed. *Mill City: A Visual History of the Minneapolis Mill District.* St. Paul: Minnesota Historical Society Press, 2003.

Peppers, Todd C., and Artemus Ward, eds. *In Chambers: Stories of Supreme Court Law Clerks and Their Justices.* Charlottesville: University of Virginia Press, 2012.

Perry, Susan, and Jim Dawson. *Nightmare: Women and the Dalkon Shield.* New York: MacMillan Publishing Company, 1985.

Posner, Richard A. *Reflections on Judging.* Cambridge, Mass.: Harvard University Press, 2013.

Price, Polly J. *Judge Richard S. Arnold: A Legacy of Justice on the Federal Bench.* Amherst, N.Y.: Prometheus Books, 2009.

Pringle, Peter. *Cornered: Big Tobacco at the Bar of Justice.* New York: Henry Holt and Company, 1998.

Roberts, Kate. *Minnesota 150: The People, Places and Things That Shape Our State.* St. Paul: Minnesota Historical Society Press, 2007.

Sandbrook, Dominic. *Eugene McCarthy and the Rise and Fall of Postwar American Liberalism.* New York: Anchor Books, 2005.

Schaumburg, Frank D. *Judgment Reserved: A Landmark Environmental Case.* Reston, Va.: Reston Publishing Company, 1976.

Sherman, Norman *From Nowhere to Somewhere: My Political Journey.* Minneapolis: First Avenue Editions, 2016.

Sobol, Richard B. *Bending the Law: The Story of the Dalkon Shield Bankruptcy.* Chicago: University of Chicago Press, 1991.

Solberg, Carl. *Hubert Humphrey: A Biography.* St. Paul: Borealis Books, 2003.

Tilsen, Kenneth E. *Judging the Judges: Justice, Punishment, Resistance, and the Minnesota Court During the War in Vietnam.* St. Cloud, Minn.: North Star Press of St. Cloud, 2002.

Tweton, D. Jerome. *Depression: Minnesota in the Thirties.* Fargo: North Dakota Institute for Regional Studies, 1981.

White, Theodore H. *The Making of the President, 1968.* New York: HarperPerennial, 1969.

Wilson, Betty. *Rudy! The People's Governor.* Minneapolis: Nodin Press, 2005.

Zwick, David, and Marcy Benstock. *Water Wasteland: Ralph Nader's Study Group Report on Water Pollution.* New York: Grossman Publishers, 1971.

Index

Roberta Walburn is an attorney and former journalist in Minneapolis, Minnesota. She has practiced law for more than twenty-five years, focusing on high-stakes civil litigation. Previously, she worked as a reporter for the *Minneapolis Star Tribune* and *Buffalo (N.Y.) Evening News* and as a legislative assistant to U.S. Senator Paul Wellstone, as well as serving as a law clerk to U.S. District Judge Miles Lord.